KU-573-298

Modern Introductions to Philosophy

General Editor: D. J. O'CONNOR

The titles of the volumes in this series are:

W. D. HUDSON is a Senior Lecturer in Philosophy at the University of Exeter. He received his Ph.D. from the University of London and his books include *Ethical Intuitionism*, *Ludwig Wittgenstein*, *Reason and Right*, and *The Is-Ought Question*.

MODERN MORAL PHILOSOPHY

W. D. Hudson

MACMILLAN

© W. D. Hudson 1970

All rights reserved. No part of this publication
may be reproduced or transmitted, in any
form or by any means, without permission.

First published in the United States 1970
First published in the United Kingdom 1970

Published by
MACMILLAN AND CO LTD
London and Basingstoke
Associated companies in New York Toronto
Dublin Melbourne Johannesburg and Madras

SBN (boards) 333 11554 6
(paper) 333 11555 4

Printed in Great Britain by
RICHARD CLAY (THE CHAUCER PRESS) LTD
Bungay, Suffolk

The Papermac edition of this book is sold subject to the
condition that it shall not, by way of trade or otherwise,
be lent, resold, hired out, or otherwise circulated without the publisher's prior consent, in any form of binding
or cover other than that in which it is published and
without a similar condition including this condition
being imposed on the subsequent purchaser.

TO ROSEMARY

CONTENTS

PREFACE

I should like to express my sincere thanks to those who have helped me in the writing of this book and, in particular, to the following persons.

Professor D. J. O'Connor, Head of the Department of Philosophy in this University, added to the many debts of gratitude which I owe him by his willingness to discuss with me, from time to time, points which arose in the planning and preparation of this book. I am most grateful for his unfailing help and encouragement.

Professor R. M. Hare, White's Professor of Moral Philosophy in the University of Oxford, very kindly read and talked over with me a first draft of Chapter 5 and of parts of Chapter 6. I am greatly indebted to him, not only for his many helpful comments, but for the generosity with which he has made available to me some of his unpublished papers and has allowed me to refer to them in my treatment of prescriptivism.

It hardly needs to be added that neither of the philosophers whom I have named must be held in any way responsible for what I say in this book or for any mistakes which I may have made.

The former secretary to this department, Mrs. Ann Smith, cheerfully and painstakingly attended to much of the typing and my thanks are due to her; as they are also to the faculty secretary, Mrs. E. Ridgeon, who helped me with the proof-reading.

My wife has also helped me greatly and to her I dedicate the book.

Department of Philosophy　　　　　W. D. HUDSON
University of Exeter

ABBREVIATIONS USED IN THIS VOLUME

A: *Analysis*

EL: *Ethics and Language* by C. L. Stevenson (New Haven and London, 1944)

FE: *Foundations of Ethics* by W. D. Ross (Oxford, 1939)

FR: *Freedom and Reason* by R. M. Hare (Oxford, 1963)

LM: *The Language of Morals* by R. M. Hare (Oxford, 1952)

M: *Mind*

MO: *Moral Obligation* by H. A. Prichard (Oxford, 1949)

P: *Philosophy*

PAS: *Proceedings of the Aristotelian Society*

PE: *Principia Ethica* by G. E. Moore (Cambridge, 1903)

PI: *Philosophical Investigations* by L. Wittgenstein (2nd ed., Oxford, 1958)

PQ: *The Philosophical Quarterly*

PR: *The Philosophical Review*

RG: *The Right and the Good* by W. D. Ross (Oxford, 1930)

T: *Tractatus Logico-Philosophicus* by L. Wittgenstein (1961 translation by Pears and McGuinness)

CHAPTER 1. MORAL DISCOURSE AND MORAL PHILOSOPHY

This book is not about what people ought to do. It is about what they are doing when they *talk* about what they ought to do. Moral philosophy, as I understand it, must not be confused with moralizing. A moralist is someone who uses moral language in what may be called a first-order way. He, qua moralist, engages in reflection, argument, or discussion about what is morally right or wrong, good or evil. He talks about what people ought to do. I suppose the expression "moral philosopher" is sometimes used to mean a particularly wise or well-informed moralist. But I shall not so use it. By a moral philosopher I mean someone who engages in what may be called second-order discourse. Qua moral philosopher, he thinks and speaks about the ways in which moral terms, like "right" or "good," are used by moralists when they are delivering their moral judgments. What are the defining characteristics of moral language as such? How is it like, and how unlike, language used for other purposes, such as for stating empirical facts or uttering commands? What *are* people doing when they talk about what they ought to do? That is the moral philosopher's concern. The distinction which I draw here is sometimes expressed by saying that a moralist, as such, is interested in ethics; and a moral philosopher, as such, in metaethics.

An Example of Moral Discourse

As an example of first-order moral discourse, let us take the Parliamentary debate which, as I write, has just occurred at an all-night sitting of the House of Commons when the Divorce Reform Bill (1969) was receiving its second and third readings.[1] This bill recognized the breakdown of marriage as the sole ground for divorce. To put the matter summarily, there have been hitherto in England four main grounds on which one party to a marriage could petition for divorce from the other party, viz. adultery, desertion, cruelty, and insanity. The "guilty" party could, in no instance, petition for divorce on the ground of his own "guilt." The new bill abolishes this distinction between "guilty" and "innocent" parties. It allows either party to petition for divorce on the ground of the break-down of the marriage. What constitutes breakdown is, within certain limits, for the divorce court judge to decide. Five years' separation, other things being equal, could mean that the marriage had broken down. If a husband (or wife) walked out on his (or her) spouse, then, after five years he (or she) could, if this bill becomes law, petition for divorce with considerable chance of success.

The moral question which arises is: ought divorce law to be reformed along these lines? That was the question debated at the all-night sitting to which I have referred. We may safely take this debate as an example of moral discourse. The participants put forward what purported to be their own answers to a moral question. They supported these with what they considered reasons appropriate to the settlement of a moral issue.

What were they doing when they talked through the night about what they ought to do? That is the question which would interest a moral philosopher, as I have defined him. He would not wish to participate in the first-order debate; not, that is, qua philosopher. Nor would he want to reopen the moral question, when the debate was ended, by discussing whether or not the House ought really to do what those present had said that it ought to do about divorce. It is the logical features of the debate itself which would interest him, as a philosopher. What had these people been doing when they talked about what they ought to do? I will indicate one or two points which I think might have occurred to a moral philosopher as he reflected upon that question.

[1] See *Weekly Hansard* No. 798, June 16–19, 1969, pp. 1798–2074.

He might have asked himself, for instance, whether they were trying to make some sort of discovery or to reach some sort of decision. Which of these would be the more appropriate account of what had occurred? Some philosophers would say that trying to answer a moral question is trying to make a discovery. Some others would say that it is trying to reach a decision. Whichever answer he gave, however, a philosopher would recognize that what goes on in moral discourse is not quite like what goes on in other contexts where it is appropriate to talk about making discoveries or reaching decisions. In science, for example, men claim to make discoveries. It is true enough that when they claim to have done so, they are sometimes mistaken; and that when they really have done so, it sometimes takes other scientists a long time to agree that they have. Nevertheless, in science, there are accepted objective tests for determining when a discovery has really been made and when it has not. Moreover, you cannot be a scientist unless you are willing to submit your claims to these tests. In morals, however, there seems to be no counterpart to such tests. Moralists, it appears, can go on disagreeing with one another forever. It is not a necessary condition of being a moralist that one should be willing to submit one's claim to have made a discovery to certain specific, agreed, objective tests which verify, or falsify, it.

Turning now to the taking of decisions, compare what goes on in morals with what goes on, say, in a sport. In a sport, decisions have to be taken. A coin is tossed, for instance, to decide who shall bat first. If any captain came back from the tossup claiming that it had not really decided who should bat first, what could we make of that? It wouldn't be cricket, not only in the sense that we should take a poor view of the man's sportmanship, but because it would be opting out of the game. Unless you abide by the tossup you cannot (logically) play cricket, since one of the rules of the game is that the tossup decides who shall bat or bowl—or perhaps it would be more accurate to say decides who shall decide, since it is the captain winning the toss who chooses to do one or the other. The point to take is that the tossup is the recognized "authority" which settles the matter. This is a very simple example of decision-making. But, in far more complicated examples, the same point can be observed. In trying a criminal or deciding a lawsuit, for instance, there is a recognized authority to which appeal is made. All who participate in such legal activities accept this authority. It is true, of course, that lawyers may disagree as to what the law says about some sort of case, as captains of cricket teams can hardly disagree as to whether an upturned coin is "heads" or "tails." But the point remains that, without the law to appeal to, there could (logically) be no trials and no lawsuits. Now, where is the "authority" to which appeal is made in taking moral decisions? In morals, there appears to be no counterpart to the authority of the tossup or the law. It is not a necessary condition of being a moralist that one should be prepared to decide things by invoking a recognized authority. Cricketers, as such, abide by the tossup, and lawyers, as such, by the law; but where is the authority, the invoking of which makes a moralist a moralist?

Such reflections as these suggest that moral discourse, while in many ways resembling other sorts of discourse, nevertheless has something distinctive about it. Most modern moral philosophers, whether they think of a moral judgment as a discovery or a decision, conceive of it as *sui generis*. What reflections confirm them in that opinion?

I turn for an answer to the Parliamentary debate upon which we are supposing a moral philosopher to be reflecting. (It should be recognized that those members of Parliament whom I quote had all far more to say than I indicate. The quotations which I give should not be taken to represent their entire, or indeed their most important, remarks on the subject of divorce reform.) Take at random two things which were said in the course of the debate. Sir Tufton Beamish, member for Lewes, who opposed the bill, said: "It is bound to have the effect of unnecessarily increasing the number of broken homes"; and under it, a woman "would suffer . . . the misery that is part and parcel of being a deserted wife and of course in many cases the children would stand to suffer as well." Another opponent of the bill, Sir Lionel Heald, member for Chertsey, was troubled by the passage in it which

deals with financial provision by the petitioner for the re-
spondent. Such provision, says the bill, must be reasonable
and fair "or the best that can be made in the circumstances."
Sir Lionel said of the words in quotation marks, "I have never
seen anything like that in a statute," and implied that they
introduced a new principle into British law.

The appeal of both Sir Tufton and Sir Lionel was to *fact*,
or putative fact. Sir Tufton appealed to what, as a matter of
fact, in his opinion, would happen to some women and children if the bill became law. Sir Lionel appealed to what, as
a matter of fact, can or cannot be found in the statute book
of England. Both speakers could conceivably have been mistaken in what they took the facts to be. And indeed, so far
as Sir Tufton was concerned, that is the argument with which
Mrs. Lena Jeger, member for Holborn and St. Pancras, South,
in effect, countered his remarks. She said that a law which
made breakdown of marriage the sole ground of divorce
would raise the status of both parties to a marriage. So far
from it increasing the miseries of women, the women of the
future would rejoice in it because it would give them greater
equality with men.

All of this might suggest that the only difference between
supporters and opponents of the bill lies in what they take
the facts of the matter to be. A moral philosopher, reflecting
upon such remarks as I have quoted, will ask himself: does
this tell us what supporters of the bill *meant* when they said
that it ought to become law, or opponents when they said
that it ought not? Did the supporters mean by "ought" simply
that, if the bill becomes law, it will, in fact, increase the happiness of the women of the future, or that its terms are not, in
fact, unique in the statute book, or something like that? Did
its opponents mean, by "ought not," the opposite? It may
seem, superficially, that the answer is yes, because so much
of the debate about what ought or ought not to be done was
concerned with matter of fact. But the moral philosopher, as
such, will not leave it there. He will notice that it *made sense*,
when someone agreed with the bill's opponents as to the facts
but said that nevertheless it *ought* to become law; and again,
when someone agreed with the bill's supporters as to the facts

but said that it *ought not*. In the course of the debate, for example, the Solicitor General, Sir Arthur Irvine, appeared to agree in effect with Sir Lionel Heald that the words "or the best that can be made in the circumstances" would be new to the statute book, but spoke *in favor* of the bill. Again, Quintin Hogg, member for St. Marylebone, agreed with supporters of the bill that it would end misery for many people; nevertheless, he inclined to the view that the bill ought not to be passed into law. To the ordinary listener in the public gallery, neither the Solicitor General nor Mr. Hogg would have appeared to be contradicting themselves. But the former would certainly have done so if "ought to be done," as ordinarily used, *meant* "is not new to the statute book," and the latter, if it *meant* "will prevent misery."

Considerations such as these suggest to the moral philosopher that the meaning of "ought" and "ought not" must be very carefully distinguished from the meaning of expressions such as "is new to the statute book," "prevents misery," and so on. He may wonder, of course, whether the trouble is simply that he has not yet come across the expression of this kind which *is* equivalent in meaning to "ought (or ought not) to be done." He may try other expressions not unlike "is new to the statute book" or "prevents misery." Many moral philosophers have tried to find some such factual description with which to replace moral terms like "ought." But many of them have come to the conclusion that none can be found. Just as it makes sense to say "Ought what prevents misery to be done?" or "Ought what is new to the statute book to be enacted?" so, whatever expression is suggested as equivalent in meaning to "ought," or "ought not," some such question can be asked. When I say that it "can" be asked, I use "can" in a logical sense. The point is that none of such questions would seem to somebody who uses English normally to be self-answering. But at least one of them would have to do so (logically), if there were some factual description which could be substituted, without loss or change of meaning, for a moral judgment. *If* "ought to be done" *meant* "is X," where X is some matter of fact, then "Ought what is X to be done?" would be self-answering. It would be meaningless in the sense that it was a question which there is no point in raising because anyone who knew the meaning of the words used to ask it would thereby know the answer. But this question *is* meaningful. People who know the meaning of all the expressions used may differ as to the answer. Some may say that what is X ought to be done, some that it ought not. We may, of course, *disagree* with either side. But we should not consider that those who said that what is X ought to be done were merely uttering a *tautology,* or those who said that it ought not were *contradicting* themselves. This applies, be it emphasized, *whatever* matter of fact X refers to.

Reflections upon these lines lie behind the view now widely held among moral philosophers that it is logically impossible to define moral language in terms of nonmoral, or to derive "ought" from "is." "Ought to be" or "ought to be done" does *not mean* that something is, or is not, the case.

What then does it mean? What are people doing when they talk about what they ought to do, if not stating some specific fact about the consequences of doing it, or what some authority says on the subject, etc?

In this connection there is one thing which a philosopher, reflecting upon the Parliamentary debate about divorce reform, would have noted. Let us take, as an example of it, what Peter Mahon, member for Preston, South, had to say, when speaking against the bill. "This is legislation for marital pandemonium, or if you prefer it, the law of the jungle. . . . With the bill we are trying to pledge this country to eternal promiscuity. . . . If the bill makes its mark, Britain will indubitably be a philanderer's paradise." Mr. Mahon did not like the bill and wanted others not to like it; hence, his emotionally-charged language. "Marital pandemonium," "the law of the jungle," "eternal promiscuity," "a philanderer's paradise"—these are angry noises. They give vent to what Mr. Mahon feels on the subject and are intended to arouse similar feelings in others. The member for Preston, South, was doing what people often do in the heat of moral argument. He was using language in the way that propagandists and advertisers frequently use it, to play upon the emotions of his hearers rather than to appeal to their reason. Who

wants "pandemonium" or a return to "the jungle"? Who
would wish to be thought "promiscuous"—eternally so, to
boot—or a "philanderer"? Mr. Mahon's intention was clearly
to saddle the bill with these descriptions and so to direct upon
it the opprobrium incapsulated within them. Anyone who
uses English normally and who assents to Mr. Mahon's description of the bill will necessarily feel some disgust for it. He
will be assenting, not so much to description, as to abuse.

The moral philosopher notices this emotive element in
moral discourse, but he asks: is that all there is to it? He may
well decide that it is not. The great majority of those members
of Parliament who participated in the debate did not use
Mr. Mahon's sort of language. They gave reasons for their
judgments. And they worked with these reasons, to some
degree at least, as rational men work with reasons in uni-
verses of discourse other than the moral. In a word, they
recognized the need for *consistency*.

As an example of one thing which I have in mind here,
let us take what Kenneth Lewis, member for Rutland and
Stamford, said following upon Sir Lionel Heald's remarks referred to above. He claimed that it was self-contradictory to
say that provision for a divorced wife should be "fair" and
"reasonable," as the bill does, and then to go on to add "or
the best that can be made in the circumstances." His point
was that for the bill to say that the provision must be "fair
and reasonable" and then, as he claimed it did, to say that
the provision may be *either* that *or* "the best that can be
made in the circumstances" *is* self-contradictory, because the
latter expression admits the possibility of an unfair and unreasonable provision being made. One cannot meaningfully
offer as a reason for action that which is self-contradictory.
Anything follows from a contradiction. And where anything
follows, no reason has been given for one thing rather than
another.

The recognition of reason, or consistency, in the debate,
however, went much further than this demand that the phras-
ing of the bill should not be self-contradictory. In effect,
every speaker who offered a reason for saying that the bill
ought, or ought not, to become law was appealing for con-

sistency. Sir Tufton Beamish, as we saw, said that if it does
become law it will cause unnecessary misery to many women.
In effect, he was saying: "You believe, do you not, that
whatever causes unnecessary misery to women is morally
wrong? I am pointing out that this bill will cause it. I call on
you, as rational men, to be consistent and oppose the bill."
Mrs. Jeger, in her turn, was saying in effect: "You believe,
do you not, that whatever gives women greater equality with
men is morally right? I am pointing out that this bill will do
so. I invite you, as reasonable men and women, therefore, to
support it."

A distinction can be drawn between reasons which appeal
for consistency in moral beliefs which everyone does, as a
matter of fact, hold and those which appeal for consistency
in beliefs which only some hold. Sir Tufton's appeal is an
instance of the former. It may make sense to ask: ought one
to do what will cause misery? But this is not a question which
normal people *do*, in fact, ask. One can safely assume that,
other things being equal, any member of our society will
profess assent to the principle that one ought not to cause
unnecessary misery. Sir Tufton was invoking a principle to
which everybody who is not sick subscribes. Whether he was
correct in saying that the passing of the Divorce Reform Bill
would cause misery is, of course, another matter. But his
appeal was for consistency in what everybody believes. Contrast it with the appeal which Mr. Emery, member for
Honiton, made. He claimed, in effect, that the bill ought to
become law because in divorce, there is never just one guilty
party. But many people would say that if a bill is based on
this belief it ought not to become law. "We ought to do whatever instantiates the opinion that, in divorce, there is never
just one guilty party" is not a principle to which everyone,
by any means, subscribes. Mr. Emery was setting up, rather
than using, a standard of what ought to be done. Here the
question which arises for the moral philosopher is: can moral
discourse claim to be based in reason, as other types of discourse (e.g., scientific) are, if, as we have just seen, it allows
those who participate in it to set up their own standards of
what ought, or ought not, to be done? What should we make

of a scientist who said: "I have my own method of determining what is true or false. Many scientists have other methods. But I am consistent in adhering to mine. So my discourse is grounded in reason"? Moral judgments, since they appear to allow those who pass them to make up their own reasons for doing so, are not like scientific hypotheses.

Such reflections may well lead the moral philosopher to another, and a deeper, question. Namely: <u>how, then, are the reasons which are given for moral judgments related to them?</u> I pointed out above that there seems to be a logical gap of some kind between factual reasons such as "This will prevent misery" and moral judgments such as "This ought to be done." <u>Is there really such a gap between "is" and "ought";</u> and if so, how is it to be bridged? Are we to say that "the passing of this bill will prevent misery," though it has the appearance solely of a statement of fact concerning a particular bill, is really such a statement *together with* an incapsulated universal principle to the effect that whatever prevents misery ought to be done? Or are we to say that the expression "prevents misery" states a fact of a peculiar kind, a morally-loaded fact so to speak, such that, when you have said that anything "prevents misery" you have said that it ought to be done? If we take the former line, we are saying that there certainly *is* a logical gap between "is" and "ought." We are saying that an ought conclusion can only follow from an ought premise. No one could, therefore, get from the factual premise "This bill will prevent misery" to the ought conclusion "This bill ought to become law" without the aid of a major premise, "Whatever will prevent misery ought to become law." People do argue from the factual premise to the ought conclusion and what they say does not have the appearance of nonsense. What they are really saying, therefore, must include the major premise. If we take the latter of the above lines, on the other hand, we are, in effect, saying that there *is no* logical gap between "is" and "ought," in some instances at any rate. To say "X is what prevents misery" is to say "X ought to be done." Moral philosophers are at present busily engaged in debating the relative merits of these two ways of explaining what men are doing when they talk about what they ought to do.[2]

I hope that the *kind* of question with which the moral philosopher, as I have defined him, deals, will now have been made clear. In this book I shall be concerned with the sort of questions which we have seen would arise for a moral philosopher who reflected on the Parliamentary debate about the Divorce Reform Bill. Recall some of these questions.

Are moral judgments more like discoveries than decisions, or vice versa? We shall see why the intuitionists said that they are more like the former; and the prescriptivists, more like the latter.[3]

Can moral judgments be replaced, without loss or change of meaning, by any statements of nonmoral fact? We shall see why some philosophers, ethical naturalists as they may be called, have thought that the answer is yes; while others—intuitionists, emotivists, prescriptivists—have thought that the answer is no.[4]

Is the appeal in moral discourse primarily to emotion or to reason? This question raises many issues with which I shall deal in due course. We shall see what emotivists have meant when they said that the meaning of moral language is primarily emotive; and we shall see what criticisms can be brought against their point of view.[5] We shall see what prescriptivists mean when they say that reasoned argument on moral questions is possible.[6] And we shall see that their critics, the descriptivists, think that prescriptivism does not show this to be so because, on the prescriptivist analysis of moral discourse, it is logically possible for anyone who participates not only to form his own opinion on a moral issue but to choose for himself what shall, or shall not, count as evidence, and this, they hold, is not reasoning.[7] Descriptivists claim to have found a firmer ground in reason for moral discourse than the prescriptivists. There are, they maintain, certain specific con-

[2] See Chap. VI.
[3] Chaps. III and V.
[4] See especially pp. 69–71.
[5] Chap. IV.
[6] Chap. V.
[7] Chap. VI.

siderations, or kinds of consideration, which must (logically) count as evidence for, or against, a moral judgment in the minds of all reasonable men. We shall see that their view, in its turn, has not gone unchallenged by contemporary philosophers who hold fast to emotivism or prescriptivism.[8]

In all of this, the fundamental question is: what is the *meaning* of *moral* discourse? That will be our main concern throughout this book. Behind the question just stated, however, lies another and an even more fundamental one, namely: what *is* meaning? We can hardly see the meaning of moral discourse, if we have no view of meaning as such. First of all, then, I shall consider in the next chapter some of the theories of meaning to which modern moral philosophers have subscribed. I shall go on to show in subsequent chapters how these theories of meaning respectively form the background to the main types of modern metaethical theory.

The story which I have to tell in this book is of a discussion which has gone on for more than fifty years. It has become more interesting with each decade. At the present time, one of the liveliest areas of philosophical debate is that concerned with the meaning of moral language. I shall of necessity have to tell the story as it appears to me, selecting for attention those thinkers and developments which seem to me to have most notably advanced the subject. No two philosophers, I suspect, would tell the story in exactly the same way, for opinions are bound to differ as to what has been, or what is, most notable in modern moral philosophy. I can only hope that I shall be able to tell the story in sufficient detail and with enough accuracy and fairness for the reader to understand what, in the main, has been going on and to form a judgment of his own on some, at least, of the crucial points which have been, and are, at issue.

Is There a Connection between Moral Philosophy and First-Order Moral Discourse?

I have differentiated very sharply between moral philosophy and first-order moral discourse in this chapter—some may

[8] *Ibid.*

feel, too sharply. Even as I define it, is there not a connection between moral philosophy and what has been called first-order moral discourse?

I stand by my insistence that the two must not be confused. When we come to consider prescriptivism, I shall refer to the criticism that its foremost exponent mixes up what is called "the universalizability thesis" with the liberal principle that one ought to apply to oneself the same standards as one applies when judging others.[9] The thesis referred to is a *logical* one; the principle, a *moral* one. The former is a theory about what people are doing when they talk about what they ought to do; the latter is what some people say that they ought to do. One belongs to moral philosophy, the other to what may be called (in an entirely non-pejorative sense) moralizing. Below, I shall discuss this particular criticism of prescriptivism and argue that it is not well founded. All I wish to point out at the moment is that if anyone were unaware of the fact that it is one thing to make the moral judgment "We ought to be impartial," and quite another to offer the logical analysis "Moral judgments, as such, are universalizable," he would, indeed, be guilty of a great confusion. The two activities are quite distinct.

However, where two activities are distinct, the one may nevertheless imply the other. Is there any such connection between moral philosophy and first-order moral discourse? Obviously, there is. Just because philosophy is second-order talk, it implies the existence of the first-order talk which it is about. In that sense, moral philosophy implies moralizing. It is perhaps worth emphasizing something which follows from this. A moral philosopher, as such, needs to know as much as possible about what goes on in first-order moral discourse. If he has not taken part in very much moral argument or discussion, there is a presumption that he will not be a very good moral philosopher. There is always a danger that philosophers will go astray because they do not know enough about what they are talking *about*. It is notorious, for example, that in the philosophy of science and the philosophy

9 See pp. 230–31.

of religion, the instances of first-order discourse upon which philosophers, specializing in these fields, base their analyses, often strike practicing scientists and religious believers respectively as naive to the point of misrepresentation. A philosopher who writes about the logic of scientific discovery without having been a scientist, or who sets out to analyze religious belief without knowing at firsthand what it is like to be, or at least to have been, a believer, must, to say the least, be careful. The same point can be made about moral philosophy. Here, perhaps, there is much less possibility of a philosopher not really knowing what he is talking about. One could know little of science, and have no acquaintance with religious belief, but still feel quite at home in our contemporary society. But one would hardly feel at home if one were totally inexperienced in moral discourse. There is some distaste for such discourse nowadays, it is true, but it would be difficult to find anyone who has managed to opt out of moralizing, however pejorative that word may have become in his usage.

This connection, then, exists between moralizing (in my non-pejorative sense) and moral philosophy. The latter presupposes the former. Although I have said that it is an advantage for a moral philosopher to participate in first-order moral discourse, I must make it quite clear that I am not saying that he must (logically) do so in order to be a moral philosopher. I am only saying that he must have some acquaintance with what it is that he exists to analyze. If he reads a newspaper, watches television, or listens to people on trains and buses, he will not lack for material. He can (logically) know what he is talking about simply by listening to other people moralizing. It remains true that, for any individual, to philosophize about moral discourse is to do one thing and to moralize is to do another.

However, it may be instructive to pursue a little further the question: can the opinions which someone holds, as a moral philosopher, make any difference to any views, other than purely philosophical ones, which he holds where moral discourse is concerned? I am taking the "can" here to be a logical "can." It is very important, of course, to keep clearly in mind the distinction between *understanding* a universe of discourse and *participating* in it. But, given that distinction, does the understanding which anybody thinks that he has gained from moral philosophy have any important logical consequences beyond the realm of moral philosophy? In concluding this chapter, I shall refer to three respects in which I think that it does, or rather that it may.

First, from the opinions which a moral philosopher, as such, holds there will follow certain opinions as to what constitutes moral education and as to how the latter should be conducted. I am not saying, for a moment, that anybody has to be a moral philosopher in order to be a moral educator. Many parents and teachers make excellent moral educators without knowing anything about the sort of questions with which this book will deal. But if they do happen to be interested in moral philosophy, then from their opinions on certain philosophical questions, conclusions necessarily follow as to what it is *in* which they are educating their pupils. From these, in turn, there will follow certain conclusions as to how one must go about giving a moral education.

Take, for example, the very basic question: what makes a judgment moral? Some philosophers contend that it is the *form* of the judgment, or rather of the reasoning in support of it, which does so; others, that it is the *content*. I shall be writing at length about these two points of view in the sequel.[10] All I want to point out here is that if anyone thinks that what makes a piece of thinking moral is its *form*, then it would be logical for him to say that moral education is education in that form of reasoning. He might say, "We must give our pupils every opportunity to practice arguing with one another in the specifically moral way and it doesn't matter what they are arguing about." On the other hand, if anyone thinks that what makes a piece of thinking moral is its *content*, that for instance it is about the interests or wants which human beings have, then it would be logical for him to say that a moral education ought to make those who receive it aware of the interests or wants which people have. He might say, "We must

[10] Chaps. V and VI.

show our pupils what miseries such-and-such things (e.g., apartheid, divorce, drugs, war, or whatever) cause." Perhaps, in practice, the difference noted here in moral philosophy will not make all that much difference to what anyone does in a moral education class. But it is enough for my purpose if it could make some difference. And I have tried to show that it could. From one's answer to the question "What makes a judgment moral?" there follows logically a certain answer to the question "What must we do in order to give a moral education?" There is, then, that connection between moral philosophy and training in first-order moral discourse. But it should be born clearly in mind that the question to which I have just referred, viz. "What must we do in order to give a moral education?" is an educational or a logical question, but *not* a moral one. The same goes for any answers to it. We have not here shown that a conclusion in first-order moral discourse can be derived from a premise in moral philosophy.

Secondly, the opinions which a moral philosopher, as such, holds may provide him with what he sees as a logical foundation for a point of view within first-order moral discourse. Take, for example, a philosopher who holds what is called "the universalizability thesis." We have already noted that this is a metaethical theory about what makes discourse moral, and I shall have much more to say about it below.[11] Putting things crudely for the moment, it is the theory that a judgment is moral if, and only if, the reasons given for it could conceivably apply to other cases than that which is being judged. If, for example, we give the fact that we are in situation S as a reason why we ourselves ought (morally) to do a certain action, A, we imply that anyone else in a situation of the same kind as S ought to do an action of the same kind as A. That is, we cannot (logically) make exceptions in our own case, if we are judging morally. From which it could conceivably follow that we are not judging *morally* unless we are judging a situation from a utilitarian point of view, i.e., the view that the greatest happiness ought to be aimed at and, in

[11] Chap. V.

assessing it, everybody ought to count for one and nobody
for more than one. This conclusion has been drawn by some.
What does their inference amount to? It may look as though
a philosophical view (the universalizability thesis) has implied a moral point of view (the greatest happiness principle).
But has it? Let us assume that it can be shown that a judgment is not moral unless it is delivered from a utilitarian
point of view. If it can, it is important to be clear what has
been shown and what has not. So to speak, the rules of the
moral "language-game," i.e., first-order moral discourse, have
been made clearer. It has been shown that it is a rule of that
"game" that unless we are judging with a view to what will
maximize happiness we are not judging morally. In other
words, if anyone says that something ought morally to be
done, but does not support what he says by reasons which
have regard to the maximization of happiness, then what
he has said will make no sense. In moralizing, as in any other
"game," we must (logically) keep the rules or the game is at
an end. But we should bear clearly in mind that enunciating
the rules of a game is different from playing it. To explain
the conditions under which a goal may be scored is not to
score one. To show what would constitute a reason within
moral discourse is not to give a reason within that discourse.
Once again, it has not been shown that a conclusion in first-
order moral discourse can be drawn from a premise in moral
philosophy.

Thirdly, it is generally true that philosophical reflection
upon any type of first-order discourse can (logically and
empirically) enable one to participate in such discourse more
effectively. We may safely assume that this is so where moral
discourse is concerned. I am not saying that a moral philosopher will always be a better moralist than a non-philosopher
—far from it. In any " game," to draw that analogy once more,
there are some who know the rules of the game but are very
inexpert in playing it. If a team is playing football badly, what
it needs is not more people who know the rules (every well-
informed spectator does), but some better players. Similarly,
if a society is deteriorating morally, what it needs is not more

moral philosophers but more good men.[12] However, understanding what one is doing is seldom a disadvantage and, as I have said, we may assume that this applies to morality. A moral philosopher, as we have seen above, draws distinctions within moral discourse between matters of fact and matters of evaluation. He recognizes the points at which consistency is vital, if moral thinking is not to fall apart. He reflects on what considerations make a reason a *moral* reason. He is alive to the emotive nature of the language often used in moral argument, and so on. After all this, he ought to be able to think in a reasonably clearheaded way about moral issues, if he chooses to do so. Everyone knows, of course, that philosophers are frequently just as prejudiced and irrational in their moral opinions as anybody else. But not always. It was fashionable, a little time ago, for moral philosophers to say that they had nothing to do with first-order moral questions, and to leave these alone. There is some evidence that moral philosophers are turning their attention again to practical problems, such as what we ought to do about sex or war.[13] Such problems will not concern us directly in this book. But one may venture to hope that a reader who has worked through this book will be able to think about such matters more clearly than he might otherwise have done.

[12] I realize, of course, that, whereas a good football player may be defined simply as someone who plays football well, there is more to being a good man than being a good moralizer. Nevertheless, it would make sense to say that one of the necessary conditions of being a good man is that one should engage effectively in first-order moral discourse and the form of life which it constitutes. The fact that the word "effectively" in the last sentence covers a nest of metaethical problems does not affect this point.

[13] See, e.g., R. F. Atkinson, *Sexual Morality* (1965); and R. M. Hare's lecture *Peace* (Canberra, 1966). I am currently editing a series of monographs, *New Studies in Practical Philosophy*, to be published by Macmillan, which will include *inter alia* studies by analytical philosophers of a number of practical moral problems.

CHAPTER 2. MORAL DISCOURSE AND THEORIES OF MEANING

We saw in the last chapter that the main question with which modern moral philosophers have concerned themselves is: what is the meaning of moral language? Their differing answers to it have taken shape under the influence of theories about the meaning of language in general, not simply of moral discourse. During the period of philosophy with which I am concerned in this book there have been important developments in the general theory of meaning. For an understanding of modern moral philosophy it is essential to have some knowledge of these. In this chapter, therefore, my aim will be threefold. Within the limited space available, I will try: (i) to outline the theories of meaning which lie behind the main types of modern ethical theory; (ii) to show why some of them are mistaken; (iii) to give some indication of the influence upon modern moral philosophy which each theory of meaning has had.

Each of the theories of meaning to which I shall refer has been the subject of long and detailed argument among philosophers. To do these theories justice would require a whole book rather than a chapter. I can only hope that my treatment will not appear too superficial or hasty. But even at the risk of that, some attempt at an exposition of the relevant theories of meaning must be made. We cannot get into a position to assess the merits or demerits of the different types of modern ethical theory without considering the general theories of meaning to which they are related. In order to answer the question "What is the meaning of moral language?" it is necessary not only to be clear what moral discourse is, but also to have an opinion as to what meaning is.

The word "mean" and its cognates have many differing uses. It is important to emphasize that the sense in which I am using "mean" in this chapter is that in which it applies to *language*. Consider the following examples of other uses. In the case of each I will provide a synonym for "mean" or its cognate.

> I mean to go. (intend)
> Excess of expenditure over income means bankruptcy. (results in)
> Life has lost its meaning for me. (purpose)
> What is the meaning of your lateness? (explanation)
> If he takes the 6:30, that means that he will be there before us. (implies)

There are numerous other uses, in which, as in these examples, "mean" and its cognates are used to talk about persons, actions, events, or things. But the sense of "mean" etc. which concerns us is different from all of these. To take one of the above examples, it is perfectly clear that there is a sense in which "excess of expenditure over income" does *not* mean "bankruptcy," because, if anyone substituted one of these expressions for the other in a speech-act, he would change its meaning. The quotation marks indicate that what we are talking about here is the *words* "excess of expenditure over income" and "bankruptcy." It is with the meaning of words, phrases, sentences, as used in speech-acts, that we are concerned in this chapter. Language is used to communicate something. Through it something is, or is not, understood. Its *meaning* is what it communicates, what is, or is not, understood. But to the question: what precisely *is* meaning in this sense? philosophers have given differing answers. Some of these I shall consider.

First, I shall turn to the referential theory of meaning, which seems to lie behind the ethical theory of those recent moral philosophers who are called intuitionists and, with a different result, behind the early Wittgenstein's views on ethics. Next, the verificationist and the causal, or psychological, theories of meaning will be discussed. These may be said

to undergird the ethical theory called emotivism. The verificationist theory undergirds the emotivism of the early logical
positivists; the causal, or psychological, theory, that of Professor C. L. Stevenson. In the final section, called *Meaning as
Use*, I shall turn to some of the opinions about language held
by the later Wittgenstein and J. L. Austin respectively. These
opinions form a foundation for the ethical theories of the
prescriptivists and descriptivists.

I. THE REFERENTIAL THEORY

Simplest Form of the Theory

This is the theory that the meaning of language is that
which it names or to which it refers. There are different ways
of indicating what language means, of course. We can define
it ostensively, i.e., by pointing to its referent; or we can define
it verbally, i.e., by naming, or referring to, its referent in other
terms. If anyone asks what "the Prime Minister of Great
Britain," for example, means, we may either point to a certain
individual or say something like "the man who presides
over the Cabinet." Language is about things, activities, qualities of objects, states of affairs, relations, etc.; but it all, according to the theory which we are now considering, means
that to which it refers. If, in the last analysis, there is nothing
in existence which a word names, then it has no meaning.

Some immediate objections to this theory spring to mind.
It is sometimes represented as the theory of meaning which
reflection on the ordinary use of language most naturally
suggests. But, even with expressions which from the point
of view of this theory are least problematic, i.e., the names of
objects or persons, an appeal to ordinary language soon shows
that the meanings and the referents of such expressions are
not, in such language, to be equated. To take examples
which others have used, according to the referential theory
the meaning of the expression "the morning star" is the planet
Venus. But whereas it would mean one thing to say "Venus
has just exploded" or "The object referred to by the expression 'the morning star' has just exploded," it would surely

mean something different, if indeed it meant anything at all, to say "The meaning of the expression 'the morning star' has just exploded." We might say naturally enough on some occasion "The person called N has gone away," or with the same meaning, simply "N has gone away," but it would be unnatural to the point of nonsense to say "The meaning of the name 'N' has gone away."[1] Two pieces of language may have the same referent but different meanings; or, again, the same meaning but different referents.[2] For example, the expressions "the son who was born to James Herbert and Ethel Wilson on March 11, 1916" and "the man who became Prime Minister of this country in October 1964" have the same referent. But that their meanings are different is clear from the fact that "the son who was born to James Herbert and Ethel Wilson on March 11, 1916, became Prime Minister of this country in October 1964" is not tautologous. For example again, the expression "Prime Minister" at this moment has at least two referents, viz. Harold Wilson and Ian Smith. But, as it stands, its meaning is the same with reference to either of them. "Harold Wilson is Prime Minister" and "Ian Smith is Prime Minister" convey the same information about their different subjects.

A More Sophisticated Version of the Theory

The referential theory of meaning is said to be capable of a formulation which avoids the sort of objections just noted. This "more sophisticated view" of it has been given as follows: "that the meaning of the expression is to be identified with the relation between the expression and its referent, that the referential connection constitutes the meaning."[3] One instance of this more sophisticated formulation, sometimes quoted, is Bertrand Russell's remark: "When we ask what constitutes meaning . . . we are asking, not who is the individual meant, but what is the relation of the word to the

---

[1] Cf. F. Waismann, *The Principles of Linguistic Philosophy* (London, 1965), pp. 312–13.

[2] Cf. W. P. Alston, *Philosophy of Language* (Englewood Cliffs, N.J., 1964), p. 13.

[3] Alston, *op. cit.*, pp. 12–13.

individual which makes the one mean the other."[4] Let us
consider again the expression "Prime Minister." We saw
that its meaning cannot be equated with any individual
referent because it will have the same meaning when it refers to some other individual. We must note further that its
meaning cannot be the *class* of Prime Ministers. If we wished
to say "The class of Prime Ministers isn't what it was," we
could not render this as "Prime Minister isn't what it was."[5]
But, despite such considerations, it is in line with the more
sophisticated version of the referential theory of which I am
now speaking, to hold that the meaning of "Prime Minister"
consists in the referential relation which subsists between this
expression and the persons whom it denotes or connotes. The
expression "Prime Minister" can be applied to all members
of the class of Prime Ministers, whereas it cannot, to the members of any other class of persons (denotation). A necessary
and sufficient condition of its being asserted correctly of anyone that he is a Prime Minister is (if the verbal definition suggested above is accepted) that he should preside over a
Cabinet (connotation). The referential theory, in this sophisticated form, is to the effect that the meaning of language is
made clear only by indicating that in the world to which it
applies, or of which it can be asserted. You cannot say baldly
that the meaning *is* the referent. But you can say that the
meaning of language is not known until the persons or things,
of whom or of which the language is asserted, are known.[6]

There seem to be at least two objections to this more sophisticated version of the referential theory. (i) If language
is meaningful, only when there is that in the world of which
it can be asserted, what are we to make of such elements in
language as prepositions, conjunctions, or the modal auxiliaries of verbs? What things in the world are there to which
words like "at" or "in" refer; or words like "and" or "but";
or "would" in "He would do it if he could?" These words are
not meaningless and any theory which implies that they are

[4] Cf. Alston, *op. cit.*, p. 14; from B. Russell, *Analysis of Mind* (1921),
p. 191.
[5] Cf. Alston, *op. cit.*, pp. 14–15.
[6] Cf. Alston, *op. cit.*, pp. 16–18.

must be mistaken. (ii) But even if there is some way of over-coming that objection, the referential theory oversimplifies the concept of meaning. Take the speech-act "X is good," as an example. It might, with certain safeguards, be true to say that it is meaningless, if it is not *about* anything, i.e., if there is no such thing as X. But you have not revealed what its meaning is when you have simply shown *what* it is about. *How* is it about what it is about? Is it about X in the way that a commendation is about its subject matter, or in the way that a description is, or in what way? Until you have shown, not simply *what* a piece of language is about, but *how* it is about it, you have not shown the meaning of that piece of language. The referential theory puts all the emphasis on "what about." We are entitled, therefore, in the light of the distinction just drawn, to say that it oversimplifies the concept of meaning.

Wittgenstein's "Picture Theory"

One extremely sophisticated version of the referential theory of meaning is that developed by Ludwig Wittgenstein in his *Tractatus Logico-Philosophicus* (completed in 1918 and first published in German in 1921 and in English in 1922).

Wittgenstein's earliest recorded remark concerning this pic-ture theory is to be found in his *Notebooks 1914–16* and runs, "In the proposition a world is, as it were, put together experi-mentally. (As when in the law-court in Paris a motor accident is represented by means of dolls, etc.)" (entry dated Septem-ber 29, 1914).[7] It is said that this picture theory occurred to Wittgenstein while he was serving in the trenches as a mem-ber of the Austrian army. He there read a magazine which contained an account of how an accident had been repre-sented in the above way during a lawsuit. To the making of any such model three things would go, namely: (i) objects such as dolls, toy cars, etc. which symbolize the vehicles, persons, or whatever, involved; (ii) a certain arrangement, or configuration, of these symbols which represents the ar-rangement of the vehicles, persons, or whatever, in the modeled situation; (iii) a convention, understood and ac-

[7] Cf. *T* 4.031.

cepted by all who use the model, whereby its several elements are related to their counterparts in the actual situation. (Where objects such as dolls and toy cars are used, of course it is obvious what they symbolize; but a model could be constructed in which, for example, matchsticks represented people, ink pots stood for cars, and so on). Wittgenstein claimed that language models, mirrors, or pictures reality as that model in the law courts represented the accident. It *refers* to the world in a similar way. A proposition presents a *logical picture* of a situation. What follows, concerning (a) language and (b) the world, from this theory of meaning?

(a) So far as language is concerned, Wittgenstein said that all meaningful language is analyzable into "elementary propositions."[8] He defined an elementary proposition as a "concatenation of names."[9] By "names" here he meant logically proper names; in that sense, a name is a simple sign which does not describe but designates, or denotes, that of which it is the name. Names are the elements of language. Each of them refers to one element in reality and to no other; and each element in reality has one name and no other. Of course, the propositions expressed in language, as it is normally used, are far from elementary in Wittgenstein's sense. The terms used in them can be replaced by other terms without loss or change of meaning, and these in their turn by yet others, and so on. But this replacing of words with words must have an end. Wittgenstein said: "A proposition has one and only one complete analysis."[10] A point will be reached eventually in the analysis of a proposition's meaning at which the signs used to express it are "simple" signs. That is, there is a one-to-one correspondence between each of them and some element of reality. It is logically necessary that we should reach such a point before we can know the precise meaning of a proposition. "The requirement that simple signs be possible," said Wittgenstein, "is the requirement that sense be determinate."[11] Language consists, in the last analysis, of elemen-

[8] *T* 4.221.
[9] *T* 4.22.
[10] *T* 3.25.
[11] *T* 3.23.

tary propositions, which in turn consist of simple signs or names.

(b) What follows from Wittgenstein's theory of meaning concerning the world to which language is taken to refer? Just as language consists of simple signs, so the world must consist of—to use Wittgenstein's term for the elements of reality—simple "objects." These "objects" are simple in the sense that we can refer to them only by naming them: we cannot describe them because this would only be possible if they were analyzable into other elements, as for instance a watch can be reduced to its parts. If there is to be meaning at all, on Wittgenstein's theory, then, just as language must break down into elements which determinately refer to reality, so reality must logically consist of elements to which determinate reference can be made. "Objects," said Wittgenstein, "make up the substance of the world."[12] He did not, however, think that they exist in isolation. He said: "The world divides into facts";[13] that is, into *Sachlagen* (situations or molecular facts) and, in the last analysis, into *Sachverhalten* (states of affairs or atomic facts). An atomic fact is a "combination of objects."[14] Language reduces, in the last analysis, to elementary propositions, i.e., "concatenations of names"; the world, to atomic facts, i.e., "combinations of objects."

A point, with regard to both language and the world, which we may note in passing, is that there is a difference, according to Wittgenstein, in the way that elementary propositions and names respectively refer to the world. He marked this difference by saying that names have *Bedeutung,* and elementary propositions, *Sinn.* In the light of this distinction he said: "The meanings (*Bedeutungen*) of simple signs (words) must be explained to us, if we are to understand them. With propositions, however, we make ourselves understood. It belongs to the essence of a proposition that it should be able to communicate a *new* sense (*Sinn*) to us."[15] What this means is as follows. We need to be told to what object a name refers

[12] *T* 2.021.
[13] *T* 1.2.
[14] *T* 2.01.
[15] *T* 4.026, 4.027.

but names do not change their meanings. If, however, we know to what objects the names within a proposition refer, then, even though we have never encountered these names in this particular configuration before, we can understand what the proposition means. A name which does not refer to an existing object has *no Bedeutung;* but a proposition which does not correspond to reality, provided the names of which it is composed are the names of existing objects, may nevertheless have *Sinn.* If there is in reality no object X, then the name "X" is meaningless; but though a proposition, e.g., "Exeter is in Cornwall," is false it is not thereby necessarily meaningless. "The world divides into facts": and facts may not only change, they may be imagined to be other than they really are. We can construct a world as it were experimentally. "Objects are what is unalterable and subsistent; their configuration is what is changing and unstable."[16]

I mentioned three elements which would go to the making of a model such as that used in the Paris court. We are now in a position to see that these correspond to the three conditions which according to Wittgenstein must be fulfilled if a proposition is to be, as he said it was, a logical picture of a situation or state of affairs. These conditions are:

(i) "In a proposition there must be exactly as many distinguishable parts as in the situation that it represents."[17] In the last analysis, a proposition consists of names only and it can therefore only represent a situation (which, in the last analysis, consists of atomic facts, these in turn consisting only of objects) if for every object in the situation there is a name in the elementary proposition which pictures it.

(ii) "The configuration of objects in a situation corresponds to the configuration of simple signs in the propositional sign."[18] This is illuminated by Wittgenstein's remark: "Only facts can express a sense, a set of names cannot."[19] The proposition pictures reality only because its elements (names) have the configuration which they do have, this configuration

[16] *T* 2.0271.
[17] *T* 4.04.
[18] *T* 3.21.
[19] *T* 3.142.

corresponding to that of the elements (objects) of the situation.

(iii) ". . . A proposition is a propositional sign in its projective relation to the world."[20] A proposition is not a propositional sign *simpliciter*. A propositional sign consists of words which express the proposition. This does not mean that a proposition, according to Wittgenstein, is a mysterious metaphysical entity. A proposition, he said, is a propositional sign (i.e., a sentence, written or spoken) *intended and understood to refer to reality*. He spoke of a "law of projection."[21] The elements of the propositional sign are related by laws, or rules, of projection with the elements of reality—as, for instance, certain notes on a musical score are related by convention to certain sounds. By intending the signs to have such references in the particular configuration which they have in this propositional sign, we "think of the sense of the proposition,"[22] i.e., we think of the situation which it represents.

It is important to remember that what Wittgenstein was concerned with was the analysis of the concept of meaning. He deemed his conclusions to follow with logical necessity from that concept. If there was to be meaning, then language and the world *must* consist in the last analysis of the "simples" of which he conceived. Asked for examples of a "name" or an "object," he replied that it was no part of his business, as a logician, to supply them.[23] He considered that he had fulfilled his analytical task simply when he had shown that "names" and "objects" there must be, if there is to be meaning.

I noted, in the last subsection, two objections to the sophisticated version of the referential theory of meaning; viz.: (i) it fails to explain the meanings of words like "in," "and," "would," etc.; (ii) it oversimplifies the concept of meaning. Wittgenstein was alive to the former of these at the time when he wrote the *Tractatus*, and we shall see how he tried to

[20] *T* 3.12.
[21] *T* 4.0141.
[22] *T* 3.11.
[23] N. Malcolm, *Ludwig Wittgenstein: a Memoir* (1958), p. 86.

dispose of it in that book. To the latter objection he became increasingly alive after the *Tractatus* was written, and eventually, in view of this objection, rejected his "picture theory" of meaning. I will say something about his treatment of each of these objections in turn.

(a) Prepositions, conjunctions, and modal auxiliaries, i.e., words like "in," "and," "would," etc., appear to correspond to nothing in the world but they are undoubtedly meaningful. What, on a referential theory, can their meaning be? Wittgenstein was clear in the *Tractatus* that words like "and," "not," "or," "if—then"—logical constants or connectives as they are sometimes called—are "not representatives."[24] Take "not" for instance. If "not" represented something, then the situation referred to by the expression "not not p" would contain two more things than that represented by "p" on its own. But "not not p" and "p" are normally taken to mean the same. Again, take "and" as an example. The proposition (A) "Fred is in his car and Bill is on his bike" may be analyzed into two more elementary propositions (A1) "Fred is in his car" and (A2) "Bill is on his bike." If (A1) is true and (A2) is true, then (A) is true. If (A1) is false or (A2) is false, or both are, then (A) is false. So the truth value of (A) depends only on the truth values of (A1) and (A2) respectively. We do not need to ask whether or not there is anything which "and" represents before we can know that A is true, if we know that (A1) and (A2) are true.

(b) In *Philosophical Investigations* (completed in 1949 and published posthumously in 1953) Wittgenstein realized that the *Tractatus* had oversimplified the concept of meaning. He set out the following objections among others to his own picture theory. I will arrange the following objections so as to show their bearing upon the three elements which go to the making of a model such as that used in the Paris law court, and upon the three conditions, corresponding to these, which, I said above, must be fulfilled if a proposition is to present a logical picture of a situation.

(i) It makes no sense, Wittgenstein said, to speak of an ab-

solute one-to-one correlation between the simples of language and those of reality because reality cannot be broken
down *absolutely* into simples. "What are the simple constituent parts of which reality is composed?" he queried. "What
are the simple constituent parts of a chair?—The bits of wood
of which it is made? Or the molecules, or the atoms?—'Simple' means: not composite. And here the point is: in what
sense 'composite'? It makes no sense at all, to speak absolutely
of the 'simple parts of a chair.'" He pointed out that "we
use the word 'composite' (and therefore the word 'simple')
in an enormous number of different and differently related
ways." The visual image of a tree, for example, cannot be
said to consist of one kind of simples. You could break it
down into the different colors of which it is composed or alternatively into the tiny straight lines of which its outline is
composed. It makes sense to ask what the simples of any given
piece of reality are only when we have decided what kind
of simplicity is in question. "Is the color of a square on a
chessboard simple, or does it consist of pure white and pure
yellow? And is white simple or does it consist of the colors
of the rainbow?—Is this length of 2 cm. simple, or does it
consist of two parts, each 1 cm. long? But why not of one bit
3 cm. long, and one bit 1 cm. long measured in the opposite
direction?"[25] Questions which presuppose—as the picture theory presupposed—absolute complexity and simplicity, quite
apart from context, are unanswerable.

(ii) When you have analyzed a complex proposition into
elementary propositions—i.e., into simpler configurations of
words—you have not, said Wittgenstein, necessarily made the
sense of the original proposition thereby clearer. According
to the theory of meaning which he is now rejecting, the statement "My broom is in the corner" could be "further
analyzed," according to Wittgenstein, into a statement giving
the position of the stick and the position of the brush. "If the
broom is there, that surely means that the stick and the brush
must be there, and in a particular relation to one another."
This analysis is, as it were, "hidden in the sense of" the first

[25] *PI*, 47.

statement and "is *expressed* in" the *analysans*. But now he questions all this. "Then does someone who says that the broom is in the corner really mean: the broomstick is there, and so is the brush, and the broomstick is fixed in the brush? —If we were to ask anyone if he meant this he would probably say that he had not thought specially of the broomstick or specially of the brush at all. And that would be the *right* answer, for he meant to speak neither of the stick nor of the brush in particular. Suppose that, instead of saying 'Bring me the broom,' you said, 'Bring me the broomstick and the brush which is fitted on to it!' Isn't the answer: 'Do you want the broom? Why do you put it so oddly?'—Is he going to understand the further analyzed sentence better?"[26] The answer is, obviously, that he is not.

(iii) The *Tractatus* had said in effect that meaning is given to a proposition by a mental act, distinct from the publishing of the propositional sign, namely by "thinking of the sense of the proposition."[27] It would seem to follow from this that any sign could be used to mean anything, provided some such mental act gives it this meaning. Wittgenstein now said: "Make the following experiment: *say* 'It's cold here' and *mean* 'It's warm here.' Can you do it?"[28] He thought not. You cannot take a remark out of its appropriate language-game and give it any meaning you decide upon simply by thinking of that sense for the proposition.

With such arguments, then, Wittgenstein expressly repudiated his earlier referential theory of meaning and replaced it by one which takes account, not only of what language is about, but of *how* it is about what it is about. We shall turn to this later theory below.

The Referential Theory and Moral Discourse

There are two ways in which, given the referential theory of meaning, it is possible to deal with a moral judgment, such as "X is good." One of these ways was taken by the intuitionists, whose moral philosophy will be considered below in

---

[26] *PI*, 60.
[27] *T* 3.11; cf. above, p. 28.
[28] *PI*, 510.

Chapter 3. The other was taken by the early Wittgenstein, to whose opinions about ethics I shall refer in the early part of Chapter 4.

If one subscribes to the former of the two ways of dealing with "X is good," one has to say that "good" must refer to something. The judgment "X is good" is meaningful. Given the referential theory, then, there must be some quality to which "good" refers. But whatever goodness may be, it is not a quality or property which can be apprehended by the physical senses, like redness or sweetness. It must, then, be assumed: (a) that there are such things as "nonnatural" qualities or properties of actions or states of affairs, to which words used in moral discourse, like "right," "good," "obligatory," refer; and (b) that men possess a faculty which apprehends these and which is distinct from the physical senses, that is, the faculty commonly called conscience and conceived of either as reason or as a peculiar "moral sense." The intuitionists believed that these assumptions can be justified. We shall consider in Chapter 3 how well founded that belief was.

According to the other way of dealing with "X is good," it is possible to say that "X is good" must be meaningless. It is a value judgment. As such, it is about what *ought* to be the case. If you hold to a picture theory you hold to the view that language is meaningful only when it refers to reality. But reality is what *is*, not what ought to be, the case. Therefore, a value judgment is not about reality and so it cannot (logically) be meaningful. In Chapter 4 we shall look more closely at Wittgenstein's development of this line of thought about ethics.

II. THE VERIFICATIONIST THEORY

Logical Positivism

The verificationist theory was propounded by the logical positivists. Originally, they were a group of philosophers, scientists, and mathematicians, who during the 1920's gathered around Moritz Schlick, professor of philosophy at Vienna, and became known as the Vienna Circle. Many of those who belonged to this Circle became renowned in philosophy, e.g., Carnap, Waismann, Neurath, Feigl, and others.

Wittgenstein was never a member but he associated with Schlick; and the Circle were deeply influenced by his *Tractatus*. The best-known British exponent of logical positivism is Professor A. J. Ayer, who attended the meetings of the Circle during the early 1930's. With the rise of the Nazis and the outbreak of war, the Vienna Circle dissolved.

Logical positivism has had a profound influence on philosophy during the past fifty years and this influence has extended to moral philosophy. To appreciate its influence on moral philosophy we need to understand the verficationist theory of meaning, to which the logical positivists subscribed, and of that theory I will offer a brief account.

Its classic formulation is that the meaning of a proposition is the mode of its verification. What precisely does that mean? Ayer expanded it thus: "A statement is held to be literally meaningful if and only if it is analytic or empirically verifiable."[29] By "literally meaningful" he intended "capable of being shown to be true or false." Put very summarily, what the logical positivists said about meaning comes to this. Analytic statements are verified, or falsified, simply by appeal to the definitions of the signs used in them. If they turn out to be tautologies, on such appeal, they are true; if contradictions, false. Mathematical and logical statements are of this kind. All other meaningful statements are such as can be verified, or falsified, by empirical observation, i.e., by the evidence of our physical senses. They are, in effect, hypotheses concerning future experience. If I say "There is a policeman in the garden," I am predicting that any normal person will, if he goes into the garden, see a policeman. If I say "There was a policeman in the garden yesterday," I am predicting what anyone would experience who set out to test this statement. If, for example, he did so by questioning my neighbors, he would hear the reply "Yes, there was." The statements of science, history, and common sense are meaningful by this criterion.

There has been a great deal of philosophical discussion about the verification principle, as the logical positivists'

[29] A. J. Ayer, *Language, Truth and Logic* (2nd ed., 1946), p. 9.

criterion of meaning is usually called. Two main questions
have been raised concerning it. The first is: what is its correct
formulation? The logical positivists themselves ran into great
difficulties when attempting a formulation of it which would
be neither too exclusive nor too inclusive. Scientific laws are
universals to the effect that all A's are B. In order to verify
this conclusively, one would need to observe all the A's in the
universe; but it is logically impossible to be certain that one
has ever done so. There may always be an A somewhere
which is not B. It follows, if statements are meaningful only
when they can be verified, that scientific laws are meaningless. If we substitute for the notion of verification that of falsification, the problem is not solved completely. A scientific
law will then be one which can be empirically falsified; e.g.,
"All A's are B" is falsified if we find one A which is not B.
We may then say that scientific laws are universal propositions
which have hitherto escaped falsification. But this formulation
of the criterion, though it may leave science intact, seems to
play havoc with common sense. For, while it would allow us
to say meaningfully, "There are no A's which are B" since
this could be falsified by finding one A which was B, it
would not allow us to say "There are some A's which are B"
because that could not be falsified.[30] To avoid such conclusions, the verification principle was reformulated to the effect
that a statement is meaningful if some observation statement
can be deduced from it in conjunction with certain other
premises, without being deducible from these other premises
alone ("observation statement" here meaning a statement
which records an actual or possible empirical observation).
Will this do? Let us take the metaphysical statement "The
Absolute is pure spirit" as the example. If this is conjoined
with the premise "If the Absolute is pure spirit, then all cats
are black," we may validly deduce from these two premises,
though not from the latter alone, the observation statement
"All cats are black." It follows that the metaphysical statement
"The Absolute is pure spirit" is, by the reformulated principle,

[30] Cf. K. R. Popper, *The Logic of Scientific Discovery* (1959), *passim.*

meaningful.[31] All these conclusions, however, were repugnant to the logical positivists. The whole point of their movement was to laud science and common sense and to discredit metaphysics. The last thing they wanted from their criterion of meaning was that it should exclude the former and include the latter. We need not go further into the intricacies of the debate. Suffice it to remark that the dilemma does not seem ever to have been resolved satisfactorily. Ayer himself in his introduction to *Logical Positivism* recognizes that the verification principle has never been adequately formulated.[32]

The second question raised concerning this principle is: does it purport to be a lexical or a stipulative definition of "meaning"? Clearly it is not the former; in the ordinary sense of the word, ethical or metaphysical statements undeniably have meaning. Ayer recognizes this and remarks:

> It seems to me fairly clear that what they [the logical positivists] were in fact doing was to adopt the verification principle as a convention. They were propounding a definition of meaning which accorded with common usage in the sense that it set out the conditions that are in fact satisfied by statements which are regarded as empirically informative. Their treatment of *a priori* statements was also intended to provide an account of the way in which such statements actually function. To this extent their work was descriptive; it became prescriptive with the suggestion that only statements of these two kinds should be regarded as either true or false, and that only statements which are capable of being either true or false should be regarded as literally meaningful.[33]

Ayer conceded that it does not follow necessarily that we should accept this prescription; but he points out quite justifiably that metaphysicians have often posed as men doing the same sort of work as scientists only doing it more profoundly, whereas, in fact, it can be shown that, since their statements are neither analytic nor empirically verifiable, they are not. If the metaphysicians are not doing what the scientists

[31] See Ayer, *op. cit.*, pp. 11–12.
[32] Ayer, *Logical Positivism* (Glencoe, Ill., 1959), p. 14.
[33] *Ibid.*, p. 15.

are doing, then it is up to them to make it clear just what they are doing and, in particular, how this differs from what poets, preachers, or writers of fiction do.[34]

The Verification Principle and Moral Discourse

What, then, of moral judgments? It seems fairly clear that they can be verified in neither of the approved ways. They cannot be shown to be true or false by definition. "X is good" is not to be verified by showing that "good" means X. Some philosophers have in the past argued that it is, but we shall see in Chapter 3 that they made a serious mistake. Briefly, this was the mistake of overlooking the fact that whatever definition (D) you give of, for example, "good," the question "Is what is D good?" is never self-answering. Again, goodness, as we have already noted in this chapter, whatever it may be, is certainly not a property which can be seen, smelled, tasted, touched, or heard. We may speak figuratively of apprehending it in one or other of these ways, but we do not "see" goodness as we see tables and chairs, and similarly with reference to the other senses. If "X is good" is not verifiable—or falsifiable—analytically or empirically, then, by the logical positivist theory of meaning, it is meaningless. Great scandal was caused when early logical positivists announced that ethics is nonsense. It seemed a monstrous thing to say. Really, though they did not always make this clear, they were using "nonsense" as a technical term. Ethics is "non-sense": i.e., it has to do with that which cannot be observed by sense. Its judgments, according to the logical positivists, are therefore uninformative; they cannot be shown to be true or false, they lack literal meaning. This, of course, does contradict the views of those who believe in an objective moral order, i.e., objective in the same sense as the physical world, and in moral truths apprehended by intuition. But it does not exclude the possibility that moral judgments have some kind of meaning, albeit not literal meaning. We shall see in Chapter 4 that the emotivist theory appealed to Ayer and other logical positivists

[34] Cf. A. J. Ayer, "The Vienna Circle" in *The Revolution in Philosophy* (1956), p. 76.

as the correct account of the meaning of moral judgments. However, Stevenson, the foremost exponent of emotivism, subscribed to a theory of meaning different from theirs. To this I shall now turn.

III. THE CAUSAL, OR PSYCHOLOGICAL, THEORY

Two Senses of Meaning

According to this theory, the meaning of language is its disposition to be caused by, or to cause, the occurrence of certain psychological processes in the speaker or the hearer respectively.

The psychological processes which cause, or are caused by, language can, of course, be investigated; and numerous investigations into this subject matter have been, and are being, carried on by psychologists. They are doubtless of absorbing theoretical interest; and profitable practical application is made of their results by advocates and advertisers of every sort. The question which concerns us, however, is not simply what psychological causes or effects language has. It is whether or not these psychological causes and effects of the use of language can be logically equated with its meaning.

We noted at the beginning of this chapter that there are different kinds of meaning, different ways in which the expression "to mean" and its cognates can be used. There are some ways in which "to mean" does appear to be equivalent to "to be caused by, or to cause, the occurrence of certain psychological processes." For example, suppose a headmaster puts on the school notice board the words "All those who were absent from prayers must see me at once." As they read it, the boys may say to each other, "That means he's in a rage." This remark is equivalent to "his saying that is caused by his rage." Again, suppose two people listen to a piece of music and afterward one of them says to the other, "That was full of meaning, wasn't it?" The meaning to which he refers is certain psychological effects, e.g., tranquillity, excitement, etc., which the music has had upon him and which he expects it to have had upon his companion. Such senses as these of "to mean" and its cognates undoubtedly exist; but we must differentiate them very sharply from another sense of "to mean" and its cognates which is quite distinct. This other sense is the one in which philosophers are primarily interested. That meaning in this other sense is logically distinct from the psychological causes or effects of the use of language can be shown, I think, in at least three ways, as follows. These considerations will make it clear what this other sense of meaning is.

(i) The meaning of a speech-act may be said to remain, whatever the psychological causes or effects of its occurrence are. Let us consider these examples of speech-acts:

(a) A command: "Get out."

(b) A statement: "He got out."

(c) A judgment: "He ought to get out."

A moment's reflection, and we realize that a speaker's utterance of any one of these might be caused by the occurrence of any one of a wide variety of psychological processes within him, e.g., anger, fear, envy, love, etc. Similarly each of the above speech-acts might, according to the nature and the circumstances of the hearer, have any one of a wide variety of psychological effects upon him, e.g., astonishment, amusement, delight, dismay, etc. The point to grasp is that, whatever the psychological process which causes, or is caused by, any of the above speech-acts, the meaning of the speech-act remains the same. "Get out" would mean the same, whether it was said because of the speaker's hatred or love for the hearer and whichever of these emotions it caused the hearer to have toward the speaker. Of course, "Get out" may not always mean the same thing. My point is not that it does. It is rather that any given meaning of this speech-act could logically remain constant, whatever variety in the psychological causes or effects of its utterance there might be. And as with commands, so with statements, judgments, and any other speech-acts. It follows that the meaning of the speech-act cannot be equated with any psychological processes whose occurrence it is caused by, or causes.

(ii) If the psychological theory of meaning were correct, some absurd consequences would follow. Consider what, if that theory were correct, it would mean to disobey a command, to disbelieve a statement, or to disagree with a judgment. According to the psychological theory of meaning (leaving aside possible refinements of this account), the meaning of a command is the activity which it causes, the meaning of a statement is the belief which it occasions, and the meaning of a judgment is the assent which it gains. Now, to disobey a command is not to act upon it; to disbelieve a statement is not to believe it; and to disagree with a judgment is to withhold assent to it. But, if the psychological theory of meaning were correct, a command which was disobeyed, a statement which was disbelieved, and judgment which occasioned disagreement, would all be meaningless. They would not cause to occur the psychological processes which constitute their meaning and so they could have no meaning. This is manifestly a *reductio ad absurdum*. For it just is not open to anyone, in this way, to make what is said to him meaningless. Suppose I said to a hearer "Get out" and he stayed where he was; or I said "He got out" and my hearer disbelieved it; or I said "He ought to get out" and my hearer replied "I don't agree." In no instance, on these suppositions, does my speech-act become meaningless. There is, then, a sense of "meaning" in which it is absurd to suggest that a speech-act could be evacuated of its meaning by any effects which followed, or failed to follow, from it.

(iii) The meaning of language (in the sense of meaning which I am here attempting to distinguish and clarify) is discovered through its logical, not its causal, explanation. To see the difference between these two types of explanation, recall the command, the statement, and the judgment instanced under (i) above. Someone might ask, in each case, why the speaker says what he does. This question can, on the one hand, be taken to seek a causal explanation. What caused him to say what he has said? The answer will reveal the mechanism which produced—that is, the train of psychological events which resulted in—the utterance, by such-and-such a man at such-and-such a time in such-and-such circumstances, of this remark. Psychologists do build up hypotheses about what

such-and-such kinds of people at such-and-such times say
in such-and-such circumstances, and then apply these generalizations to particular instances. The final appeal throughout is to the empirical observation of causally connected
psychological events. That is causal explanation.

On the other hand, when we ask why someone says what
he says, we may be seeking something else, namely its logical
explanation. We want to know, that is, not what its cause was
but what the *reason* was for saying it rather than something
else. It is true, of course, that the word "reason" is sometimes
used loosely with the same meaning as "cause." But there is
a use of "reason" in which it is logically distinct from "cause";
and that is the sense in which I am using the word here. Why
does a given speaker say X? The logically explanatory answer will be: because he purports to utter a command, or
state a fact, or express a judgment, or to perform whatever
speech-act X purports to be, *and X is how to do it.* That is the
reason for saying X rather than anything else. This explanation of what has been said appeals, not to hypotheses as to
what people *do* say, but to rules or norms concerning what
to say. A logical explanation of language explains it by showing that what the speaker is doing with it is the thing to do
with it, if you purport to communicate to your hearers what
the speaker is taken to purport to communicate. When and
only when we have shown that a speaker is doing with language the thing to do with it—that is, is using it in accordance
with such-and-such rules or conventions—have we shown that
it has meaning and what its meaning is, in the sense of meaning which I am here seeking to distinguish and to clarify.

The psychological, or causal, theory of meaning has perhaps continued to attract adherents because it is, despite all
I have been saying, nevertheless true to say that language is
meaningful when it produces a certain effect in those who
hear it. But this effect, note well, is *understanding.* The important point to take against the psychological theory is that
producing understanding in one's hearers is logically quite
unlike getting them to act on a command, or believe a statement, or agree with a judgment. Professor J. R. Searle points

this out by considering what it is to understand the sentence "Hello." He writes:

1. Understanding the sentence "Hello" is knowing its meaning.

2. The meaning of "Hello" is determined by semantic rules, which specify both its conditions of utterance and what the utterance counts as. The rules specify that under certain conditions an utterance of "Hello" counts as a greeting of the hearer by the speaker.

3. Uttering "Hello" and meaning it is a matter of (a) intending to get the hearer to recognize that he is being greeted, (b) intending to get him to recognize that he is being greeted by means of getting him to recognize one's intention to greet him, (c) intending to get him to recognize one's intention to greet him in virtue of his knowledge of the meaning of the sentence "Hello."

4. The sentence "Hello" then provides a conventional means of greeting people. If a speaker says "Hello" and means it he will have intentions (a), (b), and (c), and from the hearer's side, the hearer's understanding the utterance will simply consist in those intentions being achieved. The intentions will be achieved in general if the hearer understands the sentence "Hello," i.e., understands its meaning, i.e., understands that under certain conditions its utterance counts as a greeting.[35]

The appeal in this explanation is not to empirically observed causal connections between the utterance of language and the occurrence of psychological processes, but to rules or norms for the use of language.

F. Waismann in *The Principles of Linguistic Philosophy* sums up what I have been endeavoring to say thus: "We look upon language not as a mechanism but as a calculus."[36] He gives, as instances of transition according to a calculus, moves in chess, addressing envelopes from a list of addresses, passing from the name of a color to that color on a chart, solving

---

[35] J. R. Searle, *Speech Acts: An Essay in the Philosophy of Language* (Cambridge, 1969), p. 48–49.

[36] Waismann, *op. cit.*, p. 124.

an algebraic equation by transforming it step by step according to the rules of algebra, and drawing a conclusion from premises according to the propositional calculus. Then he says:

> What, then, is the difference between a causal connection and a transition in a calculus? What is the difference between a calculation formed by a machine, and that made by a person? Or else between a musical box playing a tune and person playing it? One point at any rate is this: the playing or calculation of a person can be justified by rules which he gives us when asked; not so the achievements of a machine, where the question "Why do these keys spring out?" can *only* be answered by describing the mechanism, that is by describing a causal nexus. On the other hand, if we ask the calculator how he comes to his results, he will explain to us what kind of calculation he is doing and then adduce certain laws of arithmetic. He will not reply describing the mode of action of a hidden machine, say, a machine in his brain.[37]

Language *can* operate as a mechanism, as we noted at the beginning of this subsection. A speech-act may be connected with certain psychological processes in the hearer or speaker in such a way that its utterance releases, or is released by, their occurrence, in much the same way that a switch can be operated by, and in its turn operate, other parts of a machine. But, says Waismann, speaking for philosophers who share his approach to the theory of meaning, "we do not *regard* language in its mechanical aspect, but in its aspect as a calculus, that is in so far as it is guided by rules."[38] The rules to which he refers are such as lay it down that "red," for instance, is the sign for a certain color. When we use the word in accordance with that rule it has meaning. It may, of course, have other meanings: there may be other rules according to which it is the word for a Communist. But if there is no rule by reference to which we can read off its meaning, then it has no meaning.

[37] *Ibid.*, p. 122.
[38] *Ibid.*

It would be one thing for a philosopher to point out that there are different kinds of meaning and, as examples, to contrast the use of the word "meaning" in the remark quoted earlier in this subsection with regard to music ("That was full of meaning, wasn't it?") with "meaning" in the sense in which I have been attempting to distinguish and clarify it later on in this subsection. But this is *not* the kind of thing which proponents of the psychological theory of meaning have done. They have entered a discussion, going on among philosophers, which, when examined carefully, is seen to be about meaning in the latter of the two senses to which I have just referred, a discussion, that is, about what it is to understand language, about its logical explanation. Then they have, in effect, said that meaning *in this sense* is equivalent to meaning in another sense: the sense in which the headmaster's notice meant that he was angry or in which the music was full of meaning for one of its hearers. And that is simply a confusion.

The Psychological Theory and Moral Discourse

Professor C. L. Stevenson, the foremost exponent of the ethical theory called emotivism, subscribes to the psychological theory of meaning. This makes it possible for him to recognize that it is not enough to ask what language is about. If we wish to get at its meaning we must ask also *how* it is about what it is about. When we ask that question about moral judgments we see that they have a dynamic character. They do not, or not simply, describe nonnatural states of affairs. Moral judgments exert a "magnetism," to use Stevenson's word; that is to say, if anyone sincerely assents to the judgment "X is good" he must *ipso facto* acquire thereby a stronger tendency to act favorably toward X. Again, moral judgments, to use Stevenson's phrase, "create an influence"; to tell anyone that X is good is to bring a kind of pressure to bear upon him, where X is concerned, so that he will act favorably toward it. This view of moral discourse ties in with the theory that the meaning of language is its disposition to cause, or be caused by, certain psychological processes in the hearer or speaker respectively. But, like all adherents of the psychological theory, Stevenson, as we shall see in Chapter 4, failed to distinguish between the causal, and the logical, explanation of language. He recognized that the question to ask is: how is moral language used? But he confused the causes of, with the reasons for, the use to which moral discourse is put.

IV. MEANING AS USE

In this section I want to say something about ideas concerning language which have been held by the later Wittgenstein and J. L. Austin. These ideas have been highly influential in contemporary analytical philosophy. To give an adequate account of either the later Wittgenstein or Austin would require far more space than is available here. In the case of each, two questions arise: what precisely did this thinker take meaning to be? and, was he correct in so far as we are able to discern what he took it to be? These questions are still being investigated in depth by modern philosophers and alternative answers to them, debated. I hope that I can say enough about them to give some impression of how the most recent developments in moral philosophy are related to the ideas about language found in Wittgenstein's *Philosophical Investigations* (Oxford, 1953) and J. L. Austin's *How To Do Things with Words* (Oxford, 1962).

The Later Wittgenstein and the Need to Look at the Use to Which Language Is Put

The central idea in Wittgenstein's picture theory of meaning was as follows: "What any picture, of whatever form, must have in common with reality, in order to be able to depict it—correctly or incorrectly—in any way at all, is logical form, i.e., the form of reality."[39] Wittgenstein eventually rejected this basic idea that, for language to be meaningful, it must represent some configuration of "objects," some "logical form," which exists in the objectively real world.

Professor Norman Malcolm in his *Memoir* on Wittgen-

[39] *T* 2.18.

stein tells a story about how the latter was weaned away
from his picture theory by his friend, P. Straffa, a lecturer in
economics at Cambridge. To the stimulus of Straffa's criticism, by the way, Wittgenstein attributes the most consequential ideas of his *Investigations* in his preface to that book.
Malcolm's story is that Straffa and Wittgenstein were travel-
ing on a train one day during the early 1930's and Wittgenstein was insisting that a proposition and what it describes
must have the same "logical form." Malcolm goes on: "Straffa
made a gesture, familiar to Neapolitans as meaning something like dislike or contempt, of brushing the underneath of
his chin with an outward sweep of the fingertips of one hand.
And he asked: 'What is the logical form of *that?*' Straffa's
example produced in Wittgenstein the feeling that there was
an absurdity in the insistence that a proposition and what
it describes must have the same 'form.' This broke the hold
on him of the conception that a proposition must literally
be a 'picture' of the reality it describes."[40] Wittgenstein's
reasons for eventually abandoning that theory—or some of
them—have already been indicated briefly.[41] We must now
see what he put in place of the picture theory of meaning.

Wittgenstein believed that he had been wrong in the *Tractatus* because he had tried to impose on language a preconceived idea of what its meaning ought to be. He came to think
that what he should have done instead is to *"look at* its use
and learn from that."[42] He added: "The difficulty is to remove the prejudice which stands in the way of doing this."[43]
When one does overcome prejudice and takes such a look at
language, one sees, said Wittgenstein, that there are a great
many different uses to which it is in fact put. He compared
words to tools and said that the functions of language are
as diverse as those of the tools in a toolbox.[44] "Look at the
sentence as an instrument," he wrote, "and at its sense (*Sinn*)

[40] Malcolm, *op. cit.*, p. 69; Malcolm notes that this story exists in
differing versions.
[41] Above, pp. 29–31.
[42] *PI*, 340.
[43] *Ibid.*
[44] *PI*, 11.

as its employment."[45] Again, he spoke of these different
uses to which language may be put as so many "language-
games." The following quotation sums up in terms of "language-games" the point of view at which Wittgenstein had
arrived when he wrote his *Investigations*.

But how many kinds of sentence are there? Say, assertion, question, and command?—There are *countless* kinds:
countless different kinds of use of what we call "symbols,"
"words," "sentences." And this multiplicity is not something
fixed, given once for all; but new types of language, new
language-games, as we may say, come into existence, and
others become obsolete and get forgotten. (We can get a
rough picture of this from the changes in mathematics.)
Here the term "language-*game*" is meant to bring into
prominence the fact that the *speaking* of language is part
of an activity, or of a form of life. Review the multiplicity
of language-games in the following examples, and in others:
Giving orders, and obeying them—
Describing the appearance of an object, or giving its
measurements—
Constructing an object from a description (a draw-
ing)—
Reporting an event—
Speculating about an event—
Forming and testing a hypothesis—
Presenting the results of an experiment in tables and
diagrams—
Making up a story; and reading it—
Play-acting—
Singing catches—
Guessing riddles—
Making a joke; telling it—
Solving a problem in practical arithmetic—
Translating from one language into another—
Asking, thanking, cursing, greeting, praying.
—It is interesting to compare the multiplicity of the tools in
language and of the ways they are used, the multiplicity of
kinds of word and sentence, with what logicians have said

[45] *PI*, 421.

about the structure of language. (Including the author of the *Tractatus Logico-Philosophicus*.)[46]

Philosophical perplexity arises, said Wittgenstein, where there is confusion between language games. An example of what he meant—though not one which he used—occurs when anyone asks with what sense moral rightness is perceived. If such a question were asked about redness or hardness, instead of moral rightness, it would be easy to understand and to answer. The person who asks this question about moral rightness assumes that to speak of the latter is to do the same kind of thing as to speak of redness or hardness. That is his mistake and the occasion of his perplexity. Since it is apparent that we do not apprehend moral rightness with one of our physical senses—as we apprehend redness with sight or hardness with touch—he concludes that there must be some other sense with which we do so. A great deal of discussion has gone on in the past among moral philosophers as to what this "moral sense" might be. But it is all based on a confusion which is, at bottom, a confusion between the language game of sense perception and that of moral judgment. A question is asked which would fit well enough into the former of these, and it is assumed that an answer to it must therefore be discoverable in the latter. We shall look into this particular confusion about "moral sense" more carefully in Chapter 3.

Depth Grammar, Forms of Life, and Moral Discourse

Wittgenstein spoke of philosophy in *Investigations* as "a battle against the bewitchment of our intelligence by means of language."[47] The sort of bewitchment which he had in mind was the kind of confusion to which I have just been referring. In two ways particularly, according to Wittgenstein, the bewitchment is effected. (i) We can be tempted "to draw some misleading analogy,"[48] or, in other words, be held

---

[46] *PI*, 23.
[47] *PI*, 109.
[48] Wittgenstein, *The Blue and Brown Books* (Oxford, 1960), p. 48.

captive by a picture. A famous example of this is St. Augustine's puzzlement as to how time can be measured. In effect, Augustine pictured time as a stream flowing past us. If we lay a measuring rod alongside this stream, in order to measure time, the task is impossible for the following reasons. Our measuring, whenever we do it, will necessarily be done in the (then) present. We cannot, therefore, measure an interval of time in the (then) past because it is no longer there in the (then) present to be measured. For the same reason, neither can we measure an interval of time in the (then) future. Moreover, the present which, in that it is the (then) present, we could measure, cannot, in fact, be measured because it is not more than a point. We cannot, therefore, measure past, present, or future. So we cannot measure time at all. This is a logical "cannot." As a matter of fact, however, we *do* measure time—we say "It took four hours," "I'll come for tea at four fifteen," and so on. How can these things be? Now, such puzzlement arose simply because Augustine succumbed to the temptation to draw a misleading analogy, viz. between how space is measured and how time is. We take spatial measurements by laying a measuring rod alongside the objects to be measured. But we measure time by agreeing that such-and-such natural events, e.g., the rising and setting of the sun, or such-and-such artificially contrived events, e.g., the point-by-point unwinding of a spring, shall constitute *termini a quo* or *ad quem*. Units in the time span are marked off by the occurrence of such events, not by laying a measuring rod against something called time.[49] Once we free ourselves from captivity to the picture of spatial measurement, the puzzle about how time can be measured dissolves.

(ii) The second way in which the bewitchment of our intelligence by means of language takes place is through the confusion of what Wittgenstein called respectively "surface grammar" and "depth grammar."[50] By the former he meant the way in which words are used in the course of a sentence; by the latter, he meant, I think, the use to which words are char-

[49] Wittgenstein refers to Augustine on time; *ibid.*, p. 26.
[50] *PI*, 664.

acteristically put in their own language game. As I pointed out in the last subsection, an example of philosophical perplexity or "bewitchment"—though not one which Wittgenstein himself used—can be found in moral discourse. The sentence "X is right" is syntactically similar to "X is red"—i.e., similar in "surface grammar." A noun, X, is coupled by the third person singular present indicative of the verb "to be" with an adjective. This sentence "X is red" describes X; it attributes to it a feature which is visible to the normally sighted. This is its "depth grammar." It is a sentence which belongs within the language game of describing physical objects in terms of their colors. Now, there is a temptation to think of "X is right" as though it were similar in depth grammar as well as surface grammar to "X is red." Of course, everyone knows that rightness is not visible as redness is. But "X is right" looks like a description of X just as much as "X is red" does. Because they have assumed that this is what it must be, "moral sense" philosophers and intuitionists generally have assumed: (a) that rightness must be a property of some kind; and (b) that we must "see" it in some sense of the word. But what if the basic error lies in regarding "X is right" as a description? Its "surface grammar" could have "bewitched" philosophers into mistakenly supposing that such was its "depth grammar." We shall find reason in Chapter 3 to think that this is just what happened.

Two further points which Wittgenstein made about language games were as follows. One concerns what he calls "forms of life." He said: ". . . the term 'language-*game*' is meant to bring into prominence the fact that the *speaking* of language is part of an activity, or of a form of life."[51] The other concerns the "tacit presuppositions" on which, according to Wittgenstein, language games are based. He said: ". . . what we do in our language-game always rests on a tacit presupposition."[52] I will take them in turn.

(i) Language does not exist in a vacuum. It is, to use Wittgenstein's own word, "woven"[53] into other activities.

[51] *PI*, 23.
[52] *PI*, p. 179.
[53] *PI*, 7.

There is a cryptic remark toward the end of *Investigations:* "If a lion could talk, we could not understand him."[54] Dr. G. Pitcher endeavors to illuminate it as follows:

> Suppose a lion says "It is now three o'clock" but without looking at a clock or his wristwatch—and we may imagine that it would be merely a stroke of luck if he should say this when it actually *is* three o'clock. Or suppose he says "Goodness, it is three o'clock; I must hurry to make that appointment," but that he continues to lie there, yawning, making no effort to move, as lions are wont to do. In these circumstances—assuming that the lion's general behavior is in every respect exactly like that of an ordinary lion, save for his amazing ability to utter English sentences—we could not say that he has *asserted* or *stated* that it is three o'clock, even though he has uttered suitable words. We could not tell what, if anything he has asserted for the modes of behavior into which his use of words is woven are too radically different from our own. We would not understand him, since he does not share the relevant forms of life with us.[55]

The point which is being made here applies to moral language. Try to imagine somebody who utters the sentence "X is morally good," but there is nothing else whatever in his behavior which we would recognize as expressive of moral approval toward X; nothing, in what the speaker does himself or refrains from doing; nothing, in his attitudes toward other people. It is true, of course, that many people fail to practice what they preach. But what I now ask the reader to imagine goes far beyond what we mean by that. It is a man whose entire behavior indicates that the putative fact that X is morally good which his judgment announces does not make any difference to him beyond the utterance of "X is morally good." Should we not naturally say of such a man that he does not mean, or does not understand, what he is saying?

[54] *PI*, p. 223.
[55] G. Pitcher, *The Philosophy of Wittgenstein* (Englewood Cliffs, N.J., 1964), p. 243.

In Chapter 6, we shall have occasion to imagine Martians[56]
arriving on earth and speaking in terms of "moral" approval
or disapproval about matters which we never think of discussing in such terms. Should we understand them or not?
Some philosophers, we shall find, are inclined to say that we
should not be able to recognize their discourse as moral in
our sense of the word at all, because what makes our discourse "moral" is its content. Other philosophers hold that, for
all its difference of content, if the Martians' discourse had the
same *form* as our moral discourse, then we should certainly
recognize it as moral. What respectively these philosophers
take the content and the form of moral discourse to be we
shall see in due course. All I wish to say at the moment is this.
If Wittgenstein was right about language being woven into
forms of life—and I am inclined to think that he was—then,
even if a Martian's "moral" discourse had both the same content and the same form as ours, unless there was something
in his behavior, besides the utterance of sentences in moral
terms, which indicated moral approval, then he would re-
semble Pitcher's lion in our eyes. We should not be able to
recognize what he was engaging in as moral discourse at all.
He would not share the relevant form of life with us.

(ii) What of Wittgenstein's view that language games, or
forms of life, are, based on "tacit presuppositions"? I think
the point to take here is that the demand for a justification
of what is said has to stop somewhere. Every language game
goes down in the last analysis to certain concepts, or rules of
inference, or both, which are tacitly presupposed and which
logically constitute that universe of discourse. An example
would be the concept of a physical object. The empirical evidence, on the basis of which we talk about physical objects,
is discontinuous. Now we see the table; now we go into the
next room and see it no longer; now we return and there it
is. Though there has been a break between our observations
of it, we nevertheless think of it as identical on the two occasions. Someone may raise the question: are we entitled to
do so? In ordinary discourse, there are accepted ways of de-

---

[56] Below, p. 314.

ciding that question: conditions which must normally be fulfilled if a table which we see on one occasion is to be taken for the same table as we saw on another. But even where such conditions are fulfilled, our questioner may persist with his question. We make statements about physical objects on the strength of our experience of them. In doing so, we speak of these objects as continuous existents, for physical objects are always so conceived though their continuity may be of short duration. But our observation of physical objects is, if not invariably, at least characteristically, discontinuous. There is a logical gap here, then, between evidence which is *discontinuous* and what it is invoked to support which is *continuous*. Are we entitled to jump this gap as we do? asks our persistent questioner. Professor P. F. Strawson, dealing with the skeptic who answers that question in the negative, points out that "a *condition* of our having this conceptual scheme is the unquestioning acceptance of particular-identity in at least some cases of non-continuous observation."[57] The skeptic, says Strawson, ". . . pretends to accept a conceptual scheme, (*sc.* that of common sense or natural science in which we speak of physical objects on the strength of empirical observation) but at the same time quietly rejects one of the conditions of its employment. Thus his doubts are unreal, not simply because they are logically irresoluble doubts, but because they amount to the rejection of the whole conceptual scheme within which alone such doubts make sense."[58] Doubts about whether or not we are entitled to regard our observations as observations of the same object make sense within the scheme of common sense or natural science, where there are accepted ways of deciding whether or not they are well founded. But doubts which strike at the rules of inference tacitly presupposed by, and constitutive of, this whole conceptual scheme itself, are in Strawson's sense "unreal." That is, they are doubts which reject any settlement of them in the only place where that kind of doubt

[57] P. F. Strawson, *Individuals* (1959), p. 35.
[58] *Ibid.*

could be settled, namely the language game in which we speak of physical objects.

All modern moral philosophers—even those who antedate the later Wittgenstein—have aimed at clarifying the ultimate concept(s) and the rules of inference of the moral universe of discourse. They have asked: in the last analysis, what *is* moral obligation? The intuitionists believed it to be something which we discover, grounded in objective reality. The emotivists have taken it for a feeling which we have toward certain courses of action. The prescriptivists have judged it to be a decision which we make. The descriptivists or neonaturalists have thought of it as, to say the least, essentially connected with certain natural properties which objects or actions have. Again, modern moral philosophers have asked: in the last analysis, what is the logical structure of moral reasoning? Does it proceed by invoking decisions of moral principle, one, or some, of which are the ultimate logical constituents in any moral judgment? Or are there moves, e.g., from what men in fact *want* to have or do to what they *ought* to have or do, which, though questioned by some skeptics, are such that their rejection amounts, to recall Strawson on skeptics, "to the rejection of the whole conceptual scheme" of moral discourse? Some say that, if the fact that all men want something does not count with you as a reason for saying that one ought to attain it, then whatever your reasoning may be, it is not moral reasoning. Others, we shall see, stoutly deny this.

The later Wittgenstein's influence becomes more and more apparent as the story of modern moral philosophy unfolds. The most recent moral philosophers have tried to take his advice and *look* at moral discourse with eyes unprejudiced by any preconceived theory of meaning. They have asked: what is moral language *for?* What job does it do? How is this job like, and how unlike, other uses to which language is put?[59] They have tried to avoid any "bewitchment" of their intelligence by means of language which would mislead them

[59] E.g., P. H. Nowell-Smith, *Ethics* (1954), pp. 95–100 and *passim.*

into oversimplifying the meaning of moral discourse or confusing it with discourse of other kinds.

J. L. Austin and What We Do with Words

In *How to Do Things with Words*[60] Austin distinguished three kinds of thing which we can do with words, calling these respectively locutionary, illocutionary, and perlocutionary acts. Much use of this distinction has been made in modern discussions about the theory of meaning. In particular, the question as to which of them, or which combination of them, constitutes the meaning of a speech-act has been, and is still being, debated. I can do little more than scratch the surface of the matter here, but I will try to give some account of it, and, in particular, to give some indication of the effects which Austin's threefold distinction, and the questions which it raises, has had on contemporary moral philosophy. First, the three kinds of thing which we can do with words must be differentiated.

(i) The locutionary action, or the locution, is the act of saying something. It is, said Austin, in effect a combination of three acts. These are: (a) a phonetic act, i.e., an act of uttering certain noises; (b) a phatic act, i.e., the uttering of certain vocables or words, i.e., noises of certain types, belonging to and as belonging to, a certain vocabulary, conforming to and as conforming to a certain grammar; (c) a rhetic act, i.e., the performing of an act of using those vocables with a certain more or less definite sense and reference. An example of a report of a phatic act would be: "He said 'The cat is on the mat.' " An example of a report of a rhetic act: "He said that the cat was on the mat."[61] This latter reports, not simply the giving vent to certain significant sounds, but the making of an assertion. That brings us to the next thing which we can do with words.

(ii) Of the illocutionary act, or illocution, Austin wrote: "To perform a locutionary act is in general, we may say, also

---

[60] J. L. Austin, *How to Do Things with Words* (Oxford, 1962), see especially Lecture VIII.
[61] Austin, *op. cit.*, p. 95.

and *eo ipso* to perform an illocutionary act, as I propose to call it. To determine what illocutionary act is so performed we must determine in what way we are using the locution."[62] The illocutionary act is what we do *in* saying something, as opposed to the locutionary act *of* saying something. "For example," wrote Austin, "it might be perfectly possible, with regard to an utterance, say 'It is going to charge,' to make entirely plain 'what we were saying' in issuing the utterance, in all the senses so far distinguished, and yet not at all to have cleared up whether or not in issuing the utterance I was performing the act of *warning* or not."[63] If we perform the act of saying something, then the question can always be raised as to what we are saying *in* saying that, the type of answer looked for being that which will make it clear whether we are answering a question, issuing a warning, making a statement, or whatever. Austin gives a list of possible illocutionary acts which is, in many ways, reminiscent of the list of the uses of language, given by Wittgenstein in *Investigations* and quoted above (p. 46). Austin's list runs:

> asking or answering a question,
> giving some information or an assurance or a warning,
> announcing a verdict or an intention,
> pronouncing a sentence,
> making an appointment or an appeal or a criticism,
> making an identification or giving a description.

This list is not, of course, exhaustive. These different kinds of function which language may be used to fulfill are sometimes referred to by Austin as its illocutionary "forces."[64]

(iii) When Austin spoke of a *perlocutionary* act, or of perlocutionary force, what he had in mind was as follows. "Saying something will often, or even normally, produce certain consequential effects upon the feelings, thoughts, or actions of the audience, or of the speaker, or of other persons:

[62] *Ibid.,* p. 98.
[63] *Ibid.*
[64] *Ibid.*

and it may be done with the design, intention, or purpose of producing them; and we may then say, thinking of this, that the speaker has performed an act in the nomenclature of which reference is made either (*C.a*) only obliquely, or even (*C.b*) not at all, to the performance of the locutionary, or illocutionary act. We shall call the performance of an act of this kind the performance of a *perlocutionary* act or *perlocution.*"[65]

Austin offered, among others, the following examples of reports of locutionary, illocutionary, and perlocutionary acts.

Locution: He said to me "Shoot her!" meaning by "shoot" shoot and referring by "her" to *her*.

Illocution: He urged (or advised, ordered, etc.) me to shoot her.

Perlocution: (What he calls above *C.a*) He persuaded me to shoot her.
(What he calls above *C.b*) He got me to (or made me, etc.) shoot her.[66]

How do we know the illocutionary and perlocutionary force of anything which is said? Austin brings out an important difference between them here.[67] Consider how we tell that an utterance is, for instance, a warning. Suppose the utterance is "It is going to charge." The most obvious way in which we can tell that this is a warning is if the speaker prefixes it with what Austin would have called the explicitly performative formula, "I warn you that. . . ." But there are other possible ways as well. For instance, tone of voice or emphasis could tell us that "It is going to charge" was a warning. In other examples, the mood of the verb (the fact, for instance, that it is imperative, indicating that a command is being issued) is sometimes a sufficient clue to illocutionary force. Adverbs or adverbial phrases can serve this purpose too: e.g., "I'll come without fail" indicates that a promise is being made. Connecting particles may do the job: e.g., "still"

[65] *Ibid.,* p. 101.
[66] *Ibid.,* pp. 101–2.
[67] *Ibid.,* p. 103.

can have the force of "I insist that"—"Still, do it"; and "therefore" can show that a conclusion is being drawn. Gestures
(e.g., winks or frowns), ceremonial nonverbal actions (e.g.,
bowing as one speaks), or the circumstances of the utterance
(e.g., "Coming from *him*, that was an order"), may all determine illocutionary force.[68] The important point to take
here is that all these are conventional devices, or *rules* for
the use of language. It is by reference to these that we know
what the illocutionary force of an utterance is. But the case
is quite different when we turn to perlocutionary force. The
psychological effects which utterances, or kinds of utterance,
produce can be discovered only by empirical observation of
what happens to hearers when they are said. Linguistic rules
constitute illocutionary force, but not perlocutionary force.
In the light of what has already been said above (p. 42),
this fact leaves open the possibility that the illocutionary force
of a speech-act may have something to do with its meaning,
whereas its perlocutionary force does not.

Meaning, Illocutionary Force, and Moral Discourse

We will turn now to consider something of the influence
which Austin's differentiation of locution, illocution, and perlocution has had upon modern moral philosophy. One part
of it is easy to understand and we have already foreshadowed
it. Austin himself wrote: "to speak of the 'use' of language
can . . . blur the distinction between the illocutionary and
perlocutionary act."[69] The emergence of interest in the use
to which moral language is put has been, as we noted, very
important. It could be said with some truth that the transfor-
mation which has taken place in moral philosophy over the
last fifty years reflects that which took place in the thought of
Wittgenstein. Moral philosophers have been weaned away
from the belief that moral discourse pictures some objective
reality and from the consequent puzzlement which afflicted
their philosophical forebears as to what that reality is and
how we apprehend it. They have come to concern them-

[68] *Ibid.,* pp. 73–76.
[69] *Ibid.,* p. 103.

selves rather with the use, or uses, to which moral language is put. But to leave the matter there would blur the distinction between some modern moral philosophers, the emotivists, who conceive of this "use" as perlocutionary force, and others, the prescriptivists, who conceive of it as illocutionary force. In dealing with the psychological theory of meaning, we have already seen, following Waismann, that the meaning of language requires that it be considered, not as a mechanism, but as a calculus. This is much the same distinction as that between perlocutionary and illocutionary force. We shall see in Chapter 5 what advances were made when philosophers recognized that the question about the meaning of moral language is not to be answered by considering its perlocutionary force.

But now we must turn to a much more complicated and difficult question: can the meaning of moral discourse be *equated* with its illocutionary force? Austin himself, at first sight anyway, seems to have thought not. He does not consider moral language in particular, but what he would have said in its case follows from what he said in general terms. He said explicitly: "I want to distinguish *force* (*sc.* illocutionary force) and meaning in the sense in which meaning is equivalent to sense and reference. . . ."[70] Sense and reference Austin located in the locutionary act as we have already seen. However, it is arguable that Austin's whole object was to show that philosophers had failed at all fully to understand how language works just because they have been held captive by, and concentrated far too much attention on, meaning as sense and reference. When Austin said, as he did, that the expression "meaning" "can blur the distinction between locutionary and illocutionary acts,"[71] it is at least arguable that he was making a point against the traditional interpretation of meaning as sense and reference rather than putting up the shutters against any attempt to equate meaning and illocutionary force. Austin's intention, it would not be absurd to suppose, was to clarify the concept of meaning and

[70] *Ibid.,* p. 100.
[71] *Ibid.,* p. 103.

deliver it from the misunderstandings of traditional philosophers. His scant use of, and seeming distaste for, the word
"meaning" would be in line with this.

Different disciples of Austin, at any rate from among those
who have turned their attention to moral philosophy, tend to
claim either (a) that they are following him by maintaining
a sharp distinction between meaning and illocutionary force
or, alternatively, (b) that they are following him by enlarging
the concept of meaning so as to include illocutionary force,
and even by equating meaning with the latter. G. J. Warnock
and R. M. Hare are respectively cases in point.

Warnock seems to take the former course (at least it is
Hare's charge against him that he does).[72] In his *Contemporary Moral Philosophy,* he argues that what is definitive of
moral discourse is that it has, as such, a particular content;
and in one place he gives this as: "human happiness or interests, needs, wants, or desires."[73] Given this subject matter,
then, according to Warnock, speakers in making moral judgments may be doing as many different things as they may be
doing in discourse at large.[74] He thinks it is a great mistake
of prescriptivists to conceive of moral judgments as having
only one kind of illocutionary force. There are dozens of
things which those who employ moral words may *therein* be
doing, says Warnock, and goes on: "They may be prescribing,
certainly; but also they may be advising, exhorting, imploring;
commanding, condemning, deploring; resolving, confessing,
undertaking; and so on and so on."[75] Approvingly, Warnock
quotes P. H. Nowell-Smith: "The words with which moral
philosophers have especially to do . . . play many different
parts. They are used to express tastes and preferences, to express decisions and choices, to criticise, grade, and evaluate,
to advise, admonish, warn, persuade and dissuade, to praise,
encourage and reprove, to promulgate and draw attention to

---

[72] See Hare's review of Warnock's *Contemporary Moral Philosophy*
in *M* LXXVII (1968), 437.
[73] G. J. Warnock, *Contemporary Moral Philosophy* (1967), p. 55.
[74] *Ibid.,* p. 40.
[75] *Ibid.,* p. 75.

rules; and doubtless for other purposes also."[76] I doubt if it could be said that Warnock follows Austin here in conceiving of the meaning of moral discourse as its sense and reference. But he is clearly drawing, or at least implying, a distinction between meaning and illocutionary force. For if the illocutionary forces of moral judgments can be as diversified as those of speech-acts in discourse as a whole, then what makes a judgment a moral judgment cannot (logically) be its illocutionary force. Whatever illocutionary force we fastened on as constituting its meaning we could adduce counterexamples of speech-acts with a different illocutionary force which were nevertheless moral.

Hare takes the latter of the two courses which, I suggested above, a disciple of Austin's might take. He goes so far as to equate illocutionary force and meaning.[77] Austin located meaning in the locutionary act. But can we know the meaning of a speech-act before we know its illocutionary force? Take the example "You will arrive at six thirty." This could be either an order or a statement. Do we know its meaning until we know which it is? The answer is clearly that we do not, and that, I think, is why Hare insists, as we shall see that he does, upon his point that no speech-act is complete without what he calls its "tropic."[78] The latter, in Hare's terminology, is the logical particle which gives a speech-act its illocutionary force. Most obviously, this may be the sign of mood (hence the word "tropic"). In the example "You will come at six thirty" the mood of the verb is indicative and normally that would mean that a statement is being made. However, emphasis, e.g., "You *will* come at six thirty," or circumstances, e.g., the fact that it is said by an officer to a private, can make this seeming statement into a command. Notice that, even in the case of "Come at six thirty," where the mood is imperative, we cannot, without reference to something beyond the mood of the verb, be sure whether it is a command, a request, or a piece of advice. Its "tropic" may be a complicated element in a speech-act. Hare does not deny this. He simply in-

[76] *Ibid.*, p. 40; Nowell-Smith, *op. cit.*, p. 98.
[77] See *M* LXXVII (1968), 438.
[78] See below, p. 232.

sists that no speech-act is complete, i.e., meaningful, without a tropic. If this is so, then meaning cannot logically be separated altogether from illocutionary force. This shows that Austin was wrong to locate it exclusively in the locutionary act. But it does not show that there is nothing more to meaning than illocutionary force.

Against Warnock's contention, or what Hare takes to have been his contention,[79] that the meaning of moral discourse cannot be equated with its illocutionary force because the latter is as diverse in moral discourse as it is in discourse at large, Hare claims that a distinction can be drawn between a genus, and its species, of illocutionary force. He says that all the speech-acts listed by Warnock and Nowell-Smith (see above) can be regarded as species of one genus, which it is legitimate to call "prescribing." In Chapter 5, relying upon hitherto unpublished papers of Hare's, I shall consider his defense of his own position against those who contend that there are, in ordinary language, numerous examples of words such as "good" being used with their literal meaning, but without being used to prescribe or commend. If Hare's position here can be sustained, it still does not prove that the meaning and the illocutionary force of moral discourse can be equated, but it does dispose of the particular argument, attributed above to Warnock, as to why they cannot.

It has been argued[80] that, in the case of an explicitly performative speech-act, e.g., the warning, "I warn you that it is going to charge," *no* distinction can be drawn between the illocutionary force of such an utterance and its meaning. To say "I warn you that it is going to charge" is not to report or describe your warning. It is simply to warn. If your speech-act is to be assigned a meaning at all, then this meaning must be of a performative, or illocutionary, kind. Your meaning lies solely in the issuing of the warning. Where else could it lie? If somebody asked, "What did you say?" and you replied, "I warned him that it was going to charge," is not that a per-

[79] Cf. *M* LXXVII (1968), 438.
[80] Cf. L. J. Cohen, "Do Illocutionary Forces Exist?" *PQ* 14 (1964), 122.

fectly satisfactory answer? Do you need to separate out a
locution, viz. "It is going to charge," because the meaning of
what you said resides in that, as distinct from what you were
doing in saying that?

Considerations of this kind might suggest that the difference between meaning and illocutionary force can be eliminated. To anticipate matters which will occupy our attention
in Chapter 5, the sense and reference of a speech-act can be
located in what Hare called its "phrastic," i.e., the logical
particle of a speech-act which may be common to speech-
acts with differing illocutionary force. For instance, the
phrastic "Going by you to the station" is common to the
statement "You go to the station" and the command "Go to
the station." Everything except what Hare called the "tropic"
can (logically) be located in the phrastic. Now, phrastics by
themselves have no meaning because they are incomplete
as speech-acts. Meaning resides in the complete speech-act.
This is evident from the fact that we do not learn the meanings of individual words and then learn how to string them
together in speech-acts. Language, however primitive, consists
of speech-acts, and it is learned—can only be learned—by par-
ticipation in these speech-acts. Phrastics, then, have meaning
when, and only when, tropics are added to them. It is the
tropic which completes the speech-act and so gives it meaning. The tropic makes it possible to reply to the question
"What did you say?" with "I warned him that . . . ," "I
asked him whether . . . ," etc. And such replies, as we have
noted, can legitimately be taken to give the meanings of the
utterances concerned.

However, the question with which this discussion began—
can the meaning of moral discourse be equated with its illocutionary force?—cannot, I think, be regarded as finally settled.
Illocutionary force is undoubtedly a necessary condition of
meaning, but is it a sufficient? True, phrastics by themselves
are meaningless. But are not tropics by themselves equally so?
While the meaning of a speech-act lies in the whole speech-
act, is it not legitimate to draw distinctions between elements
in that meaning—e.g., between *what* the speech-act is about

and *how* it is about what it is about? Considerations such as these give one pause. Perhaps we cannot give an unqualified yes in reply to the question: can the meaning of moral discourse be equated with its illocutionary force? Even so, those who have said yes to this question, it seems to me, are much nearer the mark than those who hold that the meaning of a speech-act resides in a locutionary act which is logically quite distinct from its illocutionary force. Of that point of view I would say, not that it may need some qualification, but that it is flatly mistaken and should be rejected.

CHAPTER 3. THE INTUITIONIST THEORY

In the early part of the present century, the main point at issue in British moral philosophy was that which arose between ethical naturalists and nonnaturalists. "Ethical naturalist" is the name given to a thinker who has—or is taken to have—defined moral words, such as "good" or "right," in terms of natural properties. Anyone who defined "good" or "right" as, for examples, "producing happiness," "conducing to evolution," or "fulfilling the will of God," would be an ethical naturalist. G. E. Moore set himself to refute those whom he took to have defined "good" in these, or similar, ways. The book in which he attempted to do so, *Principia Ethica* (London, 1903), has a good claim to be regarded as the *terminus a quo* of modern moral philosophy. The point of view which Moore defended in it may be described as ethical nonnaturalism.

In the opening pages of *Principia Ethica*, Moore said that his sole business was with "that object or idea" which the word "good" "is generally used to stand for."[1] It is dangerous to generalize, but I think it would be true to say that the referential theory of meaning, in some form or other, is largely taken for granted in the work of those ethical naturalists and nonnaturalists whom we shall consider. The former believed that moral terms mean, i.e., refer to, certain natural properties of actions or states of affairs and that these properties can be observed by one or other of the physical senses. Nonnaturalists, by contrast, believed that moral terms mean,

[1] *PE*, p. 6. I take this to imply a referential theory of meaning, but I do not suggest, of course, that no other theory is to be found in Moore's writings.

i.e., refer to, nonnatural properties which can only be apprehended by moral intuition.

In this chapter, I will first outline what I take to have been Moore's conception of the mistake which ethical naturalists make and for which he coined the expression "the naturalistic fallacy." I will then consider some of the questions which arise in this connection. Next, two other thinkers, H. A. Prichard and W. D. Ross, will engage our attention. They held views similar to Moore's but, as I shall try to show, extended them more widely over the field of moral language than he had done. Finally I shall ask whether or not the underlying assumption of the type of ethical theory with which this chapter is concerned, namely, the assumption that moral right and wrong, good and evil, can be known by intuition, is well founded.

I. MOORE AND THE REJECTION OF ETHICAL NATURALISM

The principal discovery which Moore claimed to have made concerning "that object or idea" which the word "good" is generally used to stand for, was that it is *indefinable*. We must try first to answer two questions: (i) what precisely did Moore mean when he said that "good" stands for something indefinable? and (ii) what precisely were his grounds for saying so? I will take them in turn.

Good as Indefinable

Moore differentiated three kinds of definition.[2] The first two were stipulative and lexical definition respectively. He recognized that on the one hand, anyone could, logically and empirically, stipulate a meaning of his own for "good"; and on the other hand, that if one looked in a dictionary one would find that there are generally accepted rules for the use of the word. But he held that there is definition of a third kind which is much more important than either of these other two. Definitions of this third kind "describe the

[2] *PE*, p. 8.

real nature of the object or notion denoted by a word, and
. . . do not merely tell us what the word is used to mean."[3]
The point to grasp, Moore contended, is that such definitions
"are only possible when the object or notion in question is
something complex."[4] He went on to explain what he meant.
"You can give a definition of a horse, because a horse has
many different properties and qualities, all of which you can
enumerate. But when you have enumerated them all, when
you have reduced a horse to his simplest terms, then you can
no longer define those terms. They are simply something
which you think of or perceive, and to anyone who cannot
think of or perceive them, you can never, by any definition,
make their nature known."[5] He noted the possible objection
to this, that we are able to describe things to people which
they have not previously thought of or perceived; but maintained that such things are always composed of parts, with
which we and they are familiar, combined in ways with which
we and they are also familiar. Moore continued:

"Good" then, if we mean by it that quality which we
assert to belong to a thing, when we say that the thing is
good, is incapable of any definition, in the most important
sense of that word. The most important sense of "definition" is that in which a definition states what are the parts
which invariably compose a certain whole; and in this
sense "good" has no definition because it is simple and has
no parts. It is one of those innumerable objects of thought
which are themselves incapable of definition, because they
are the ultimate terms by reference to which whatever *is*
capable of definition must be defined. That there must be
an indefinite number of such terms is obvious, on reflection; since we cannot define anything except by an analysis,
which, when carried as far as it will go, refers us to something, which is simply different from anything else, and
which by that ultimate difference explains the peculiarity
of the whole which we are defining: for every whole contains some parts which are common to other wholes also.

[3] *PE*, p. 7.
[4] *Ibid.*
[5] *Ibid.*

There is, therefore, no intrinsic difficulty in the contention that "good" denotes a simple and indefinable quality. There are many other instances of such qualities.[6]

Yellow was one such instance to which Moore referred. "My point is," he said, "that 'good' is a simple notion, just as 'yellow' is a simple notion; that, just as you cannot, by any manner of means, explain to any one who does not already know it, what yellow is, so you cannot explain what good is."[7] All things which are yellow do produce a certain kind of vibration in the light; and similarly all things which are good may be things which produce pleasure. But Moore maintained, just as "yellow" *does not mean* "productive of a certain kind of vibration in the light," so "good" *does not mean* "productive of pleasure." He recognized it as the aim of ethics to discover the other property, or properties, besides being good, which all good things possess. But he argued that "far too many philosophers have thought that when they named those other properties they were actually defining good." For this mistake he invented the name "the naturalistic fallacy,"[8] and we shall return to it shortly.

It may further illuminate what Moore meant by saying that good is indefinable, if we recall two distinctions which he drew. The first is that between analytic and synthetic propositions. The former can be shown to be true simply by reference to the definitions of the terms used (e.g., "A bachelor is an unmarried male"); the latter cannot. Moore said: "Propositions about the good are all of them synthetic and never analytic."[9] The reference here to "the good" brings us to the other distinction which Moore drew, namely, that between the substantive "the good" and the adjective "good." The good (that which is good) is what the adjective "good" applies to; but, said Moore, "if it is that to which the adjective will apply, it must be something different from that adjective

[6] *PE*, pp. 9–10.
[7] *PE*, p. 7.
[8] *PE*, p. 10.
[9] *PE*, p. 7.

itself."[10] Moore recognized that "the good" is certainly definable: we can indicate what it is by denotation or connotation. We can, for instance, enumerate all those things which produce pleasure and say "These are what 'the good' denotes"; and we can show what "the good" connotes by saying such things as "Whatever produces pleasure is also either part or the whole of the good." Moore's crucial point is that it does not follow from this that "good" is definable; *indeed the very reverse follows.* For "there is no meaning in saying that pleasure is good unless good is something different from pleasure."[11] We shall see the force of this remark if we turn now to the second of the questions which, I said, we must try to answer.

The Naturalistic Fallacy

This was the question: what precisely were Moore's grounds for saying that "good" stands for something indefinable? He held that there are two, *and only two,* conceivable alternatives to such a view and "a simple appeal to the facts" will show that neither is tenable.[12] These alternatives were: (i) that "good" denotes "a complex, a given whole, about the correct analysis of which there may be disagreement" and (ii) that "good" "means nothing at all, and there is no such subject as Ethics."[13] He attempted to establish his own view by a *reductio ad absurdum* of these alternatives.

The former, said Moore, is seen to be incorrect from the fact that "whatever definition be offered, it may be always asked, with significance, of the complex so defined, whether it is itself good."[14] This is now sometimes referred to as "the open-question argument."[15] It runs as follows. Take any proposed definition of "good," e.g., "good" means produces pleasure. Given this definition, if we ask whether or not any-

[10] *PE*, p. 9.
[11] *PE*, p. 14.
[12] *PE*, p. 15.
[13] *Ibid.*
[14] *Ibid.*
[15] G. C. Kerner, *The Revolution in Ethical Theory* (Oxford, 1966), p. 16.

thing is good, we shall be asking in effect whether or not it produces pleasure. But suppose someone asks "Is what produces pleasure good?" If the foregoing definition is correct, this question will be self-answering; that is, it will be equivalent to "Does what produces pleasure produce pleasure?" Of course, it could (logically) be the case, that whatever produces pleasure is always also good; but that is beside the present point. The force of the argument lies here: would even a hedonist suppose that anyone who doubted whether what produces pleasure is really good simply be wondering whether what produces pleasure produces pleasure? Moore thought it perfectly clear that he would not. Whatever *definiens* of "good" were proposed, he went on to say, it would make perfectly good sense to doubt whether this *definiens* was good; and "the mere fact that we understand very well what is meant by doubting it, shows clearly that we have two different notions before our minds,"[16] viz. the *definiens* in question and goodness. To put the same point another way, no one—least of all a hedonist—would consider the proposition "whatever produces pleasure is good" to be an insignificant tautology, meaning no more than "whatever produces pleasure produces pleasure." But if "good" *means* produces pleasure, then "whatever produces pleasure is good" *is* an insignificant tautology.

Moore saw that moralists have frequently made a move which is self-defeating. He had in mind writers such as Bentham or Mill, Spencer, and Green, whom he believed to have been guilty of this move, or at least to have been "influenced" by it.[17] They have tried to win assent to their particular view about what is good by the knockdown argument that this view follows from the very meaning of the word "good" and so it cannot (logically) be denied. True enough, if "good" means X, then anyone who says "X is not good" will be guilty of self-contradiction. But, by the same token, anyone who says "X is good" will then be uttering an analytic triviality, a remark which is undeniable simply because it is uninformative. Moore saw that the very last thing which any of the moralists whom he had in mind would have wanted to say was that a statement of their view—"Maximizing happiness is good," "Conduct is better as it is more evolved," "What satisfies desire is good," or whatever it might be—amounted to nothing more than an insignificant tautology. He said, with hedonists particularly in mind, "When they say 'Pleasure is good' we cannot believe that they merely mean 'Pleasure is pleasure' and nothing more than that."[18] Moralists cannot have it both ways; the statement of their view cannot be both a significant and informative remark and at the same time true by definition of the word "good."

The second of the alternatives, to his own view, which Moore said was conceivable, is the view that "good" means nothing at all and there is no such subject as ethics. Against this Moore appealed to what he thought any man may observe by introspection. "But whoever will attentively consider with himself what is actually before his mind when he asks the question 'Is pleasure (or whatever it may be) after all good?' can easily satisfy himself that he is not merely wondering whether pleasure is pleasant. And if he will try this experiment with each suggested definition in succession, he may become expert enough to recognise that in every case he has before his mind a unique object, with regard to the connection of which with any other object, a distinct question may be asked. Every one does in fact understand the question 'Is this good?' When he thinks of it, his state of mind is different from what it would be, were he asked 'Is this pleasant, or desired, or approved?' "[19] The point is that for a man to feel the difference between goodness and other things there must be some "unique object" before his mind and so there must be some subject matter for ethics. A man may not be aware of this difference without being put on the alert for it; but according to Moore it is the point of analysis to make him alert to it.

[18] *PE*, p. 12.
[19] *PE*, pp. 16–17.

Moore's Predecessors

We have seen, then, what Moore meant by saying that "good" is indefinable and what his grounds were for saying it. Before considering these arguments any further, some comment is called for on Moore's remarks about other philosophers. He said, it will be remembered, that "far too many" moral philosophers have been guilty of the naturalistic fallacy.[20] Another remark which he made was that only one writer had anticipated him in his arguments for the indefinability of good, and against the naturalistic fallacy, namely Henry Sidgwick.[21] Both of these remarks can be challenged. The latter is certainly mistaken, as we shall see in a moment. As for the former, it has recently been argued that at least some of those to whom Moore attributed the naturalistic fallacy were not guilty of it. Mill was Moore's particular target, and in the next subsection I shall refer to some recent attempts to defend Mill against his criticisms.

But first: did only Sidgwick anticipate Moore? No. If Moore had read *A Review of the Principal Questions in Morals* by the eighteenth-century rational intuitionist, Richard Price, for instance, he would have found his own distinction between a significant ethical generalization and the definition of an ethical term as clearly drawn in Price's early pages as in those of the *Principia*, and the doctrine that basic ethical terms are simple and indefinable defended by a *reductio ad absurdum* of its denial which exactly paralleled his own. It is true that Price wrote about the word "right" rather than "good," but that does not affect the claim that he was alive to what Moore called the naturalistic fallacy. Price wrote: "As to the schemes which found morality on self-love, on positive laws and compacts, or the Divine will; they must either mean, that moral good and evil are only other words for *advantageous* and *disadvantageous, willed* or *forbidden.* Or they relate to a very different question; that is, not to the question, what is the nature and true account of virtue; but,

---

[20] See note 8.
[21] *PE*, p. 17; Moore refers to H. Sidgwick's *Methods of Ethics* I. iii. 1 (6th ed.).

what is the *subject matter* of it." This parallels Moore's distinction between what "good" means and what things are good. Price wrote again: "Right and wrong when applied to actions which are commanded or forbidden by the will of God, or that produce good or harm, do not signify merely, that such actions are commanded or forbidden, or that they are useful or hurtful, but a *sentiment* concerning them and our consequent approbation or disapprobation of the performance of them. Were not this true, it would be palpably absurd in any case to ask, whether it is *right* to obey a command or *wrong* to disobey it; and the propositions, *obeying a command is right*, or *producing happiness is right*, would be most trifling, as expressing no more than that obeying a command, is obeying a command, or producing happiness, is producing happiness."[22] This parallels exactly Moore's grounds for saying that good is simple and indefinable.

Other classical moral philosophers besides Price were aware that what is morally good, right, or obligatory cannot be proved to be so by appeal to definitions of these terms. In the eighteenth century both sides of the great debate between rational intuitionists and the "moral sense" school, despite all their differences, were at one in their opposition to Hobbes's social compact theory of morals on the ground that it is one thing to say that men have contracted together to obey the will of a sovereign but quite another to say that what this sovereign wills or commands is good or bad, right or wrong, what ought to be done or not done. It is interesting to see that they rejected such a view, even supposing the sovereign to be God. On the "moral sense" side we find Shaftesbury saying: "If the mere will, decree, or law of God be said absolutely to constitute right or wrong, then are these latter words of no significancy at all";[23] and Hutcheson, in similar vein: "To call the laws of the Supreme Deity good, or holy,

[22] Price, *Review,* edited by D. D. Raphael (Oxford, 1948), pp. 16–17. For "most trifling" Price's first edition reads "most triflingly identical." For a critical study of Price's *Review* see my *Reason and Right* (London, 1970).

[23] *Inquiry concerning Virtue or Merit* I. iii. 2; quoted by A. N. Prior, *Logic and the Basis of Ethics* (Oxford, 1949), p. 96.

or just, if all goodness, holiness and justice be constituted by laws or by the will of a superior any way revealed, must be an insignificant tautology, amounting to no more than this, 'That God wills what he wills.' "[24] On the rational intuitionist side, besides Price, we find Cudworth contending that, if moral terms are defined as meaning willed or commanded by any agencies, human or divine, then they become "mere names without any signification, or names for nothing else, but willed and commanded."[25] It is, then, simply not true that only Sidgwick anticipated Moore on this point.

Did Mill Commit the Naturalistic Fallacy?

Is it true that those to whom Moore attributed the naturalistic fallacy actually committed it? Some of them did so, but in the case of others, doubts can be raised. It is not possible to examine each case in depth. There has been much controversy about John Stuart Mill and so I will confine the question to his case. Mill's *Utilitarianism* provides, according to Moore, "as naive and artless a use of the naturalistic fallacy as anybody could desire."[26] Was Moore fair to Mill? The offending passage in *Utilitarianism* ran thus:

> The only proof capable of being given that a thing is visible, is that people actually see it. . . . In like manner, I apprehend, the sole evidence it is possible to produce that anything is desirable, is that people do actually desire it. If the end which the utilitarian doctrine proposes to itself were not, in theory and in practice, acknowledged to be an end, nothing could ever convince any person that it was so. No reason can be given why the general happiness is desirable, except that each person, so far as he believes it to be attainable, desires his own happiness. This, however, being a fact, we have not only all the proof which the case admits of, but all which it is possible to require, that happiness is a good: that each person's happiness is a good to

[24] *Inquiry concerning Virtue or Moral Good* VII. vi; L. A. Selby-Bigge, *British Moralists*, p. 173; quoted by Prior, *op. cit.*, p. 96.
[25] Quoted by Prior, *op. cit.*, p. 17.
[26] *PE*, p. 66.

that person, and the general happiness, therefore, a good to the aggregate of all persons.[27]

Moore, and countless critics following him, have claimed that these words of Mill's contain a mass of confusions. For one thing, while it undoubtedly follows from the fact that X is actually seen that X is visible, because "visible" means "able to be seen," Mill should have realized that "desirable" does not mean "able to be desired" but "ought to be desired" or "deserves to be desired"; and it is, to say the least, not obvious that this follows from "is actually desired." Again, Mill commits the fallacy of composition in supposing that, from the fact, if it is a fact, that A's happiness (AH) is a good to A, B's happiness (BH) a good to B, C's happiness (CH) a good to C, it follows that the entity, AH plus BH plus CH, is a good to each of A, B, and C respectively. But Mill's most serious error, Moore contended, was that he here defined "desirable" as "desired" and so rendered "X is good" equivalent in meaning to "X is desired." If this is so, then all Moore's reasons for contending that good is indefinable can be marshaled against Mill's utilitarianism.

Recently, however, some philosophers[28] have objected that to accuse Mill of committing the naturalistic fallacy is to misunderstand the above passage. It is pointed out that Mill expressly rejected the possibility of such a proof as he is accused of having fabricated: he said that questions of ultimate ends do not admit of proof in the ordinary meaning of the term.[29] Moreover, in his *System of Logic* he showed why. He differentiated quite clearly between propositions which "assert that anything is" and those which "enjoin or recommend that something should be." The latter form "a class by themselves." So "a proposition of which the predicate is expressed by the words *ought* or *should be* is generically different from

---

[27] Fontana edition, edited by M. Warnock (1962), pp. 288–89, cf. 254–55. Quoted and criticized by Moore, *PE*, pp. 66 ff.

[28] E.g., M. Warnock's introduction to the Fontana edition of Mill's *Utilitarianism*, pp. 25–26; A. Ryan, "Mill and the Naturalistic Fallacy," *M* LXXV (1966).

[29] Mill, *op. cit.*, pp. 254, 288.

one which is expressed by *is* or *will be*."[30] He could hardly
have been more explicit about the logical gap between "is"
and "ought," between statements of natural or empirical fact
and moral judgments. Did Mill then change his mind when
he came to write *Utilitarianism?* Such a possibility is excluded by the fact that Mill revised his *System of Logic* after
writing *Utilitarianism* but without altering any of the relevant
passages in it.[31] Only two possibilities, then, remain: either
Mill was simply inconsistent in the two works; or his meaning
in *Utilitarianism* has been misunderstood by Moore and those
who echo his criticisms. The former does, admittedly, seem
unlikely. But if we exclude it, we are left with the question,
what precisely did Mill mean by the passage from *Utilitarianism* which has given such offense? None of the answers which
have been proposed to that question seems to me to defend
Mill altogether satisfactorily against Moore's criticism.

Attention has been called by his defenders to the fact that
Mill said that he was offering a proof, not in an "ordinary"
sense of the word, but in "a larger meaning" of it. According
to this larger meaning, said Mill, "the subject is within the
cognizance of the rational faculty" because "considerations
may be presented capable of determining the intellect either
to give or withhold its assent to the doctrine; and this is equivalent to proof."[32] The first thing to say in reply to this is that
it is one thing to present considerations which "determine the
intellect" in the sense of persuading people to believe something and quite another to present considerations which show
the belief in question to be rational. If the contention of Mill's
defenders is that the former was what he was doing, then
against them it suffices to say that he may well have been, but,
once the logical flaw in his argument is pointed out, it will
cease to be persuasive, at least with rational men. However,
Mill's defenders seem to be saying that the latter of the above
alternatives was what Mill purported to be doing, namely presenting considerations which show the belief in question (the

[30] VI. xii. 6, quoted by Ryan, *op. cit.*, p. 422; italics mine.
[31] Ryan, *op. cit.*, p. 423.
[32] Mill, *op. cit.*, pp. 255, 288.

greatest happiness of the greatest number is the ultimate end)
to be rational. How do they support this contention?

Mrs. Warnock, in her introduction to Mill's *Utilitarianism*,
writes:

> When Mill uses his much-criticised argument from the
> analogy between "visible" and "desirable," he is attempting
> to establish what things are good. He holds that, if people
> did not already regard some things as ends, and therefore
> desire them, it would be impossible to prove to them that
> these things were ends. He asks "How is it possible to prove
> that health is good?" The answer is that it is not possible,
> but neither is it necessary. For everyone knows that it is
> good, and shows this by desiring it. When he says that "the
> sole evidence it is possible to produce that anything is de-
> sirable is that people actually desire it," he is making the
> same point. He is not trying to *prove* that happiness is good
> but to produce evidence that people already know, without
> waiting for any proof, that it is good. You can find out
> what people recognise as ultimate ends by finding out what
> they desire. What they desire, Mill goes on to say, is hap-
> piness.[33]

Here presumably the "proof" which Mill is *not* trying to effect
is proof in the "ordinary" meaning of the word; and the "evidence" which he *is* trying to produce is that which constitutes
proof in the "larger" meaning of the word. But what does
this "larger" "proof" amount to? Mrs. Warnock says that he
is producing evidence that people already "know" that happiness is good. But the only sense which it seems possible to give
to "know" here is "firmly believe." If Mill was grounding his
case in the putative fact that people firmly believe that happiness is good, what about the distinction between true belief
and mere opinion? This appears to have been obliterated. It
could be that Mill was right and there is no possibility of prov-
ing that anything is, or is not, desirable; in which case the most
we might hope to show would be whether or not any given
end is, or is not, *thought* to be desirable. But this would then
be entirely a psychological discovery, not an ethical one. If all

[33] Warnock, *op. cit.*, p. 26.

we can talk about is what men think desirable without any means of deciding whether their opinions are correct or mistaken, then—to recall Moore's second alternative to his own view—there is no such subject as ethics. I find it hard to believe that Mill would have been content to accept that as the point which he was making in his *Utilitarianism*.

Other possible interpretations of Mill's offending passage in *Utilitarianism* have been suggested.[34] According to one of these, Mill was attempting to deduce the greatest happiness principle from (a) every man's natural desire for his own happiness, and (b) the principle of universalizability. On this interpretation, Mill's argument purported to be as follows.

> As a sentient being, every man has a desire for his own happiness.
> As a rational being, every man recognizes that all others have as much right to their happiness as he has to his own.
> As both a sentient and a rational being, therefore, every man must (logically) recognize that the ultimate moral end is the greatest happiness equitably distributed.

According to another interpretation of Mill's offending passage, he was attempting to show that morality is logically connected with human happiness; or, more precisely, that if a rule is a *moral* rule, then it follows from the meaning of the word "moral" that it will be a rule directed to the maximization of happiness and its equal distribution.

It seems to me far from proved—perhaps far from provable—that Mill intended to put forward either of these arguments in the passage in which he was accused by Moore of committing the naturalistic fallacy. At best, one would have to say that if he was putting either of them forward, he was doing so with far less than his customary clarity. It is true, as we shall see in due course, that, in more sophisticated forms, both these latter arguments, attributed to Mill, have been put forward by modern moral philosophers in support of utilitarian-

[34] See Ryan, *op. cit.*, pp. 424–25.

ism. There is something very like the former of them in Professor R. M. Hare's writings,[35] and something very like the latter in Mrs. P. Foot's.[36] But this is to anticipate matters which will concern us in Chapters 5 and 6. All that need be said at the moment is that attempts so far made to absolve Mill from Moore's accusations, by reinterpreting the offending passage, do not seem to me to be convincing.

Are Moore's Arguments Good Ones?

We must now consider whether the case which Moore made out for the indefinability of good is convincing or not. He rested it, remember, upon the contention that there are only two possible alternatives to his own view and both of them are untenable. The first of these unacceptable alternatives was that "good" denotes a complex object; the second, that men do not have a unique object before their minds when they think or speak of good. I will consider them in a moment.

But first a brief word about Moore's "open question" argument (see above, p. 69). In ordinary discourse, there are contexts where no *definiens* will serve as a substitute for "good" without loss or change of meaning. If for the evaluative question "Was his action good?" we substitute "Did his action produce pleasure (conduce to evolution, fulfill the will of God, etc.)?" then we change the meaning of the question. This is seen, as Moore rightly pointed out, from the fact that the further question "But is what produces pleasure (etc.), good?" always makes sense. If "good" meant "produces pleasure" or any of the alternatives referred to by "etc.," that question would not make sense. There is, then, a logical gap of some kind between "good," used in this evaluative sense, and any such naturalistic description as "produces pleasure (etc.)." A great deal of modern moral philosophy has been concerned with this gap between naturalistic, or supernaturalistic, description and moral evaluation. Does it really exist? What precisely is its nature? And so on. Moore may justly be

[35] See below, pp. 227–30.
[36] See below, pp. 304–7.

said to have given ethics in this century its direction by his
"open question" argument. It called attention to a problem
which has been discussed ever since and is still not finally settled. When, however, we turn to Moore's own reasons for
thinking that the gap referred to exists, they do not seem to
have been very good ones. If we recall the two alternatives to
his own view which he considered untenable, we shall see
what those reasons were.

The first appears to have been that we see what the nature
of the gap is, and we know that it exists, when we recognize
that "good" denotes a simple, not a complex, object. Moore
himself says explicitly that there are as good grounds, and
the same sort of grounds, for holding that "yellow" denotes a
simple object as for holding that "good" does so. Moreover,
he sees that it follows from this that any attempt to define
"yellow" will be "the same fallacy"[37] as any attempt to define "good." Now, it is obviously impossible to establish that a
gap exists between what "good" denotes and what any naturalistic description denotes by means of an argument which
simply brings out the logical similarity between "good" and
"yellow" because "yellow" is a naturalistic description. No
doubt, because he was alive to this fact, Moore himself
tried to establish some difference between "good" and "yellow." He said that, if anyone attempted to define "yellow,"
the *definiens* and *definiendum* would both denote "natural
objects"; and so this could not be called a case of the naturalistic fallacy, i.e., the fallacy of defining naturalistically something which is nonnatural. But "good," he contended, is different: ". . . if [anyone] confuses 'good,' which is not in the
same sense a natural object, with any natural object whatever,
then there is reason for calling that a naturalistic fallacy; its
being made with regard to 'good' marks it as something quite
specific, and this specific mistake deserves a name because it is
so common."[38] This leaves the crucial question unanswered,
namely, what *is* the reason for saying that "good" denotes
something nonnatural? That question is certainly not an-

[37] *PE*, p. 13.
[38] *Ibid.*

swered by an argument which simply shows that what "good" denotes is simple, in the sense in which what "yellow" denotes is simple.

Moore's second reason for thinking that a logical gap exists between what "good" denotes and what any naturalistic description denotes appears to have been his belief that we know this by intuition. The second alternative to his own view, viz. the opinion that there is nothing to which "good" refers, is, he held, untenable because we all know, when we look into our own minds, that what "good" denotes is "a unique object." In other words, we know by intuition that this object is logically different from whatever is denoted by expressions such as "producing happiness," "conducing to evolution," "fulfilling the will of God," etc.

I will digress for a moment to consider a question which arises at this point. Was Moore really an intuitionist? There is considerable room for doubt. He says himself in the preface to *Principia Ethica:* "I am not an 'Intuitionist,' in the ordinary sense of the term."[39] From what he goes on to say it is clear what he means. First, he denies, in effect, that he is a deontological intuitionist, i.e., one who thinks that judgments concerning *right* or *duty* are incapable of proof by consideration of the results to which different courses of action lead, or would lead. He does *not* believe in the intrinsic rightness or obligatoriness of certain kinds of action. We shall consider in the next section contemporaries of Moore who did, namely H. A. Prichard and W. D. Ross. But the Moore of the *Principia* certainly did not, though, as we shall see, in his later book *Ethics* he seems to have been coming around to a view similar to that of Ross and Prichard. In *Principia* Moore judged actions right or wrong, our duty or otherwise, in accordance with how much good they effected or failed to effect. Moore also dissociated himself from intuitionism thus: "I would wish it observed that, when I call such propositions [*sc.* propositions as to what kind of things ought to exist for their own sakes] 'Intuitions,' I mean *merely* to assert that they are incapable of proof; I imply nothing whatever as to the

[39] *PE*, p. x.

manner or origin of our cognition of them."[40] The classical intuitionists of the seventeenth and eighteenth centuries engaged in a great debate concerning the nature of the moral faculty.[41] Some, like Shaftesbury and Hutcheson, believed it to be a kind of sense; others, like Cudworth, Clarke, Balguy, and Price, believed it to be reason. Prichard and Ross appear, on the whole, to have sided with the latter school of thought and are generally classified as rational intuitionists. Moore, however, was not interested in this question of how moral intuitions originate and had nothing to say on the subject.

The third aspect of intuitionism from which Moore dissociated himself was the claim that moral intuition is infallible. He said, "Still less do I imply (as most Intuitionists have done) that any proposition whatever is true, *because* we cognise it in a particular way or by the exercise of any particular faculty: I hold, on the contrary, that in every way in which it is possible to cognise a true proposition, it is also possible to cognise a false one."[42] This seems to reject what is surely the bedrock belief of intuitionism, namely the belief that men have a faculty which is unerring in its apprehension of certain truths. This faculty, it is conceded by most intuitionists, may be impaired or obstructed by certain conditions, but, given the nonfulfillment of these conditions, it cannot err. I think the important questions are two: does Moore's view that it is possible to cognize falsely, as well as truly, by intuition, avoid any of the problems concerning the claim to know by intuition which arise in the case of traditional intuitionism, and, does Moore consistently adhere to this view? The answer in both cases appears to be no.

As we shall see in the next section, the difficulty about the claim to know X by intuition is how this can amount to more than the claim to believe X. Moore thinks intuition may be true or false. This does not lessen the difficulty of differentiating it from mere belief. Indeed all Moore has done is to add a further problem: how are we to differentiate between true

[40] *Ibid.*
[41] Cf. my *Ethical Intuitionism* (1967), Chap. VII.
[42] *PE*, p. x.

and false intuitions? His view that they may be either does not
make intuitionism more credible. Did he adhere to his view
consistently? When we recall what he said in the *Principia*
about "the Ideal," it is hard to reconcile this with his view
that intuitions may be true or false. He wrote: "No one, probably, who has asked himself the question, has ever doubted
that personal affection and the appreciation of what is beautiful in Art or Nature, are good in themselves." He describes
this as "the ultimate and fundamental truth of Moral Philosophy," and goes on, "It is only for the sake of these things—
in order that as much of them as possible may at some time
exist—that any one can be justified in performing any public
or private duty; . . . they are the *raison d'être* of virtue; . . .
it is they . . . that form the rational ultimate end of human
action and the sole criterion of social progress. . . ." He
does add that "these appear to be truths which have been
generally overlooked"; but he does not appear to conceive it
possible that they are *not* truths at all.[43]

I return from this digression to Moore's reason for thinking
that there is a logical gap between "good" and any naturalistic description. That reason was, in effect, that we all know
by intuition that there is such a gap because we all apprehend
that to which "good" refers as a unique object. Two points
can be made against this. First, do all men have before their
minds this unique object when they think about good? In
order to answer that we would have to do two things: one, to
decide what are the appropriate criteria for determining
when a man has this unique object before his mind and when
he has not; and the other, to test all men by these criteria in
order to see whether or not they all do have that unique object before their minds when they think of good. It is difficult
to decide what such criteria could be; and certainly no one has
ever conducted the consequent investigation. If anyone says,
therefore, that he does not have a unique object before his
mind when he thinks of good—and we shall see in the next
sub-section that some say this—then we cannot refute him.
The logical gap between "good" and any naturalistic descrip-

[43] *PE*, pp. 188–89.

tion cannot be established by Moore's appeal to introspection.

But, even if that appeal were successful, what would it prove? If all men did have a unique object before their minds when they thought of "good," this would not prove that to fail to have such an object before one's mind when one thinks of good is to be guilty of a fallacy. It would show simply what is the case, not what logically must be the case. The logical gap between "good" and naturalistic descriptions concerns something which cannot (logically) be said. One cannot (logically) say "good" and mean "producing happiness." If this is so, it is so because of the rules for the use of these expressions. It is not so because of anything which does or does not happen inside men's minds. Introspection may lead to psychological discoveries. But it cannot settle questions of logical validity.

Is Ethical Naturalism Defensible?

It is instructive to ask how an ethical naturalist might attempt to counter Moore's attack upon his position. He could, as we have already noted, deny that he is aware of good as a unique object. Before such a denial, in default of any satisfactory method of testing the claim that all men are aware of "good" as such, Moore would have been helpless.

Can an ethical naturalist equally effectively dispose of the rest of Moore's case against him? Moore rejected the view that "good" refers to a complex object on the ground that, if it does, some analytic propositions about good will be true, and the "open question argument" shows that none, in fact, are. In other words, nothing is true *by definition* of "good." To this, the ethical naturalist may reply that, given what *he* himself means by "good," certain propositions about good *are* true analytically, or by definition. Suppose he says that by "good" he means "producing happiness." Then it is analytically true that anything which is good produces happiness. But Moore, in his turn, could have pointed out, in reply to this, that the naturalist's definition of "good" is stipulative. Of course anyone can (logically) stipulate whatever definition he chooses for "good," as for any other word. Moore never denied it. All he did say was, in effect, that anyone who stipulates a definition of "good" is thereby opting out of the ordinary use to which "good" is put. Lexically, as distinct from stipulatively, "good" is indefinable.

It has been suggested[44] that the ethical naturalist could return to the attack by contending that there is a simple explanation of the fact that "good" is lexically indefinable. This is the explanation which Mill offered. Mill said that a word may be "first applied to one thing, and then extended by a series of transitions . . . from one object to another, until it becomes applied to things having nothing in common with the first things . . . so that it at last denotes a confused huddle of objects, having nothing whatever in common; and connotes nothing, not even a vague and general resemblance."[45] This, the ethical naturalist might say, is what has happened in the case of "good." It is just because so many definitions of "good" are, in fact, current, that it appears to be indefinable. Mill went on to argue that, when a word has fallen into this state, "it has become unfit for the purposes either of thought or of the communication of thought; and can only be made serviceable by stripping it of some part of its multifarious denotation and confining it to objects possessed of some attributes in common, which it may be made to connote."[46] In a similar vein, the ethical naturalist may go on to claim that all he is attempting to do is to tidy up the lexical definition of "good." He is not trying to define the indefinable. He is simply proposing that the sense and reference of "good" should be restricted to one object, or type of object, rather than to a "confused huddle" of objects. He may further claim that the restricted use which he proposes is, in fact, the most common use of the word. In the interests of clarity of thought and communication, he could go on, it is desirable that the "multifarious denotation" of "good" should be stripped away from it and its meaning restricted as he proposes to restrict it. Prima facie this line of argument seems plausible.

---

[44] Cf. Prior, *op. cit.*, pp. 10–11.
[45] *System of Logic* I. viii. 7, quoted by Prior, *op. cit.*, p. 10.
[46] *Ibid.*

Against ethical naturalists, however, Moore had one very powerful argument, as we have already seen (above, pp. 70–71). He accused them with justice of inconsistency. They contended that "good" means "produces happiness" (etc.); and, in effect, they also contended that the statement, "what produces happiness (etc.) is good," is more than an insignificant tautology. Both these propositions cannot be true. The ethical naturalists believed that they had a triumphant argument in their point that "good" means whatever, as utilitarians, evolutionists, etc., they took it to mean. If "good" means "produces happiness (etc.)," then to say "what produces happiness (etc.) is *not* good" is to contradict oneself. By making this point, they thought that they had shown the position of anyone who rejected their utilitarianism, evolutionism, or whatever, to be irrational. But when, on their platforms and in their pamphlets, they advocated courses of action which produce happiness (etc.) *as good,* they intended to say more than that what produces happiness (etc.) simply does what it does. They intended to say that it is the end to be chosen, sought, achieved. But this they could *not* say by using "good," if their own definition of "good" was correct. All they could say was that what produces happiness (etc.) produces happiness (etc.). Moore may have been wrong about what "good" and similar words mean but he saw clearly that to call anything good cannot be to give it a naturalistic description. And he saw that there was a fundamental inconsistency in those ethical naturalists who thought that it can. He made the point in his own way:

They [*sc.* ethical naturalists] are all so anxious to persuade us that what they call good is what we really ought to do. "Do, pray, act so, because the word 'good' is generally used to denote actions of this nature": such . . . would be the substance of their teaching. And in so far as they tell us how we ought to act, their teaching is truly ethical, as they mean it to be. But how perfectly absurd is the reason they would give for it! "You are to do this, because most people use a certain word to denote conduct such as this." . . . My dear sirs, what we want to know

from you as ethical teachers, is not how people use a word
. . . what we want to know is simply what *is* good.[47]

The ethical naturalists set themselves up as able to do two
things with the word "good": viz., (i) to point out that it was
used only to describe certain natural properties; and (ii) to
use it in ethical teaching. Moore's achievement was to see
that they could not (logically) do both.

II. THE INTUITIONISM OF PRICHARD AND ROSS

Moore was a teleologist whereas many intuitionists have
been deontologists. The difference, summarily put, between
these two types of ethical thinkers is that teleologists consider
the moral value, positive or negative, of actions to be determined by the end to which such actions are a means; while
deontologists hold that the rightness or wrongness, goodness
or evil, of an action is intrinsic to the action itself. Moore, as I
say, held the former view. He argued that all men, if they
reflect carefully on the nature of goodness, will discern by
intuition that "by far the most valuable things, which we know
or can imagine, are certain states of consciousness, which may
be roughly described as the pleasures of human intercourse
and the enjoyment of beautiful objects."[48] Personal affections
and aesthetic enjoyments constitute ends to the attainment or
fulfillment of which actions may be the means. Actions are
right or *wrong,* such as *ought,* or *ought not* to be done, as they
maximize, or fail to maximize, the pleasures of human intercourse or the enjoyment of beautiful objects. Here is what
Moore had to say on the subject in *Principia Ethica:* "What I
wish . . . to point out is that 'right' does and can mean nothing but 'cause of a good result,' and is thus identical with 'useful'; whence it follows that . . . no action which is not justified
by its results can be right. . . . Our 'duty' . . . can only be defined as that action which will cause more good to exist in
the Universe than any possible alternative. And what is 'right'
or 'morally permissible' only differs from this, as what will not

[47] *PE*, p. 12.
[48] *PE*, p. 188.

cause *less* good than any possible alternative."[49] On Moore's view we know by intuition the ends which are good. But, of course, this does not mean that it will be self-evident in any situation what it is right to do or what we ought to do. We shall have to work that out. What courses of action are open to us? What amount of good will each cause to exist? Only when we have discovered the answers to such questions by discursive reasoning shall we be able to say where our duty lies or what it is morally permissible to do.

Over against Moore, within intuitionism, stood his contemporaries H. A. Prichard and W. D. Ross. Prichard's most important work has been collected in his *Moral Obligation* (Oxford, 1949) and in *Moral Obligation and Duty and Interest* (Oxford, 1968), edited by J. O. Urmson. Ross's moral philosophy is contained in his *The Right and the Good* (Oxford, 1930) and *Foundations of Ethics* (Oxford, 1939). Prichard and Ross were deontologists. They built, however, on the foundation which Moore had laid. Ross pointed out that Moore's arguments for the indefinability of "good" apply equally in the case of "right" or "obligatory." Whatever *definiens* (D) is proposed for "right" or "obligatory," the question "Is what is D right or obligatory?" is not self-answering and the proposition "What is D is right or obligatory" is not tautologous. We see this in the case of "right" and "obligatory" just as clearly as in the case of "good," whether we appeal to our own intuitions or to the ordinary use of words. Ross claimed moreover, that Moore, in his later book *Ethics* (London, 1912), was coming around to this way of thinking.[50] In *Principia Ethica* Moore had said, "If I ask whether an action is *really* my duty or *really* expedient, the predicate of which I question the applicability to the action in question is precisely the same."[51] But in *Ethics* we find him saying that we cannot discover "any characteristic, over and above the mere fact that they are right, which belongs to absolutely *all* voluntary actions which are right, and which at the same time does not

[49] *PE*, pp. 147–48.
[50] *RG*, pp. 10–11.
[51] *PE*, p. 169.

belong to any except those which are right."[52] And he arrives
at the conclusion that "it is, indeed, quite plain, I think, that
the meaning of the two words [*sc.* 'duty' and 'expediency']
is *not* the same; for, if it were, then it would be a mere tautology to say that it is always our duty to do what will have
the best possible consequences."[53]

H. A. Prichard

Prichard contended that with regard to any situation, we
can know by intuition what action would be right or obligatory within it, but a certain amount of discursive reasoning
may be necessary first in order to clear the ground for this
intuition. Prichard defined the rightness of an action thus:
it "consists in its being the origination of something of a certain kind A in a situation of a certain kind, a situation consisting in a certain relation B of the agent to others or to his
own nature."[54] We may need to think out carefully what the
action would originate. To quote his example: "We may not
appreciate the wrongness of telling a certain story until we
realize that we should thereby be hurting the feelings of one
of our audience."[55] And in order thus to appreciate what an
action would originate we may need to look into the facts of
the situation to ensure that we have in mind every relevant
relation of the agent to others or to his own nature. To quote
Prichard again: "For instance, we may not appreciate the
obligation to give *X* a present, until we remember that he
has done us an act of kindness."[56] Getting all this clear—
what the action originates, how the agent is related to himself or others—demands what Prichard called "general thinking." But having got it clear, we perceive what ought to be
done by what he calls an act of "moral thinking." He explains
what he means by moral thinking thus: "This apprehension is
immediate, in precisely the sense in which a mathematical

[52] *Ethics* (1947 pagination), p. 13.
[53] *Ethics*, p. 107.
[54] "Does Moral Philosophy Rest on a Mistake?" *M* XXI (1912), reprinted in *MO*.
[55] *MO*, pp. 7–8.
[56] *MO*, p. 8.

apprehension is immediate, e.g., the apprehension that this three-sided figure, in virtue of its being three-sided, must have three angles. Both apprehensions are immediate in the sense that in both, insight into the nature of the subject directly leads us to recognise its possession of the predicate; and it is only stating this fact from the other side to say that in both cases the fact apprehended is self-evident."[57] These quotations are from an article entitled "Does Moral Philosophy Rest on a Mistake?" first published in *Mind* in 1912. Prichard's answer to the question in his title was that moral philosophy *does* rest on a mistake in so far as moral philosophers have tried to answer the question "Is there really a reason why I should act in the ways in which hitherto I have thought I ought to act?"[58] There is, he held, no such reason. It is not possible to prove what is right or what ought to be done; this "can only be apprehended directly by an act of moral thinking."[59]

It occurred to Prichard that there are possible objections to his view that duty is self-evident.[60] How, in the light of it, are we to explain irresoluble differences of opinion about what ought to be done? And if obligations are self-evident, how are we to know what to do when they conflict as, not infrequently, they do? His answer to the former question was: men are at varying degrees of moral development and some have clearer intuitions than others. Failure to recognize a particular obligation is usually due to some mistake in the preliminary "general" thinking. Even the best men are sometimes blind to their obligations because the general thinking which has to be done in order to be aware of every obligation is so extensive and complicated. Granted Prichard's basic assumption—that discerning duty is like discerning that two plus two equals four—his answer to this first objection seems reasonable enough. It is, of course, rather odd to say that something is self-evident and then to add that many men cannot see it even when told where to look, and not even the best men can see it

[57] *Ibid.*
[58] *MO*, p. 1.
[59] *MO*, p. 16.
[60] *MO*, p. 9 n.

altogether clearly and consistently. Nevertheless, Prichard could have countered any such objection by pointing out that many people are unable to perform elementary mathematical calculations even after instruction; and even the greatest mathematicians are sometimes stumped by a problem. Just as these latter facts, in themselves, do not impugn a Cartesian account of mathematics, so the fact that intuition is sometimes defective does not, in itself, preclude an intuitionist account of moral thinking.

Prichard's answer to the latter of the two above objections —how are we to know what to do when obligations conflict?— does not, at first, seem so defensible. It ran: "To the second objection I should reply that obligation admits of degrees, and that where obligations conflict, the decision of what we ought to do turns not on the question 'Which of the alternative courses of action will originate the greater good?' but on the question 'Which is the greater obligation?' "[61] Against this it might be said that, in fact, we often do decide between conflicting obligations by asking which will realize the greater good. However, I think Prichard would—or could—have replied thus. The obligation to realize the greater good is *one* obligation among others and even if, unlike any other obligation, it is instantiated in *every* situation where a moral question arises, nevertheless it cannot just be taken for granted that the question "Which action will originate the greater good?" settles conflicts of obligation. We may well decide that it is the question to ask; but if we do so, we have, in effect, answered the logically prior question: which is the greatest of obligations?

A difficulty about conflicting obligations remains, of which Prichard does not appear to have been aware. He said, as we noted, that the sense in which moral intuitions are immediate or self-evident is "precisely" the same as that in which mathematical ones are. But, in fact, there is a difference. In the mathematical case, these self-evident apprehensions never conflict. If two or more axioms are instantiated in one example, we never have to choose between them as we some-

[61] *Ibid.*

times have to choose between conflicting obligations in a
given situation. It may well be, even if we reject Cartesian
intuitionism, that there is a close parallel between mathematical and moral thinking. But there is also the divergence
to which I have just referred, and Prichard does not account
for it, even on his own presuppositions.

Prichard developed in later writings the views of his 1912
paper with great subtlety, but never changed them substantially at any rate in his hitherto published work.

W. D. Ross

In the writings of W. D. Ross we find careful distinctions
drawn between right, duty, and moral goodness.

"'Right'" he said, "means 'suitable, in a unique and indefinable way which we may express by the phrase "morally
suitable," to the situation in which an agent finds himself.'"[62]
To this situation there are two aspects. The *objective* aspect
which consists of certain morally relevant *facts* about the
persons or things involved, and the *subjective* aspect which
consists of certainly morally relevant *thoughts* of the agent's
about the persons or things involved.[63] A number of questions arise concerning this account of right, some of which
take us on to a consideration of the related concept, duty.
We will deal with these questions in turn.

(i) The first of them is: what renders the facts or thoughts
just referred to, in differentiating subjective and objective
rightness, morally relevant? Ross believed that there are certain general principles of conduct—prima facie duties or obligations as he called them—which all men of developed moral
consciousness intuit, such as promise-keeping, fidelity (i.e.,
not lying), reparation, gratitude, justice, beneficence, self-
improvement, non-maleficence. He compared these prima
facie obligations to mathematical axioms.[64] Expressly, he
repudiated any claim to finality or completeness for his list;
presumably because he thought that he might have over-

[62] *FE*, p. 146.
[63] *FE*, Chap. VII.
[64] *RG*, pp. 29–30.

looked some prima facie obligations which are apparent to other people. But if they are self-evident, would it not be strange if anyone who had reflected on morality as much as Ross had done, had overlooked any prima facie obligations? Alternatively, he might have thought that some further prima facie obligations, which no one had so far perceived, might eventually come to light. But again this would be strange, if they are comparable to mathematical axioms, for what should we make of it if someone said that he had just perceived an axiom of Euclid which no one had known before?

(ii) How did Ross explain the relationship between, for example, the natural property of being the fulfillment of a promise and the ethical property of being right or being one's duty? His way of differentiating between natural and ethical properties was to call the former *constitutive* characteristics and the latter *consequential*. But he does not offer any explanation of how, for instance, being the fulfillment of a promise constitutes rightness, or why rightness is a consequence of it. He thinks of the connection simply as perceived by intuition. We "see" that if X is the keeping of a promise, then X is right. Ross, like Prichard, compares this to mathematics, to seeing that if a triangle is equilateral it is equiangular. But Ross did realize that there is one difference: the relation in the case of triangles is reversible (if equilateral, then equiangular; if equiangular, then equilateral); but it is not in the case of actions (if keeping a promise, then right; but not necessarily, if right, then keeping a promise).[65]

(iii) How did Ross conceive of the relationship between rightness and duty? It will be recalled that he differentiates subjective from objective rightness. Is it our duty to do the objectively right, or the subjectively right, action? Ross originally held that it is our duty to do the former but under Prichard's influence he changed his mind.[66] In any given case it is possible to perform actions which are right in one or other of four senses:

[65] Cf. *RG*, p. 121.
[66] See *FE*, pp. 148 ff. It was Prichard's "Duty and Ignorance of Fact," Hertz Lecture 1932, reprinted in *MO*, which changed his opinion.

(a) an act which is *in fact* right in the situation as it *in fact* is;

(b) an act which the agent *thinks* right in the situation as it *in fact* is;

(c) an act which is *in fact* right in the situation as the agent *thinks* it to be;

(d) an act which the agent *thinks* right in the situation as he *thinks* it to be.

Which of these is it the agent's duty to perform? Ross, following Prichard, held that the answer is the fourth. If any of the other three were one's duty, then before I could (logically) know what any agent ought to do, I would need to have complete knowledge of what, in the case of each of the actions open to him, he would be doing, i.e., what this action would do to him and everyone else concerned; and, logically prior to this, I should need complete knowledge also of the situation in which each of such acts would have to be done, so that I would be perfectly certain that no morally relevant feature of it was being overlooked. But such completeness of knowledge is unobtainable, if not in principle then at least in practice. We do not have the time or the facilities to obtain it. If, therefore, in order to know what ought to be, or to have been, done, one needs to possess such knowledge, two consequences necessarily follow: viz., an agent can never know what his duty is; and he may do, or fail to do, his duty without knowing that he is doing, or failing to do, it.[67] An analysis of the concept of duty which lands us with these conclusions must be mistaken. They are so plainly at variance with the word "duty" as normally used. Ross pointed out that, if we consider that it is an agent's duty to do what is right in sense (d) above, we do not thereby obliterate the distinction between what an agent *really* ought to do and what he thinks that he ought to do.[68] We should consider that he ought *really* to do what is right in sense (d) above. Someone else may think that an agent ought to do what is right in senses (a), (b), or (c); but we would not concede that the

[67] Cf. *FE*, pp. 149–50.
[68] See *FE*, p. 156.

fact that he thinks this, makes it so. Such a person would, in our view, simply be mistaken. The belief that there is a correct opinion, as distinct from mistaken ones, can (logically) only be held where the distinction is preserved between what really is the case and what is merely thought to be so. Ross did not forego that distinction.

(iv) How did Ross relate prima facie rightness or obligatoriness to rightness or obligatoriness *sans phrase?* Prima facie rightness or obligatoriness, i.e., tendency to be right, or one's duty, he said, is a "parti-resultant attribute" of an action—"i.e. one which belongs to an act in virtue of some one component in its nature." Being right or obligatory *sans phrase,* on the other hand, is a "toti-resultant attribute"—i.e., "one which belongs to an act in virtue of its whole nature and of nothing less than this."[69] An action could, for instance, be right in that it was the keeping of a promise but wrong in that it was a case of maleficence. In such an instance its morally relevant features have to be "weighed" against one another. An act is right [or obligatory] when "of all acts possible for the agent in the circumstances, it is that whose *prima facie* rightness [or obligatoriness] in the respects in which it is *prima facie* right [or obligatory] most outweighs its *prima facie* wrongness [or disobligatoriness] in any respects in which it is *prima facie* wrong [or disobligatory]."[70] The difficulty which immediately arises about this view is as follows: upon what *scales,* so to speak, is this "weighing" to be done? We must weigh certain features of an act against one another, but how? Ross's answer is: by intuition. The man of developed moral consciousness, he thinks, will simply "see" in which act rightness most outweighs wrongness.

(v) What is a "tendency to be" right, or one's duty? Reference was made to this a moment ago. If an action is, for example, the fulfillment of a promise or an act of gratitude, then each of these particular features of it instantiates a prima

[69] *RG,* p. 28.
[70] *RG,* p. 46; cf. *FE,* p. 85, which differs in reading "obligatoriness" where *RG* reads "rightness" and "disobligatoriness" where *RG* reads "wrongness."

facie obligation and gives it what Ross called "a tendency to be one's duty."[71] He seemed to think that "tendency to be one's duty" is some sort of positive property which an action may have. But, as Professor P. F. Strawson has pointed out, it is not. To say, for instance, that all acts of gratitude have a tendency to be right is simply to say that most, but not all, of the class, acts of gratitude, are right.[72] It is, therefore, self-contradictory to say that *all* acts which are acts of gratitude have a tendency to be right, which is what Ross wished to say.

Before turning from right and duty to moral goodness we should note a point about duty which Prichard made and Ross took up. Duty or obligation is not really a property of actions but a fact about agents. Prichard put it: "But, as we recognize when we reflect, there are no such characteristics of an action as ought-to-be-doneness and ought-not-to-be-doneness. This is obvious; for, since the existence of an obligation to do some action cannot possibly depend on actual performance of the action, the obligation cannot itself be a property which the action would have, if it were done. What does exist is the fact that you, or that I, ought, or ought not, to do a certain action, or rather to set ourselves to do a certain action. And when we make an assertion containing the term 'ought' or 'ought not,' that to which we are attributing a certain character is not a certain activity but a certain man."[73] This point is valid and important. We might well say of some possible, but as yet unperformed, action that it would be *right, if it were done*. But we should not say that an act would be our duty, *if it were done;* we should say that it is our duty to do this act (period).

Another important distinction which Ross usefully brought out is that between moral goodness and right or duty. Moral goodness, he said, is a characteristic: (a) of certain kinds of voluntary actions, such as those done from a desire to fulfill

[71] *RG*, p. 28.
[72] Strawson, "Ethical Intuitionism," *P* XXIII (1949).
[73] "Duty and Ignorance of Fact" in *MO*, p. 37; quoted approvingly by Ross, *FE*, p. 155.

duty, to relieve pain, to extend knowledge, etc.; (b) of the
desire for such ends even when it fails to issue in action; (c)
of the satisfaction experienced at seeing such ends attained,
or dissatisfaction at seeing them not realized; and (d) of dispositions, embodied in character, to act for the sake of such
ends. All these, according to Ross, we call morally good.[74]
We see that moral goodness is distinct from right or duty
when we recognize that it is possible to do one's duty from a
bad motive as well as a good; for instance, to give one's weak
or promising pupils extra tuition, not from a desire to assist
them or to justify one's salary but in order to embarrass a col-
league. Equally, one may do what is morally good and thereby
fail in one's duty; for instance, toil at one's research from a
desire to extend knowledge and in the process neglect one's
teaching function. An agent's motives—with which moral
goodness always has to do—are not under his control as his intentions—with which rightness and duty have to do—are. He
can set himself to perform a certain action and carry this intention through as far as circumstances permit; but he cannot,
at will, find one end desirable and another not so. He may indeed set himself to cultivate good motives or dispositions; he
will then do whatever he thinks will achieve that result. But
"ought" implies "can"; and we cannot desire whatever we
choose to desire. It would not make sense to say that one
ought to love knowledge as it would to say that one ought
to pursue it.

Ross, then, highlights the distinctions between moral
goodness, right, and duty. But there are basic similarities in
his accounts of each of the three. These similarities are as
follows. All are discerned intuitively. All are indefinable.
All are nonnatural characteristics consequential upon constitutive, natural characteristics. All may require us to
"weigh" certain morally relevant considerations against others.
This brief attempt to clarify Ross's position has been sufficient to show that, in his case as in Moore's and Prichard's, at
every vital point in the analysis of moral thinking, a claim
is made to knowledge gained by intuition. In the next main

[74] See *FE*, Chap. XII.

section we shall challenge the view that there is any such knowledge.

A Predecessor of Prichard and Ross

We noted above that the eighteenth-century British moral philosopher Richard Price anticipated Moore's argument against "the naturalistic fallacy" in his *Review*. In that work, he also anticipated the leading ideas of Prichard and Ross.

The former's contention, that moral thinking, like mathematical, consists, in the last analysis, of the immediate apprehension by intuition of self-evident truths, he clearly enunciated. Price differentiated two acts of the understanding: "deduction," by which he meant discursive reasoning and under which he classified what we should call induction as well as what we call deduction; and "intuition" (i.e., Cartesian intuition).[75] Taking Locke's view that it is the work of the understanding to perceive agreement or disagreement between ideas and that this produces knowledge, Price contended that the ideas of such agreement or disagreement are themselves new simple ideas. For example, the equality between the two angles, made by any right line standing in any direction on another, and two right angles is a new simple idea clearly and distinctly perceived by the understanding, wholly different from that of the angles compared and denoting self-evident truth. He went on to claim that, besides such mathematical ideas, logical ideas (e.g., necessity), physical ideas (e.g., cause) and *moral ideas* (e.g., right, fit, good, duty) are likewise new simple ideas perceived by the understanding. Such ideas shine by their own light. They are the ultimate constituents of knowledge and without them all reasoning would be impossible. To such self-evident truths the last appeal in reasoning must always be made.[76]

Ross's views are also paralleled in Price. Price gives a list of "heads of virtue," as he calls them, which is very similar to Ross's list of prima facie obligations.[77] And the underlying

[75] Price, *op. cit.*, p. 18 n.

[76] Price, *op. cit.*, pp. 97–103. Price drew very largely on the Cambridge Platonist, Ralph Cudworth, for his leading ideas. See my *Reason and Right* for a full-length study of R. Price's moral philosophy.

[77] Price, *op. cit.*, Chap. VII.

idea is the same in both authors: that these general principles are directly intuited and one or more of them is instantiated in every moral situation. Ross's idea that the right or obligatory action is that which "suits" or "fits" its situation in a way which is intuited after weighing against each other the prima facie obligations, or "heads of virtue," which the situation instantiates, is also to be found in Price.[78] The objections to this view and a possible line of defense against them can be seen in the case of both authors.

First, the objections. Hume, Price's contemporary, charged rational intuitionists, like Price, with having simply assumed that virtue is some kind of relation, viz., fitness or suitableness, and vice its opposite, because they took it for granted that the moral faculty is the understanding. He contended that if virtue, or vice, does consist in a relation, then, whatever this relation might be, it could conceivably hold between material objects or animals just as well as between human beings. A sapling overtopping its parent tree must then be morally like a child crushing its parent; and incest between animals, the same kind of occurrence morally as it is between human beings. We do not believe objects and animals to be "susceptible of the same morality" as ourselves, and so the relational account of virtue and vice must be mistaken.[79] A further possible objection is that, if moral rightness is some sort of relation, such as fitness, we end in absurdity. An act, to be relationally fit, must be fit, for example, as an instance of a standard. But the question inevitably arises: is this standard right? If this question means "Is it fit?" further or higher standards are implied. Eventually, however, we come to our ultimate standard. We wish to say—and indeed need to say or all our moral judgments are forfeit—that this too is right. But what sense does that make, on the present view, unless there is some higher standard still? And, by definition, there can be none in the case of an ultimate standard.

What defense can be offered, on behalf of Price or Ross, to such objections? It is important to distinguish between two

[78] Price, *op. cit.*, p. vi.
[79] *A Treatise of Human Nature* III. i. 1; Selby-Bigge edition, pp. 464–68.

possible conceptions of moral rightness from the rationalist's viewpoint. One is that such rightness is simply a *relation* between acts and situations or persons, comparable to mathematical equality; the other, that it is a property of acts, in situations, *entailed* by certain of their nonmoral properties, comparable to the equilaterality entailed by equiangularity in triangles. The latter conception has certain advantages over the former; and I think that there is good reason to say that it is the view to which Price[80] and Ross[81] subscribed. If rightness is, as these authors evidently thought, what Ross calls a consequential characteristic entailed by what he calls constitutive characteristics, such as being the fulfillment of a promise, then the latter characteristics can (logically) be so defined that they restrict the entailment to instances where persons are concerned. Trees and animals do not for instance make promises. I think the rational intuitionists would be unanimous on the point that the grounds of rightness *always* involve persons in some way or other; and so they safeguard themselves in advance against Hume's objection. As we have just interpreted their view, it is proof also against the other objection given above. The entailment of rightness by the grounds of rightness is the same entailment in the case of the ultimate standard as in that of the particular instance. In so far as there is promise-keeping, for example, there is rightness; we intuit this in the same sense of "intuit," whether we are thinking in general terms of a prima facie obligation or engaged in "weighing" out the rightness of a particular act. This interpretation does not involve any regress into absurdity.

III. THE CLAIM TO KNOW BY MORAL INTUITION

We must now call in question the very idea of knowing by intuition. All ethical intuitionists—and this includes Moore even though he thought that intuition may sometimes be mistaken—subscribe to the belief that there are moral truths known to us by intuition. They would say that we know there

---

[80] Cf. Raphael's introduction, Price, *op. cit.*, pp. xxxii–xxxiii.
[81] See above, p. 93.

to be a nonnatural property of goodness or rightness and that it attaches to such-and-such acts or states of affairs. In assessing this claim, we must first consider what it means to say that we *know* that something is the case; and then whether it is consistent with this to speak of knowing *by intuition*.

What conditions must be fulfilled before I can say "I know that X"? If we follow A. J. Ayer,[82] these appear to be three in number. (i) It must be true that X. I cannot know, for example, that two and two make five or that Brazil is in Europe. Of course, ways of establishing the truth or falsity of propositions vary and some of these may be questionable in themselves. But, given whatever it is that we usually mean by saying that X is true, we must be able to say this, if we are going to say "I know that X." (ii) I must believe that X. It would be nonsense, whatever value we gave to X, to say "I know that X but I don't believe that X." This is self-contradictory, not, of course, because "know" and "believe" mean entirely the same thing, but because part of what I am saying in saying that I know anything to be the case is that I believe it to be such. (iii) I must be able to give an appropriate answer to the question: how do you know that X? There are, in a phrase of Ayer's, "accredited routes to knowledge."[83] These differ. The route to discoveries in mathematics or logic is different from that to discoveries in the natural or social sciences. Epistemologists have to make clear what an appropriate answer to "How do you know?" would amount to in any given instance. They also have to show us exactly where we are when we have arrived at "knowledge" by any accredited route, for these routes do not all lead to the same destination. Analytical and empirical knowledge are clearly not the same thing, and there may be further distinctions which need to be drawn within the concept of knowledge. Nevertheless, when all such qualifications have been added, I think it remains true that, when I say I know that something is the case, I must be prepared to say how I know.

I ask the reader now to consider two illustrations. The first is of a mother who says that she knows her son is alive even

[82] *The Problem of Knowledge* (1956), pp. 31 ff.
[83] *Ibid.*, p. 33.

though he has been classified as killed in action. "But *how* do you know?" asks a somewhat insensitive person with whom she has the misfortune to be acquainted. "I can't answer that," she replies. "I just know." In such a case there is no doubt that she believes her son to be alive; and so one of the necessary conditions of a claim to know is fulfilled—viz., (ii) above. Suppose it turns out that her son was incorrectly classified as killed and she is told that he is in fact a prisoner of war. "There you are," she says, "I knew it all along." This seems a natural enough use of the verb "to know," but I think it seems so only because a distinction, which it is perfectly legitimate to draw, namely that between true belief and knowledge, is so commonly blurred in ordinary discourse. Even in the latter, if someone says "She didn't really know. She only guessed right," that will not seem an odd, or in any way a puzzling, remark.

This brings us to the second illustration. An entertainer invites members of his audience to select cards from a pack unseen by him and each time tells them correctly which card they have taken. In such a case there are certain possibilities. (i) He may have planted an assistant who can observe the denominations of the cards and communicate these to him secretly. He could, then, answer the question "How do you know?" if he chose to do so. (ii) He may—a fantastic supposition no doubt, but conceivable—have formerly made some such arrangements but then, through the operation of unusual psychological factors, now no longer be aware of having made such arrangements or of their operation. If asked, "How do you know the cards?" he will reply, "I just do." (iii) We, observing his performance, may be aware that either one or other of the foregoing possibilities is realized and if asked, "How does he know?" be able to explain accordingly. (iv) We may be unaware of any explanation, and if asked, "How does he know?" be unable to say anything beyond, "He just does."

It is important to notice that "By intuition" purports to give an answer to "How do you know?" comparable to that which the entertainer might give if possibility (i) were realized, or to "How does he know?" comparable to that which we might give if possibility (iii) were realized. Intuition, it is claimed, *entitles* a speaker to say that he knows that X; or it *explains* how it comes about that he knows that X. But, when we examine the notion of intuition carefully, both these claims evaporate. If, to take them in reverse order, when we are asked, "How does this entertainer know which cards members of his audience have selected?" we reply to the effect that either of possibilities (i) or (ii) above is realized, what are we doing? We are setting this particular event—his getting the cards right—within a framework of covering laws physical, psychological, or both. We are not just saying that this event occurred, but tying it in with what we know about the way the world, as a whole, works. For this is what it means, in common speech, to explain such an event. But if we say that the entertainer knows *by intuition* which card is selected each time, what more have we said than that he knows which card is selected each time (period)? All that which we would be saying amounts to is that he is the sort of man who gets cards right. But we know that already. It is like saying that opium sends people to sleep because it has a *virtus dormitiva*.

Does "By intuition" fare any better as an answer to "How do *you* know?" That is, does it *entitle* a speaker to claim that he knows such-and-such to be the case? Does it give him, in another of Ayer's phrases, "the right to be sure"?[84] Let us look back to the mother in the first of our two illustrations. Suppose that she had answered the question "But how do you know?" with "By intuition." This reply would have been unsatisfactory for the following reasons.

Firstly, we can form no clear idea of what more she would have said by this than if she had said only that she firmly believed her son to be alive, or "knew" him to be alive in that sense of the verb "to know." The answer "By intuition" to the question "How do you know?" in such a case simply re-iterates what was given above as the second condition which must be fulfilled if one is to say "I know that X," namely, the speaker must believe that X. But the whole point of the

84 *Ibid.*

third condition—that the speaker must be able to give an appropriate answer to the question "How do you know that X?"—is to take us beyond the fulfillment of the second condition. What *more* than "I believe that X" does "I know by intuition that X" tell us? The answer seems to be that it tells us nothing more.

Secondly, we supposed in the above illustration that the mother's belief that her son was alive turned out to be true. But now conceive of the alternative, that it turned out to be false. How would the mother's intuition—her feeling of certainty, that is—have differed in the two cases? Can she herself tell us? Can we discover, apart from what she may say, any distinction in the intuition itself as between the two cases? There are numerous examples of people feeling absolutely sure of something and being right; and apparently equally numerous examples of them so feeling and being wrong. But, as far as any evidence that is available to us may go, there does not seem to be anything necessarily different about the intuition, i.e., the feeling of certainty, in the two kinds of examples.

Thirdly, if the mother's belief that her son was alive had turned out to be false, if evidence had come to light which convinced even her that he had died—as for instance the discovery of a body which she could not but identify as his —what would she have said? Surely not, "I knew before that he was alive, but now I know that he is dead." Rather she would have said, "I felt sure he was alive but now I know that he is dead." Only crazy people insist that their intuitions are correct if evidence against them comes to light which, along some accredited route, leads to what would be generally accepted as knowledge.

The *moral* intuitionist is really in an even more exposed position than these considerations about intuition in general place him. The entertainer mentioned above, if he had said that he knew by intuition which cards members of his audience had selected, would have been claiming to know by this route what could be shown by other accredited routes to be, or not to be, the case. That A has in his hand the six of diamonds is, or is not, a fact, and whether it is, or is not, can be ascertained by appeal to something other than the entertainer's intuition. But the ethical intuitionists do not claim that men know by intuition what can be shown in any other way to be, or not to be, the case. There is, in their opinion, no check beyond intuition on what ethically is, or is not, the case. That promise-breaking is wrong, for example, can be known, and only known, by intuition. Intuitionists say, in effect, that, when it comes to moral values, men are like an entertainer who does not give the names *of* the cards which his audience select but gives names *to* the cards; and he then claims that his names for them are the correct ones. If he says a card is the six of diamonds, it *is*, quite apart from any other considerations. To claim that any such process is an accredited route to the knowledge that something is the case is obviously fantastic.

The casualty here is not, of course, morality, but only a particular account of it. This discredited account starts from the assumption that, if we talk about right and wrong, good and evil, we must be referring to properties of actions or states of affairs which, nonnatural though they be, are objectively there. If such a starting point is accepted, it follows— since we do talk about right and wrong, good and evil—that there must be some way in which we know that they are there, some faculty which apprehends them. Thus moral intuition was conceived of. The difficulties which we have exposed in any claim to know by this faculty make it hardly surprising that Moore did not wish to be identified *tout court* with the intuitionists. But it is not just the conclusion—that we know moral truths (or, *pace* Moore, falsehoods) by intuition—which is at fault. The starting point—viz., that the meaning of language in general, and ethical language in particular, is that to which it refers—is mistaken. What is needed is a new point of departure. We have seen that there are other theories of meaning besides the referential theory. We shall see in subsequent chapters to what ethical theories these have given rise.

CHAPTER 4. THE EMOTIVIST THEORY

I. THE REJECTION OF NONNATURALISM

The intuitionists disposed of ethical naturalism. But they replaced it by a nonnaturalism which most modern philosophers have found equally repugnant. Two main lines of criticism[1] have been directed against their nonnaturalism. (i) It shrouds the matter in mystery. Moral terms are taken to refer to metaphysical entities, mysterious supersensible properties of actions or state of affairs apprehended by an equally mysterious supersensory faculty of intuition. (ii) It fails to explain one essential feature of moral language, namely its close connection with action, or what may be called its essentially dynamic character.

Wittgenstein and the Logical Positivists

The first line of criticism proceeds from certain assumptions about meaning and, carried through to its conclusion, seems to render moral discourse meaningless. The early Wittgenstein and the logical positivists were protagonists in this line of attack.

We saw in the second chapter that, according to Wittgenstein's picture theory, meaningful language, as such, mirrors what *is* the case. Its elements refer to the simples of reality. Ethical discourse, however, has to do with value rather than fact. If it were to refer to anything, it would have to refer to what *ought* to be the case and this is logically different from what *is* the case. As Wittgenstein wrote in the *Tractatus:* "If there is any value that does have value, it must lie outside

[1] Cf. J. O. Urmson, *The Emotive Theory of Ethics* (1968), Chap. 2.

the whole sphere of what happens and is the case."[2] In that sense, he held, "ethics is transcendental."[3] It follows—given the picture theory of meaning—that ethical statements must be meaningless. In concluding a public lecture on ethics, which he delivered in Cambridge at the end of the thirties, Wittgenstein considered the possibility that, since we are constantly tempted to speak in ethical terms, they cannot be dismissed as meaningless, and so his own perplexity about their meaning might be due to the fact that he had not yet discovered the correct logical analysis of that meaning. To this he replied:

> Now when this is urged against me, I at once see clearly, as it were in a flash of light, not only that no description that I can think of would do to describe what I mean by absolute value, but that I would reject every significant description that anybody could possibly suggest, *ab initio*, on the ground of its significance. That is to say: I see now that these nonsensical expressions [*sc.* moral judgments] were not nonsensical because I had not yet found the correct expressions, but that their nonsensicality was their very essence. For all I wanted to do with them was just *to go beyond* the world and that is to say beyond significant language. My whole tendency and I believe the tendency of all men who ever tried to write or talk Ethics . . . was to run against the boundaries of language. This running against the walls of our cage is perfectly, absolutely hopeless. Ethics so far as it springs from the desire to say something about the ultimate meaning of life, the absolute good, the absolute valuable, can be no science. What it says does not add to our knowledge in any sense. But it is a document of a tendency in the human mind which I personally cannot help respecting deeply and I would not for my life ridicule it.[4]

All this seems to point clearly to the conclusion that ethical statements are meaningless; but it is difficult, perhaps impossible, to be sure that Wittgenstein was, in fact, drawing

[2] *T* 6.41.
[3] *T* 6.421.
[4] "A Lecture on Ethics," *PR* LXXIV (1965), 11–12.

that conclusion. Rush Rhees interprets the remark quoted a moment ago—"if there is any value that does have value, it must lie outside the whole sphere of what happens and is the case"—to mean: "because of what judgments of good and evil *do* mean . . . it is pointless to look for their meaning in any events or facts that might be found by science."[5] On this interpretation, so far· from designating ethical judgments meaningless, Wittgenstein would have been simply clarifying their real meaning; that is, drawing a line between the logic of moral discourse and the logic of scientific. It is tempting so to interpret him, especially in the light of his later philosophy. But where the picture theory of the *Tractatus* is accepted, it seems impossible to avoid the conclusion that ethics is "transcendental" in the sense of meaningless.

The logical positivists were less problematic in their treatment of ethics. We considered their theory of meaning in Chapter 2. They had only to turn to the intuitionists for arguments which showed that moral judgments are neither analytic nor empirically verifiable. Moore's arguments against the naturalistic fallacy had established: (i) that there is no moral judgment which is true by definition; (ii) that there is nothing natural, i.e., empirically observable, to which moral terms such as "good" or "right" refer. On the logical positivists' presuppositions, it followed that moral judgments are literally meaningless. As Ayer expressed it:

> The fundamental ethical concepts are unanalysable, inasmuch as there is no criterion by which one can test the validity of the judgments in which they occur. . . . The reason why they are unanalysable is that they are mere pseudo-concepts. The presence of an ethical symbol in a proposition adds nothing to its factual content. Thus if I say to someone "You acted wrongly in stealing that money," I am not stating anything more than if I had simply said "You stole that money." In adding that the action is wrong, I am not making any further statement about it.[6]

[5] "Some Developments in Wittgenstein's View of Ethics," *ibid.*, p. 17; italics mine.

[6] Ayer, *Language, Truth and Logic* (2nd ed., 1946), p. 107.

A moral judgment because it has no literal meaning can be neither true nor false, valid nor invalid. It cannot, therefore, be argued about. Ayer, in drawing this conclusion, realized its paradoxical nature, for it is a fact of common experience that moral judgments are disputed. He claimed, however, that such disputes are not really ever about a question of value but always one of fact. In contesting a man's moral opinions, we call his attention to matters of fact which we think he must have overlooked; for instance, the motives, effects, or circumstances, of particular actions or classes of action, which he has judged to be right or wrong. Underlying our argument is the assumption that fundamentally our opponent has the same moral attitudes as ourselves. Since he usually lives in the same social order and will usually have received much the same moral education as we have, this assumption is, as a rule, justified. But if ever we find so great a radical disagreement between ourselves and an opponent that, although he agrees with every factual consideration which we can bring forward, he still does not share our moral assessment of the action or situation in question, then, says Ayer, "we abandon the attempt to convince him by argument."[7]

It is important to remember that the logical positivists directed their opinions against ethical subjectivists and objectivists alike. According to the former, moral judgments are equivalent in meaning to factual statements about the feelings of those who utter them, e.g., "This is good" means "I (We) have a feeling of liking or approval for this." According to objectivists, moral judgments state facts of a *sui generis*, nonnatural kind. Both subjectivists and objectivists believe that moral judgments have what Ayer called "literal meaning," and it was this which the logical positivists were concerned to deny. They did not say that moral judgments are nonsensical in the way that the gibbering of a madman or the rhymes of a nonsense poet are. Some said that moral judgments should be understood as imperatives of a sort; others, as ejaculations of a kind; yet others, as a combination of the two. "Go!" is not meaningless; neither is "Ugh!" It seemed, however, to

[7] *Ibid.,* p. 111.

the logical positivists, important to point out that it would be nonsensical to reply to either of those remarks with talk of truth or falsity. The collocutions:

"Go!"

"Is that true?"

and

"Ugh!"

"You lie."

make no sense. And it seemed equally clear to them that, in the last analysis, any claim that a moral judgment is the valid, or invalid, conclusion of an argument can be shown to have begged the question. Whatever factual considerations are adduced in its support, talk of the wrongness of stealing, for instance, is grounded ultimately in assumption, not proof. It is based on commitment to some principle, or principles, from which it follows. For instance, if we say that stealing is wrong because it undermines peace and order in the society and therefore diminishes human happiness, the wrongness of what diminishes human happiness is, so to say, brought to this argument, not derived from it. We shall have to consider eventually whether the fact that it boils down in the last analysis to assumptions of that kind makes moral thinking different in principle from thinking of other kinds, such as mathematical, scientific, historical, etc.[8] But enough has been said to serve our present purpose of showing how nonnaturalism was rejected along the first of the two lines of criticism mentioned above—i.e., the criticism that it took moral terms to refer to metaphysical entities.

The Dynamic Character of Moral Discourse

The second line of criticism—that nonnaturalism fails to account for the essentially dynamic character of moral judgments—opened up the way for a discussion of the kind of meaning which moral judgments really do have.

Two points seem clear. (i) When a *fact* has been stated, it is logically possible to say that any attitude whatever has been adopted toward it, or any action taken with regard to it. Of

[8] See below, e.g., pp. 192–93.

course we may think the attitude or action concerned foolish or irrational but that is beside the point. Given that X is the case, we can (logically though not, as a rule, empirically) adopt any attitude whatever or take any course of action we choose with regard to X. (ii) When a *moral* judgment has been delivered, it would be, to use Professor P. H. Nowell-Smith's expression, "logically odd" in ordinary speech to add certain remarks.[9] For example, if I say that X is wrong, it would be, not a formal contradiction, but nevertheless odd for me to add, "Now shall I do X?" Again, if I said that state of affairs Y is good, it would, similarly, be odd if I added, "Shall I seek to bring it about?" The same sort of oddness would attach to any recommendation that others should perform X or not pursue Y. True, a *ceteris paribus* clause needs adding in each case, for we can conceive of circumstances in which it might not be logically odd to say these things. We do, in practice, sometimes ask ourselves whether or not we should do what we think wrong, or try to bring about what we think morally good; and sometimes we urge others to do what we think wrong or to spurn what we would say is good. But these considerations do not dispose of the point that *in* judging X to be wrong or Y to be good one commits oneself to certain attitudes or courses of action with regard to them. I must make it clear that it is not the *moral* principles, that one ought to be sincere or practice what one preaches, which I am invoking here. It is a logical point about moral language to which I am referring. The connection between "X is wrong" and "Shall I do X?" or between "Y is good" and "Shall I seek to obtain it?" is *not*, as I have already recognized, that the latter, in each case, formally contradicts the former. Nevertheless, there *is* a logical connection between them in the sense that, in each case, if the latter is said, once the former has been said, it is as though one were reopening a subject which has been closed, or asking a question which has just been answered. This is one thing at least which is meant by the dynamic character of moral judgments: they commit those who utter them to certain attitudes or courses of action.

[9] Cf. P. H. Nowell-Smith, *Ethics* (1954), pp. 83–84.

What is the relevance of all this to the rejection of non-naturalism? From the two points indicated in the last paragraph it follows that an utterance cannot be both (i) factual and (ii) dynamic. Moral judgments, for the reasons given in the last paragraph, are clearly dynamic. It was the mistake of the nonnaturalists to think that they can also be statements of (nonnatural) fact.

If nonnaturalism is thus disposed of, the question which remains to be answered is: what is the correct logical analysis of this essentially *dynamic* character of moral discourse? To that question emotivists, and Stevenson in particular, addressed themselves.

II. STEVENSON'S ACCOUNT OF EMOTIVISM

Origins of Emotivism

The theory known as emotivism, according to J. O. Urmson's recent study *The Emotive Theory of Ethics* (London, 1968), was adumbrated by a number of English-speaking philosophers[10] who were interested only incidentally in ethics, before it found definitive expression in the work of C. L. Stevenson. The first to propose it appear to have been I. A. Richards and C. K. Ogden in their *The Meaning of Meaning* (London, 1923). They wrote:

> "Good" is alleged to stand for a unique, unanalyzable concept . . . [which] is the subject matter of ethics. This peculiar ethical use of "good" is, we suggest, a purely emotive use. When so used the word stands for nothing whatever. . . . Thus, when we so use it in the sentence, *"This is good,"* we merely refer to *this,* and the addition of "is good" makes no difference whatever to our reference . . . it serves only as an emotive sign expressing our attitude to *this,* and perhaps evoking similar attitudes in other persons, or inciting them to actions of one kind or another.[11]

[10] A form of it had been developed by the Swedish philosopher A. Hagerstrom (1868–1939), but his work does not appear to have been known to those named here.

[11] I. A. Richards and C. K. Ogden, *The Meaning of Meaning* (2nd ed., 1946), p. 125.

Urmson also refers to the following early forms of emotivism. In a short paper in *Analysis,* 1934, W. H. F. Barnes suggested that "value judgments in their origin are not strictly judgments at all. They are exclamations expressive of approval." C. D. Broad, in a contribution to the *Proceedings of the Aristotelian Society,* 1934, entitled "Is 'Goodness' the Name of a Simple Non-natural Property?" attributed to A. S. Duncan-Jones an emotivist theory of ethics. Others, e.g., Susan Stebbing and Karl Britton, were thinking at the time along similar lines.[12] As we have seen, A. J. Ayer in *Language, Truth and Logic* (1934) rejected the literal meaning of ethical judgments. He went on to offer suggestions as to the meaning which they do have and these are still considered by many the best brief statement of the case for emotivism. That theory came to complete expression in the writings of C. L. Stevenson, particularly in his two articles "The Emotive Meaning of Ethical Terms" (*Mind,* XLVI, 1937) and "Persuasive Definitions" (*Mind,* XLVII, 1938) and in his book *Ethics and Language* (New Haven and London, 1944). To Stevenson's views we now turn.

Stevenson's Three Features of Moral Discourse

Stevenson's starting point was what he called "observations of ethical discussions in daily life."[13] What do people actually do with moral language? This was the question which opened up the way for all the important developments in recent moral philosophy. Stevenson must be given full credit for having made it his point of departure. He maintained that any account of the meaning of ethical terms, which accords with typical usage, must allow for the following three features of moral discourse:[14]

(i) *The fact that genuine agreements and disagreements occur within it.*

[12] See S. Stebbing, *A Modern Introduction to Logic* (7th ed., 1965), pp. 16–19; K. Britton, *Communication* (1939), pp. 8–10 and Chap. IX.
[13] *EL,* p. 13.
[14] "The Emotive Meaning of Ethical Terms," *M* XLVI (1937), reprinted in C. L. Stevenson, *Facts and Values* (New Haven, 1963), p. 15.

(ii) *The fact that moral terms have, so to speak, a "magnetism."*

What he had in mind here was the dynamic character of moral language which we have already noted. He explained his term "magnetism" thus: "A person who recognizes X to be 'good' must ipso facto acquire a stronger tendency to act in its favour than he otherwise would have had."[15]

(iii) *The fact that the scientific, or empirical, method of verification is not sufficient for ethics.*

In explanation of this feature, he recalled Moore's objection to naturalistic definitions of "good," and in effect rejected the ethical naturalist's reply that "good" refers to "a confused huddle" of objects.[16] Stevenson said:

> G. E. Moore's familiar objection about the open question is chiefly pertinent in this regard. No matter what set of scientifically knowable properties a thing may have (says Moore in effect), you will find, on careful inspection, that it is an open question to ask whether anything having these properties is *good*. It is difficult to believe that this recurrent question is a totally confused one, or that it seems open only because of the ambiguity of "good." Rather we must be using some sense of "good" which is not definable, relevantly, in terms of anything scientifically knowable. That is, the scientific method is not sufficient for ethics.[17]

Stevenson's moral philosophy was an attempt to provide a clarification of the meaning of ethical terms which would allow full recognition of each of these three features. I will arrange my exposition of his ethical theory in three subsections, corresponding to these three features, though, of necessity, there will be some overlap between one subsection and another.

---

[15] *Ibid.*, p. 13.
[16] See above, p. 85.
[17] Stevenson, *op. cit.*, p. 15. On the word "relevantly" cf. Stevenson's comment: ."A defined meaning will be called 'relevant' to the original meaning under these circumstances: Those who have understood the definition must be able to say all that they then want to say by using the term in the defined way. They must never have occasion to use the term in the old, unclear sense" (*ibid.*, p. 11).

Disagreement in Attitude and Belief

The first feature of moral discourse which Stevenson wished to explain was the possibility of genuine agreement and disagreement within it. In order to do so he drew a distinction between *beliefs* and *attitudes*.

We took note above[18] of Ayer's view that men never really dispute about value but only about fact; that, if we cannot show our opponent in a moral argument that he is mistaken on some matter of fact, we abandon our attempt to convince him. Though he does not dissent fundamentally from Ayer's view, it seemed to Stevenson that the matter is somewhat more complicated than Ayer's bald statement makes it appear. There are, said Stevenson, *two* sorts of agreement or disagreement in moral argument. The one is in belief; the other, in attitude. Only by differentiating them and recognizing the presence of both can "a full picture" of "the varied functions" of ethical language, which is "in touch with practice," be drawn.[19]

The difference is obvious enough. For instance, in his highly controversial encyclical *Humanae Vitae* (1968), Pope Paul gave, as one reason for his refusal to declare the use of contraceptives licit, the fact that, were he to do so, governments might apply "to the solution of the problems of the community those means acknowledged to be licit for married couples in the solution of a family problem." Presumably, this means compulsory sterilization. He takes it for granted that, if this consequence occurred, it would constitute a "lowering of morality." We can disagree with the Pope here on either, or both, of two counts: (i) His *belief* that his declaring licit the use of contraceptives might have had such a consequence may not be one which we share. (ii) His *attitude* of total disapproval toward compulsory sterilization may not be one with which we sympathize. Stevenson argued that, whenever a moral judgment is voiced, it is possible to draw this kind of distinction: between (i) what is said, or assumed, to be the factual state of affairs under judgment, and (ii) the

18 P. 110.
19 *EL*, pp. 11–13.

positive or negative evaluation which is placed upon that state of affairs.

Concerning agreement and disagreement in attitude, it is important to emphasize that Stevenson took moral judgments to *express*—not to *report*—attitudes. He compared two simple "working models" of the analysis of "This is good," insisting that the former, not the latter, corresponded to his own theory. They were: (i) "I approve of this; do so as well" and (ii) "I approve of this and I want you to do so as well" (where the last clause is taken to have simply descriptive, not any imperative, force). If moral disagreements are to be genuine, the former analysis is required for the following reason. When A says "This is good" and B says "It is not" then, on the first analysis, there *is* a disagreement between them: one is saying "Approve of this!" the other is saying "Don't!" By contrast, on the second analysis, there is *no* neccessary disagreement between them: one is saying "I want you to approve of this" and the other, "I don't," and each of them could acknowledge both these statements to be true without self-contradiction.[20]

It is of course customary for persons who share the same beliefs to share the same attitudes, or vice versa, and a great deal of moral argument is concerned to secure agreement in belief concerning the facts of the case. Opponents of the Pope, to revert to our example, have spent a lot of time arguing that he is mistaken about the probable effect of his making contraceptives licit. Even though it is undeniable that two disputants may be at one in their beliefs concerning the object of moral judgment, while remaining divided in their attitudes to it, we can never be quite certain that further discussion would not reveal that there are relevant factual beliefs which one of them holds while the other does not. For example, those who do not sympathize with the Pope's abhorrence of compulsory sterilization, while agreeing with him that it would have been a probable effect of permitting contraception, might well be found, if a more exhaustive investigation were conducted, to differ significantly from the

[20] *EL*, Chap. II.

Pope in their beliefs concerning what is involved in, or consequent upon, compulsory sterilization. Stevenson nowhere denied that, *in practice,* certain beliefs and attitudes do go so closely together that frequently, perhaps invariably, if you bring anyone to accept the beliefs, you bring him to adopt the attitudes, and vice versa. But, nevertheless, he insisted that the connection between agreement or disagreement in belief and in attitude "is always factual never logical." It is always logically possible that the beliefs concerned should be adopted and the attitudes rejected or vice versa. In moral judgment, every attitude is, no doubt, accompanied by some belief about its object, but the beliefs which attend opposed attitudes, or the attitudes which attend opposed beliefs, need not be incompatible. "Since it may . . . happen that both sorts of disagreement occur conjointly, or that neither should occur, the logical possibilities are all open."[21]

This logical distinction between disagreement in belief and in attitude, if it really exists, implies that, wherever a moral disagreement occurs, the disagreement in belief (if any) can (logically) always be stated without any reference to attitudes. But is this so? Take, for example, the Pope's words in the encyclical to which we have already referred: "It is also to be feared that the man, growing used to the employment of anti-conceptive practices, may finally lose respect for the woman and, no longer caring for her physical and psychological equilibrium, may come to the point of considering her as a mere instrument of selfish enjoyment and no longer his respected and beloved companion." This purports to be simply a statement of belief about one probable consequence of permitting the use of contraceptives; but such expressions as "respect," "equilibrium," "mere instrument," "selfish enjoyment," are clearly attitude-impregnated. However, on Stevenson's view, it should be possible to rewrite the above passage in attitude-free terms, thereby stating the precise factual belief which the Pope affirms and which those who disagree with him (i.e., those who differ from him at this point not only in attitude but also in belief) deny. Can that be done?

[21] *EL,* p. 6.

Let us try. "It is probable that the man will have sexual intercourse with the woman more frequently than she desires."
This, we may say, is the Pope's factual belief which those
who disagree with him deny. But it is important to remember
that there are two ways at least in which people may disagree
as to the facts: (i) they may make two factual statements,
the only difference between them being that one is the assertion of X and the other the denial of X; (ii) they may be
unable to accept any common statement of fact (X) which
one wishes to assert and the other to deny. Confronted by
our rewriting of the Pope's belief, his defenders, for example,
may well say, "You haven't adequately stated his belief" and
perhaps add, "If only you appreciated what he is saying, you
would be more ready to agree with him." So let us suppose
that we try again and rewrite the Pope's words thus: "It is
probable that the man will have sexual intercourse with the
woman more frequently than she desires and this will cause
her nervous distress and will make the man insensitive to her
feelings." Is that what the Pope means? "No," his defenders
may say again, "he means more than that." Now, how long
can this go on? We want to get at the Pope's precise factual
belief so that we can test it for truth or falsity; we want to
know whether or not, on the available evidence, there is a
significant degree of probability that permitting the use of
contraceptives will have the effects which he thinks likely. His
defenders may go on blocking all our attempts to state these
effects in attitude-free terms, declaring any statement which
we propose to be inadequate to state the full content of the
Pope's belief. The interesting question is: could they conceivably be right? Stevenson says very confidently that the
connection between belief and attitude is always factual, never
logical; but what if this is simply dogmatism on his part? Is
it conceivable that in order to agree with the Pope about the
facts of the case, you must agree to some degree with his
attitudes? Are there some statements of fact which cannot be
made in what Stevenson would have called attitude-free
terms? Here I simply point out that the question can be raised.

I shall return to it[22] when we consider the views of some, in recent moral philosophy, who think that there are such facts.

Leaving that for the time being, how did Stevenson conceive of the logical structure of the argument by which agreement is reached, and disagreement resolved, in ethics? It seemed to him beyond question that the "reasons" given for moral judgments do not support them in the way that scientific hypotheses or mathematical theorems are supported. He was left with the question whether or not there is, as he phrases it, "a *different sort* of proof": "whether there is some 'substitute for proof' in ethics, some support or reasoned argument which, although different from a proof in science, will be equally serviceable in removing the hesitations that usually prompt people to ask for a proof."[23] He thinks that there is and we shall go into his account of its methodology more fully below.[24] At the moment notice the main feature of this "support" or "reasoned argument" which Stevenson had in mind. He said that it "describes the situation" which the moral judgment concerned seeks to alter or preserve, or the new situation which it seeks to bring about, and if something in this description promises to satisfy "a preponderance of the hearer's desires," he will hesitate to agree no longer.[25] That is to say, in ethics, "a reasoned agreement . . . is theoretically possible only to the extent that agreement in belief will *cause* people to agree in attitude."[26] It will be seen at once that this is indeed "a substitute for proof." There is the world of difference between providing one's hearer with *reasons* for adopting an attitude (or for anything else) and saying things which will *cause* him to do so. This is the feature which characterizes, and vitiates, Stevenson's whole ethical theory.

[22] See the discussion of "institutional facts" below, pp. 282 ff. The expression "to lose respect," for example, as used by the Pope, may well be similar to the expression "to promise," discussed in Chapter VI. Both expressions state "institutional facts." If it follows that when anything is a promise it ought to be kept, it may follow that when anything is the losing of respect it ought not to be done.

[23] *EL,* p. 27.
[24] See below, pp. 126 ff.
[25] *EL,* p. 27.
[26] *EL,* p. 31; italics mine.

Subtle and, in many ways, illuminating as that theory is, in the last analysis it fails because it reduces logical to psychological considerations.

The Meaning of Moral Judgments

The second feature of moral discourse which seemed to Stevenson to be evident from its ordinary use was its dynamic character, or to use his word, the "magnetism," which it has. He said that a person who recognizes X to be good thereby acquires a stronger tendency to act in its favor than he would otherwise have. In saying that X is good, that is, I am not simply expressing a belief about it; what I am really doing is expressing, and seeking to evoke, an attitude toward it. The "major use" of moral judgments, Stevenson declared, "is not to indicate facts but to *create an influence*."[27] What, therefore, is in need of explanation is how such expression, or evocation, of an attitude can be part of the *meaning* of moral judgment. Stevenson deliberately turned for the answer from the notion of meaning as referent to that of the use which is made of language.[28] But he located this answer, not primarily in the rules or conventions in accordance with which language is used, but in the psychological processes of those who use it or on whom it is used. He attempted to show: (i) that this is a correct account of the genus, meaning; and (ii) that the meaning of moral discourse is a combination of two species of it, viz., *descriptive* and *emotive* meaning, the former corresponding to the expression of belief; the latter, of attitude. According to Stevenson, the relation between a sign and the psychological processes of those who use it, or hear it used, is causal. The meaning of the sign, however, is not some specific psychological process which serves as the cause, or effect, of its use at any one time, for such causes or effects may vary widely from person to person and time to time; and the meaning of signs must not vary unless there is to be wholesale confusion. The meaning of a sign, therefore, is "a dispositional property" of the sign to cause, or be caused by,

[27] *Facts and Values*, p. 16.
[28] *EL*, pp. 13 and 42.

certain psychological processes in hearers and speakers of it respectively.[29] This dispositional property can be called its "meaning" "only if it has been caused by, and would not have developed without, an elaborate process of conditioning which has attended the sign's use in communication."[30] Stevenson explains in detail what he means by an unchanging disposition and he is careful to recognize such points as that the statement "This sign has such-and-such a meaning" is elliptical for "This sign has such-and-such a meaning for people of such-and-such a kind."[31]

How does Stevenson apply this general psychological or causal theory of meaning to the particular case of moral discourse? In his "working model"[32] of an analysis of "This is good," namely "I approve of this; do so as well," belief and attitude, that is, descriptive and emotive meaning, are combined. But he hastened to point out that both are, to some extent, misrepresented, or at least oversimplified, in this analysis. "I approve of this" describes only the speaker's own attitude; but the descriptive meaning of moral terms may have far wider reference than that. When I say that something is good, I may be describing the motives from which it springs, the consequences which it has, the standards to which it conforms, etc. Again, ". . . do so as well" is a straightforward imperative, but emotive meaning is not simply imperative force. Stevenson said, "Emotive terms present the subject of which they are predicated in a bright or dim light, so to speak, and thereby *lead* people, rather than command them, to alter their attitudes."[33]

In accordance with his general "psychological" theory of meaning, Stevenson held that the *descriptive* meaning of a sign is its disposition to affect cognition. By cognition he meant such mental activities as believing, thinking, supposing, presuming, etc. And he tended to the behaviorist view that the

[29] *EL*, p. 54.
[30] *EL*, p. 57.
[31] *EL*, p. 56.
[32] See above, p. 117.
[33] *EL*, p. 33.

latter are dispositions to action.[84] The most interesting part of his discussion, however, for our purposes is concerned with the question: how does descriptive meaning become as precise as it does? The answer, he thought, lies in linguistic rules which relate signs to each other. For instance, a child may learn first that "100" means simply many; but this sign comes to have a more precise meaning as he learns, albeit by rote, that "100" means "10 times 10." Dictionary definitions, similarly, fix precisely the reference of descriptive signs.

This possibility of precise descriptive meaning, effected by linguistic rules, has two consequences which, we shall see, are important in Stevenson's emotivism. The linguistic rules referred to: (i) make possible a distinction between what a sign means and what it suggests;[35] and (ii) help us to measure change in a sign more exactly by providing precise criteria for the use of the sign at any given time.[36] The distinction between what a sign means and what it suggests applies, according to Stevenson, to descriptive, but not to emotive, meaning. The latter is simply a "flexible mechanism of *suggestion*."[37] Emotive words, like "Bah!" do not mean anything more than they suggest. Two of Stevenson's oft-quoted definitions of *emotive* meaning are as follows. "Emotive meaning is a meaning in which the response (from the hearer's point of view) or the stimulus (from the speaker's point of view) is a range of emotions."[38] "The emotive meaning of a word is the power that the word acquires on account of its history in emotional situations, to evoke or directly express attitudes, as distinct from describing or designating them."[39] Both these are in line with Stevenson's general causal theory of meaning. It will be noted that in the first he speaks of *emotions* and in the second of *attitudes*. He is well aware that these two expressions are not synonymous and warns against confusing them. "Emotion" or "feeling" he takes to designate "an affective

[84] *EL*, pp. 62–63; but cf. p. 66.
[35] On this see below, pp. 142–43.
[36] *EL*, pp. 68–71.
[37] *EL*, p. 33.
[38] *EL*, p. 59.
[39] *EL*, p. 33.

state that reveals its full nature to immediate introspection"; "attitude," "a complicated conjunction of dispositional properties . . . marked by stimuli and responses which relate to hindering or assisting whatever it is that is called the 'object' of the attitude."[40] Urmson[41] is right, however, to criticize Stevenson for not drawing the distinction between emotion and attitude more firmly than these definitions do. Stevenson recognized that it is a more complicated business to express, or evoke, an attitude than it is an emotion. But he did not bring out the "category differences" between emotion and attitude which are apparent in the ordinary usage of these terms. It makes sense to speak of deliberately choosing, or taking up, one's attitudes, or of being responsible for them, as it does not, of one's emotions; and again, of maintaining, being consistent in, being argued into or out of, attitudes, as it does not, emotions. Stevenson calls an attitude a "disposition" to act in certain ways and to experience certain feelings;[42] but even this is not altogether satisfactory for we do not normally speak of choosing, maintaining, being argued out of, dispositions. If Stevenson had been more sensitive to these logical differences between emotions and attitudes, he might not have been so ready to accept the conclusion that arguments for or against moral judgments, as attitude-directing, cannot be either valid or invalid.[43] Emotions, unlike attitudes, are often thought of as lying beyond reason; consider how naturally a man, if asked why he had certain feelings, would recount what had *caused* them, whereas if asked why he had certain attitudes, would give the *reasons* for them. It is easy to persuade oneself that no questions of validity arise in connection with moral judgments, if like Stevenson, one thinks of the "attitudes" which they express as like emotions or dispositions.

A moral judgment has *both descriptive and emotive* meaning, according to Stevenson. How does he relate them within it? Both kinds of meaning are said to grow up over a period

[40] *EL*, p. 60.
[41] Urmson, *op. cit.*, pp. 40–48.
[42] *EL*, p. 90.
[43] See below, pp. 145–47.

of time and may change. Frequently they grow up together, but it does not follow that they change together. It is this latter fact which Stevenson had in mind when he spoke of the "inertia" of meaning.[44] "Democracy" is used to illustrate what he meant. This word has a descriptive meaning: "government by the people, direct or representative." It also has an emotive meaning, i.e., the power to express, or evoke, an attitude. Its emotive meaning may change while its descriptive remains constant: for instance, in the eighteenth century "democracy" meant, as now, government by the people, but writers and preachers used it then with strong pejorative overtones. Now, by contrast, the emotive meaning of the word is universally laudatory, but its descriptive meaning is very different in Communist countries from what it is in the West.

Stevenson differentiated three possibilities so far as the dependence of emotive upon descriptive meaning is concerned. (i) Emotive meaning may be *dependent* on descriptive; that is to say, changes in the latter may be followed immediately, or very soon, by changes in the former. (ii) Emotive meaning may be *independent* of descriptive to varying degrees. Expressions such as "Hurrah!" or "Boo!" have an emotive meaning which is absolutely independent, cut off from all anchorage in descriptive meaning. Most emotive expressions, however, are such that a point may always come when a change in the descriptive meaning disturbs the inertia of the emotive. (iii) Emotive meaning may be *quasi-dependent* on descriptive. In this case it is contingent upon what Stevenson calls the "cognitive suggestiveness of a sign"[45] rather than on its precise descriptive meaning. For example, the emotive meaning of "pig" in "That man is a pig" is dependent, not on the precise definition of "pig" but upon what, when applied metaphorically to men, it suggests.[46] We shall return in a moment to this subject of the relationship between emotive and descriptive meaning when we consider persuasive definitions.

[44] *EL*, p. 72.
[45] *EL*, p. 78.
[46] *EL*, p. 75.

Stevenson's Patterns of Analysis and the Methodology of Moral Argument

We come now to the third feature of ordinary moral discourse which Stevenson noted: that the scientific method of verification is not sufficient for ethics. The key to this methodological difference between science and ethics lies in the fact that moral judgments have *both* emotive *and* descriptive meaning and not only the latter. Stevenson brought this out in both his *patterns of analysis* of a typical moral judgment. He said that two patterns of analysis, not just one, are necessary because only so could justice be done to the "flexibility" of moral discourse.[47] They were intended to be complementary to one another. He uses "good" to illustrate his analyses, but he said that they applied equally to other ethical terms, such as "right," "ought," and their opposites and cognates.

(i) The first pattern is based on his working model that "This is good" means "I approve of this; do so as well." "I approve of this" constitutes the descriptive meaning; and ". . . do so as well," the emotive. (We have already noted his caveat that this analysis oversimplifies both.)[48] Stevenson said that emotive meaning, because it does not mean more than it suggests,[49] cannot be defined but only "characterised."[50] An example of such characterization is the dictionary definition of "nigger": "negro—now usually contemptuous." This cannot be defined "Negro-bah!" because the "bah!" does not tell us how the precise force and quality of the contempt varies from one occasion of use to another.

(ii) Stevenson stated his second pattern of analysis thus: "'This is good' has the meaning of 'This has qualities or relations X, Y, Z . . . ,' except that 'good' has as well a laudatory emotive meaning which permits it to express the speaker's approval, and tends to evoke the approval of the hearer."[51] He pointed out, (a) that here again the emotive

[47] *EL*, p. 89.
[48] Above, p. 122.
[49] Cf. above, p. 123.
[50] *EL*, p. 82.
[51] *EL*, p. 207.

meaning has to be characterized rather than included in the definition, (b) that reference to the speaker's attitudes is not mentioned here, though it is suggested by the presence of emotive meaning, and (c) the variables "X, Y, Z . . ." must be replaced by ordinary words before the above schema serves as a definition of "good."

Not just any ordinary words, however, can be substituted for these latter variables. If that were so, Stevenson remarks, " 'good' would be a possible synonym for any term in the language which has both a laudatory and a descriptive meaning; and although 'good' is vague, it is not so vague as that."[52] The terms replacing these variables must lie within the "boundaries of common usage,"[53] though, of course, what constitutes common usage may vary. "Good" does not have any descriptive meaning unless there are accepted standards or criteria of goodness, but these differ from age to age, community to community, locale to locale, occasion to occasion. It does not follow that the emotive meaning of "good" is, to any degree, lost. But it does follow that, whereas, according to Stevenson's first pattern of analysis, attitudes are altered only by the expression of approval or disapproval directed to things or classes of things, according to his second pattern, there is an additional way in which they can be, and frequently are, altered, namely by "persuasive definition." It is one of the chief merits of Stevenson's work that he brought out so clearly the role which such definitions play in moral discourse.

He defined persuasive definition as follows: "In any 'persuasive definition' the term defined is a familiar one, whose meaning is both descriptive and strongly emotive. The purport of the definition is to alter the descriptive meaning of the term, usually by giving it greater precision within the boundaries of its customary vagueness; but the definition does *not* make any substantial change in the term's emotive meaning. And the definition is used, consciously or unconsciously, in an effort to secure, by this interplay between emotive and

[52] *Ibid.*
[53] *EL*, p. 208.

descriptive meaning, a redirection of people's attitudes."[54]
The illustration which he uses is two men, A and B, arguing
as to whether a mutual acquaintance, C, is "cultured" or
not. A points out C's limited education, inelegant manner of
expressing his thoughts, lack of subtlety in argument, and
claims that he is uncultured. B concedes that C has all these
defects, but insists that he is cultured, claiming that in the
true sense of the word a cultured man is one who has imaginative sensitivity and originality, and that C possesses these
qualities to a higher degree than many men who are better
educated, etc., than he is.[55] Here, as in many instances, the
persuasive definition which B offers of "culture" is doubly
persuasive: it seeks to take A's attitude of approval away from
one thing *and* to attach it to another, to take it away from
education, elegant forms of speech, subtlety of mind, and to
attach it to imaginative sensitivity and originality.

It will be seen that the effect of such persuasive definitions is
achieved by a combined use of descriptive and emotive meaning. In its emotive meaning the relevant word commends or
discommends, while in its descriptive, it indicates the object
upon which this praise or condemnation is bestowed. The
former gives persuasion force; the latter, direction.[56] The
emotive meaning must, in some degree, be both dependent
upon, and independent of, the descriptive; the former in the
sense that, when descriptive meaning changes, the emotive
changes direction accordingly; the latter in the sense that such
changes in descriptive meaning do not destroy the emotive
meaning's force. Persuasive definitions are possible only where
the emotive meaning of a word is strong and its descriptive
meaning, in a measure, vague. The former condition must be
fulfilled, if the persuasive definition is to result in any significant redirection of attitude; the latter must be fulfilled to allow
room for the maneuver of persuasive definition to take place
at all. "Culture" is one word which has the requisite strength
and vagueness. Stevenson claims that there are hundreds of

[54] *EL*, p. 210.
[55] *EL*, p. 211.
[56] *EL*, p. 227.

words like it in this respect. Where persuasive definition is taking place there is frequently talk of the "true" or "real" meaning of words. What is true democracy? What is the real meaning of culture? And so on. Stevenson rightly remarks that "true" and "real" themselves, in such contexts, have persuasive force.[57] People usually accept what they consider true, and rely upon what they think real, and so these words carry with them the persuasive force "to be accepted" or "to be relied upon." In philosophy itself persuasive definition is not at all uncommon. Philosophical illustrations of it which Stevenson gives are Socrates' definition of "justice," Spinoza's of "God," and the logical positivists' of "meaning."[58]

Such then, were Stevenson's two patterns of analysis, but what was the relationship between them? His central thesis, remember, was that the point of all moral judgments is to exert an influence, to direct attitudes. This may be done by *predication*, as in the first pattern, or by *definition*, as in the second, either by predicating "good" of X or defining "good" as X. If we take the second course, however, we thereby implicitly predicate "good" of X, for as Stevenson remarks, words like "culture" are "prizes which each man seeks to bestow on the qualities of his choice."[59] The two patterns are alternatives, but it seems that, to Stevenson's mind, the first is logically prior to the second.

What difference did Stevenson see between the analysis of "good" ("right," "ought," etc.) in a *moral*, and in a *nonmoral*, sense? He said that "morally good" refers not to *any* kind of favor that the speaker has, but only to the kind that is "marked by a special seriousness or urgency."[60] This seems quite inadequate to mark the difference. Stevenson was presumably thinking of feelings of guilt and responsibility which burden those of sensitive conscience, but these can hardly serve as a sufficient criterion of morality. They often attach to objects which are not really matters of moral obligation:

[57] *EL*, pp. 213–14.
[58] *EL*, pp. 224–26; cf. "Persuasive definitions," *M* XLVII (1938), reprinted in *Facts and Values*, pp. 41–48.
[59] *Facts and Values*, p. 35.
[60] *EL*, p. 90.

for instance, to avoiding the cracks in the pavement or going back again and again to make sure that one has locked the door. Not only other people, but even the victims of such obsessions themselves, while still feeling guilt and responsibility in connection with them, can say with good sense that they are not really part of morality.[61]

Stevenson said that there are two main ways of resolving moral disagreement, the logical and the psychological. Within the latter he drew a distinction between rational and non-rational methods.[62]

The *logical* way calls in question the consistency either of the predication (first pattern) or of the use of the definition (second pattern) of "good." Suppose I say "X is good" and when asked why, reply, "Because X is P." If then, although Y is also P, I deny that Y is good, I am guilty of inconsistency. A great deal of moral argument, though not the whole of it by any means, is, Stevenson said, concerned with pointing out this sort of inconsistency.

The *rational psychological* way calls in question (a) the *comprehensiveness* of the reasons which are given for the predication, or definition, of "good" or (b) the *truth* of the beliefs which these reasons express; or both. Suppose I say that X is good because it is P. Is there something else—call it Q, etc.—about X, other than the fact that it is P, which, if I took a more *comprehensive* view, would lead me to say that X is not good? Again: is it *true* that X is P (and, if applicable, Q, etc.)? In predicating "good" of X, or defining "good" as X, one may not have taken into account, or be mistaken about, such matters as the nature and consequences of X, the motive from which X is done, the origin of one's attitude to X, how X stands in the judgment of some authority, etc. When it is pointed out that one has not taken account of, or been mistaken about, such matters, one can, and should, revise one's judgment that X is good.

All these are matters of *belief*. But, as Stevenson notes, the assumption throughout is certain logically fundamental

[61] Cf. G. J. Warnock, *Contemporary Moral Philosophy* (1967), p. 53.
[62] *EL*, pp. 111–15, 231–37.

attitudes to which appeal is being made. They are attitudes of approval or disapproval toward P (and if applicable, Q, etc.). It is only where these are presupposed that whether or not X is P (or, if applicable, Q, etc.) becomes relevant to whether or not X is good. If, and only if, there is this presumption of attitude do the beliefs that X is, or is not, P (or Q, etc.) become reasons for or against X's goodness.

The *nonrational psychological* way of supporting predications or definitions of "good" relies upon the emotive force of language entirely. An example, according to the first pattern, which Stevenson gives is:[63]

A: He has no right to act without consulting us.
B: After all, he is the chairman.
A: Yes, but not the dictator.

Here the emotive force of "dictator" is brought to bear upon B in order to change his attitude toward the chairman. In the case of the second pattern, persuasive definitions are in themselves examples of the same technique, viz. cashing in on the emotive force of the language used. It should be noted, however, that they can be supported by reasons, i.e., by statements of belief about matters of fact.[64] In seeking to persuade you that X is good by presenting it to you as really Y, where Y is something of which you approve, I make a statement about X which is either true or false and can be tested in whatever is the appropriate way.

Disagreements in ethics are resolved by all these methods, not only as between individuals, but in the case of any given individual himself when he has to make up his mind on a moral issue. He may put to himself, so to speak, considerations similar to any of those which we have just considered, calling in question his own consistency or the comprehensiveness and truth of the reasons which he would give for his judgment. And he may present the situation to himself in highly emotional language. Rationalization, as psychologists call it, is a species of persuasive definition.

[63] *EL*, p. 141.
[64] *EL*, p. 235.

III. CRITICISM OF EMOTIVISM

The emergence of emotivism was one of the most important developments in ethical theory of modern times. It provided a point of new departure. Its exponents led moral philosophy out of the blind alley of nonnaturalism and directed it along new lines of inquiry into the dynamic character of moral discourse. Stevenson asked the right question: to what use is moral language put? If he made mistakes in answering it, they were fruitful ones, the sort from which other philosophers have learned. The significant developments in ethical theory which have occurred since, such as prescriptivism and neo-naturalism, can only be understood, explained, and evaluated against the back cloth of emotivism.

In the remainder of this chapter I shall attempt a critical assessment of emotivism. I shall dispose first of one very superficial and mistaken criticism. Next I shall correct a couple of confusions about the emotivism of Stevenson and others. Then I shall consider whether or not Stevenson was self-consistent. Turning from defense to attack, I shall finally marshal what appear to me to be some major objections, first to Stevenson's theory of meaning in general, and then to his account of moral discourse in particular.

Moral Effects of Emotivism

Emotivists have been charged with undermining morality. Their theory, it has been said, produces within those who accept it a loss of interest in, or of seriousness about, moral issues. Some would have us think that if the meaning of moral judgments is basically emotive, then, it follows, and is taken by emotivists to follow, that in the realm of morals, anything goes. As one critic wrote with emotivism in mind:

> If we accept in bitter earnest the theory that all differences of opinion about what is morally good and morally evil are merely differences of personal taste, we shall find ourselves driven to the unhappy conclusion that it is impossible to justify on rational grounds the conviction that any particular form of conduct is really any better than

any other, however apparently barbarous that other may be. Further we shall be unable to offer any rational defence for our own national or international policies, when they conflict with the purely aggressive policies of leaders like Hitler or Stalin. In the final resort this would seem to imply that conflicting policies that arise from differences of opinion can only be settled by an appeal to force. . . . In short, we seem to be driven to accept the motto of all dictators, "Might is Right." There are very few who will be prepared to accept such a conclusion with an easy mind.[65]

Indeed there are. But are we really driven to accept that conclusion, if we accept emotivism?

A distinction must be drawn between the questions: (a) have some people, as a matter of fact, been driven to it? and (b) does anyone, as a matter of logic, need to be driven to it? The answer to the former is perhaps yes. I have had pupils who claimed that the study of emotivism had robbed them of their assurance about what is right or wrong, good or evil. Sometimes they have offered this claim as the explanation of their own conduct where most people would have said that the latter was irresponsible or immoral, and one has had the choice of accepting their claim as either the true explanation or a mere rationalization. All I am saying is that it could conceivably have been the former. If you have been taught a certain code of conduct by instructors who claimed that it embodied the law of nature, or if you have been conditioned in arguments about morals to appeal to conscience, conceived as a faculty which intuits objective moral truths—and such is the context within which many people have their first thoughts about morals—then it is understandable if emotivism appears to you to knock the bottom out of morality. From which it may well follow, not that emotivism is morally objectionable, but that objectivist theories of morality are.

The answer to the second of our two questions—Does anyone as a matter of logic have to accept such conclusions as "might is right," if he accepts emotivism?—is emphatically no.

[65] R. Corkey, *A Philosophy of Christian Morals for Today* (1961), pp. 22–23.

Rejecting any such implication, Ayer remarked, "In fact the [emotivist] theory only explores the consequences of a sound and respectable point of logic which was already made by Hume; that normative statements are not derivable from descriptive statements, or, as Hume puts it, that 'ought' does not follow from 'is.' To say that moral judgments are not fact-stating is not to say that they are unimportant, or even that there cannot be arguments in their favour. But these arguments do not work in the way that logical or scientific arguments do."[66] It may be debatable, as we shall see below in Chapter 6, whether Hume's point of logic is as sound and respectable as all that, but, whether it is or not, there is certainly no inconsistency in denying the foundations of morality which objectivists persuade themselves that they have discovered and at the same time holding, with reasoned conviction, some moral views rather than others. Theories such as emotivism are metaethics, not ethics.[67] The very existence of emotivism as a theory of morality entails the existence of morality. It is as absurd to say that emotivism destroys morality as it would be to say that some cartographer had drawn a map of a country which showed that the country was not really there.

As a matter of fact some of the foremost exponents of various forms of emotivism have shown themselves almost fanatical in their seriousness about moral issues. Witness Ayer marching down the Strand in a procession to protest against apartheid, or Bertrand Russell depositing his aged bones on the London pavement in protest against the manufacture of nuclear armaments.[68]

Two Confusions

Emotivists have been accused of *subjectivism* and *relativism,* but, as emotivists, they are not necessarily guilty of either.

I am using the expression *subjectivist* to mean a philosopher

[66] A. J. Ayer, *Logical Positivism* (Glencoe, Ill., 1959), p. 22.
[67] Cf. A. J. Ayer, "On the Analysis of Moral Judgments," *Horizon* XX. 117 (1949), reprinted in *Philosophical Essays* (1963), pp. 245–57.
[68] On Russell's views about ethics see his *Human Society in Ethics and Politics* (1954).

who thinks that ethical terms convey psychological information about the speaker and nothing more. In brief, that "X is
good" means "I (We) like X." I touched on this above in my
subsection on *Disagreement in Attitude and Belief*. From the
very beginning, Stevenson was at pains to dissociate himself
from any such view. He began his earliest published paper
on emotivism by emphasizing the difference between it and
what he called "interest" theories; and he gave, as one example of the latter, Hobbes's view that "good" means "desired by me."[69] Though, on his first pattern of analysis, "I
approve of X" is included in the meaning of "X is good"; and,
on his second, may replace one of the variables, "X, Y,
Z . . . ," it must be remembered that this descriptive meaning
was, in both cases, *only part* of the meaning of "X is good."
The "major use" of moral judgments, he said, is "not to indicate facts but to create an influence. . . . They *recommend*
an interest in an object, rather than state that the interest
already exists. . . . The difference between the traditional interest theories and my view is like the difference between
describing a desert and irrigating it."[70]

Other emotivists have been more explicit even than Stevenson in dissociating their theory from all forms of subjectivism.
Ayer, for example, says that although his theory is subjectivist in the sense that it denies objective validity to moral judgments, it differs in an important way from the orthodox
subjectivist theory. "We reject the subjectivist view that to
call an action right, or a thing good, is to say that it is generally approved of, because it is not self-contradictory to assert
that some actions which are generally approved of are not
right, or that some things which are generally approved of are
not good. And we reject the alternative subjectivist view that
a man who asserts that a certain action is right, or that a
certain thing is good, is saying that he himself approves of
it, on the ground that a man who confessed that he sometimes
approved of what was bad or wrong would not be contradicting himself."[71] This is, in effect, Moore's argument against

[69] *Facts and Values*, p. 11.
[70] *Ibid.*, pp. 15–16.
[71] *Language, Truth and Logic*, p. 104.

"the naturalistic fallacy" applied explicitly to subjectivism. In a later paper, entitled "On the Analysis of Moral Judgments," Ayer seems to dislike the expression "subjectivist" even when it is used to mark the difference between his own theory and any theory which takes moral language to describe objective properties of actions or of states of affairs. Insisting that moral judgments are not in any sense at all concerned with the applicability of a description, he writes:

> The familiar subjective-objective antithesis is out of place in moral philosophy. The problem is not that the subjectivist denies that certain wild, or domesticated animals, "objective values," exist and the objectivist triumphantly produces them; or that the objectivist returns like an explorer with tales from the kingdom of values and the subjectivist says he is a liar. It does not matter what the explorer finds or does not find. For talking about values is not a matter of describing what may or may not be there, the problem being whether it really is there. There is no such problem. The moral problem is: What am I to do? What attitude am I to take? And moral judgments are directives in this sense.[72]

A *relativist* in ethics is, to take the view in its most extreme form, someone who thinks that whatever anyone approves of is good. Stevenson's first pattern of analysis, if not his second, might appear to reduce moral judgment to that absurdity, but Stevenson firmly and effectively rebutted the charge that it does so.[73] For any X and any speaker, "I approve of X" is, according to the first pattern, equivalent in descriptive meaning to "X is good"; but again remember that this is *only part* of the latter's meaning. If I say "Whatever anyone approves of is good," I am saying, according to the first pattern of analysis, "I approve of whatever anyone approves of; do so as well"; and according to the second pattern, I am supplying "whatever anyone approves of" as one possible value for the variables "X, Y, Z . . ." According to both, I am commending something, namely whatever anyone approves of.

[72] "On the Analysis of Moral Judgments," p. 242.
[73] *EL*, pp. 102–8.

That is, then, my moral position. Whatever anyone approves of has my moral approval. This is a logically possible moral position, though it is doubtful whether anyone really holds it. However, the important point is that there is *no* reason at all to suppose that everyone, or anyone, who accepts Stevenson's emotivism is under a logical necessity to hold it.

Is Stevenson Self-Consistent?

Stevenson's exposition of both his patterns of analysis has been criticized as internally inconsistent. Was he guilty of this fault? Let us look at two points where, it is alleged, he was.

(i) Urmson has pointed out[74] that Stevenson speaks of "I approve of this . . ." throughout the first pattern of analysis as the *purely* descriptive meaning of "This is good." That is to say, it has to do only with belief, not at all with attitude. But, in the course of his account of the first pattern of analysis, Stevenson gives this example. A says, "This is good" and B replies, "I fully agree. It is indeed good." Stevenson analyzes A's remark as "I approve of this; do so as well" and B's as "I fully concur in approving of it; [continue] to do so as well." Then he comments, ". . . the *declarative* parts of these remarks, testifying to convergent *attitudes,* are sufficient to imply the agreement [in attitude]."[75] But this takes "I approve of this . . ." and "I fully concur in approving of it . . ." to be *not* purely descriptive, i.e., not attitude-free. Here, then, Stevenson seems to be plainly inconsistent.

(ii) Again, Urmson has pointed out,[76] with respect to Stevenson's second pattern of analysis, that at one point he put some limitation on what may be substituted for "X, Y, Z. . . ." He remarked that although "good" is vague, it is not so vague that any words whatever can be substituted for these variables.[77] But then he went on, according to Urmson, to introduce, not just vagueness, but a "double dose of ambiguity" into his account of "good." He gave, that is to say, no indication why what "good" means should not vary limitlessly

[74] Urmson, *op. cit.,* p. 54.
[75] *EL,* p. 22; italics mine.
[76] Urmson, *op. cit.,* pp. 78–79.
[77] Cf. above, p. 127.

(a) when used of different things in one person's vocabulary
and (b) when used of the same thing by persons differing in
attitude. Therefore, Stevenson seems to argue for an application of "good" which is both limited and limitless. Once more,
then, he is apparently inconsistent.

Urmson said that Stevenson was confused in these ways
because he failed to recognize certain features of the language which he was using.

In the case of the first inconsistency, (i) above, Stevenson
was, in effect, recognizing the illocutionary force of "I approve of this." This utterance does not—or does not simply—
report a fact, as "I have a feeling of liking for this" would
normally do. It also registers a pro-attitude toward the object of the approval. In saying "I approve of this" I am commending this. The utterance has, in Stevenson's terminology,
emotive meaning. That is the feature of it which Stevenson
was recognizing when he spoke of "the *declarative* parts of
these remarks, testifying to convergent *attitudes*. . . ." But
the rest of his exposition of the first pattern of analysis allows no room for an emotive meaning of "I approve of
this," and so Stevenson's present point is inconsistent with it.

It is perhaps of some interest to digress for a moment at
this point and to notice that Moore raised the question why
Stevenson required "I approve of this" in his analysis of "This
is good" at all. Why should Stevenson not simply have said
that "This is good" means "Do approve of this!"—an emotive
utterance with no cognitive, or declarative, meaning whatever? On such an analysis, when you said "This is good," you
would not be asserting anything which could be true or false
except perhaps that this exists; though, Moore said, you would
be "implying" that you approve of this. You would be doing
the latter in a sense which Moore stated thus: "The fact
that you *imply* that you approve of or have some such attitude
to this . . . simply arises from the fact, which we have all
learnt by experience, that a man who makes this kind of
assertion does in the vast majority of cases approve of" this.[78]

[78] See "A reply to my critics" in *The Philosophy of G. E. Moore*,
edited by L. A. Schilpp (Evanston, 1942), p. 543. Moore was, in fact,
discussing "right" rather than "good," but his points can apply to both.

It is perhaps the more surprising that Stevenson did not in fact adopt some such first pattern of analysis as Moore suggested, when we bear in mind, (a) that Stevenson did have a second pattern which provided for the descriptive meaning of "good," and (b) that he evidently thought of the first pattern as logically prior to the second. The answer may well be that he considered it plausible to include "I approve of this . . ." in his first pattern because, as we have seen, he thought, however inconsistently, of this "declarative part" of the analysis as "testifying to . . . attitudes"—i.e., he realized subconsciously the attitude-expressing illocutionary force of the performative "I approve of this."

The second example of inconsistency, (ii) above, is attributed by Urmson to Stevenson's failure to differentiate clearly between the *meaning* of "good" and the *criteria* for its application. Stevenson, Urmson holds, failed to see that, though the criteria for the use of "good" may vary endlessly, it does not follow that the meaning of "good" does so. I am not convinced that he did fail to see this or that he really tried to have an application of "good" which was both limited and limitless. It was surely his whole point that the emotive meaning of "good" has a more or less constant characterization, although its application will vary according to what objects its users happen to approve of. Is not this the distinction between the meaning of "good" and the criteria for its application? Again, what he said about limitations on the possible criteria for the use of "good" is not really self-contradictory. He recognized (a) that all communities and all individuals who engage in talk of what is good will have certain, to some degree, settled criteria, but also (b) that these criteria may differ very widely indeed from case to case. If we concentrate on (a), we shall be aware of restriction on the use of "good"; if on (b), of the seemingly infinite variety in its use. Stevenson was never in the position of holding that the application of "good" is, in the same *sense* and the same *respects,* both limited and unlimited. What he did hold to was that, by drawing a distinction between emotive and descriptive meaning, one could account for both the restriction and the infinite variety in its use.

I think, then, that Stevenson can be largely exonerated from the charge of internal inconsistency, at any rate so far as the putative examples of such inconsistency which we noted above are concerned. So far as the second of these, (ii) above, is concerned, there seem to be no grounds for saying that he was inconsistent. And as for the former, (i) above, while Stevenson does seem to have been inconsistent, it could perhaps be argued in extenuation of his misdemeanor that this was due to a creditable, if subconscious and momentary, recognition of the inadequacies of his own ethical theory.

Stevenson's Psychological Theory of Meaning

There is a difference between language (a) having, or not having, a natural power or disposition to produce, or be produced by, certain psychological processes and (b) being, or not being, in accordance with certain linguistic conventions or rules. Is the distinction between being meaningful and meaningless that noted in (a) or in (b)? I argued in the second chapter, when criticizing the psychological theory of meaning, that it is the latter. Stevenson made the mistake of supposing that it is the former.

He recognized that some place must be allowed for the operation of linguistic rules, but the only function which he took them to fulfill was, as we have seen, to make descriptive meaning more precise.[79] They are a part of the conditioning process whereby the power of language is built up, but this is to say no more than that they "render more fixed any rough meanings that may have developed in other ways."[80] The development of the power or disposition of language to produce, or be produced by, psychological processes is therefore logically prior to the rules which make it more precise. When linguistic rules do operate, and only then, Stevenson further recognized, can distinctions be drawn between meaning and suggestion, truth and falsity, validity and invalidity. Because he thought that emotive meaning is not susceptible of linguistic regulation, he held that these distinctions do not apply to it.

[79] See above, p. 123.
[80] *EL*, pp. 68–69.

Whether or not a piece of language produces, or is produced by, certain psychological processes is a matter of contingent fact. Stevenson seeks to reduce the question whether or not language is meaningful to this question. In other words, he seeks to reduce a normative question to one of contingent fact. Now, whether or not language has meaning, i.e., makes sense, logically depends upon some standard or criterion which prescribes what is sense and what is nonsense. Such a norm lays down, in effect, what language *ought* to be. But this "ought" cannot (logically) be reduced to an "is"; or at the least, it is clear that it cannot in the facile way in which Stevenson seeks so to reduce it. For, even if you say, as he chose to do, that the meaningfulness of language is its causal efficacy, you have, by implication, chosen the latter as your standard of meaning. In the last analysis, meaning is constituted by the conventional rules which govern the use of expressions, which determine whether they are appropriate or inappropriate to the occasions and circumstances of their use. This conclusion is reinforced by considering the characteristics which meanings share with rules but not with the dispositions to which Stevenson likened them. Meanings can be learned, remembered or forgotten, adhered to or departed from, as rules can. In learning one may certainly acquire a disposition, but one does not learn a disposition. Nor does one remember or forget, adhere to or depart from a disposition, even though to do any of these things with regard to a piece of language may be evidence that one has such-and-such a disposition.

If rules constitute meaning and *if* we admit emotive as well as descriptive meaning, then obviously we must depart from Stevenson's conclusion that rules do not apply to emotive meaning. Are there any good grounds for rejecting this conclusion? Undoubtedly, there are possibilities of precision in language which describes, that are not paralleled in language which expresses or evokes a range of emotions. But it does not follow that there are no rules governing the use of emotive language. Take the emotive expression "Oh!" for example. Given the right tone of voice, it is used to express

or evoke alarm; and it is appropriately used in certain kinds
of circumstances and on certain kinds of occasions, in a word,
unusual ones. There would be a failure in communication,
if anyone, for instance, said "Oh!" (in a surprised tone of
voice) every time he got on the bus to work, so that his
fellow passengers had come to expect it. His remark would
be nonsense. Take again the dependently emotive word "nigger" and suppose that the cultured and liberal-minded chairman at a learned society introduced a colored lecturer with
the words, "Our visitor, this nigger. . . ." The reaction would
not be one so much of outrage as of puzzlement. What on
earth did he mean? Conventional rules, admittedly much less
precise in their application, do provide a criterion for differentiating sense from nonsense in the case of emotive, as well
as descriptive, language.

The interesting question which therefore arises is: does it
follow that distinctions between meaning and suggestion, validity and invalidity, truth and falsehood, contrary to Stevenson's opinion, *can* be drawn in the case of emotive language?

Meaning and Suggestion

Stevenson said that, so far as emotive language is concerned, we cannot differentiate between what language means
and what it suggests, as we can, for instance, between the
precise definition of "pig" and what it suggests when applied
to a man. He thought that this lent support to his view that
linguistic rules do not apply to emotive meaning. He was
mistaken. There is certainly a distinction, within the descriptive meaning of a word like "pig," between its precise definition and what it suggests about a man if you call him a pig.
Linguistic rules apply in both cases, but they are, so to say,
tighter in the former case than in the latter. It is no doubt
true that one could not offer any similar examples of a
"tight" and a "loose" use of "Oh!" and to that extent Stevenson is correct. But it does not follow that there are no linguistic rules for the use of "Oh!" We have seen that there
are.

Dr. G. C. Kerner[81] thinks that Stevenson was deceived by his own idea that emotive language operates through "a flexible mechanism of suggestion."[82] "Suggestion" admits of two interpretations: (i) "to suggest" may be taken to mean "to induce or arouse a thought or feeling." In that sense, any utterance, descriptive, emotive, or whatever, may be suggestive and what it induces a hearer to think or feel will depend upon any of an infinite number of factors; but this is logically quite distinct from what the utterance means. This kind of suggestiveness is not the *differentia* of emotive meaning. (ii) Suggestion may be a linguistic performance comparable, say, to stating, promising, questioning. In this sense, emotive language does suggest as descriptive does not; and one could say that such suggestiveness is its meaning. But, in this latter sense, what makes any utterance a suggestion is conformity to the linguistic rules for suggesting. To succeed in suggesting, all I need to do is to keep these rules. In the former sense, on the other hand, I could succeed in suggesting only if my hearer had the thoughts or feelings which I was trying to induce him to have. The alternatives, therefore, where emotive language is concerned are: (i) to say that it can suggest apart from rules, which is true but does not differentiate it from any other sort of language; or (ii) to say that it suggests in accordance with rules, which contradicts Stevenson's view that linguistic rules do not apply to it.

Truth and Falsity

Stevenson contended that the distinction between truth and falsity does not apply to utterances with emotive meaning. A description may be true or false and in so far as moral judgments are descriptive, this distinction does apply to them. If I say "This is good," it may be true or false that "I approve of this . . ." or that this can replace the variables "X, Y, Z. . . ." But ". . . do so as well," and the laudatory

[81] G. C. Kerner, *The Revolution in Ethical Theory* (Oxford, 1966), pp. 45–52.
[82] *EL,* p. 33.

emotive meaning of "good" are neither true nor false. Stevenson concedes that someone who agreed with my "This is good" might express agreement by "That's true," but in such a case the remark would, in effect, be equivalent to an ethical judgment of the speaker's own.[83]

Urmson rejects[84] Stevenson's contention. He asks whether or not it would make sense to say, for instance, "Is it true that killing is wrong?" This question seems to him no less meaningful than, for instance, "Is it true that it is six o'clock?" It would, as a rule, be odd to say "Is it true that killing is wrong?"; but then it would be equally odd to ask "Is it true that it is six o'clock?" rather than "Is it six o'clock?" The conditions which have to be fulfilled to remove the oddness are in both cases: (i) it must have been put to us that such-and-such is the case and we are surprised or doubtful; and (ii) we must be addressing our question to someone whom we consider to be an authority. Admittedly, authorities on the time are easier to come by than on right and wrong; and we may not in fact believe that there are any of the latter sort at all, in which case we shall have no use for the question "Is it true that killing is wrong?" But whether such an authority exists or not is a separate issue from whether or not this latter question makes sense. "Is it true that it is six o'clock?" would make sense even if all the timepieces in the world had suddenly stopped. So, whether or not we believe it empirically possible to find the answer, the question "Is it true that killing is wrong?" makes just as much sense as "Is it true that it is six o'clock?" according to Urmson's view.

This seems plausible enough, but the fact remains that in asking some putative authority whether or not it is true that it is six o'clock, we are asking a question, his answer to which can in its turn be checked for truth or falsity in accordance with known and generally accepted tests. But what generally accepted tests are there for checking a moral authority's answer to "Is it true that killing is wrong?"

[83] *EL*, p. 169.
[84] Urmson, *op. cit.*, pp. 83–85.

Validity and Invalidity

Stevenson appears to have had two main arguments to offer in support of his view that moral judgments cannot be valid or invalid: (i) He held that an argument is valid, if, and only if, its premises being true, its conclusion is true; and therefore where there is no possibility of truth, there is none of validity either.[85] (ii) As we have seen,[86] he held that the connection between beliefs and attitudes is always factual, never logical, and this of course cuts out all talk of validity or invalidity concerning that connection.

Against the first of these Urmson puts the case well:

> The criterion of the validity of an argument may well be that if its premises are true its conclusion must be true; but this no more shows that the notion of validity has to be explained in terms of truth than the fact that a criterion of a valid marriage is that both parties must be without an existing spouse shows that the notion of validity has to be defined in terms of the concept of spinsterhood. It is indeed much more plausible to hold that the notion of argument is bound up with the notion of validity and invalidity; it might well be thought to be analytic that every argument is either valid or invalid, somewhat as it is analytic that every statement is true or false—in fact I am more certain of the former of these two than of the latter.[87]

What of Stevenson's second argument? He never denied that when a moral judgment has been delivered two questions can always be asked: (i) is the reason given for it true?; and (ii) does the person who has given this reason hold consistently to the moral commitment implicit within it? When he said that the connection between beliefs and attitudes is not logical, he was not, of course, going back on either of these points. He was simply making the further point that, in the last analysis, there is always an attitude (or attitudes) to which a moralist holds and which does not follow from any belief which he holds. This is the moralist's ultimate com-

[85] *EL*, pp. 151–55.
[86] Above, p. 118.
[87] Urmson, *op. cit.*, p. 86.

mitment and with regard to it questions of validity or invalidity cannot arise. At every stage of ethical reasoning, this commitment is implicit and determines what moves the moralist makes; and so the whole process can only be called reasoning in a qualified sense of that word, according to Stevenson.

There is, however, a distinction which needs to be drawn in this connection. It is between: (i) questions about the validity or invalidity of a whole system of reasoning, e.g., "Is induction valid?" and (ii) questions about the validity or invalidity of particular moves within any system of reasoning. Whether or not the axioms of the system are acceptable is one thing; whether or not an inference is in accordance with them is another. This latter question *can* certainly be raised with reference to any particular piece of moral argument; the latter's conclusion may not follow logically from its premises. Some commentators[88] seem to think that Stevenson was unaware of this point but I do not think that they are right. Nothing in Stevenson's ethical theory is necessarily at variance with it.

There is one point, however, where Stevenson does seem to be overconfident about validity and moral argument. He takes it for granted that *any* belief whatever could logically serve as a reason for a moral attitude. In his view, it makes perfectly good sense to say "X is good (or bad) because it is Y," where Y is any putative fact whatever. Suppose, for instance, I say that apartheid is morally wrong, and when asked why, I reply, "Because it occurs in South Africa." I back this up by saying that I am morally opposed to everything which happens in South Africa. Have I given what is recognizable as a reason for a *moral* judgment? To say the least, this question gives one pause. If the answer is no, then my reason is invalid. It is not so because I refuse to work with it consistently. I am, remember, opposed to *everything* which occurs in South Africa. Rather, my reason is invalid in the way that it would be invalid, if I said at a cricket match, "The umpire ought to send that fielder off," and when asked

[88] Cf. Kerner, *op. cit.,* pp. 80–83, and Urmson, *op. cit.,* pp. 86–87.

why, replied, "He persistently handles the ball." This is invalid because it runs counter to the rules of cricket which permit, indeed necessitate, that fielders persistently handle the ball. Are there similar rules of "the moral language game" so that not simply *anything* which I could choose to give as a *moral* reason will serve as such? This is a question into which we must go further below; but it certainly cannot be answered with an obvious "No" as Stevenson appears to think. What makes a move part of the moral language game is a more complicated matter than he takes it to be.

Does Stevenson's Theory Fit the Facts?

Stevenson claimed to have formulated his theory by paying careful attention to the way in which moral language is ordinarily used. How accurate was his observation? Most of what has already been said by way of criticism bears upon this question. To recall one instance, we saw reason to think that he conceived of the attitudes which moral judgments express too much as though they were simply emotions. A more accurate observation of moral discourse would have made him alive to the logical differences, which we noted above,[89] between what is ordinarily said of moral judgments and what is said of emotions. We may deliberately choose or take up our stand in morals, we are held responsible for it, said to maintain it. We can be consistent or inconsistent in it, argued into or out of it. If asked why we take it, we most naturally reply in terms of reasons rather than causes. In all these respects, our talk of moral judgments differs logically from our talk of emotions.

Is it any more in accordance with the facts to say, as Stevenson did, that the purpose for which moral language is used is primarily "to create an influence"?[90] G. J. Warnock has pointed out that, if one is setting out to create an influence when one utters a moral judgment, then certain assumptions are in order: (i) one takes one's hearer not to share one's moral opinion; (ii) one wishes him to do so; (iii) one thinks

[89] Above, p. 124.
[90] *Facts and Values*, p. 16.

that by delivering the judgment, one will cause, or tend to cause, him to adopt it.[91] All these assumptions, however, may *not* apply and yet it be *not* absurd for me to issue my moral judgment. My hearer may already hold the same moral opinion as I; I may not care whether he does so or not; and I may not consider it likely that my giving my opinion will have any effect on his. But even so, it may make perfectly good sense to deliver my opinion. Frequently moral judgments are delivered where these latter conditions are fulfilled. It would be ridiculously dogmatic to say that all such cases of moral utterance are pointless or nonsensical. Absurdity lies rather in an analysis of their meaning from which such a conclusion follows.

Stevenson is very sensitive to the objection that his account of ethical argument reduces it to the level of propaganda or even blunt coercion.[92] If the point of ethical judgments is to exert an influence and if no question of validity arises concerning the connection between the attitudes recommended and the "reasons" given in their support, then it does seem to follow that the only test left for an argument in morals is whether or not it will be efficacious in producing the desired attitudes. Stevenson replies that "it would be a gross distortion of people's motivation to say this factor is always the decisive one"[93] and he protests that he is doing no such thing. He is right of course. Martin Luther King's advocacy of civil rights was not characterized by that complete indifference to all considerations of truth which marked Goebbels' Nazi propaganda; and no one supposes that Stevenson would have said that it was. But these are not the points at issue. What is at issue is whether or not Stevenson misrepresents the logical structure of moral argument, not the motives of those who participate in it.

He does not say that anything goes in moral discourse so long as it produces the desired attitudes. But the considerations which, in his opinion, determine what does, or does not, "go" are *moral* and *utilitarian* rather than *logical*. How

[91] Warnock, *op. cit.*, p. 25.
[92] *EL*, p. 157 and Chap. XI.
[93] *EL*, p. 157.

shall I treat my opponent in a moral argument? If he is a cold fish who has "let his reflective habits devitalise his emotional ones," then, says Stevenson, maybe "persuasion will assist, whereas rational methods will actually hinder, any quickening of his practical attitudes."[94] So I ought to weigh in with heavily emotive language. On the other hand, I myself may not be absolutely firm in my own attitudes and conceive of the possibility that, if I considered certain aspects of the relevant situation more carefully than I have hitherto done, I might change my attitudes. In that case, when commending my view to a hearer, or a fortiori an opponent, I must choose rational methods, says Stevenson, "to open the way to a counteruse of them."[95] This will be a useful move on my part because it gives me a chance of hearing the other side of the argument, and will help to confirm, or to correct, my attitude. Stevenson has, therefore, substituted for the distinction between an argument's being valid and its producing conviction, a distinction between an argument's being moral or useful and its producing conviction.

In this account of what is permissible or desirable, and what is not, in moral argument, is Stevenson telling us (a) how he thinks people ought *morally* to behave in moral argument or (b) that recognition of such moral or utilitarian considerations as he instances is part of the *logic* of moral discourse, i.e., part of what it means to say that an argument is moral? If the former, it doubtless does him credit but sheds no light on the nature of moral discourse as such. And why restrict the point to talk about morals? What is the difference between, say, scientific discourse and moral discourse which makes sensitivity to the effect of the moves which one makes upon the character of one's opponent or on the well-foundedness of one's own opinions applicable in the one instance but not the other? If, on the other hand, Stevenson is saying that it is a rule of the moral language game that these moral or utilitarian considerations must logically be taken into account when making a move within it, then he is simply mistaken. The

[94] *Ibid.*
[95] *Ibid.*

statement, "I am saying that you ought *morally* to do to X, *but* I am quite deliberately *not* putting my point in language calculated to quicken the emotions which you have devitalized through excessive ratiocination, nor supporting my point with arguments calculated to invoke a counteruse of argument by you which will correct or confirm my own uncertain attitude" —is *not* a self-contradictory statement. A *moral* judgment can (logically) be such quite apart from any considerations about the effect of the way in which it is expressed or supported upon the hearer or speaker.

Urmson accuses Stevenson—and says that this is the basic defect of his theory—of failing to distinguish clearly between setting up a standard and using it.[96] The distinction itself is obvious enough. I use "good" in deciding that my criteria for goodness in cars, students, or whatever shall be C; and then I proceed to use "good" in accordance with C when I say that X is a good car, student, or whatever. Notice that this is *not* simply the distinction between "good" and criteria for its use; it is a distinction between two uses, or meanings, of "good." According to Urmson, Stevenson failed to bring out two important points about the meaning of "good": (i) that "This is good" is *normally* a standard-using evaluation;[97] and (ii) that there is *no point* in setting up a standard unless it is a preliminary to using it.[98]

Because he failed to recognize the former, it is said, he spoke as though the remark "X is good" were always analyzable as setting up a standard. Most of the time, though, we are not doing that at all when we say that things are good. We are evaluating them in accordance with the *accepted* criteria. Did not Stevenson, however, recognize this in his second pattern of analysis? If, as I think, he did then, Urmson's criticism loses its force on this count.

On the second count: did Stevenson fail to see that the only point of setting up a standard is to use it? Here again I think that, although we might be inclined to say that he did, if we take account only of his first pattern of analysis, the thing to

[96] Urmson, *op. cit.*, pp. 64–71, 77–80.
[97] *Ibid.*, p. 68.
[98] *Ibid.*, p. 79.

notice is that his whole discussion of persuasive definition is about how people get, or try to get, certain standards *used*. What other purpose is he supposed to have thought that persuasive definition serves? None that one can think of.

Does Stevenson's theory fit the facts so far as our use of the word "moral" is concerned? What logical features of the moral use of "good" differentiate it from wider evaluative uses? Stevenson's answer, as we have already noted, is this: "We may recognise a sense where 'good' abbreviates 'morally good' and refers not to *any* kind of favour that the speaker has, but only to the kind that is marked by a special seriousness and urgency."[99] It would seem to follow from this that one could take *any* action or state of affairs and intelligibly predicate "morally good" of it (according to Stevenson's first pattern of analysis), or one could take the expression "morally good" and intelligibly define it in terms of *any* set of qualities or relations (according to his second pattern of analysis) *provided only* that one did so with "special seriousness and urgency." But is that how we normally use "moral" and its cognates? Suppose I announce that it seems good to me to spend my life taking one step forward and two steps backward and recommend this way of life to others as "good" with intense seriousness and urgency. Would my serious and urgent use of "good," in itself, make my point of view generally recognized as a "moral" one? Surely not. At first blush, then, it seems absurd to locate the difference, between the moral use of "good" and wider evaluative uses, where Stevenson does. But is what he says entirely absurd?

The question of what makes a moral judgment moral has aroused much controversy in the quarter-century since Stevenson published his *Ethics and Language,* as we shall see in the next two chapters. Some philosophers locate the defining characteristics of moral discourse in its form; others in its content; and others in a combination of form and content. There are some grounds for wondering whether any definition of moral judgment can be enunciated which will net *only* those judgments which we would normally call moral.

[99] *EL,* p. 90.

If, with the prescriptivist, we say that a moral judgment is a commendation, or discommendation, for which a reason must be given on demand and this reason must be consistently adhered to in argument, counterexamples like that at the end of the last subsection spring to mind. We supposed, it will be remembered, that I condemn apartheid as morally wrong because it happens in South Africa and that I am prepared to see this reason universalized and to maintain that everything which happens in South Africa is morally wrong just because it does so. Such a point of view, we noted, would not naturally be described by ordinary users of English as a *moral* one.

If, with the descriptivist, we say that a moral judgment, as such, is concerned with some specific content, e.g., what all men want, then it immediately occurs to us that other sorts of discourse besides moral have the same content. Advertising consultants, for example, may discuss what all men want.

If we put form and content together and say that moral judgments, as such, have the content which descriptivists would attribute to them *and* the form which prescriptivists say that they have, does such a definition net *only* moral judgments? Compare the judgments passed in our society upon abortion with those passed on the scattering of litter. Both these activities, it may be said, concern what all men want, namely freedom from hazard to life, health, or beauty. Again, it may be pointed out, those who deliver judgments upon either abortion or litter-scattering are prepared to give reasons for their judgments and to see these universalized in argument. So, in both cases, content and form are the same. Yet, in our society, while almost everyone would say that abortion is a moral issue, not everyone would agree—or, at any rate, not so readily and naturally—that scattering litter is.

The appeal to content, or form, or a combination of the two, therefore, does not seem to be sufficient to net only moral judgments. Is "special seriousness and urgency" of any use in supplying a criterion which will differentiate judgments which we readily and naturally call moral from those which we do not? It is true, of course, that advertising consultants can be just as serious and urgent in their talk of what men want as moralists are. Again, it is true, to revert to the above example, that my condemnation of everything which happens in South Africa could be just as serious and urgent as it is consistent. We may be inclined, then, to say that seriousness and urgency do not come into it. So long as we think only of cases like the difference between advertising consultants and moralists, or of cases like the difference between my supposed view about everything which happens in South Africa and a moral point of view, we might be inclined to say that recognizing the difference between moral and nonmoral discourse is a matter of recognizing a differentiating moral *form*, where both are about what all men want, or a differentiating moral *content*, wherein both reasons are given and universalized. But the whole point of my example above of the difference in opinion about abortion and scattering litter lay in the fact that, in both these cases, there is a common form *and* a common content. Why, then, is the one more readily and naturally thought of as a moral issue rather than the other? It is hard to resist the conclusion that this is because in our society at the present time what we do about abortion is felt to be a more serious and urgent matter than what we do about the scattering of litter. I do not, of course, for a moment say that the whole difference between what is a moral judgment and what is not lies in this special seriousness and urgency. It is, at most, only one necessary condition of a judgment being a moral one. Other necessary conditions concerning form or content or both must be added to it before we have a sufficient condition. All I am saying is that *some* room must be left for seriousness and urgency. When writers of leading articles and others urge their publics that this, that, or the other *is* a moral issue, they may not be pointing out that it has such-and-such a form or such-and-such a content. Form and content may be well known. These guides of public opinion may simply be calling upon their hearers to regard the matter with greater seriousness and urgency than they are wont to do. Stevenson's criterion of the difference between "good" and "morally good," therefore, though it might with justice be said to have oversimplified the matter to the point of naiveté, was not entirely and absolutely wide of the mark. His error was to treat a necessary condition as a sufficient one, an error by no means rare in philosophy.

CHAPTER 5. PRESCRIPTIVISM

We turn now to a second type of ethical theory which was developed under the influence of the view that the meaning of language is to be looked for in the use to which it is put. This is known as prescriptivism and its foremost exponent is Professor R. M. Hare. Hare's moral philosophy has some affinities with emotivism but differs from it in certain important respects. Like the emotivists, Hare rejects all forms of descriptivism, that is all theories of moral judgment which take it to be logically equivalent to factual statement, whether the fact concerned be natural, as in the case of those whom Moore accused of the naturalistic fallacy, or nonnatural, as in the case of Moore, Prichard, and Ross. Why then does Hare also reject emotivism? I think one could say, as a preliminary statement of his position, that he does so on two closely related grounds: (i) because emotivism confuses reasons for action with causes of action; and (ii) because it confuses the perlocutionary force of language with its meaning.

I. THE REJECTION OF EMOTIVISM

Reasons and Causes

Two points may be recalled from the discussion, in the last chapter, of the emotivists' account of the methodology of moral argument. First, we saw[1] that Stevenson allowed a place within that methodology to what he called "non-rational psychological" ways of getting people to change their feelings or attitudes. His examples of moral argument included the predication of moral terms (first pattern of analysis), supported by nothing more than the emotive force of a word such

[1] Above, p. 131.

as "dictator," and the persuasive definition of moral terms (second pattern of analysis), likewise supported by arguments which appeal to attitudes rather than beliefs. Since he thought that the aim of moral argument is to get people to change their attitudes, and since these irrational methods of argument are sometimes effective to that end, it seemed to Stevenson perfectly legitimate to regard them as part of the methodology of morals. The second point[2] which may be recalled is Stevenson's opinion that the "reasons" given for moral judgments never support them in the way that reasons support a scientific hypothesis or a mathematical theorem, and his consequent quest for a "different sort of proof" or some "substitute for proof" in ethics. This "proof" he claimed to have discovered. But his account of it was, to say the least, unfortunate. One can change one's hearer's beliefs about a situation, Stevenson said, and thereby swing "a preponderance of the hearer's desires" behind one's judgment that a given situation should be altered, or preserved, or brought into being, as the case might be. By this means, in his own phrase, one "removes the hesitations" which prompt people to ask for proof of a moral judgment. All that this amounts to, in other words, is that one "proves" one's moral judgments by calling attention to various considerations which will *cause* one's hearers to assent to these judgments. As Stevenson himself put it: "A reasoned agreement . . . is theoretically possible only to the extent that agreement in belief will *cause* people to agree in attitude."[3] As we have already remarked, this is indeed a substitute for proof or reasoned argument. To effect such psychological conditioning in order to secure assent to one's opinions is logically a quite different procedure from offering valid reasons for what one says.

It is hardly surprising, there being such elements as these in emotivism, that its critics have condemned it as rendering the rational justification of moral judgments impossible. From the point of view of these critics, it is not simply the case that emotivism offends their prejudice that morality is a solemn

---

[2] Above, p. 120.
[3] *EL*, p. 31; italics mine.

and serious matter. They are of the opinion that a little reflection upon moral discourse as it actually occurs will show quite clearly that it is far from being irrationalist in character. In it reasons are given for what is said; and distinctions are drawn between good reasons and bad ones, between conclusions which follow and ones which do not. A theory which appears to put morality beyond reason flies in the face of these facts. Thus it was that prescriptivism took shape. Hare has remarked that this was why he entered the lists. After the war, when he began to do moral philosophy, emotivism was the height of fashion. He found its rejection of ethical naturalism entirely convincing. But he could not bring himself to accept its denial that reasoned argument in ethics is possible. He therefore set himself to work out—as he himself has called it—"a rationalist kind of non-descriptivism."[4]

There is undoubtedly a good deal in emotivism to give ground for the conclusion that it takes moral thinking to be irrationalist. At the conclusion of his early paper, "The Emotive Meaning of Ethical Terms," for example, Stevenson included in a summary of his position, the regrettable remark that "to ask whether [a thing] is good is to ask for *influence*."[5] This seems patently false. Even someone who knows all about the "hidden persuaders" of the advertising world does not page through magazine advertisements or watch television commercials in search of influence. If he has any conscious purpose in mind at all, it is to discover what is worth buying. Albeit warily, he takes the advertisements and commercials to be answering that question. A fortiori when it comes to moral questions, no one who asks "Is this good?" or "What ought I to do?" is looking for influence. He is looking for guidance.[6] He wants to be told what is good or what he ought to do. And if he has doubts about the guidance which he receives, it will not be because he wonders whether or not it will *cause* him to choose, or act, accordingly. It will be be-

---

[4] In unpublished introductory lectures on moral philosophy.
[5] *M* XLVI (1937), reprinted in *Fact and Value*, p. 30.
[6] Cf. R. M. Hare's paper, "The Freedom of the Will," *PAS*, Supp. Vol. XXIX (1955).

cause he wonders whether or not there is good *reason* why he should do so. At many points in the literature of emotivism, there is this failure to differentiate clearly between causes and reasons.

However, something can be said on the other side. Stevenson found a place in his methodology for other elements besides the "non-rational psychological." And, when we take account of all he had to say in his mature writings the question does arise: is prescriptivism's methodology of moral argument radically different from his?

Two methods which Stevenson named, besides the "non-rational psychological," were, as we saw above, respectively the "logical" and the "rational psychological."[7] By the former, we may call in question the *consistency* with which "good," or any other moral expression, is predicated or defined; by the latter, the *comprehensiveness* of the reasons which are given for any such predication or definition, and the *truth* of the beliefs which these reasons express. What Stevenson had in mind in the case of the former is obvious enough: I can shake an opponent by showing him that he is using the same words in different senses at different points in his argument. What he had in mind in the case of the latter method is the fact that one may not have taken into account (comprehensiveness), or be mistaken about (truth), such matters as the nature and consequences of an act, the motive from which it is done, and so on, all of which are relevant when assessing its morality. His fundamental position was that both the "logical" and the "rational psychological" ways of supporting moral judgments presuppose logically anterior attitudes to which the last appeal is always made. He recognized, of course, that the nature and consequences of an act or the motive from which it is done are matters of belief, but he thought that they are only relevant because of underlying attitudes. And so a rational man who applies either the "logical" or the "rational psychological" method in moral discussion is really asking such questions as: Are the relevant attitudes being consistently expressed? Are these attitudes

[7] Cf. above, p. 130.

narrow-minded? Is the belief that such-and-such a case falls under them true? The final determinant of what is right or wrong, good or evil, is always the attitude, or attitudes, which have been adopted.

Now, how far removed is all this from what a prescriptivist, such as Hare, would say about rational procedure in moral thinking? We are not yet in a position to answer that question; but, anticipating, one can indicate some of the points at which it may well come into focus. Hare, we shall find, speaks of morality as grounded logically in decisions of principle—we are entitled to ask whether these differ radically from Stevenson's logically fundamental attitudes. Hare recognizes that one way of rationally defeating an opponent in moral discussion is to show that the reason which he offers for his judgment is in fact untrue; and he considered that rational moral thinking would range over all morally relevant aspects of an act or state of affairs before pronouncing judgment upon it. Are not these the very points which Stevenson was making when, in explaining his "rational psychological" method, he dwelt upon the necessity for comprehensiveness and truth in the reasons with which attitudes are supported? Again, Hare, as we shall see, considered that it is constitutive of moral argument, as moral, that the reasons given within it shall be universalizable. At this point perhaps we have come to the parting of the ways. Stevenson's "logical" method of supporting a moral judgment was by consistency in the attitude expressed or in the reasons given for it. He thought, however, that this is simply *one* method, among others, of moral argument or deliberation. Hare, on the other hand, thought of the universalizability of the reasons offered within it as a *sine qua non* of moral argument, or deliberation, as moral.

We shall return below to the matters upon which I have just touched. But first I must outline a second ground—closely related to the charge of confusing reasons with causes—upon which Hare rejected emotivism. There is a difference between him and the emotivists more radical than that which lies in what respectively they take the methodology of morals to be. It lies in what they take meaning to be.

Meaning and Perlocutionary Force

We have seen in the last two chapters that Stevenson's emotivism was based on a general theory of meaning. I will recapitulate briefly. The psychological theory of meaning is to the effect that the meaning of a sign is its dispositional property to cause, or to be caused by, certain psychological processes in the hearer or the speaker respectively. To this Stevenson subscribed. If this theory were true, then we should have explained the meaning of any given piece of language when we had shown either what psychological process in the speaker had caused it, or what psychological processes it itself had caused in the hearer, or possibly both. We noted the basic defect in this conception of meaning. There is a logical distinction between empirical generalizations to the effect that such-and-such psychological processes cause, or are caused by, the utterance of such-and-such language, on the one hand, and normative rules or conventions, which lay down when it is appropriate or inappropriate to use such-and-such language, on the other. Whether or not language is meaningful is determined, not by whether or not it has such-and-such a cause or effect, but by whether it is or is not in accordance with certain conventions or rules for its use.

We see that what causes a *speaker* to say something is clearly a different matter from the meaning of whatever it is that the speaker says, when we recognize that what he says can have the same meaning, though conceivably quite different causes. Suppose two colleagues of Smith, Jones and Brown, are members of an academic committee which is considering Smith for promotion. Both say "Smith is a poor scholar. Don't promote him." Jones says these things because he feels malice toward Smith and wants to prevent the latter's advancement. Brown says them because he sincerely believes that Smith does not deserve promotion and feels bound to express his opinion honestly to the committee. In this example, the psychological processes which caused Jones and Brown respectively to speak about Smith as they did were radically different, but even so the *meaning* of what each of them said was precisely the same.

If we turn now to the view that the meaning of language is its dispositional property to cause certain psychological processes in the *hearer,* then a similar logical distinction has to be drawn. The meaning of an utterance cannot (logically) be identified with its effects, or even with what it is intended to effect. Depending on the circumstances and on the hearers concerned, the remark "Smith is a poor scholar. Don't promote him" could cause a wide variety of psychological processes to occur: surprise, resentment, contempt, amusement—the list is endless. But the meaning of "Smith is a poor scholar. Don't promote him" would remain the same whatever the effect which it produced. Hare has pointed out[8] that what a speaker *gets* his hearers to do by saying something is logically distinct from what he *tells* them to do in saying it. Jones or Brown would have *succeeded* in telling their committee that Smith is a poor scholar simply when they had uttered the words "Smith is a poor scholar," and in telling it not to promote Smith when they had simply said "Don't promote him." But they might *not* have succeeded thereby in getting the committee to believe the former or act upon the latter. A speaker may—indeed if he is sincere, usually will—intend to effect something by whatever it is that he says. If you tell people that Smith is a poor scholar, you normally intend thereby to get them to believe it; and if you say, "Don't promote him," you normally intend thereby to stop them from promoting him. But—and this is the important point—in neither case is what is said meaningless if it does *not* have the intended effect. The difference which must be recognized here is that between the *perlocutionary force* of an utterance—what the speaker intends to do by making it—and the *meaning* of the utterance.[9] Hare, with full justification, maintained that a basic defect in emotivism is the failure of its exponents to draw this distinction clearly—or indeed at all—in their theory of ethics.

Notice that they could (logically) have done so. Within

[8] Cf. Hare, *op. cit.*.
[9] Cf. above, pp. 54–63.

their own conception of emotive meaning, the distinction just referred to could have been drawn. Suppose moral utterances are logically comparable to *ejaculations,* as some early emotivists thought. There are rules by reference to which expressions such as "Boo" or "Hurrah" make sense or nonsense on any given occasion.[10] "Boo" and "Hurrah" are *words* and, as such, should be distinguished clearly from expressions of emotion such as tears or giggles, sighs or screams, grunts or groans, etc. Frequently these latter expressions of emotion are involuntary. If, in such a case, one asked what, for instance, a groan "meant," one would really be looking for some causal explanation of the groan—such as, for instance, "He's groaning because he's lost all his money." This would explain it because there is a common connection in our experience between losing all one's money and involuntary groaning. It is important to differentiate such a use of the verb "to mean" from the sense in which I have been using it in this section so far.[11] Perhaps Stevenson's mistakes about meaning are due to a failure on his part to mark this difference and all that it implies. In the sense in which I have been using "to mean," an involuntary groan does not mean anything. There are no rules or conventions for its appropriate use. And so there is no point in the question "Does this groan make sense or nonsense?" In so far as a groan, or similar expression of emotion, is voluntary, there will be rules or conventions which determine whether it is meaningless. But this is to say no more than that, in such a case, a groan functions as a word (or words), not a mere exhalation of breath. Where *words,* i.e., conventional signs of one sort or another, are concerned, their meaning consists in rules for their correct use. And so, if we say that moral judgments are logically similar to ejaculations such as "Boo" or "Hurrah," we must still recognize that there is a distinction which can be drawn between: (i) what they mean; and (ii) each of the following—(ii.a) what causes anyone to utter them, (ii.b) what effect they have on those who hear them, (ii.c) what effect they are intended to have by the speaker on those who hear them.

[10] Cf. above, pp. 141–42.
[11] Cf. above, p. 40.

If we suppose, as some other early emotivists taught, that moral judgments are logically comparable, not so much to ejaculations as to *imperatives*, exactly the same distinctions can be drawn. What an imperative, and any utterance comparable in logical character, means is determined by rules or conventions for its use. Its meaning is distinct from what causes anyone to utter it, from whatever effect its utterance may have, and from whatever effect it may be intended to have. We have seen that the imperative, "Don't promote Smith!" could be caused by malice or conscientiousness on the part of the speaker; and that it could produce varying reactions—surprise, resentment, etc.—in those who hear it. It is true that if we ask what effect an imperative is intended to have the normal answer will be: the doing of whatever it is that we are telling our hearers to do. But this need not be the invariable answer. To revert to our example, it is conceivable that Jones and Brown should not have been motivated by malice and a sense of duty respectively as we supposed, but have been both of them eager to see Smith promoted, and yet still said precisely what we supposed them to say. On the committee with them, let us imagine, are three other colleagues. Jones and Brown do not feel sure of carrying any one of these with them in support of Smith by expatiating upon the latter's good qualities. But they do know that all the other three members of the committee dislike them and lose no opportunity to disagree with them. They therefore decide to say "Don't promote Smith," confident that this will unite the other three in saying "Let us promote him" and thereby secure a majority in favor of Smith. A fantastic example, perhaps, though stranger things have happened on academic committees. The point is that in such an example the meaning of "Don't promote Smith" would be exactly the same as if, by uttering that imperative, Jones and Brown were trying to get the committee *not* to promote him. The perlocutionary force of their imperative is different in the two instances, but its meaning is the same.

So, the emotivists *could* have drawn—on either an "ejaculatory" or an "imperative" interpretation of the emotive meaning of moral judgments—the distinction between perlocutionary force and meaning, which Hare rightly accuses them of overlooking.

II. HARE'S ACCOUNT OF PRESCRIPTIVISM

Hare lists the following as the "three most important truths about moral judgments":[12] (i) They are a kind of prescriptive judgment. (ii) They are distinguished from other prescriptive judgments by being universalizable. (iii) There can be rational procedure in moral thinking and argument because logical relations between prescriptive judgments are possible. I will attempt an exposition of Hare's moral philosophy under three corresponding heads.

(I) PRESCRIPTIVITY

Supervenience

Value-words, i.e., words such as "good," "right," and "ought," have, according to Hare, a "supervenient character." He arrived at this conclusion by reflecting upon certain features of their ordinary use. It is, for instance, *always* logically legitimate to ask for a reason when value judgments have been delivered.[13] Take these examples: "This is a good book," "This is the right road," "You ought to pay your tailor's bill." In every case it would be in order for the person so addressed to ask "Why?" And the answer to the question typically would be some naturalistic description of the thing concerned, e.g., "The characters in this book are very funny," "This road will take us to our destination," "Your tailor made you a suit on the understanding that you would pay for it." The justification, or ground, of goodness, rightness, or oughtness respectively lies in certain non-evaluative characteristics of the thing or action being judged. To take another, closely related, feature of the ordinary use of "good," "right," and "ought," there is something which it is *never* logically legitimate to say.[14] You would puzzle your hearers if you said that two things, A and B, are alike in every respect except

[12] *FR*, pp. 4–5.
[13] *LM*, p. 176; *FR*, pp. 36–37.
[14] *LM*, pp. 81, 153.

that A is good and B is not; or if you said that two actions, C and D, were exactly the same except that C was right, or obligatory, and D was not. They would insist that there must be some other difference to account for this one. But if you said, for instance, "This book is exactly like that one except that this has a red cover," no such insistence would be forthcoming. Differences in value have to be accounted for by differences of another kind as other sorts of difference do not.

Why then do value words have this supervenient character? Hare rejected two ways of explaining it: those of the ethical naturalist and the ethical intuitionist respectively. According to the naturalist, there are certain natural properties—call them P—which acts or states of affairs may have, such that the statement "X has P" entails "X is good" (or "right," or "obligatory"). This is so because "having P" is what "being good" means. We have already discussed[15] Moore's famous refutation of any such naturalistic theory. It is a mistake to suppose that "good" *means* "producing happiness," or whatever, because, in ordinary use, "Is what produces happiness (etc.) good?" is always an open question and "What produces happiness (etc.) is good" is never an insignificant tautology. Hare thinks that this argument of Moore's "rests, albeit insecurely, upon a secure foundation."[16] We shall see where the insecurity lies in a moment. But note first that Hare goes along with Moore in the view that the relationship between value judgments and the naturalistic descriptions upon which they are supervenient is not one of entailment due to equivalence of meaning.

Neither—and here we come to the insecurity in Moore's view and the second account of supervenience which Hare rejects—is it an entailment apprehended by intuition. According to Moore, and more explicitly to Ross, the relationship between, for example, "giving aesthetic enjoyment" and "being good," or between "fulfilling a promise" and "being right," respectively, is a self-evident one of which all rational beings, as such, are aware. The natural properties are, to be

[15] Pp. 69–74.
[16] *LM*, p. 83.

sure, logically distinct from the nonnatural. The former statement in each of the pairs just quoted does not mean the same as the latter. Nevertheless, the former in each case entails the latter in the sense that if anything is describable as "giving aesthetic enjoyment" all rational beings as such will see that it is also describable as "being good," or if as "fulfilling a promise," also as "being right." This view—that words like "good" and "right" describe nonnatural properties intuitively perceived to be entailed by natural ones—Hare finds just as unacceptable as the naturalists' view that value judgments have the same meaning as certain naturalistic descriptions. The "insecurity" which he detects in Moore's view is Moore's failure to perceive that value words, in their typical primary use, *do not describe at all.*

Whereas Moore and Ross had asked to what value-words refer, Hare asked what job they are used to do. Reflection upon their ordinary use convinced him that they "are used primarily for giving advice or instruction, or in general for guiding choices."[17] In a word, their use is *prescriptive.* Hare recognizes that prescribing is a many-sided activity: it includes such diverse uses of language as, for example, commending pictures, instructing pupils, or deciding questions of duty. His main point against both the naturalist and the intuitionist explanations of supervenience was that, if you take value words to be descriptive, you put them out of work; it is then logically impossible for them to do any of the jobs which they are primarily used to do. Says Hare: "Let us generalise. If 'P is a good picture' is held to mean the same as 'P is a picture and P is C,' then it will become impossible to commend pictures for being C; it will be possible only to say that they are C. It is important to realize that this difficulty has nothing to do with the particular example that I have chosen. It is not because we have chosen the wrong defining characteristics; it is because, whatever defining characteristics we choose, this objection arises, that we can no longer commend an object for possessing those characteristics."[18]

[17] *LM,* p. 155.
[18] *LM,* p. 85.

Given, then, the primarily prescriptive character of value words, how does Hare account for their supervenience? He says that the reason for the latter is that value words are used in order to teach, or affirm, or otherwise draw attention to, standards, rules, or principles for choosing between actions or states of affairs.[19] In order to see how this explains it, we must anticipate the next section so far as to notice one further feature of the ordinary use of words like "good," "right," and "ought." We have already noted the logical legitimacy of asking why, for instance, a certain book is said to be good. Suppose the answer is "Because the characters in it are very funny." Anyone who then wished to refute the judgment that the book is good could—and typically would—challenge this reason for thinking it good by taking either of two steps. He might dispute the factual claim that the characters in the book are amusing. Alternatively, he might call attention to another book which also has amusing characters but which he hopes those with whom he is arguing would not consider a good book. In making this latter move, he would be universalizing the reason which had been given. He would treat it as setting up a standard of goodness and challenge it accordingly. This shows us what constitutes the relationship of supervenience between "This is a good book" and "The characters in this book are very funny." When we give the latter as a reason for the former, we are invoking or applying a general criterion—a standard, rule, or principle. It is our subscription to that general criterion, not any equivalence in meaning or mysterious intuition, which logically constitutes the supervenience. To this subject I shall return below.[20]

Value-Judgments and Imperatives

We must now look a little more closely at the notion of prescriptivity to see precisely what Hare meant by it. He makes it true by definition that value judgments entail imperatives: "I propose to say that the test, whether someone is using the judgment 'I ought to do X' as a value-judgment or

[19] *LM*, p. 159.
[20] See pp. 182–84.

not is, 'Does he or does he not recognize that if he assents
to the judgment, he must also assent to the command 'Let
me do X'?"[21] With particular reference to moral value judgments he writes as follows in *The Language of Morals*.

> All the words discussed . . . [i.e. "good," "right," and
> "ought"] have it as their distinctive function either to com-
> mend or in some other way to guide choices or actions; and
> it is this essential feature which defies any analysis in purely
> factual terms. But to guide choices or actions, a moral judg-
> ment has to be such that if a person assents to it, he must
> assent to some imperative sentence derivable from it; in
> other words, if a person does not assent to some imperative
> sentence, that is knock-down evidence that he does not as-
> sent to the moral judgment in an evaluative sense—though
> of course he may assent to it in some other sense. . . .
> This is true by my definition of the word evaluative. But to
> say this is to say that if he professes to assent to the moral
> judgment, but does not assent to the imperative, he must
> have misunderstood the moral judgment (by taking it to be
> non-evaluative, though the speaker intended it to be evalu-
> ative). We are therefore clearly entitled to say that the
> moral judgment entails the imperative; for to say that one
> judgment entails another is simply to say that you cannot
> assent to the first and dissent from the second unless you
> have misunderstood one or the other; and this "cannot" is
> a logical "cannot"—if someone assents to the first and not
> to the second, this is in itself a sufficient criterion for say-
> ing that he has misunderstood the meaning of one or the
> other. Thus to say that moral judgments guide actions, and
> to say that they entail imperatives, comes to much the same
> thing.[22]

A number of questions arise here, in answering which we
shall, I hope, get the notion of prescriptivity into clearer
focus.

(i) Is Hare's definition of a value judgment arbitrary?
While admitting that he has carried his point by definition,
Hare claims that this definition is in accordance with ordinary

[21] *LM*, pp. 168–69.
[22] *LM*, pp. 171–72.

usage. Value-judgments in general, and moral ones in particular, are used to guide choices, i.e., to tell people to select one thing rather than another or to do one thing rather than another. They prescribe action. We shall see shortly that as Hare recognized, this statement requires some qualification, but it undoubtedly represents *one* typical use to which value judgments are put. When people get into arguments about what is good, right, or obligatory, it would be absurd to say that these are normally arguments the conclusion of which has no direct bearing on what anybody is to do.[23] Hare's definition is therefore not arbitrary.

(ii) How precisely did Hare conceive of the connection between value judgments and action? He recognized that someone might assent to the value judgment "I ought to do X" but dissent from the command "Let me do X." But he held that there are only two possible explanations of this occurrence: either the speaker does not understand the meaning of the words which he is using or he is insincere. Hare's claim is that, where these two conditions *are* fulfilled—that the speaker understands what he is saying and is sincere—a speaker who is using "I ought to do X" as a value judgment will assent to the command "Let me do X."

Given the sincerity of the value judgment, what constitutes sincere assent to the entailed command? Hare's answer is: "It is a tautology to say that we cannot sincerely assent to a command addressed to ourselves, and *at the same time* not perform it, if now is the occasion for performing it, and it is in our (physical and psychological) power to do so."[24] One common objection to Hare's prescriptivism, which he thinks so important that he devotes a whole chapter of *Freedom and Reason* to its rebuttal, is as follows. If value judgments implied sincere assent to an imperative, as such assent has just been defined, then it would be logically impossible to assent sincerely to any such judgment and yet act contrary to it. But manifestly this is *not* logically impossible. Sincere people can be morally weak. It makes perfectly good sense to say that someone thinks he ought to do X but is failing to do it. Hare's

[23] Cf. *FR*, p. 90.
[24] *LM*, p. 20; cf. *FR*, p. 79.

reply is that it is to meet just such an objection that he has
included in his above defini on of sincere assent to a command the condition, "if . . . it is in our (physical and psychological) power to do so [i.e., to perform the command]";
and he drives his point home: "Nobody in his senses would
maintain that a person who assents to an imperative must
(analytically) act on it even when he is unable to do so."[25]
This of course is so; it is logically possible to conceive of the
following train of events, for example. I think that I ought
to pay my tailor's bill. I assent to the entailed imperative "Let
me pay it." I draw a check and then *either* (a) find that I
have no money with which to honor the check *or* (b) put
it in my pocket and forget to post it. In this example, I am
supposing that it is not in my power (a) to avoid bankruptcy
or (b) to avoid such lapses of memory as that supposed. To
deny, with such cases in mind, that I can sincerely assent to
a value judgment and yet act contrary to it would be absurd.
Hare maintains (a) that he does not deny this and (b) that it
is precisely what he would have to be denying if the sort of
counterexamples which his critics quote against him served
their purpose.

Hare refers to two such counterexamples commonly used.
One is Medea's case—*video meliora proboque deteriora
sequor;*[26] the other St. Paul's—"The good that I would I do
not; but the evil which I would not, that I do."[27] Both Medea
and St. Paul were patently sincere in their judgments of what
is morally good but lamentably contrary to these in their actions. However, they would only serve as counterexamples
to Hare's prescriptivism, if we wished to say that (a) Medea
and St. Paul failed to act in accordance with their moral
judgments *though able to do so* and (b) were nevertheless
sincere. But no one does wish to say this. It is common
ground between Hare and his critics that (a) Medea and St.
Paul were not merely pretending to be unable to do what was
good; and (b) if they had been, they could properly have been
called insincere. The very common metaphorical interpreta-

[25] *FR*, p. 79.
[26] Ovid, *Metamorph.* vii. 30.
[27] *Romans* 7:19.

tion—divided personality—of conditions such as that of Medea and St. Paul, Hare maintains, witnesses to the truth of his prescriptivism. St. Paul, for instance, speaks as if there were two selves within him, one which gives orders to the other, the latter being too weak to obey. Notice that it is the self which makes moral judgments that gives the orders; but it is the other self, i.e., *not* the one which makes these judgments, which fails to obey them. So it is perfectly consistent with this divided-personality account of St. Paul's condition to say that (a) value judgments entail commands and (b) they are insincere if the one who delivers them does not act upon them.[28] These are the very points which Hare is intent upon making.

(iii) Is there a legitimate use of value judgments in which they do *not* entail imperatives? I have spoken so far as though Hare thought that the *only* meaning which value judgments have is prescriptive, and the time has come to put this right. In *Freedom and Reason* Hare differentiates three kinds of meaning. "An expression which, in a certain context, has descriptive meaning and no other, I call a *descriptive* term, word, or expression, as used in that context; one which has prescriptive meaning (whether or not it also has descriptive meaning) I call a *prescriptive* term; and one which has both kinds of meaning I call an *evaluative* term."[29] This, as Hare notes, is rather different from the terminology of *The Language of Morals*, where he uses "evaluative meaning" for the prescriptive meaning of evaluative expressions.

In what sense do all value judgments have descriptive meaning? We noted above the essentially supervenient character of value words and that this is to be explained, according to Hare, by the fact that they are invariably used in accordance with standards or principles. It follows on this view that when you call anything good, for instance, you are, in effect, saying that it conforms to some standard; and thereby you are describing it for those who know what your standard is. "This is a good book." tells anyone who knows that your standard of goodness in books is that they have funny char-

[28] *FR*, pp. 77–82.
[29] *FR*, pp. 26–27; italics mine.

acters that the characters in this book are, in your opinion, funny. Of course, he needs to know that this is your standard before your remark has any such descriptive meaning for him, since not everyone assesses the goodness of books by that criterion. However, sometimes the standards or principles invoked when a value judgment is expressed are so firmly fixed and well known that one does not need to ask what they are. For instance, if, in academic circles, anyone says that Jones is a good scholar, we can safely assume that they are thereby describing him as one who has read a great deal, who backs up his judgments with relevant facts, who carefully checks references, and so on. Or, to take an example which Hare borrows from Stevenson, if a clergyman says that a girl is a good girl, we can safely assume that she is devout and chaste.[30] True, it is not as safe as it once was to make assumptions of this kind, especially where moral value judgments are concerned; standards are much less fixed than they used to be, even among clergymen. But, with that proviso, there are certainly some value judgments which have a firmly fixed and well-known descriptive meaning.

It is important not to lose sight of the fact that the parallel between the descriptive meaning of value judgments and that of other sorts of utterance is not exact. Compare the descriptive meanings of the expressions "good" and "motor car." If the defining characteristics of a motor car are a, b, and c, then "X is a, b, and c" is equivalent in meaning to "X is a motor car." But if the standard of goodness for some kind of thing is G, and even if this standard has become so fixed that to call anything of that kind good is tantamount to calling it an instance of G, nevertheless a distinction between the meaning of "good" and the criteria for its application can —and must—still be drawn. From the fact that value words have descriptive meaning it does not follow that the naturalists were right after all. The descriptive meaning of value words, as we shall see in a moment, is subject to another kind of meaning, namely prescriptive, as the descriptive meaning of other sorts of expression is not.

[30] See *EL*, p. 85.

(iv) We turn then to the question: in what relationship does the descriptive meaning of evaluative terms stand to their prescriptive meaning? We are concerned here with what Hare calls "primarily evaluative" words. In passing, however, we must note his distinction between "primarily" and "secondarily" evaluative words. "Industrious" is an example of a secondarily evaluative word. It is so called because its descriptive meaning is more firmly attached to it than its prescriptive, according to Hare. By "industrious" we describe certain qualities and express our approval of them. If, through some change of social circumstances, we came to disapprove of these qualities, we could hardly retain the commendatory force of "industrious" while altering its descriptive meaning so that it referred to the qualities which we now call dilatoriness, carelessness, or whatever. Its descriptive meaning is too firmly attached to it for that. With a primarily evaluative word like "good" the case is different. We can, usually at any rate, detach from the word "good" the criteria for its application and substitute others. Here the prescriptive meaning of the word is logically prior to its descriptive. This, as Hare points out, can be seen from the following two considerations.[31] (a) The prescriptive meaning is constant for every class of object of which a value word may be used. This meaning of "good," for example, is identical in "a good book," "a good road," and "a good act." And it is identical whatever may be the standards of goodness invoked; "good" in "a good road" means the same prescriptively, whether the person using that expression judges roads by their surface or the surrounding scenery. Hare says that we learn the prescriptive meaning of "good" in our earliest years and it remains the same; but we have constantly to be learning, or devising, its descriptive meaning. Sometimes we get the latter from others by accepting their standards of goodness; sometimes we make it up for ourselves by creating our own standards. But amid all this change and variation in descriptive meaning, the prescriptive meaning remains constant.

[31] See *FR*, pp. 24, 27, 189; also *LM*, Chap. 7, where Hare uses "evaluative" for "prescriptive."

(b) Changes in a value word's descriptive meaning are effected by using it with its prescriptive meaning. To recall Moore's point against the naturalists, whatever reason is given why something is good (i.e., whatever descriptive meaning the word may have) it is always open to a reformer to propose a new standard of goodness (i.e., a new descriptive meaning). There is no standard, S, such that "Whatever is an instance of S is good" is tautologous. "Is whatever is an instance of S good?" always makes sense. Notice, this is so not only where changes in descriptive meaning are being effected. Prescriptive meaning is *always* logically prior to descriptive. Any standard must (logically) be accepted before it is invoked; and its acceptance is (logically) an instance of the prescriptive use of the value word concerned. If I say that books are good if they have funny characters, it must (logically) be because I have accepted that books with funny characters are good.

(v) Has Hare, by defining value judgments as entailing imperatives, reduced them to the status of mere universal commands? It should be clear by now that he has not. The universal imperative "No smoking," for example, entails "Do not smoke!" just as, according to Hare, the value judgment "You ought not to smoke" does. But these utterances do not amount to the same thing. Hare is perfectly explicit as to why they do not. Value judgments, remember, are supervenient. They are so, as we saw, because it is always legitimate to ask "Why?" when one has been delivered; and because it is never legitimate to deliver a different value-judgment on something which, in the respects indicated by the answer to "Why?" is exactly like the thing already judged. Now, would it not be absurd if some traveler, pointing out to the railroad officials that the carriages to which "No Smoking" signs are attached do not differ in any noticeable respect from those to which they are not, claimed that it was unreasonable therefore to have put these signs on the said carriages? But it would not be in the least absurd if this traveler accused you of being unreasonable when you had said that he *ought* not to smoke in a given compartment and, when he asked you why, been unable to point to anything which made the given compart-

ment different from those in which you would consider him
at liberty to smoke.[32] It might be, of course, that the difference to which you pointed in reply to his question was the
fact that the given carriage had a "No Smoking" sign on the
window; you could say that he ought not to smoke because
of that. But this does not affect the point. The point is that
"No smoking," as a universal command, does not have to
be supervenient, as "You ought not to smoke" does.

Hare says that value judgments are "proper universals"
but universal commands are not. "No smoking" is short for
"Do not ever smoke in *this* compartment" and refers implicitly to an individual. True, "You ought not to smoke in
this compartment" also contains references to individuals
(you and this compartment). But a reason can always be
asked for the value judgment. This reason, as we have seen,
invokes a standard or principle. And, as we shall see in the
next section, Hare believed that where ought judgments, and
in particular moral ones, were concerned this standard or
principle must be completely universal. "Thus," he writes,
"the particular moral judgment 'You ought not to smoke in
this compartment' depends on a proper universal, even though
it is not itself one. But this is not true of the imperative 'Do
not ever smoke in this compartment.' This invokes no more
general principle, it is itself as general as it requires to be,
and this is not general enough to make it a proper universal."[33]

(vi) What account does Hare give of the difference between intrinsic and instrumental goodness, or between the
hypothetical and categorical uses of "ought"? Compare:

	(1) He is a good poisoner. (instrumental)
with:	(2) He is a good man. (instrinsic)
And:	

| | (3) You ought to give a second dose. (said to a would-be poisoner) (hypothetical) |
| with: | (4) You ought to tell the truth. (categorical) |

[32] Cf. *LM*, pp. 175–79.
[33] *LM*, p. 176.

A poisoner is, so to say, *for* poisoning; a good poisoner is therefore one who fulfills this function well. But a man is *not* for anything; his goodness, if he is good, makes him good in himself, not as a means to something beyond himself. Again: one ought to give a second dose (in certain supposed circumstances) *if* one wants to kill one's victim. But one ought to tell the truth *without* condition.

Is there, therefore, some difference in the meanings of "good" in (1) and (2) and of "ought" in (3) and (4)? Hare says not. The primary—or evaluative—meaning of "good" is the same in (1) and (2): in both it commends. The primary meaning of "ought" is the same in (3) and (4): in both it prescribes. The secondary—or descriptive—meaning of "good" in (1) and (2), and of "ought" in (3) and (4) respectively is, of course, different. But this is not relevant to the difference between instrumental and intrinsic uses of "good" or hypothetical and categorical uses of "ought," because descriptive meaning differs *within* each of these uses and not simply between them. The standard applied by "He is a good poisoner" differs from that by "He is a good watchmaker"; the principle invoked by "You ought to give a double dose," from that by "You ought to fasten your safety belt." There is certainly one very important difference between (1) and (2) and between (3) and (4). It has to do with the extent of the class of comparison. As Hare points out, we commend or prescribe "within a class of comparison." (1) commends one man ("he") within the class of poisoners; (3) prescribes one act (giving a double dose) within the class of acts which would-be poisoners as such perform. But notice the *universality* of the class of comparison in (2) and (4). (2) commends one man ("he") as a man; and though we are not all poisoners we are all men. (4) prescribes one act (telling the truth) within the class of actions which we all perform; and, though we do not all poison, we all communicate with others.

The nature of this difference must not be mistaken. Notice that (1), (2), (3), and (4) are all *universalizable*. The difference between (1) or (3) on the one hand, and (2) or (4) on the other, is not a difference in logic. They are all value judgments and share the logical characteristics of value judgments. If we utter any of them, we can legitimately be asked why, and our reason be universalized. If we utter (3), for instance, we are committed thereby to saying that, if we ourselves were would-be poisoners in the given circumstances, we ought to give a double dose. But the point is that we have an option as to whether or not we ever will be in that position. On the other hand, as Hare puts it, "We cannot get out being men."[34] He goes on: ". . . and therefore moral principles, which are principles for the conduct of men as men—and not as poisoners or architects or batsmen—cannot be accepted without having a potential bearing upon the way that we conduct ourselves. If I say to a certain person 'You ought to tell the truth,' I signify my acceptance of a principle to tell the truth in the sort of circumstances in which he is; and *I may find myself placed unavoidably in similar circumstances.* But I can always choose whether or not to take up poisoning or cricketing as a profession. This is bound to make the *spirit* in which we consider moral questions very different from that in which we consider how we ought to poison Jones, or build him a house; but the logic of the word 'ought' is not markedly different in the two cases."[35]

(vii) Does Hare's prescriptivist theory apply to all value-words? There are, of course, differences in meaning between value words. "Right" does not mean, in ordinary use, the same as "good," nor either the same as "ought." A right act might not be good, at any rate if "right" is defined as "in accordance with such-and-such a rule or principle" and "good" as "done from such-and-such a motive"; and these words are in fact frequently so defined in ordinary use. For example, a schoolmaster might inflict statutory punishment on a pupil and there be no doubt that his act was morally right, but if he derives pleasure from it, it would not be morally good. Again, a good act may not be right; a philanthropist's act, for instance, may well be good in the sense of being done from the motive of kindness, but wrong in the sense that it is the kind of thing which encourages shiftless-

[34] *LM*, pp. 142, 162.
[35] *LM*, p. 162.

ness. "Ought" is distinct from both "right" and "good." The philanthropist's act, for all its goodness, and the schoolmaster's, for all its rightness, were not, in either case, what they ought to have done. However, Hare concentrates on "ought." Much of his moral philosophy, as readers will see in what follows, is derived from the analysis of ought judgments. So we have to ask whether his conclusions with regard to "ought" apply equally to value-judgments in terms of "right" or "good." In the concluding chapter of *The Language of Morals,* Hare argues that "artificial" words *right* and *good* (italicized to indicate their artificial character) can be invented, which are definable in terms of "ought," as that word is used in natural language; and that so defined, these artificial words will do *most* of the jobs done by "right" and "good" respectively in natural language. Undoubtedly, there are many instances in which judgments in terms of "right" and "good," as naturally used, can be translated without loss of meaning into ought judgments. "It is right (or not right) to do X" means the same as "one ought (or ought not) to do X"; and "The right X" can be rendered "The X which ought to be chosen." Again, "A is a better X that B," Hare claims, means the same as "If one is choosing an X, then, if one chooses B, one ought to choose A." These judgments in terms of "right" or "better than" guide choices in the same way as ought judgments. Hare's argument, that this sort of translation can be made from "right" and (at least in the comparative degree) "good" into "ought," is complicated and to some degree tentative. If it fails, then presumably Hare will have to say that his conclusions concerning the logical character of ought judgments apply to judgments in terms of "right" and "good" *only in so far as the latter* (i.e., judgments in terms of "right" and "good") can be translated into terms of the former (i.e., ought judgments). Although in his later writings Hare has been interested almost exclusively in "ought," I think that he takes his prescriptivist account of value judgments to apply to every such judgment, whether in terms of "ought," "right," or "good." I do not say here that he is not entitled to do so; only that, even if he were not, that would not necessarily diminish the illumination which his theory might cast over part of the field. If Hare is correct in his analysis of "ought," then he is correct also about many uses of "right" and "good."

So much, then, for the prescriptivity of value judgments, as Hare conceived of it. I have once or twice already used the words "universalizable" or "universalizability." The latter is the second of those "three most important truths about moral judgments" which Hare lists. We must turn now to consider it more carefully.

(II) UNIVERSALIZABILITY

How and Why Are Value Judgments Universalizable?

What Hare meant by universalizability is grounded fundamentally in the very notion of meaning itself. For language to be meaningful it must be used in accordance with rules. And if its use is to be intelligible, i.e., if language is not to lose whatever meaning it has, then that use must be consistent. Of course, this is not to deny that meanings may change, or that the same piece of language may have a number of different meanings, or that the rules for the use of language may be very complex. Allowing for all such qualifications, however, the fact remains that if there were no meaning-rules, there would be no meaning; and if there were no meaning, there would be no language. Words with descriptive meaning are universalizable in the sense that, if they refer to one thing, then they refer to everything else which is like it in the respects specified by their descriptive meaning-rule.

However, what Hare means by the universalizability of value judgments goes beyond that. To make clear what he does mean, he compares and contrasts evaluative and descriptive terms with regard to their universalizability. True, he says, ". . . the feature of value-judgments which I call universalisability is simply that which they share with descriptive judgments; namely the fact that they both carry descriptive meaning."[36] But he soon makes it clear that there are differences as well as similarities between the two sorts of

[36] *FR*, p. 15.

judgment with regard to their universalizability. As far as I understand him, I will try to say what Hare thinks these differences and similarities are.

First the similarities. Hare writes, "If I call a thing red, I am committed to calling anything else like it red. And if I call a thing a good X, I am committed to calling any X like it good."[37] I may define a descriptive expression ostensively or verbally. If, for example, I say "X is red" and, when asked what "red" means, define it by pointing to a patch of color (C), then I must also call anything else red which resembles C as closely as X does. Or again if I say "X is a postbox," then, whatever the verbal definition (V) of "postbox" might be, I am committed to calling anything else which conforms to V a postbox as well. Evaluative language is similar in that, if you call anything, for example, good, then you must so speak of anything else which is identical with it in those respects on account of which you call it good. Universalizability is thus a common characteristic of evaluative and descriptive language.

But it is when you ask what precisely we are doing if, for example, we call something good, as contrasted with what we are doing if we call something red or a postbox, that the differences begin to appear. Immediately after the remark quoted a moment ago, Hare adds, "But whereas the reason in the former case is that I must be using the word 'red' in accordance with some *meaning*-rule, the reason in the latter case is much more complicated."[38] How and why? Succinctly, the answer to both questions, which Hare gives, is: in the case of evaluative language "the descriptive meaning-rule becomes more than a mere meaning-rule."[39] How is the universalizability of value judgments more complicated than that of descriptive ones? By the fact that questions of value cannot—to recall Moore's open-question argument and Hare's restatement of it—be settled merely by reference to the meanings of the words used. And why not? Because a value judg-

[37] *Ibid.*
[38] *FR*, pp. 15–16.
[39] *FR*, p. 23.

ment always applies, or invokes, something more than a meaning-rule, namely a synthetic standard or principle.

Contrast these two cases. (i) An American says, "These are suspenders." "Oh no," says an Englishman, "they're braces." (ii) A Powellite says, "We ought to encourage immigrants to go back where they came from" and a left-wing socialist replies, "Oh no, we ought not." In the former case the disagreement is entirely verbal. It can be settled simply by pointing out that Americans use the word "suspenders" to mean what the English mean, not by that word, but by "braces." No sane person will then ask "Who is right?" They are both right. But would anyone suggest that the Powellite and the socialist are both right? Following Hare, we may say that in case (i) an analytic point is at issue, in case (ii), a synthetic one. The *ground* of the universalizability of "These are suspenders" is a meaning-rule; that of "We ought to encourage immigrants to go back where they came from," a principle of action. It doubtless makes sense to say that a Powellite and a socialist can agree to differ about this point at issue between them. But what would that mean? It might mean that they agree to suspend further argument until certain questions of fact (e.g., facts about the effect on a locality of a large influx of immigrants) have been settled; or perhaps that they agree not to badger one another on the point but to talk about something else; or whatever. But one thing which "agree to differ" could not mean in such a case is the kind of thing that the phrase would mean if anyone said that Americans and Englishmen "agree to differ" about the use of the word "suspenders." If *per impossible* Enoch Powell and Lord Constantine announced that they had agreed to differ as to what ought to be done about immigration, then, whatever they might mean, they could not conceivably mean simply that they had recognized the fact that they subscribed to different meaning-rules for the word "ought." Their disagreement is not about that; it is about standards or principles for the treatment of human beings in situations like that of immigrants. They could therefore not, in any sense, resolve it simply by an agreement as to meaning-rules.

What is the connection between the supervenience of value judgments, which was noted in the last section, and their universalizability? We took Hare, it will be remembered, to be saying that value judgments are supervenient in the sense that when one has been delivered, e.g., "X is good," it is: (a) always logically legitimate to ask why X is good; and (b) never logically legitimate, when the answer is given, to deny that anything else like X in the relevant respects is also good. In other words, we can always ask a reason for a value judgment and then always universalize that reason. But it may now be objected that a rational being, as such, will give reasons for many things which he says besides value judgments, and that reasons, by their very nature, are universalizable, whether given for value judgments or for anything else. If you said to me "Go to the station" and I asked "Why?" I should not expect the reply "Just do." Even if that were your reply, I should assume that you had a reason for the command which, for some other reason, you were concealing from me. Suppose your reply was, "Then you can collect my luggage." Since this was your reason for sending me to the station on the present occasion, I should be entitled to assume that *ceteris paribus,* on any other occasion, if you wanted your luggage from the station and I could collect it, you would instruct me to do so.[40] Now, it may seem to follow from all this that, given Hare's account of the matter, (a) it is not only value judgments which are supervenient, and (b) the universalizability of value judgments amounts to no more than their supervenience. But these conclusions would be mistaken.

[40] The distinction between ought judgments and singular imperatives is not, therefore, that the former require reasons while the latter do not. However, there are *some* singular imperatives which, unlike ought sentences and other singular imperatives, do not require reasons, e.g., orders in the Forces. D. H. Monro, noting this in *Empiricism and Ethics* (Cambridge, 1967), p. 173, writes: "In the order-giving situation it is the man who gives the order who takes the responsibility for the action. That is why the reason for the action need not concern the agent. But if you accept advice, the responsibility for the action is still yours, and the principle behind it does concern you. To accept advice, then, is to accept the principle behind the advice; but to carry out an order is not *necessarily* to accept the principle behind it."

(a) According to Hare, value judgments alone are supervenient. What he meant by supervenience has, perhaps, been slightly misrepresented in my account of it this far. The point which he notes about, e.g., "X is good," is not simply that one may ask a reason why and universalize the answer. It is rather that one can always ask "What is good about it?" and that the answer can *never* be "Just its goodness." This is where "X is good" differs from e.g., "X is yellow." To "What is yellow about it?" the answer may, though it need not, be "Just its yellowness." Goodness (and, equally, rightness or oughtness) is always necessarily supervenient upon other characteristics, as yellowness (or any other non-evaluative characteristic) is not.

(b) Universalizability is a characteristic distinct from supervenience. We shall see in the next subsection that Hare recognized only a certain type of reason as valid for a moral judgment and, eventually, for any ought judgment. This was a reason which did not contain any reference to particular individuals—or, as we shall see that he calls it, a "U-type" reason. If someone says, "The Chancellor's action was right because it will help Britain's balance of payments," the rightness here is supervenient. But the judgment is not, as it stands, a moral one. And why? Because the reason given is not, in the required sense, universalizable. It refers to a particular individual country, "Britain." The speaker gives a reason; if he is a rational being, he will *ceteris paribus* consistently commend as right any action in other situations which would help Britain's balance of payments; but his judgment could, nevertheless, be one of expediency rather than of moral rightness. Notice that there is a difference between supervenience and universalizability. The necessary and sufficient conditions of supervenience are here fulfilled; but not those of universalizability. For these latter to be fulfilled, the speaker would have to agree that for the Chancellor of another country, or anyone similarly placed, to act in like manner to help the balance of payments of that *other* country, when it was situated as Britain is, would also be right. This the speaker may not be willing to admit. In which case it could not, according to Hare, be moral rightness of which he was speaking. Universalizability is more than supervenience, though Hare does not bring this out.

Hare notes a difference between value judgments in terms of "ought" or "right" and those in terms of "good." Because "good" has a comparative "better than" whereas "ought" and "right" have none, there is a difference in the way in which they are universalizable. Hare says, ". . . whereas the judgment that I ought in a certain situation *to do* a certain thing commits me to the view that no similar person in a precisely similar situation ought to *fail to do* the same thing, this is not the case with a judgment framed in terms of 'good.' "[41] To say, for example, that we ought to encourage immigrants to return to their countries of origin is to say that no one, placed as we are, ought to fail to encourage them to do so. But to say that Enoch Powell is a good politician is to imply only that, if anyone acted on the political scene as he does, that man would be a good politician also. It is not to say that anyone who fails to act on that scene as he does must be a bad politician. One could say that both Mr. Powell and Lord Constantine are good politicians.[42] In the light of this distinction—between "ought" and "right" on the one hand and "good" on the other—Hare acknowledges the persuasiveness of Professor P. F. Strawson's view that morality should be divided into two parts: one aimed at producing uniformity of practice (what ought to be done), the other, diversity of kinds of life (what is good).[43]

What Makes a Value Judgment Moral?

The time has now come to face the question: how, if at all in Hare's opinion, do moral value judgments differ from those of other kinds? In his paper "Universalizability,"[44] he represents the difference as entirely a matter of differing degrees of universality in the reasons given for moral judg-

[41] *FR*, p. 153; italics mine.
[42] Cf. *FR*, pp. 153–54.
[43] *FR*, pp. 151–55; cf. P. F. Strawson, "Social Morality and Individual Ideal," *P* XXXVI (1961).
[44] *PAS* LV (1954–55).

ments, and in those given for value judgments of other kinds, respectively. Compare the following:

(a) "The Chancellor's squeeze was right."
"Why?"
"It resulted in an improvement in Britain's balance of payments."

Following Professor E. A. Gellner,[45] Hare calls this an E-type valuation.

(b) "You ought to write to him."
"Why?"
"You promised to do so."

Following Gellner, Hare calls this a U-type valuation.

Implicit in each reason is a standard or principle: "Whatever results in an improvement of Britain's balance of payments is right" and "One ought always to keep one's promises," respectively. Hare recognizes that people might give the reason in (a) who only consider it a reason for the rightness of the Chancellor's squeeze because it refers to Britain's balance of payments; they would not necessarily consider the Chancellor of another country right to institute a squeeze if by so doing he improved that country's balance of payments. By contrast, the reason in (b) does not contain any reference to a particular individual and so could not be regarded in a similar light. This is the difference between E-type and U-type valuations: it lies in the degree of universality possessed by the reasons given for them. The thesis which Hare is arguing in his paper is that moral judgments are U-type valuations. He points out that he cannot be accused of making this analytic in virtue of the meaning of the word "reason," for he is ready to admit that reasons such as that given in (a) are reasons. Nevertheless, he insists that his thesis is analytic. It is true by definition of the word "moral."[46] Hare's point, it should be noted, is a logical one. It is true, as he recognizes,

[45] See "Ethics and Logic," *ibid.*
[46] Hare, *op. cit.*, p. 302.

that any reason which is given for A to do X is, in some
sense, universalizable. If it is a reason for A to do X, it is a
reason for anyone like A in the relevant respects to do
something like X in similar circumstances. But notice carefully what this means. It does not mean that, if X's being,
for example, in Britain's interest is a reason for Britain's Chancellor to do X, then Y's being in some other country's interest is a reason for that country's Chancellor to do Y. It
simply means that, if X's being in Britain's interest is a reason
for Britain's Chancellor to do it, it is a reason for anyone
else in his position to do it. That is, anyone who is Britain's
Chancellor. The reference to an individual in the reason can
be as particular as you like and the reason still be universalizable in this sense. To distinguish between two things on
the basis of a particular relational characteristic—e.g., being
in the interest of one's country—is not to be irrational. That is
to say, it is a distinction to which one can consistently adhere
in thought and practice. But it is certainly to be partial, to be
biased in a certain direction. Inconsistency is a logical fault;
partiality, a moral defect. Hare has been accused of confusing the two in his account of universalizability. In saying that
it is a logical characteristic of moral judgments that U-type
reasons are required for them, it is contended, Hare has smug-
gled in his own moral commitment to the principle of impartiality. I think this contention misses Hare's point. I take
the latter to be that in any judgment, which according to the
normal use of "moral" we should call a *moral* judgment,
there will be some recognition of the principle of impartiality.
That is a logical point pure and simple. It is about the defining characteristics of morality.

   In a footnote to his article,[47] Hare raises, only to dismiss
as not his present concern, the question whether or not E-type
valuations can properly be called valuations. By the time he
wrote *Freedom and Reason* (1963), he appears to have decided that all ought judgments, not simply moral ones, are
U-type valuations. He writes: "The word 'moral' plays here a
far smaller role than I was at one time tempted to assign to

[47] P. 295, note 2.

it. It is the logic of the word 'ought' in its typical uses that requires universalisability, not that of the word 'moral'; the word 'moral' needs to be brought in only in order to identify one class of the typical uses, and that with which as moral philosophers we are most concerned."[48] I have found some difficulty in harmonizing Hare's views at this point. In the words just quoted, he is claiming universalizability for *all* ought judgments. At the end of the last section, I noted his view that what characterizes moral judgments, and indeed all ought judgments, as distinct from all other value judgments, is that the former are necessarily universalizable (that U-type reasons are required for them) and not merely supervenient. In this respect, they differ, for instance, from a value judgment such as "The Chancellor's action is right because it will help Britain's balance of payments." But at the end of the section on *Prescriptivity*, we noted Hare's contention that his prescriptivism holds for *all* value judgments because those in terms of "right" and "good" can be translated into judgments in terms of "ought." So, presumably, we could rewrite the above judgment ("The Chancellor's action is *right* because it will help Britain's balance of payments") thus: "The Chancellor is doing what he *ought* to do because his action will help Britain's balance of payments."

But then: (a) If Hare thinks that these two sentences *are* equivalent in meaning, he is landed with an ought judgment which is not, in the required sense, universalizable (i.e., not U-type). (b) If he thinks that the two sentences are not equivalent in meaning, he is landed with an evaluative use of "right" which cannot be translated into terms of "ought," and so which may fall outside the prescriptivist theory of value judgments which Hare derives from his analysis of ought judgments. It does seem that Hare must forego either (a) the view that all ought judgments, not just moral ones, are universalizable, or (b) the view that all evaluations in terms of "right" could conceivably be translated into terms of "ought" without loss or change of meaning.

What then constitutes a typically *moral* piece of thinking? Hare says that there are four "necessary ingredients" of moral

[48] *FR*, p. 37.

argument, "four factors . . . whose combination governs a man's moral opinion on a given matter."[49] They do not appear to be exactly necessary conditions of moral reasoning, for Hare is able to conceive of an argument's being moral where one of them is unfulfilled: he says that ". . . the absence of even one of these ingredients may render the rest ineffective."[50] Note: "may," not "will." However, it is clear that he thinks all four ingredients will normally be present in any example of moral reasoning. The four are: (i) a logical framework provided by prescriptivity and universalizability; (ii) an appeal to fact; (iii) an appeal to inclination or interest; (iv) an appeal to imagination. The first factor—the logical framework—is said to be common to all ought judgments. I will deal briefly with the other three in turn.

(i) Appeal to Fact

In moral reasoning there is invariably some appeal to the facts of the case. Take this example:

> The sale of pornographic literature ought to be prohibited. Why?
> Because the sale of such literature leads to an increase of sex crimes.

The reason given here is a statement of fact which may be true or false. The first thing to notice is that this putative fact is stated only because it instantiates a universal principle. The above piece of moral reasoning, set out in the form of a syllogism, would read:

> A: Whatever literature leads to an increase in sex crimes ought not to be sold.
> B: Pornographic literature leads to an increase in sex crimes.
> C: Therefore pornographic literature ought not to be sold.

A, the major premises, is a universal ought principle; B, the minor premises, is a statement of fact; C, a particular ought

[49] FR, pp. 92, 97.
[50] FR, p. 94.

judgment, is the conclusion. Now, there are, after all, an indefinite number of factual statements which could be made about pornographic literature, e.g., who writes, prints, sells, reads it, how many such works exist, what prices are charged for them, etc. When, in the above argument, one putative fact—that it leads to an increase in sex crime—was selected as a reason for condemning it, this was because the speaker who selected that fact subscribed to a principle which made it, rather than any of the other facts about pornographic literature, relevant. If those with whom he is arguing do not subscribe to the same principle, they will of course reject his reason out of hand. But if they do subscribe to it then they might call in question the truth of the reason which he has given. *Does* pornographic literature in fact lead to an increase in sex crime? That is certainly debatable. In June 1967 the Danish Parliament largely repealed the law under which purveyors of pornographic literature were liable to prosecution. If newspaper reports[51] can be believed, the incidence of sex crime in Copenhagen fell last year (1968) by 25 per cent. This fact, if it is a fact, certainly impugns the reason given for the judgment that the sale of pornographic literature ought to be prohibited.

Appeal to fact is undoubtedly a feature of moral reasoning, but it is not of course the *differentia* of that kind of argument. To the reason given in such an example as:

This wine is good.
Why?
It has an unusual aftertaste.

Everything which was said of the reason in the pornographic literature example could *mutatis mutandis* be applied. The appeal to fact in the two cases is of exactly the same kind.

(ii) *Appeal to Inclination and Interest*

To what extent do moral valuations involve an *appeal to inclination or interest?* By "inclination or interest" is meant

[51] E.g., B. Norman, "The Total Truth about Sex," *Daily Mail,* Nov. 27, 1968.

here any wants or desires which those involved have, or may
have,[52] and feel it important to gratify. It is true that if we
had none, if it made no difference to us what happened, we
should have no use for moral argument.[53] The universalizability of value judgments, according to Hare, has two logical
consequences so far as inclinations or interests are concerned.[54] First, we can—and in moral argument frequently
do—universalize a prescription in order to test it against the
inclinations of those with whom we are arguing. Hare uses
the illustration of a man who is owed money by another man
(call the latter X). If the first man says that he ought to
prosecute X because X owes him money, he implies, this
judgment being universalizable, that if he owed money himself, he ought to be dealt with similarly. But this would be
against his inclination; he would not want to be prosecuted.[55]
So from appeal to inclination, within the logical framework
of universalizability, it seems to follow that the creditor in
such a case ought not to prosecute. Universalizability, together with appeal to inclination, is the logical basis of "golden
rule" morality.[56] Hare uses another illustration to bring out
the second logical consequence of universalizability in this
connection. A judge has to deal with a criminal. What the
judge does he will, in effect, do to many people; not just to
the criminal but also to those whom the latter may rob, etc.[57]
In such a case, Hare says, it follows from the universalizability
of ought judgments that "everyone is entitled to equal consideration"; "the principle often accepted by utilitarians,
'Everybody to count for one, nobody for more than one' can
. . . be justified by the appeal to the demand for universal-

[52] Inclination and interest are not identical. A subject may have interests but no inclinations. In an unpublished paper on abortion, Hare
notes this distinction. He says that, when deciding what ought to be
done about a fetus and its mother, one matter which may have to be
taken into consideration is the interests of the children yet unborn (e.g.,
the probability of their not existing if this present pregnancy is not
terminated). The unborn, however, cannot have inclinations.

[53] *FR*, pp. 92–93.
[54] Cf. *FR*, p. 195.
[55] *FR*, pp. 90–91.
[56] *FR*, p. 108.
[57] *FR*, pp. 115–17.

isability. . . ."[58] From the appeal to inclination, within the framework or universalizability, it follows that the judge in such a case ought to impose a penalty on the criminal. Universalizability together with appeal to inclination, is the logical basis of utilitarian morality.[59]

I have been trying to show how Hare thought that appeal to inclination or interest gives a value judgment a moral character. It must be noted, however, that he recognized the possibility of a person rejecting any such appeal and still insisting with justification that his reasoning is moral. Such a person may, so to speak, refuse to let certain of his *own* inclinations count; he may be what Hare calls a *fanatic*. Take the case of a Nazi who thinks that Jews ought to be exterminated. Suppose we trick this Nazi into believing that his own parents were in fact Jews. Then we show him that it was just a trick. Hare thinks it not at all likely that, while this Nazi believes himself of Jewish birth, he will say, "All right. Let me and my family be exterminated"; and that it is very likely, once the Nazi has thus faced the question "What ought to be done with me if I were a Jew?" he will no longer think that Jews ought to be exterminated. Perhaps Hare is right on both counts. But nevertheless he sees that it *is logically possible* for the Nazi to accept the implication, "Let me be exterminated if I am a Jew," contrary as that may be to his inclination to go on living, and *still* persist in his view that Jews ought to be exterminated. If he does so, his view will be a *moral* view.[60]

Again, a man may refuse to let the inclinations of *others* count. He may be concerned with what Hare calls an *ideal*, rather than anyone's inclination. Hare's example is a person who thinks it wrong for girls to undress themselves in strip clubs for the pleasure of middle-aged men. He remarks: ". . . those who call such exhibitions immoral do not do so because of their effect on other people's interests; for, since

[58] *FR*, p. 118.
[59] *FR*, p. 123.
[60] *FR*, pp. 171–72. G. J. Warnock in *Contemporary Moral Philosophy* (1967), p. 59, says that "moral" would not be applicable in such cases. Cf. below, pp. 227–30.

everybody gets what he or she wants, nobody's interests are harmed. They are likely, rather, to use such words as 'degrading.' This gives us a clue to the sort of moral question with which we are dealing. It is a question not of interests but of *ideals*. Such conduct offends against an ideal of human excellence held by many people; that is why they condemn it."[61] We referred above[62] to the view of Strawson, and Hare, that morality should perhaps be divided into two parts, one aiming at uniformity of practice (the realm of "ought" and "right"), the other at diversity of ideal (the realm of "good"); but notice that our anti-strip-club "idealist" would not simply say that strip clubs are not good but that they ought to be closed. And he would mean that no one who has the opportunity ought to fail to close them. He would regard the issue as a moral one in that sense and it is surely impossible to claim that he would be opting out of the ordinary use of the word "ought" in its moral sense. *Ex hypothesi* he firmly refuses to take the interests of others into account; but he does not thereby render his judgment nonmoral.[63]

(iii) Appeal to Imagination

In some of the above examples—those of the creditor, the judge, the fanatical Nazi—an effort had to be made by the person judging morally to put himself in the place of someone else. An *appeal to imagination* was involved. Such an appeal is the third of Hare's necessary ingredients of moral argument.

At this point Hare draws a parallel between his account of moral thinking and the hypothetico-deductive account of scientific thinking. Both reveal the exploratory character of the thinking with which they are concerned. According to the hypothetico-deductive theory, of which Professor K. R. Popper is the foremost exponent, the logic of scientific discovery is as follows. From a hypothesis, together with certain initial conditions, an empirically testable predication is deduced and if this prediction is fulfilled, the original hypothesis

[61] *FR*, p. 147.
[62] P. 184.
[63] Warnock, *op. cit.*, would not agree here either.

is, to that extent, corroborated.[64] To take a very familiar example, the logic of the discovery of the planet Neptune was as follows: (i) hypothesis: the theory of gravitation; (ii) initial conditions: the orbit of the planet Uranus, which could not be accounted for by this theory, given simply the gravitational pull of the hitherto observed planets; (iii) empirically testable prediction deduced: if a telescope of sufficient strength is used, it will be seen that there is a planet of the size and orbit of Neptune exerting a gravitational pull on Uranus. Powerful telescopes were used and, at the appropriate time, the planet we now call Neptune was observed. Hare's claim is that the logic of moral discovery follows a similar pattern. For example:

> *"Hypothesis"*: All debtors ought to be prosecuted.
> *"Initial conditions"*: I am a debtor.
> *"Prediction"*: I ought to be prosecuted.

The creditor in our example rejected this "prediction" and so he rejected the "hypothesis" also—i.e., he rejected the reason "Because he is a debtor" which he had originally given for "He ought to be prosecuted."

There is, of course, an important difference between scientific and moral reasoning as thus conceived. The initial conditions in the scientific example (i.e., the movement of Uranus) are matter of *fact*. Those in the moral example (the thought of himself as a debtor) are matter of *supposition* only. This is where the appeal to imagination comes into moral argument and this is the sense in which Hare speaks of moral thinking as exploratory.[65] He writes: "Just as science, seriously pursued, is the search for hypotheses and the testing of them by the attempt to falsify their particular consequences, so morals, as a serious endeavour, consists in the search for principles and the testing of them against particular cases. Any rational activity has its discipline, and this is the discipline of moral thought: to test the moral principles that suggest themselves

[64] K. R. Popper, *The Logic of Scientific Discovery* (1959), Chap. X.
[65] *FR*, p. 88.

to us by following out their consequences and *seeing whether we can accept them.*⁶⁶ The sphere within which the exploration goes on is the imagination. The reasons given for moral judgments are universalized in the imagination and accepted or rejected there.

Two comments are called for on the phrase "seeing whether we can accept them." (i) The fact that the exploration is conducted in the realm of supposition, not of fact, does not destroy the analogy with scientific reasoning. Hare writes:

> If we enter imaginatively into a hypothetical situation, and think about it *as if* it were going really to happen to us, we logically cannot have desires about it which are different from those which we would have if it *were* going to be real. This is because, whenever we desire anything, we desire it because of something about it; and, since being hypothetical and being actual are not, in the required sense, "things about" objects or events (a hypothetical toothache, exactly like this actual one, *would* hurt as much as this actual one *does* hurt), it is impossible for there to be anything about the hypothetical similar situation which makes us desire something different concerning it. A hypothetical similar situation *is* similar.⁶⁷

(ii) However, it is important to recognize that the "can" in "seeing whether we can accept them" is *not* logical. On his theme of moral argument as a kind of exploration, Hare says:

> We are to go about looking for moral judgments which we can both accept for our own conduct and universalise to cover the conduct of other actual or hypothetical people. What prevents us from accepting certain moral judgments which are perfectly formulable in the language is not logic alone, but the fact that they have certain logical consequences which we cannot accept—namely certain singular prescriptions to other people in hypothetical situations. And *the "cannot" here is not a logical "cannot."* It would not be self-contradictory to accept these prescriptions; but all the same we cannot accept them except on one condition which

⁶⁶ *FR*, p. 92; italics mine.
⁶⁷ *FR*, p. 197.

is most unlikely to be fulfilled—namely that we should become what I have called "fanatics."[68]

The "other people in hypothetical situations" here may of course include the person who delivers the judgment himself; the creditor, the judge, and the Nazi, in Hare's examples, all put themselves in the position of someone else to see if they could accept the singular prescriptions, "Let me be prosecuted," "Let me be robbed," "Let me be exterminated," respectively, when they did so. But the important point is that the discovery which the moral explorer has to make is not, in the last analysis, concerned with what is or is not logically possible. It is simply whether or not he can stomach what his moral judgments, when universalized, require him to stomach. "Our argument [*sc.* against 'fanatics' and 'idealists'] . . . will rest, not upon logic by itself—though without logic [*sc.* i.e., universalizability and prescriptivity] we should never have got to this point—but upon the fortunate contingent fact that people who would take this logically possible view [i.e., of the fanatic or idealist], after they had really imagined themselves in the other man's position, are extremely rare."[69]

(III) LOGICAL RELATIONS

The third of the "three most important truths" about moral judgments which Hare enumerated was that there can be rational procedure in moral thinking because logical relations between prescriptive judgments are possible. We have already remarked that it was the conviction that this "truth" needed safeguarding which first brought him into the arena of moral philosophy.[70]

In an article called "Imperative Sentences" (*Mind,* 1949), Hare sets out to refute a view which he attributes to most logicians, namely that the proper subject matter of deductive logic is, exclusively, indicative sentences (i.e., sentences which tell us that something is, or is not, the case). He argues that exactly the same logical relations hold between imperative

---

[68] *FR,* p. 193. (italics mine)
[69] *FR,* p. 172.
[70] Above, p. 157.

sentences (i.e., sentences which tell us to make, or not to make, something the case) as hold between indicative ones. He regards all moral reasoning as deductive. Imperatives certainly seem able to entail and to contradict one another, just like indicatives. The imperative "All vehicles turn left" entails, in the appropriate circumstances, the imperative "This vehicle turn left" just as surely as "All vehicles will turn left" entails "This vehicle will turn left." And the imperative "Halt" contradicts the imperative "Proceed with caution" just as surely as "You will halt" contradicts "You will proceed with caution."[71] In "Imperative Sentences," Hare was content to claim simply that imperative sentences may be the subject matter of deductive reasoning and, when they are, can have the same logical relations with one another as indicative sentences. In *The Language of Morals,* he goes further and claims that imperative conclusions may follow from premises, one of which is imperative and the other indicative. I shall return to this "mixed" or "practical" syllogism shortly, but first it is important to notice: (i) how Hare conceives of logical relations in general; and (ii) why it seemed to him to follow from this conception of them that they can subsist between imperative sentences, and between an imperative conclusion and premises respectively indicative and imperative in the mixed syllogism.

How does Hare conceive of logical relations? He holds that "all deductive inference is analytic in character."[72] That is to say, it depends solely upon the meanings of the words being used, and particularly that of the logical words such as the sign of negation, "not," the connectives, "if," "and," "or," and the quantifiers, "all" and "some." Failure to recognize an entailment or a contradiction is failure to understand the meanings of the words, particularly the logical ones, being used. "Thus, if someone professed to admit that all men were mortal and that Socrates was a man, but refused to admit that Socrates was mortal, the correct thing to do would be not, as

---

[71] See "Imperative sentences," *M* LVIII (1949), 34.
[72] *LM,* p. 32.

has sometimes been suggested, to accuse him of some kind of logical purblindness, but to say 'You evidently don't know the meaning of the word "all"; for if you did you would *eo ipso* know how to make inferences of this sort.' "[73]

Why does it follow from this that logical relations may hold between imperatives as well as indicatives? In brief, Hare's answer in *The Language of Morals* is: because the logical words "are best treated as part of the phrastics of sentences" and "this means that they are common ground between indicatives and imperatives."[74] We need to understand what "phrastics" are and why they are said to be common ground between indicatives and imperatives.

Hare compared the following two sentences:

(1) Mary, please show Mrs. Prendergast her room.

(2) Mary will show you your room, Mrs. Prendergast.

Common to both, he argues, is a description of a series of events, namely:

(3) Showing of her room to Mrs. Prendergast by Mary at time *t*.

Sentence (1) is logically equivalent to (3) plus:

(4) please.

Sentence (2) is logically equivalent to (3) plus:

(5) yes.

So (1) may be rewritten:

Showing of her room to Mrs. Prendergast by Mary at time *t,* please.

And (2) may be rewritten:

Showing of her room to Mrs. Prendergast by Mary at time *t,* yes.

In "Imperative Sentences," Hare calls (3) the common "descriptor," and (4) and (5) the respectively imperative and indicative "dictors" of (1) and (2). In *The Language of Morals,* he revised his terminology, substituting for "descriptor," the expression *phrastic* (from a Greek word meaning "to point out or indicate"); and for "dictor," the expression *neustic* (from a Greek word meaning "to nod assent").[75]

[73] *LM,* p. 33.
[74] *LM,* p. 21.
[75] *LM,* p. 18.

Sentence (1) above is in the imperative mood; sentence
(2), in the indicative. Their moods are shown by differing
neustics: "please" for the imperative, "yes" for the indicative.
Anyone who actually uses or asserts a sentence, as distinct
from merely mentioning or quoting it, so to speak, "nods" the
sentence. Hare thus compares his neustic to the assertion
symbol in the logical systems of Frege and of Russell and
Whitehead. According to Hare,[76] affirming a statement is
different from affirming a command. (It strains the ordinary
use of "affirm" a little to speak of affirming commands but
Hare recognizes this.) One way of seeing the difference which
he has in mind is to ask what is understood where the respective meanings of an indicative and imperative are com-
municated. To understand an indicative sentence is to understand that assent to it consists in thinking or believing that
something is, or is not, the case. Understanding an imperative
sentence is understanding that assent to it consists in having a
disposition to do, or refrain from doing, something. The rules
and conventions of our language, in respect of the expression
of mood, implicitly constitute this difference of meaning between indicatives and imperatives. It is our reliance upon
these conventions to which Hare is referring when he speaks
of neustics. All sentences have a neustic, which is here conceived as the sign both of assertion *and* of mood.[77]

It is, however, according to the Hare of *The Language of
Morals,* in the other particle, the phrastic, that all the logical
words, which determine any piece of deduction, are to be
found. To take the word "not" as an example, if, instead of
telling somebody to make something the case (imperative)
or telling them that something is the case (indicative), we
wished to tell them *not* to make it the case or that it is *not*
the case, we should do this, not by any change in the mood
of the sentence, for that would remain the same, but in that
part of the sentence which does not indicate mood. In terms
of the above example, we should have to say:

No showing of her room to Mrs. Prendergast by Mary at
time *t*.

[76] *Ibid.*
[77] But cf. below, pp. 232.

and then add either "please" to make an imperative, or "yes" to make an indicative. But we have made a negation irrespective of which we add; and indeed of whether or not we add either. The phrastic is common ground to indicatives and imperatives.

"All vehicles turn left" entails "This vehicle turn left" just as surely as "All vehicles will turn left" entails "This vehicle will turn left" because the deduction is the same in both cases: from the phrastic, "Turning left by all vehicles" to the phrastic, "Turning left by this vehicle." Again, "Halt" contradicts "Proceed" as surely as "You will halt" contradicts "You will proceed" because the contradiction is the same in both cases: between the phrastics "Halting by you" and "Proceeding by you." Hare remarks:

> If we had to find out whether someone knew the meaning of the word "all" in "Take all the boxes to the station," we should have to find out whether he realized that a person who assented to this command, and also to the statement "This is one of the boxes" and yet refused to assent to the command "Take this to the station" could only do so if he had misunderstood one of these three sentences. If this sort of test were inapplicable, the word "all" (in imperatives as in indicatives) would be entirely meaningless. We may therefore say that the existence in our language of universal sentences in the imperative mood is in itself sufficient proof that our language admits of entailments of which at least one term is a command.[78]

He goes on to suggest that, since logical words appear in the phrastics, it should be possible "to reconstruct the ordinary sentential calculus in terms of phrastics only, and then apply it to indicatives and imperatives alike simply by adding the appropriate neustics."[79]

He recognizes that certain difficulties might be encountered in doing so. For example, it might be found that in ordinary speech there are a number of different rules for the uses of

words like "all," "if," etc., in different contexts; in particular,
for their use in imperative, as opposed to indicative, contexts.
But it is still tautologously true that "so long as we continue to
use our words in the same sense their entailment-relations
will remain the same":[80] as, for example, the words "all"
and "not" were used in the same senses in the imperative and
indicative sentences instanced above. Another difficulty which
Hare notes is the question: how are we to know, given two
premises in different moods, in what mood the conclusion is
to be? This brings us to his "mixed" or "practical" syllogism,
one illustration of which was quoted at the beginning of this
paragraph.

> Take all the boxes to the station (imperative).
> This is one of the boxes (indicative).
>
> *Therefore* Take this to the station (imperative).

Or:

> Taking of all the boxes by you to the station, *please.*
> This being one of the boxes, *yes.*
>
> *Therefore* Taking of this by you to the station, *please.*

The question is: why not:

> Take all the boxes to the station.
> This is one of the boxes.
>
> *Therefore* You will take this to the station

Or:

> Taking of all boxes by you to the station, *please.*
> This being one of the boxes, *yes.*
>
> *Therefore* Taking of this by you to the station, *yes.*

The latter would not be valid syllogisms; but why not? In
reply, Hare states "two of the rules that seem to govern this
matter." (i) "No indicative conclusion can be validly drawn
from a set of premises which cannot be validly drawn from
the indicatives among them alone"; and (ii) "No imperative
conclusion can be validly drawn from a set of premises which

[80] *LM*, p. 27.

does not contain at least one imperative."[81] The justification for these rules he takes to lie in the general logical consideration that nothing may be said in the conclusion of a valid deductive inference which is not said explicitly or implicitly in the conjunction of the premises—except what can be added solely on the strength of the definitions of terms.[82] The conclusion "You will take this to the station" (or: "Taking of this by you to the station, yes") *is not* said explicitly or implicitly either by "Take all these boxes to the station" ("Taking of all the boxes by you to the station, please") or by "This is one of the boxes" ("This being one of the boxes, yes") or by their conjunction. Whereas there *is* implicit in the major (imperative) premise, "Take all the boxes to the station," the singular imperative, "Take this to the station," "this" having been defined by the minor premise as one of the boxes. To deny that this conclusion is implicit in such a conjunction of premises would be to misunderstand the word "all." It should be noted, however, that Hare would not, I think, now hold to the first of his two rules. More will be said about this below in the subsection of criticism entitled *Hare's Rules* (pp. 234–37).

III. CRITICISM

(I) CRITICISM: PRESCRIPTIVITY

Hare himself has recently said that the perlocution-illocution distinction "makes the main difference between emotivism and prescriptivism."[83] As we have seen, he attacks the emotivist view that the major use of moral judgments is to create an influence. The emotivists thought that they could get at the meaning of moral discourse by asking what we do *by* engaging in it. It is true that the answer to this question may be that we influence people. I may get someone to switch on the "News at Ten" by saying "We ought to hear the news." But then again I may do so by say-

[81] *LM*, p. 28.
[82] *LM*, pp. 32–33.
[83] Review of Warnock's *Contemporary Moral Philosophy* in *M* LXXVII (1968), 437.

ing, according to circumstances, "It's ten o'clock" (factual statement), or "Switch on" (command), or "If only someone would turn on the news" (expression of a wish), or "Am I going to be allowed to hear the news or not?" (question), etc. It is not a *differentia* of moral judgments that they create an influence. Any speech-act may do so. It seemed clear to Hare that, if you want to get at the meaning of moral discourse, the question to ask does not concern its perlocutionary, but its illocutionary,[84] force. The effect which we intend to produce *by* an utterance may not be realized, and yet that utterance be perfectly meaningful. For example, none of the above remarks would lose any of its meaning if, though uttered with the intention of getting the news switched on, it failed to have that effect. The real clue to any utterance's meaning, or so it seems to Hare, is what are we doing *in* saying it. This question, or rather the relative answers to it, *would* differentiate the above speech-acts from one another. *In* saying one we are stating a fact; *in* saying the others, giving a command, expressing a wish, asking a question. And if we were not doing what we are doing *in* saying any one of them, then they *would* be meaningless. If you said "Switch on" and I said "Is that a command?" and you said "No," then I, and anyone else who overheard, would be at a loss to know what you meant. (Of course, we may have misjudged what you purport to be doing, e.g., this may be a request; but my argument assumes that we have got what you purport to be doing right.) If you do not succeed in doing what you purport to be doing *in* saying anything, then what you say is meaningless. So when we come to moral judgment the question which gets us to its meaning is: what are we doing *in* making it? I think Hare's most severe critics would concede that he has made a valuable contribution to metaethics by thus applying the perlocution-illocution distinction to moral discourse.

There is, of course, nothing like the same measure of agreement that Hare has got the right answer as there is that he is asking the right question. Briefly, his answer comes to this.

[84] On this distinction see above, pp. 54–63.

What we are doing centrally and importantly[85] in making moral judgments is prescribing. This speech-act of prescribing takes place within a logical framework which has the further feature of universalizability; and in contexts where there are normally appeals to fact, to inclination or interest, and to imagination, respectively. To say that moral, and indeed all ought judgments are prescriptive is to say, not that they are imperatives, but that they entail imperatives. In saying sincerely "Capital punishment ought to be abolished," for example, I commit myself to abolishing it in so far as this possibility is open to me; and in sincerely accepting this judgment, any of my hearers will commit himself similarly.

I shall consider two questions concerning this prescriptivism. (i) Is its account of what we are doing in uttering moral judgments plausible? (ii) How far does it really go beyond emotivism? Hare's prescriptivism has in fact been widely criticized. In the next chapter, I shall be concerned with a school of thought which has recently arisen largely in reaction against his views; and what I have to say in the rest of this section should be supplemented by what is said there.

Is Prescriptivism Plausible?

There is undoubtedly some intimate connection between moral judgments and action. Most, if not all, of Hare's critics would agree with his contention that the surest way to find out what a man's moral principles are is to discover what he does.[86] Nevertheless, they dispute two things. One is Hare's belief that, as a matter of fact, the most central and important use of moral language is prescriptive; and the other, the view, which they take Hare to hold, that the close connection between moral judgment and action can only be explained by this putative fact.

Against the former it is urged that a man may judge morally by one set of principles and conduct his life, or advise others to conduct theirs by another set. In this sense his judgment may not be prescriptive. Professor A. C. MacIntyre, for

[85] Cf. *FR*, p. 84.
[86] *LM*, p. 1; cf. Warnock, *op. cit.*, p. 37.

example, writes: "A man might commit himself to a certain moral appraisal but not use it as a guide for action—'This in the light of morality is how your action would be appraised: but don't follow the guidance of morality.'"[87] He expressly excludes, as the only possible explanation of such a remark, Hare's distinction between evaluative and descriptive meaning. Of course, "in the light of morality" might mean "by the generally accepted standards of this community"; but MacIntyre's point is that it might *not*. What if the morality concerned is the speaker's own? If prescriptivism were true, it would not make sense to say that a man could morally appraise actions by one standard and guide his own conduct by another. But MacIntyre claims that this does make sense. Notice that he is not thinking of weakness of will for which, as he recognizes, Hare provides.[88] He does not simply mean that a man can (logically) fail to live up to his moral principles; but rather that he can (logically) be said to have moral principles which he sincerely holds but does not put into practice, even when physically and psychologically able to do so.

Well, can he? I am assuming that MacIntyre would not object to the use of "sincerely" in my penultimate sentence. (There is nothing to indicate that he would. And if he would, then in effect he concedes the point which I am about to make against him and his case collapses.) Would we, in fact, call such a man as MacIntyre speaks of sincere? We saw that, according to Hare,[89] sincerity is one of the necessary conditions of its being true that a speaker who is using "I ought to do X" as a value judgment will assent to the command "Let me do X" So, for MacIntyre to carry his point against Hare, it is necessary that his man should be sincere. But I do not think it can (logically) be said that a man sincerely adheres to moral principles which he does not put into practice if he can.

MacIntyre charges Hare with building his own *moral* commitment, to the principle that one ought to be sincere, into

---

[87] A. C. MacIntyre, "What Morality Is Not," *P* XXXII (1957), 330.
[88] See above, p. 169.
[89] Above, p. 169.

his account of the logic of moral discourse;[90] but I do not think that there is anything in this. It is one thing to be committed to the principle that one ought to practice what one preaches, quite another to believe that one cannot (logically) hold sincerely to a moral principle and not, given the physical and psychological opportunity, act upon it. It may well be the case that Hare, as a liberal moralist, subscribes to the former opinion; but what makes him a prescriptivist is something quite different, namely the fact that he holds the logical belief just stated.

Against Hare's prescriptivism it is also said that he restricts far too narrowly what a man may be doing in making moral judgments. He may indeed be prescribing; but he may be doing a variety of other things. G. J. Warnock writes: ". . . there are . . . dozens of things which those who employ moral words may therein be doing. They may be prescribing, certainly; but also they may be advising, exhorting, imploring; commanding, condemning, deploring; resolving, confessing, undertaking; and so on, and so on."[91] Hare's reply is to the effect that he has never denied this variety. All the speech-acts listed by Warnock are, according to Hare, species of the genus, prescribing; that is to say, all, in their primary use, entail imperatives.[92] This reply seems to me to be justified. It does not, of course, show that Hare is right. But it does show that simply to present such a list as Warnock's will not in itself dispose of prescriptivism. It is as plausible to argue that all the "alternatives" to prescribing which Warnock lists entail imperatives as that prescribing does.

What of the view, attributed to Hare, that the undoubted connection between moral judgment and action is explicable only in terms of his prescriptivism? Warnock thinks he finds this view in Hare and he rejects it. He says:

From the fact, if it be a fact, that a man's moral principles are revealed most decisively in his behaviour, it does not follow in the least that those principles have to be con-

[90] MacIntyre, *op. cit.*, 332–33.
[91] Warnock, *op. cit.*, p. 35.
[92] *M* LXXVII (1968), 438.

ceived as, or as implying, *prescriptions*. They might, so far
as that point goes, equally well be conceived as expressions
of taste or of approval, as avowals of wants or aims, as
views about values or ideals, as resolutions, as beliefs about
interests, and in many other ways too. On this score at any
rate, "Eating people is wrong" is no more closely akin to
"Don't eat people" than it is to "I don't want people to be
eaten": for in each of these cases the eating of people, or
looking on complacently while people are eaten, would be
in some sort of conflict with, even in a sense would contradict, what is said.[93]

But need Hare dissent from any of this? I should not expect
him to deny that *if* moral judgments were expressions of taste,
avowals of wants, or beliefs about interests, the connection
between them and action would be explained by appeal to the
logical fact that part, at least, of what we would be saying in
saying that we have a taste for something, or want it, or think
it in our interest, is that, given the chance to attain it, we
would seize that chance. Hare does not say that the prescriptivity of moral judgments is the only *conceivable* account of
the connection between them and action. He would, I think,
accuse Warnock of a *petitio principii* at this point. All he
wishes to claim is that if *moral* judgments are prescriptive,
this will explain the fact that they have the intimate connection which they do have with actions.[94]

How Far Does Hare's Prescriptivism Go beyond Emotivism?
The second of the two questions which I said that I would
discuss is: how far does Hare's prescriptivism really go beyond
emotivism? Without question, it goes some distance. For one
thing, it differentiates what Stevenson called the "non-rational
psychological" from what he called the "logical" and the "rational psychological" methods of moral argument[95] by refusing to recognize the first as a method of moral argument
at all. Then again, Hare shows, as Stevenson scarcely began
to do, the use to which the consistency, or universalizability,

[93] Warnock, *op. cit.*, p. 39.
[94] Cf. *M* LXXVII (1968), 439–40.
[95] Cf. above, pp. 130–31.

test can be put in moral argument. Within this logical framework, rational argument can go on, by the adducing of
counter-examples, and by the appeal to inclination or interest
and imagination, at least up to a point where those who opt
out of it can only do so at the cost of becoming what Hare
calls "fanatics." And it is an empirical fact, as he realizes, that
most people are reluctant to end up in that position. We remarked above that Hare's early ambition was to show the
possibility of rational argument in morals. He certainly shows
the possibility of a good deal of such argument.

Some have denied this. They have said that prescriptivism,
like emotivism, "cannot find much place for argument."[96]
The telling point which they have to make is that both emotivism and prescriptivism do not simply consider it possible on
moral issues for us to make up our own mind *on* the evidence,
but no less possible for us to make up our own minds what
shall count *as* evidence. To quote Warnock again: "I do not,
it seems, decide that flogging is wrong because I *am* against
cruelty; rather, I decide that flogging is wrong because I *decide to be* against cruelty. And what, if I did make that decision, would be my ground for making it? That I am opposed
to the deliberate infliction of pain? No—rather that I *decide
to be* opposed to it. And so on."[97] There are people, he goes
on, who make up not only their own minds, but also their
own evidence; but such people are a menace, not a model, not
exemplars of, but abstainers from, reasoning. It is not enough,
for such critics, to say simply, as Hare seems to do, that
moral argument provides us with an instrument whereby we
can test the self-consistency of our opponents. Are not mad-
men and knaves often completely self-consistent? Surely moral
argument should be able to defeat them.

Two things at least need to be said about this, I think. (i)
An instrument which enables you to bring home to your opponents the fact that they are on a course which, followed
to its conclusion, leads to what Hare calls "fanaticism" should
not be despised. Most men would wish to avoid that terminus

[96] Warnock, *op. cit.*, p. 42.
[97] *Ibid.*, p. 47.

and so, if you can show them that they are heading for it, this will seem to them sufficient reason for a change of direction. (ii) Warnock calls people who want to decide for themselves what counts as evidence, a menace. And so they are in many contexts. One such context would be a moral argument in which a person said, for example, that X was wrong because it was the breaking of a promise and then refused to count the fact that Y was also the breaking of a promise as evidence of Y's wrongness. Once what counts as evidence is decided, one is a menace if one goes back on that decision. But, of course, the precise content of that decision may vary. If you decide to do mathematics you are, in effect, deciding to count a different kind of thing as evidence than you would be if you had decided to do natural science. The content of your decision differs from both of these if you decide to think morally. Why, then, should there not be a universe of discourse in which what counts as evidence is any reason which a speaker chooses to give for something being good or obligatory, the point of the discourse being to see how consistently he can adhere to that choice under cross-questioning? And why should not morality be such a universe of discourse? Warnock seems to think that, simply by representing it as such a universe of discourse, prescriptivism has represented morality as irrationalist and so discredited itself, since moral discourse is manifestly not irrationalist. But anyone who engaged in a universe of discourse such as we have just supposed would not thereby become a menace to reasoning or an abstainer from it; he would only become such if, having given his reason for a moral judgment, he refused to let himself be tested for consistency in holding it. And it is expressly no part of prescriptivism to permit such refusal.

The real issue, of course, is whether or not moral discourse *is* of this kind. There is nothing inherently absurd in the conception of such a universe of discourse, but it may be absurd so to conceive of morality. If morality *is* that kind of discourse, then it seems to follow that it would make perfectly good sense to say that *anything* whatever was good or that *any* conceivable course of action ought to be taken. I could (logically) offer *anything whatever* as a reason for a moral judgment: for instance, that a certain action ought to be performed because it will effect the greatest misery of the greatest number, or injure the health of my children, or constitute the breaking of a promise, or whatever. The same question arises here as arose when we were considering Stevenson's emotivism.[98] Would such remarks make sense? Or is there some logical limitation on what may intelligibly be offered as a reason for a *moral* judgment which would exclude them? Some think that there is and that it is a defect in Hare's philosophy that he fails to see this. I shall return to this question below.[99]

(II) CRITICISM: UNIVERSALIZABILITY

Hare's view, that universalizability is a defining characteristic of ought judgments in general and moral ones in particular, has also come in for much criticism. In his article "Universalisability," Hare speaks of U-type valuations, i.e., applications of a "rule wholly devoid of any personal reference containing merely predicates (descriptions) and logical terms."[100] His central thesis in the article is "that all *moral* valuations are of type U—or, which comes to the same thing, that whenever moral reasons are given for actions, the maxims involved are of type U."[101] In *Freedom and Reason* (particularly pp. 35–37), Hare claims that *all* uses of "ought," not only moral ones, involve a U-type maxim. He finds corroboration of this in the impossibility, which he claims, of using "ought" to make a legal judgment. A statement of law always contains an implicit reference to a particular jurisdiction: "It is illegal to marry one's sister" means "It is illegal (e.g.) in England to marry one's sister." Here "England," a singular term, prevents the maxim from being U-type. "It is illegal to marry one's sister" does not mean "One ought not to marry one's sister" for it is always open to us to ask, "Ought we to do what it is illegal to do?" What Hare says

---

[98] Above, p. 151.
[99] Below, pp. 298–304.
[100] R. M. Hare, "Universalisability," *PAS* LV (1954–55), 295. Hare takes this definition from Gellner, *ibid.*, p. 163.
[101] Hare, *op. cit.*, 304.

about the universalizability of ought judgments is intended to apply equally to moral and nonmoral ones. The wider thesis (all ought judgments are universalizable) is impugned as well as the narrower one (moral ought judgments are universalizable) if the latter cannot be sustained.

Some Misunderstandings

Hare's theory, that ought judgments apply U-type principles, has often been misunderstood and we must follow him in sweeping away some superficial misunderstandings first of all. To begin with, about principles. Sometimes, when men say that something is a matter of principle with them, they mean that they take a hard and fast line about it and do not waste time any longer wondering whether they are justified in doing so. In some degree no doubt we all have—and need to have, if we are to avoid spending so much time in reflection that we have none left over for action—some such principles. But, be that as it may, Hare most certainly does not mean that all moral reasoning is, or ought to be, of that kind. When he maintains that the grounds of moral judgment must always imply universal principles, he is simply saying that these grounds are reasons which necessarily invoke and apply universal rules; and that is quite different. Again, Hare nowhere says that to be moral is necessarily to be a busybody, always poking one's nose into other people's ethical concerns. Nor is it to be intolerant with those who disagree with one on moral issues. His point is simply that, in saying "X is wrong because it is Y," I must, if I have really given the complete reason for what I say, be saying that anything else which is Y is also to that extent wrong. The point is logical. It does not in the least imply that I must go around looking for things which are Y in order to denounce them.

A more common misunderstanding is the widespread belief that anyone who subscribes to the universalizability thesis is insensitive to the extremely complicated character of most of the situations in which moral issues arise. Hare's very careful distinction between universality and generality[102] is fre-

[102] *Ibid.,* 311; *FR,* pp. 38–39.

quently overlooked. "Specific" is the opposite of "general,"
but not of "universal." A moral judgment can be universalizable and at the same time very specific.

We may note, in passing, that the question has been raised:
how specific, given the universalizability thesis, can a moral
judgment be? It has been claimed that the universalizability
thesis cannot be formulated simply thus: "A judgment is a
moral judgment, if and only if the person who makes it accepts some universal moral principle which, together with
some true statement *about the nonmoral characteristics* of the
situation originally judged, entails the original judgment." This
formulation, it is said, must be revised to read: ". . . together
with some true statement about *some but not all of the nonmoral characteristics* of the situation originally judged." Two
assumptions seem to lie behind the proposal that the universalizability thesis should be thus reformulated: (a) that it is
logically possible to offer a description of the nonmoral characteristics of a situation, such that only that particular situation answers to it; and (b) that every item in such a description could (logically) be morally relevant—i.e., could
conceivably figure in some "true statement" about nonmoral
characteristics which, together with a universal moral principle, entails a moral judgment. It will be seen that, if both
these assumptions held good, a judgment could be moral and
not universalizable. The universalizability thesis is designed to
obviate that contingency and must be formulated accordingly.
If moral judgments can (logically) be moral and not universalizable, then of course the universalizability thesis is mistaken. Are the above assumptions well founded? (a) I am
inclined to think that the former is. It seems clear to me that,
if the description in question included an exhaustive account
of the spatial and temporal relations of the given situation,
then it could (logically) be so complete as to apply to that
situation and no other. Even if the universe within which the
given situation occurs were repetitive or symmetrical, so that
situations whose description would be in many respects identical with that of the given situation, could occur, a complete
description of the spatial and temporal relations of the given

situation could be offered, which would differentiate it from any other similar situation. This assumption raises the whole complicated problem of the identity of indiscernibles and it lies beyond the scope of this book to go any further into it. (b) The second assumption is not well founded. Suppose part of your description of a given situation were a description of its spatial and temporal relations, such that this part of the description referred to the particular location in space and time of that situation. Then this part of your description would be irrelevant to the morality of the given situation. The reason why an act is, say, wrong cannot *simply* be that it was done in such-and-such a place at such-and-such a time. You might, of course, say, for example, that Enoch Powell did wrong to make his so-called racialist speeches where and when he did. But if you do, you will not be saying that it was the place or time *in themselves* which made his speeches wrong, but the conditions obtaining at or in them. An act cannot be wrong solely because it occurred in Birmingham at one particular time.

The point which I want to bring out here is that it is not necessary to build into your formulation of the universalizability thesis some safeguard against the possibility that the reason given for your *moral* judgment will be such that it could (logically) apply *only* to something done in a certain place at a certain time, thereby rendering the moral judgment grounded in it non-universalizable. That possibility does not exist. The only reasons which would be recognizable as *moral* reasons are such as render the judgment grounded in them universalizable. So, the "true statement" referred to above in the formulation, and the reformulation of the universalizability thesis, could be about *all* the nonmoral characteristics of the situation—all, that is, which could conceivably be morally relevant. The original formulation, as given above, viz. ". . . some true statement about the nonmoral characteristics . . . ," appears to recognize that this is so. The suggested reformulation, viz. ". . . true statement about *some but not all* of the nonmoral characteristics . . . ," seems to fail to recognize that it is. The latter appears to assume falsely that there could conceivably be morally relevant nonmoral characteristics which would render a judgment based upon them non-universalizable, and therefore we need to formulate the universalizability thesis in such a way as to cut out such cases. There is no need to do that because such cases are inconceivable.[103]

Situation Ethics

If moral judgments are universalizable, it does not follow that they will be sweeping generalizations which take no account of the extremely complicated character of most situations in which moral issues arise. A recent attack on the notion of moral principles has come from a type of ethical theory which purports to show that moral judgments are "situational." It exists in both religious and secular versions. Professor Joseph Fletcher amusingly gives some indication of this viewpoint at the beginning of his *Situation Ethics:* "A friend of mine arrived in St. Louis just as a presidential campaign was ending, and the cab driver, not being above the battle, volunteered his testimony. 'I and my father and grandfather before me, and their fathers, have always been straight-ticket Republicans.' 'Ah,' said my friend, who is himself a Republican, 'I take it that means you will vote for Senator So-and-So.' 'No,' said the driver, 'there are times when a man has to push his principles aside and do the right thing.' That St. Louis cabbie is this book's hero."[104] However, it transpires in the sequel that Fletcher, a religious moralist, has, or says he has, nothing against principles provided they do not harden into rules or laws.[105] But he seems curiously unaware of the distinction between (a) hard-and-fast principles, appeal to which is made a substitute for thinking by the morally insensitive, and (b) reasons which must be given where moral thinking is rational and which are reasons only because they

[103] For the suggested reformulation see J. Bennett, "Moral Argument," *M* LXIX (1960), 544. For a recent discussion of the problem of the identity of indiscernibles see P. F. Strawson, *Individuals* (1959), especially pp. 120–30.
[104] Joseph Fletcher, *Situation Ethics* (London, 1966), p. 13.
[105] *Ibid.*, pp. 31 ff.

invoke principles or rules. The former it is empirically possible to forego; but with the latter we cannot (logically) dispense.

Avant-garde religious moralists of late have launched a fierce and sustained attack upon the rigid application of moral principles. The Cambridge theologian, H. A. Williams, for example, wrote a few years ago about the English film *The Mark*:

> It tells of the rehabilitation into normality of a man strongly attracted to small girls. His abnormality, which can do nothing but untold harm to everybody, is due to his fear of commitment to an adult woman. However, in time, a woman of his own age inspires him with enough confidence for them to go away for the week-end together. They have separate rooms at the hotel. But it is clear that until he sleeps with her he will not have established enough confidence in himself to deliver him from his utterly destructive abnormality which tends to exploitation to the nth degree. Will he be able to summon up the necessary courage or not? When he does, and they sleep together, he has been made whole. And where there is healing, there is Christ, whatever the Church may say about fornication. And the appropriate response is—Glory to God in the Highest.[106]

I am not concerned here to discuss the value of these opinions or their consistency with the Christian ethic. All I wish to argue is that, if you favor some such loosening up of traditional Christian morality, it does not follow that you are putting principles aside, in the sense of reasons which embody rules. Consider what another advocate of situation ethics, Bishop John Robinson, says in a section of his *Honest to God* entitled "Nothing Prescribed—Except Love": ". . . nothing can of itself always be labelled as wrong."[107] But he goes on to say that "because it is an act of love" states a good reason why an act ought to be done. He seems to think that we can look at situations, ask "What would love do

---

[106] H. A. Williams, *Soundings* (Cambridge, 1962), edited by A. R. Vidler, p. 82.

[107] J. A. Robinson, *Honest to God* (London, 1963), p. 118.

here?" and perceive the answer. But, unless he is advocating some extreme form of intuitionism or emotivism, he will have to say that there is always a statable reason why the act in question is, or would be, an act of love. For instance, he would have to say presumably, if he agreed with Williams about the film, that, in so far as an action helps another human being to overcome sexual perversion or inadequacy, it is an act of love. That is what "love" means in this situation and therefore that is the reason why the act embodying it is right. To say that this is the reason why this act is right, however, is to say that in so far as *any* act would help another human being to overcome sexual perversion it would be *to that extent* always right, and its omission always wrong. To deny this is to deny that one has offered a reason why the given act is right. There are really only two alternatives open to a moralist who wants to take the Bishop's line that nothing is prescribed except love: either (i) he means that no statable reason can be given why an act is an act of love; and what this would come to is that neither he nor anyone else knows what "love" means. It is then singularly unhelpful to tell anyone to do what love would do. Or (ii) he means simply that, while love is the overriding moral principle, the statement of what "love" means is a highly complex business and our minds must always be open to the possibility that we have got it wrong. Hare's form of universal prescriptivism can accommodate this latter view perfectly comfortably. It simply amounts to what, as we saw, Hare himself says about conceiving of moral reasoning as a kind of exploration.[108]

Act- and Rule-Utilitarianism

In secular ethics there has been a more or less parallel development to this so-called "new morality" of the radical Christians. It is the contention that utilitarianism should be act-, not rule-, utilitarianism. The principle of utility, that is, should be invoked directly to determine the morality of individual acts, and not simply to justify universal rules such as "Promises ought to be kept," which may then be instantiated

[108] Above, pp. 192–95.

in particular acts. Hare argues that, given the universalizability of moral judgments, act-utilitarianism and rule-
utilitarianism "collapse into each other."[109] He claims first
that "there cannot be a case which is consistent with *act*-
utilitarianism but inconsistent with *rule*-utilitarianism"[110] and
says, in support of this, substantially what I said a moment or
two ago against the situationalists: "If it were possible to apply
the principle of utility directly to actions without the inter-
mediacy of any subordinate principle, then we should have
such a case. But it can be shown that this is impossible. For
how could it be the case that an action could be known to
be such as to maximise satisfactions without it being known
that it did so *because* of the sort of action that it was?"[111]
The individual act is right because it instantiates a rule to the
effect that that sort of action maximizes satisfactions. Con-
versely, Hare claims that neither can there be "a case consistent with *rule*-utilitarianism but inconsistent with *act*-
utilitarianism."[112] Here there would have to be a rule which
we believed it right to observe, even though the individual act
which we performed in consequence was not right, e.g., keeping a promise because keeping promises effects the greatest
happiness of the greatest number, even though our promise
was made to a man now dead and many more people would
be happy if we broke it than if we kept it. It does not seem to
me that this argument need worry a rule-utilitarian. Would
any rule-utilitarian who was able to think clearly, ever have
to find himself in the position of holding to a rule, but except-
ing an individual act from it? Would he ever have to say—
would it, indeed, ever make sense if he did say—"This act instantiates the rule and is in that respect right, but in itself it is
wrong"? Would not his rule, if *that* particular act *as right*
came under it, always be such as stated the rightness of *all*
acts *of the kind*—e.g., "It is always right to keep promises
even where this causes the present degree of privation of happiness because in the end this produces the greatest happiness

[109] *FR*, p. 135.
[110] *FR*, p. 132.
[111] *FR*, p. 131.
[112] *FR*, p. 132.

of the greatest number." Unless it would, he would not be a utilitarian at all.[113]

MacIntyre's Criticism

Hare, in putting forward his view that ought judgments apply U-type principles, said that this will become clearly apparent, if we consider the following conversation between an existentialist and a Kantian.

E: "You oughtn't to do that."

K: "So you think that one oughtn't to do that kind of thing?"

E: "I think nothing of the kind; I say only that *you* oughtn't to do *that.*"

K: "Don't you even imply that a person like me in circumstances of this kind oughtn't to do that kind of thing when the other people involved are the sort of people that they are?"

E: "No; I say only that *you* oughtn't to do *that.*"

K: "Are you making a moral judgment?"

E: "Yes."

K: "In that case I fail to understand your use of the word 'moral.'"

Says Hare:

Most of us would be as baffled as the "Kantian"; and indeed we should be hard put to it to think of any use of the word "ought," moral or non-moral, in which the "Existentialist's" remarks would be comprehensible. Had the "Existentialist" said "Don't do that," instead of "You oughtn't to do that," the objections of the "Kantian" could not have been made; this illustrates one of the main differences between "ought" and ordinary imperatives. Indeed, the fault of the "Existentialists" might be characterised thus: because moral judgments are like ordinary

[113] I think that Hare's argument here is substantially correct, but I realize that the issues raised are complicated and a satisfactory discussion of the act-rule controversy would require a much more detailed, and perhaps sympathetic, treatment than that which I give it here, if justice were to be done to it. Hare, I imagine, would agree with this.

imperatives in some respects, they conclude that they are like in all respects.[114]

Criticism of Hare has taken the form of a defense of the existentialist's use of the word "moral" in this imaginary conversation. The by now famous example given by Sartre in his essay *L'Existentialisme est un humanisme* (Paris, 1946) is quoted against Hare. One of Sartre's pupils during the war lived alone with his mother. She was estranged from his father who was something of a collaborator; and her elder son had been killed fighting the Germans in 1940. She was deeply affected by the semi-treason of the one and the loss of the other. Sartre's pupil realized that his presence with his mother was her only consolation; but he was also eager to avenge his brother's death. He had the choice of going to England to join the Free French Forces or of staying with his mother and making her life tolerable. What could help him to choose? asks Sartre. Not Christianity, for it says "Love your neighbor," and he cannot say who is his neighbor, his mother or those whom he would benefit by fighting for France. Again, not the Kantian ethic, for it says "Treat persons as ends, never means"; but the problem is, which persons, his mother or those others? In a dilemma such as his, says Sartre, all we can do is "trust in our instincts," follow our "affections." But this does not mean that we can find some guidance before the action as to what it should be. "I can only estimate the strength of [an] affection," says Sartre, "if I have performed an action by which it is defined and ratified. But if I then appeal to this affection to justify my action, I find myself drawn into a vicious circle."[115]

MacIntyre, who uses this example against Hare, comments on it thus:

> Part of the force of his [Sartre's] argument is this. Someone faced with such a decision might choose either to stay or to go without attempting to legislate for anyone else in a

[114] Hare, "Universalisability," *op. cit.,* 304–5.
[115] English version, J. P. Sartre, *Existentialism and Humanism* (1948), trans. by P. Mairet, p. 37.

similar position. He might decide what to do without being willing to allow that anyone else who chose differently was blameworthy. He might legitimately announce his choice by saying, "I have decided that I ought to stay with my mother." If he did so, his use of "ought" would not express any appeal to a universalisable principle. It would not be a U-type valuation, but it would be a moral valuation.[116]

I think first of all that Hare is entitled to reply, as in fact he does,[117] that it is by no means certain that Sartre would recognize this as "part of the force of his argument." One central theme of the essay is, to be sure, the importance of making one's own moral choices and not taking them, in bad faith, second-hand from other people; but another is the responsibility and consequent anguish which, according to Sartre, lie in the very fact that, in making moral choices, we have to choose not only for ourselves but for all mankind. Sartre says, for example, "I am thus responsible for myself and for all men, and I am creating a certain image of man as I would have him to be. In fashioning myself I fashion man. . . . We are left alone, without excuse. That is what I mean when I say that man is condemned to be free. . . . Every man, without any support or help whatever, is condemned at every instant to invent man."[118] It is to illuminate remarks such as this that Sartre goes on to use the illustration of his pupil. These remarks themselves, and others like them, do seem to lend support to Hare's claim that the Sartre of *L'Existentialisme est un humanisme* is "as much of a universalist as I am, in the sense in which I am."[119]

Be that as it may, the important point is how well-founded the criticism which MacIntyre levels at the universalizability thesis is. I will take its main points in turn.

(i) "Someone faced with such a decision [as Sartre's pupil] might choose either to stay or to go *without attempting to legislate for anyone else in a similar position*" (italics mine).

[116] MacIntyre, *op. cit.*, 326.
[117] *FR*, p. 38.
[118] Sartre, *op. cit.*, pp. 30–34.
[119] *FR*, p. 38.

Notice that MacIntyre says "to stay," and makes no mention of *"ought* to stay." This makes his remark seem the more plausible. He adds, a little later in his article: "The fact that a man might on moral grounds refuse to legislate for anyone other than himself (perhaps on the grounds that to do so would be moral arrogance) would by itself be enough to show that not all moral valuation is universalisable."[120] But I do not think that it is logically possible to pass a moral judgment without legislating for anyone else in a similar position. Notice first MacIntyre's parenthesis. His man is saying, in effect, "I ought not to legislate for (i.e., to pass moral judgments upon) anyone other than myself." And, confronted with "Why?" he is replying, "Because to do so is morally arrogant." It is perfectly in order to say that his judgment instantiates the universal principle "No one in a position similar to mine ought to do what is morally arrogant." His reason does, in this sense—and it is the sense of the universalizability thesis—legislate for other people. There is nothing inconceivable in the thought of someone making a moral decision not to make any *more* moral judgments after this one. And it is in no sense self-contradictory to say that, in so far as that decision was moral, one would be entitled to ask a reason for it. Any reason given would invoke a universal principle.

(ii) "He might decide what to do *without being willing to allow that anyone else who chose differently was blameworthy"* (italics mine). MacIntyre refers, in this connection, to the "works of supererogation" attributed to saints or heroes.[121] He evidently thinks that the language which saints and heroes use about themselves, or which we use about them, is inconsistent with the universalizability thesis. The story of Captain Oates is often told to exemplify heroism. He was a member of Scott's ill-fated expedition to the Antarctic. Being disabled to a degree which was delaying his companions' return to safety, Oates, having said simply, "I am going outside for a moment," left the tent and walked away into the blizzard to certain death. On the universalizability thesis, if

[120] MacIntyre, *op. cit.,* 328.
[121] *Ibid.*

Captain Oates had said to himself, "I ought to walk away,"
or if we said of him that he did what he ought to have done,
he would have meant, and we would mean, that anyone else
so placed also ought to have done it. There are two questions:
(a) would Oates naturally have spoken, or would we naturally speak, in terms of "ought" about his case? and (b) if
he, or we, would do so, what would he have meant, or we
mean? We have already noted the distinction which Hare
draws between "ought" and "good": "ought" commits to the
view that no similar person in a similar situation ought to fail
to do the same thing; "good" only to the view that whatever
is the same in relevant respects is good.[122] Now, we should
certainly say that what Oates did was good. But should we
say that he *ought* to have done it? Prima facie it seems clear
that we would not. We should not have blamed Oates, or
anyone else in his position, if they had failed to walk away.
That is what is meant by calling this heroic act supereroga-
tory. But Oates himself doubtless thought, "I ought to walk
away." By the universalizability thesis, this commits him to
the view that no one else similarly placed ought to fail to do
so. Would Oates have rejected that implication? I doubt it.
Surely a man in his position, acting as he did, we presume
from a sense of duty, would think that anyone in the same
position who failed so to act would be blameworthy. Admittedly, we can conceive of him imagining some acquaintance,
X, in his position, and saying to himself, "If X were in my
shoes, I wouldn't think less of him if he didn't do what I'm
doing." But, if he asked himself why, the answer would reveal
some relevant respect—e.g., "I have a duty to set others an
example," "I've had a good life," "I shouldn't be able to live
with myself afterward if I didn't"—in which he took his own
situation to *differ* from X's. There may even be, as I think
Hare suggests,[123] a sense in which, not only Oates himself,
but we also are perfectly entitled to say that he ought to have
done what he did. We would naturally say that a man ought
to live up to his own ideals, even though we were not prepared

[122] *FR*, p. 153; above, p. 184.
[123] *FR*, p. 154.

to say that everyone ought to have the same ideals. If we can say of any ideal only that it is *good,* not that it ought to be embraced, we can still say that, whatever a man's ideal may be, he *ought* to live up to it. And in this sense we could say that Oates did what he ought to have done, implying thereby that anyone who failed to do the same (i.e., live up to his own ideals) would be blameworthy.

(iii) "He might legitimately announce his choice by saying, 'I have decided that *I ought* to stay with my mother'" (italics mine). MacIntyre is illuminating the point he makes here, when a moment later he adds that the use of "I ought" to announce a decision "is a performatory use . . . in that its use makes one responsible for performing a particular action where before saying 'I ought' one could not have been held responsible for performing that action rather than some alternative one." In this sense, MacIntyre goes on, one could never say "You oughtn't" but only "I oughtn't."[124] It is undoubtedly true that we cannot (logically) make other people's moral decisions for them; and if "I ought" (or "oughtn't") is used as MacIntyre says, then there is no corresponding "You ought" (or "oughtn't"). But would it be true to say of such a use of "I ought," as MacIntyre does, that "it would be a moral *valuation*"? The "I ought" of which MacIntyre speaks *commits* one to the performance of a certain action. This can be differentiated from the making of a judgment about an action. "I ought to do X"—in what I hope I shall not be accused of begging any questions, if I call the normal universalizable sense of that expression—entails an imperative. To *say* "I ought" is to say by implication "Let me." If I have *said* the former in the full realization of what I am doing, then I have *said* the latter also. This is different from actively committing myself to the fulfillment of that imperative in saying "I ought." When I am merely making a judgment, "ought" in "I ought" means the same as in "You ought." But there is a speech-act logically distinct from this. When I am committing myself, taking on responsibility to *do* the act—not just to say "Let me do it"—I mean by "ought" something which I

[124] MacIntyre, *op. cit.,* 326–27.

never can mean if I use the verb in the second or third persons. It does not seem to me that there is anything here which constitutes a denial, much less a refutation, of universal prescriptivism. Perhaps there is not, even if you call the speech-act of commitment a valuation, as MacIntyre does. A man may say "Two shillings" in answer to either the question "What is this worth?" or to "What am I bid?" He commits himself in the latter case as not in the former. Both are, if you like, valuations. But both are not the same speech-act. MacIntyre's point—that there is a special responsibility-incurring use of "I ought"—may be sound. But this does not show that Hare is mistaken in what he says about a *different* use: namely that in which "I ought" simply makes a moral judgment.

Is the Universalizability Thesis True but Trivial?

The universalizability thesis is sometimes criticized on the ground that it is true but trivial. To see what is at issue here, consider the following imaginary conversation.

A: Capital punishment ought to be discontinued.
B: Why?
A: It requires one man to take another's life.
B: So you think that whatever requires one man to take another's life ought to be discontinued?
A: Yes.
B: But do you think that doctors ought not to sacrifice the baby's life, when they know that it is probable the mother will die in childbirth if they don't?
A: No. I think they ought to sacrifice the baby's life in such circumstances.
B: Why? This is a case of one person being required to take another's life just like capital punishment.
A: The cases differ. In the doctor's case, he is saving a life thereby.
B: So you think that whatever requires one person to take another's life, if he does not save another life thereby, ought to be discontinued?
A: Yes.
B: Well now, suppose the West was faced with a choice between war and submission to, say, Russia or China.

If the West chose war it would be choosing a course
which led to death on a vast scale. Far *more* people
would suffer that fate than would if the West simply
submitted. But do you think the West would do wrong
if it chose war?

A: No. Even at that cost, I would say that the West ought
to fight.

B: So you do *not* really think that whatever requires one
man to take another's life, if he does not save another
life thereby, is wrong?

A: All right, I don't.

B: Then you have no reason for saying that capital punishment ought to be discontinued.

The point of B's moves in such a conversation is to convince
A that he (A) does not consistently adhere to the reason
which he gives for saying that capital punishment ought to be
discontinued. He elicits this reason from A and then, by adducing counter-examples (surgery, war), tries to get A to re-
nounce it. Notice that A is allowed to qualify his original reason in order to cope with these counter-examples. It is quite
legitimate in moral—as perhaps in any other form of argument—to restate one's meaning more precisely or carefully
in the face of objections. B's aim, however, is to produce a
counter-example with which A cannot cope. A's reason,
modified to cope with previous counter-examples, for condemning capital punishment would apply equally to war in
the supposed circumstances, but A does not think that such a
war ought not to be fought. He is therefore inconsistent in
disapproving of capital punishment and not of war. As a rational being, he has to abandon his reason and with it the
original judgment. With this paradigm of a moral argument
in mind, I turn again to the charge that the universalizability
thesis is true but trivial.

This charge may assume either of two forms:[125] (i) It may
turn on the purely logical point that it makes no sense to call
anything a criterion of the difference between genuine and
non-genuine X's, if it lets through any X whatever, the charge

[125] Cf. Bennett, *op. cit.*, 547–48.

being that this is what the universalizability thesis does. A could conceivably go on accepting the modifications to his original principle in order to escape the charge of inconsistency in face of B's counter-examples, until his principle referred to *nothing but* capital punishment. In the end his argument would be:

> Whatever is a, b, c, etc., ought to be discontinued.
> Capital punishment is a, b, c, etc.
> *Therefore* Capital punishment ought to be discontinued.

where "a, b, c, etc." was a *complete* description of the non-moral properties of, and so could (logically) not refer to anything but, capital punishment. His judgment "Capital punishment ought to be discontinued" would then be entirely particular—in the sense that it could (logically) apply only to capital punishment—*and yet pass the universalizability test.* That it would permit such a state of affairs to arise—so the charge runs—shows that the universalizability test is no test. (ii) Alternatively the charge of triviality may turn simply on the *practical* point that, whatever its logical status, the universalizability test does not provide us with a useful frame for moral argument because someone in A's position can, as a matter of fact, always find some difference in principle between his own example and counter-examples which he does not wish to accept. So, a moral argument, conducted in accordance with the universalizability criterion can (empirically) just go on forever.

In attempting a defense of the universalizability thesis against the first of these charges, everything will turn on whether or not it is logically possible to give a description of the situation being morally judged, such that it applies only to that situation. If it is, then the universalizability thesis will need to be reformulated in the way suggested above.[126] If it is not, then the logical point being made here against the

[126] Above, p. 211.

universalizability thesis is groundless. I tried to show above[127] that, while it is conceivable that a description of the nonmoral characteristics of a situation should apply to that situation alone, such a description could not be given as the reason for a *moral* judgment. If this argument was sound, then the universalizability thesis serves as a criterion of moral judgment and is not trivial.

In reply to the second charge—that the universalizability thesis is of no practical use—Bennett[128] concedes that a moral argument can never be lost by a moralist who has the requisite degree of perseverance and pigheadedness—that is, by one who goes on forever refusing to acknowledge defeat and modifies his major premise to cope with all counter-examples. However, pigheadedness of this extreme kind is fortunately not all that common. Within the frame of universalizability, one can constantly present one's opponents with a challenge to their own consistency. It is usually the case that they are not prepared to narrow their principles down beyond a certain point—as A in the above discussion of capital punishment was not. So the charge of practical triviality is not well founded. Moral argument does sometimes effect changes of opinion. It is true that prejudice plays no small part in much of it. Nevertheless, it is the convention that any specifically moral judgment must be, to use Bennett's phrase, "rationalisable on demand."[129] That is to say, one who makes such a judgment must, when required to do so, be prepared to see counter-examples adduced. If he is to retain whatever reputation he has for rationality, he must stand upon the principle(s) implicit in his reason(s) consistently. The point of moral argument is to put that consistency on trial. To recall Hare,[130] moral argument, whether carried on by an individual as a dialogue with himself or between more than one participant, is a form of exploration—exploration into what we find ourselves able as a matter of empirical fact to believe.

[127] See above, pp. 211–13.
[128] Bennett, *op. cit.*, 547.
[129] *Ibid.*, 546.
[130] See above, pp. 192–95.

The question remains, however, as to whether or not rationality in morals is *simply* a maker of such consistency. It is one to which I shall return.[131]

The Universalizability Thesis and Utilitarianism

Hare wishes to establish "a point of contact" between his universal prescriptivism and utilitarianism.[132] He claims that universal prescriptivism provides "a formal foundation" for utilitarianism.[133] If I understand him rightly, his argument goes as follows. Because moral judgments are *universalizable*, anyone who passes such a judgment on another person must accept that, were he himself in the other's place, the judgment would apply equally to him. And because moral judgments are *prescriptive*, anyone who assents to a moral judgment must assent to the imperative implicit within it. If, for instance, I say to someone "Because you are a Jew you ought to be exterminated," I must: (i) recognize that the same judgment would apply to me, if I were a Jew; and (ii) assent to the imperative "If I am a Jew, let me be exterminated." The *universalizability* of moral judgments requires me, in making such judgments, to go "the round of all the affected parties . . . giving equal weight to the interests of all," as Hare puts it.[134] The *prescriptivity* of moral judgments requires me, in making such judgments, to ask the question, as Hare has it, "How much (as I imagine myself in the place of each man in turn) do I want to have this, or avoid that?"[135] Here "this" and "that" refer to the content of the relevant imperative entailed by the judgment; for I think Hare would say that for someone to want to have (or to do) something is for him to be willing to assent to the imperative, "Let me do it (or have it)."[136] Bringing such universalizability and prescriptivity together, then we have the argument in Hare's own words thus: "It is in the endeavour to find lines of conduct which we can

[131] See below, pp. 294–329.
[132] *FR*, p. 122.
[133] *FR*, p. 123.
[134] *Ibid.*
[135] *Ibid.*
[136] See below, p. 316.

prescribe universally in a given situation that we find ourselves bound to give equal weight to the desires of all parties . . . and this, in turn, *leads* to such views as that we should seek to maximise satisfactions."[187] Hare, I think, is here saying that universal prescriptivism *leads* to utilitarianism in the following sense. Universalizability, in our moral judgments, requires us to take account of *all* the affected parties. Prescriptivity requires us, in our moral judgments, to take account of the *wants* of all the affected parties. To be a universal prescriptivist is, therefore, to be a utilitarian: it is to approve morally of that which maximizes satisfactions. I raise two questions: (i) Where does this place those whom Hare calls "fanatics"? (ii) Where does it leave minorities?

To deal with the former, let us take the example of the man who thinks that all Jews ought to be exterminated. If this man is a universal prescriptivist, he will have to do two things. He will have to assent to the imperative "Let all Jews be exterminated"; and he will have to put himself imaginatively in the place of each Jew in the world and, having done so, decline assent to the imperative "Let me not be exterminated." It is logically possible for him to do both of these things. But it is arguable that it would be empirically impossible. This fanatic would have to find a satisfaction in the thought of the extermination of all Jews which was greater than that which he found in the thought of the survival of all the Jews in the world after putting himself imaginatively in the place of each. No human being, it might be argued, could in fact experience such a degree of satisfaction as this fanatic would have to experience in the thought of the extermination of the Jews. On such grounds, I think Hare would wish to say that what he means by fanaticism is logically possible but does not, and indeed cannot, empirically, occur. But what if we suppose that our fanatic is not alone in his fanaticism? Suppose others in his society want all Jews to be exterminated. Then, as a universal prescriptivist, our fanatic, in considering what ought to be done with Jews, will put himself in the place of these

[187] *FR*, p. 123; italics mine.

fellow fanatics and take the satisfaction which they would derive from the extermination of the Jews into account. It is not beyond the bounds of empirical possibility that the satisfaction which one group of people derived from the extermination of another should outweigh the satisfaction which that other group would derive from avoiding extermination.

This brings me to the second question: where does Hare's universal prescriptivist utilitarianism leave minorities? The utilitarian principle of equity, to which Hare likens the universalizability thesis, requires that everybody count for one and nobody for more than one in the felicific calculation. But it provides no safeguard, once that calculation has been made, against discounting the minority completely in the interests of the majority. Hare, for example, thinks that murderers ought to be punished and says that his reasons "are utilitarian ones."[138] If you count everybody as one and nobody as more than one, you arrive at the conclusion that more people will get what they want if you punish murderers than if you do not. But would Hare be prepared to uphold a color bar on the same grounds? Evidently not, for he says, "reasons of this [utilitarian] sort are not available to racialists."[139] Why not? There is, Hare would presumably have to say, no logical difference between the "ought" in "Murderers ought not to be punished" and that in "Negroes ought not to be given civil rights." The difference is simply that, as a matter of fact, the majority get what they want if murderers are punished, but not if Negroes are denied civil rights. The wrongness of denying Negroes civil rights, then, lies in this contingent fact. But it follows from this that if it were not a fact—if the majority would get what they wanted by keeping colored people in subjection—then, that is what ought to be done. We know that, in some restricted communities, the majority would in fact get what they wanted if there were a color bar. Suppose this were true of the community formed by mankind as a whole. Would a color bar, then, be morally

[138] *FR*, p. 222.
[139] *Ibid.*

right? I can hardly think that Hare would give an affirmative answer. But to such an answer his universal prescriptivist utilitarianism seems to commit him.

Is the Universalizability Thesis a Moral Principle?

It is sometimes said, against Hare, that he deceives himself, and would deceive his readers, into thinking that he is elucidating the logic of moral discourse, when all he is really doing is commending a particular morality. I dismissed this criticism above[140] with respect to Hare's view that moral judgments are essentially prescriptive. There are no better grounds for it with regard to his universalizability thesis.

The criticism brought against him is that he only thinks moral discourse to be universalizable, as a matter of *logical* fact, because he subscribes to the liberal Protestant *moral* principle that one ought to apply to oneself the standards which one applies to others and *vice versa*.[141] Now, of course, it is possible that, as a matter of psychological fact, the universalizability thesis only took shape in Hare's mind because he was brought up a liberal Protestant. I do not know whether or not such is the case, but presumably there are psychological techniques which could establish whether it is or not. But whatever the answer to that question, it is entirely beside the point so far as any critique of Hare's moral philosophy is concerned. Hare's opinions about the *logic* of moral discourse are one thing. The *moral* principles to which he holds, or in which he was trained, are another. The universalizability thesis is one of the former (logical) opinions and purports to give an account of how moral language works. It should be discussed on its merits, logical and philosophical. To attempt to discredit it by playing the amateur psychologist and discussing its genesis within Hare's mind is ridiculous. How Hare came by it psychologically, if that can be discovered, would be of interest to his biographer, no doubt. It is of no interest whatever to those who are attempt-

---

[140] Above, p. 205.
[141] See note 90 and above, pp. 204–5.

ing to assess the correctness or otherwise of his moral philosophy.

(III) CRITICISM: LOGICAL RELATIONS

Neustics and Phrastics

In hitherto unpublished papers, Hare has pointed out inadequacies in the account of neustics and phrastics which he offered in *The Language of Morals* and which was outlined above.[142] He has recalled that, in his T. H. Green Prize Essay, which he abridged to form the first part of *The Language of Morals*, he had drawn a threefold distinction between signs of mood, completeness, and subscription. Thinking this rather pedantic and irrelevant to his argument, when he wrote the book he used the single word "neustic" to cover at least the sign of subscription; and the word "phrastic" to cover the element, common to imperatives and indicatives, which contained all the logical properties of a sentence. He has said that he now thinks this was a mistake. It is to be hoped that Hare will soon publish his further thoughts on this subject. In the light of the unpublished work which he has been kind enough to let me see, though without, of course, claiming authoritatively to represent his opinions, I suggest that his reasons for thinking his account of neustics and phrastics in *The Language of Morals* mistaken might include arguments somewhat on the following lines.

(i) Contradiction or entailment cannot be known to hold between sentences irrespective of mood, as would have to be the case if all logical properties were in the phrastic and the neustic was the sign of mood.

    (1) "Take these boxes to the station"

and

    (2) "You will not take these boxes to the station"

do not contradict one another, though, on Hare's earlier analysis, they have contradictory phrastics: "Taking of these boxes by you to the station" and "No taking of these boxes by you to the station," respectively.

    (3) "Take all these boxes to the station"

and

[142] Pp. 195–201.

(4) "You will take all these boxes to the station"
have on the earlier analysis, the same phrastic: "Taking of
all these boxes by you to the station." But we can validly
infer

(5) "Take this to the station,"
where "this" is known to refer to a box, from (3), though
we cannot validly infer it from (4). We know that (1) and
(2) do not contradict each other, and that (5) follows from
(3) but not from (4), *only* when we know the mood signs
of these sentences. That is, on Hare's earlier analysis, only
when we know their neustics. So, contrary to what he then
thought, not all logical properties reside in the phrastic; some
must reside in what he then called the neustic.

(ii) The sign of subscription or assertion, which shows that
a sentence is actually being used and not merely mentioned
or quoted, cannot be identified with the mood sign, as Hare
appeared to identify them in *The Language of Morals*. We
know that "p" and "not p" contradict one another *before*
we know whether they are being used or only mentioned; but
as we have just seen, we may *not* know this before we know
in what mood they are. Hare has now invented a term, *tropic*
(from the Greek word for mood), for the mood sign and restricts the meaning of "neustic" to subscription sign.

(iii) The third sign which Hare distinguished in his prize
essay he called the sign of completeness. It is necessary to
differentiate this from the neustic and the tropic in a sentence and to recognize that some logical properties of the
sentence depend upon it. Hare now calls it the *clistic* (from
the Greek word meaning "to close or shut"). It serves to en-
close a sentence: to show the beginning and the end of what
is being said, so that we know that nothing has been overlooked or is still to come. It is logically necessary to know
this. An illustration (framed along the same lines as one
which on occasion Hare himself has used) will make this
clear. If I say to a pupil, "You've got that wrong. Oh no,
you haven't," that is not a contradiction, but a correction.
Had I said, "You've got that wrong and you haven't," I should
have been contradicting myself. The full stop—the clistic—

makes the difference. It ends one thing which I have to say and shows that what comes next is a new beginning. So some logical properties of a sentence depend upon its clistic. The clistic is obviously distinct from the signs of subscription and mood. A sentence which is merely mentioned, not used, may nevertheless be complete. Restricting "neustic" to the meaning "sign of subscription or assertion," as Hare now seems to do, you could therefore say that two sentences both have a clistic but one lacks a neustic. Again, you might also say that an utterance possessed a tropic but lacked a clistic: for example, "Take all these boxes to . . ." is in the imperative mood, but it is incomplete. Neustics, tropics, and clistics are therefore logically distinct from one another and severally from phrastics; and the logical properties of a sentence are not all contained in the latter.

It lies beyond the scope of this book to discuss any further the intricacies of these sentential particles. How they are in fact constituted by the rules and conventions of our language; whether there are other such particles besides those named here; whether or not neustics, like tropics and clistics, contribute to the logical properties of sentences or not; and so on—these are all matters now exciting the interest of logicians. But the most important question for anyone attempting an evaluation of Hare's prescriptivism, seems to me to be whether or not, in any of this, Hare is going back—or ought to be—on his contention that mixed, or practical, syllogisms are possible. I think the answer is that he is not and ought not.

In the example:

> Take all the boxes to the station
> This is a box
> *Therefore* Take this to the station

the imperative conclusion follows from the conjunction of the two premises because (a) the minor premise shows the reference of "this" and (b) "this" having that reference, the conclusion is implicit in the major premise. To deny this would be to fail to understand the meaning of the word "all." The defects of the earlier analysis in terms of neustics and phrastics alone do not impugn the two rules which Hare gave in *The Language of Morals* as governing the practical syllogism or the general logical considerations upon which he based them.[143]

Hare's Rules

This is not to say that there are no other objections to Hare's rules.

The two rules to which reference has just been made are as follows:

(i) No indicative conclusion can be validly drawn from a set of premises which cannot be validly drawn from the indicatives among them alone.

(ii) No imperative conclusion can be validly drawn from a set of premises which does not contain at least one imperative.

In enunciating these rules, Hare was contributing to a discussion which has gone on for some time among logicians and still continues. Can there be "mixed syllogisms," i.e., syllogisms in which a conclusion in either the indicative or imperative mood is drawn from premises which are either respectively in the indicative and imperative moods, or both in that one of these two moods in which their conclusion is not. The logical issues arising in connection with Hare's two rules are complicated and technical and it lies beyond the scope of this book to deal with them in any great detail. A useful introduction to the whole subject of imperative inference, together with a valuable bibliography of the relevant literature, is provided in Professor N. Rescher's monograph *The Logic of Commands.*

As for the *first* of Hare's two rules, plausible counterexamples have been adduced against it and I do not think that Hare would wish any longer to defend it as it stands. Consider these examples, which I borrow from Rescher.

[143] *LM,* p. 28.

From:
    John, drive your car home (imperative)
we can validly infer:
    John owns a car (indicative).
And from:
    Never do anything illegal (imperative)
together with:
    Never do A (imperative)
we can validly infer:
    Doing A is illegal (indicative).

Such instances seem to dispose of Hare's first rule. True, it can be argued plausibly that the indicative conclusion is, in some cases, concealed within an imperative premise. For instance:

    John, drive your car home
could plausibly be analyzed thus:
    John, you have a car (indicative)
    Drive it home (imperative).

But it is not possible to claim that "Never do A," in the second of the above examples, is correctly analyzed thus:

    Doing A is illegal (indicative)
    Never do it (imperative).

Hare's *second* rule is the logical mainstay of his moral philosophy. He is careful to say that he is not the first to have formulated it. Henri Poincaré proposed it in "La morale et la science," *Dernières Pensées* (Paris, 1913), as did Professor K. R. Popper in "What Can Logic Do for Philosophy?," *Proceedings of the Aristotelian Society,* supplementary volume XXII (1948). I think that this second rule holds good. There are a number of logical problems which arise in connection with it, but they are problems of precise definition and correct formulation rather than doubts about the "viability" of the rule itself.

One such problem concerns hypothetical imperatives. Consider an example which Hare gives:

If you want to go to the largest grocer in Oxford, go to Grimbly Hughes.

Prima facie this seems to follow from and amount to nothing more than:

Grimbly Hughes is the largest grocer in Oxford.

However, we cannot say that it is really an indicative because, as Hare points out, someone who had learned the meaning of indicative verb-forms, but not imperative verb-forms, would not understand it. Hare thinks that there is an imperative neustic concealed in the word "want" and suggests this analysis:

Going by you to the largest grocer in Oxford, please
Grimbly Hughes being the largest grocer in Oxford, yes
_____
Going by you to Grimbly Hughes, please.

Such an analysis would bring this hypothetical imperative under his second rule. However, Hare does not claim that he has settled the matter. That his analysis of the hypothetical imperative is correct remains to be proved.

Another problem which arises in connection with Hare's second rule concerns how validity, in the case of a mixed syllogism, should be characterized. We might say perhaps that a necessary condition of valid inference in such cases is as follows. An imperative conclusion is valid, only if this imperative must (logically) be obeyed, when the imperative premise(s) is (are) obeyed and the indicative premise(s) is (are) true. But this condition, though necessary, would not be sufficient. The following syllogism fulfills the condition just referred to, but its conclusion is *not* valid.

John, do A whenever you do B
John does in fact do C whenever B
_____
John, do A and C whenever B

The question of what would constitute a sufficient condition remains to be answered.[144]

Value-Words and Speech-Acts

Hare wishes to explain the meanings of value words like "good," in terms of the speech-act—commending, prescribing, or whatever you call it—which these words are normally used to perform. Some critics have maintained that this cannot be done. They make two points among others: (i) if it tells us the literal meaning of "good," for example, to say that it is used to perform the speech-act of commendation, then wherever "good" has literal meaning it will be used to commend; *but* (ii) there are numerous examples of "good" being used with its literal meaning, though it is not being used to commend. Examples of such latter uses are:

> X is not good (negation)
> Is X good? (interrogation)
> If X is good, then Y (hypothesis).

It seems to follow from these considerations that Hare's explanation of the meaning of words like "good" must be mistaken.

Hare may be right in thinking that to call something good is to commend it; but an analysis of calling something good is not the same as an analysis of "good." This is how the argument against Hare goes. Any analysis of "good" must allow for the fact that the word is used in different speech-acts, such as those listed above. And "good" must mean the same in all of these, otherwise there will be the absurd consequences that "X is good" may not be denied by "X is not good"; may not be an answer to the question "Is X good?"; may not validate, along with the further premise "If X is good, then Y," the conclusion, "Y." "Good" must mean the same, in each of the three examples listed above, as it means in "X is good," if the latter answers the interrogation, contra-

---

[144] See *LM*, pp. 33–38, and N. Rescher, *The Logic of Commands* (London, 1966), Chaps. 7 and 8, in particular pp. 99–100.

dicts the negation, and together with the hypothesis, entails the conclusion "Y." But in none of the former three sentences (interrogation, negation, hypothesis) is "good" being used to commend, as it is in the categorical statement "X is good."[145] It seems to follow from considerations such as these that Hare's explanation of the meaning of words like "good" must be mistaken. Can that explanation be defended? Again with due acknowledgment to hitherto unpublished work which he has kindly shown me, but without any claim whatever adequately to be representing his opinions, I venture to think that Hare's position might be defended along some such lines as the following. Words like "good" must, of course, be considered as they come incorporated in appropriate sentences, uttered on appropriate occasions, before they can be understood; but, so considered, they give the utterances in which they occur a certain illocutionary force. In the case of "good," this may be called commendatory, interpreting the word in a wide sense. That this illocutionary force is retained even in interrogatives, negatives, and hypotheticals can perhaps be shown by an analysis of these various sentence-forms in the light of neustics and tropics, as Hare now uses those terms.

The *interrogative* sentence-form can be explained as an invitation, or an order, to make one of a number of assertions: to add a neustic (a sign of subscription or assertion) to, for instance, either "X is good" or "X is not good." If we added the assertion sign to the former we should be using "good" to commend. What if we added it to the latter?

Anyone who utters the *negation* "X is not good" would be performing a commendatory speech-act whose content is the negation of the content of the commendation "X is good." In doing so, he would have to rely upon the rules for the use of "not" in conjunction with the logical fact that "good" is used to commend.

The *hypothetical*, "If X is good, then Y" is more difficult. Here "X is good" is clearly not being used to commend. But

---

[145] Cf. J. R. Searle, "Meaning and Speech-Acts," *PR* LXXI (1962).

why? Simply because it is not asserted. What is asserted is not "X is good" but the whole sentence in which this occurs as part of one clause. However, the presence or absence of a neustic does not alter what Hare now calls the tropic of a sentence. He uses this word for the sign which, in accordance with the rules and conventions of our language, indicates not simply grammatical mood but to which sort of speech-act a sentence must be assigned. Its tropic shows its illocutionary force. When a categorical sentence such as "X is good" becomes part of a clause in a hypothetical sentence, there is no reason to say that it must have changed its tropic. But it does now lack a neustic. So "X is good" in "If X is good, then Y" may not be said to commend because it lacks a neustic. However, it may still be said to have commendatory force, for it retains the tropic which it has as a categorical sentence. To whatever extent this tropic is an element in the meaning of "good" in the one case, it is equally so in the other.

Kinds and Levels of Meaning

Dr. G. C. Kerner in *The Revolution in Ethical Theory* brings two criticisms, among others, to bear on Hare's moral philosophy: (i) that Hare was mistaken in the view that moral judgments may have two kinds of meaning, descriptive and evaluative; and (ii) that he failed to recognize the *total* difference in meaning between imperatives and ought judgments. Kerner thinks that if only Hare had made better use of his own distinction between phrastics and neustics in *The Language of Morals,* he might have avoided both these errors. Any speech-act, Kerner argues, has, so to say, two "levels" of meaning: (i) certain criteria of application (the phrastic element: what has traditionally been known as sense and reference); and (ii) a performative, or illocutionary, force (the neustic element). To apply words is simply to correlate them with something in the world, says Kerner. The rules or conventions of sense and reference effect this. They are logically prior to the rules or conventions which constitute illocutionary force, i.e., in the phraseology of *The Language*

of Morals the neustics of description, interrogation, impera-
tion, or whatever.[146] A speech-act involves reliance upon
both sorts of rule or convention. That is, I have not said
anything, if I have merely applied words to things in the
world. I have not described, commanded, questioned, recommended, etc. But neither have I said anything unless I have
said something specific.[147] I have not described, etc., unless
I have singled some thing(s) out for description, etc. Against
this background, Kerner criticizes Hare on the two counts
noted above. I will try to make clear what Kerner's criticisms
are and then to say whether or not they prevail against Hare.
First, I will outline more fully the two criticisms, noted above,
in reverse order.

(i) Kerner charges Hare with failing to recognize the
"total difference" in meaning between imperatives and ought
judgments.[148] Hare said that ought judgments entail imperatives; this implies that there is some similarity of meaning
between them. Of course, Hare recognized that there are also
differences, two in particular: (a) imperatives cannot occur
in the past tense and are predominantly in the second person,
whereas ought judgments come naturally in any tense or
person; (b) ought judgments are universalizable. It is, as I
have already suggested, arguable that a reasonable man will
have reasons for the commands which he utters no less than
for his moral judgments; but even if that is so, these reasons
need not be in the former case, as according to Hare they
need to be in the latter, U-type.[149] If I said "Form fours"
and, when asked "Why?" replied "Because I say so," this
would not offend against, so to say, the rules of the commanding game. But if, when asked why I had said that capital punishment ought to be abolished, I replied "Because I
say so," that, to someone of Hare's persuasion at least,
would seem bizarre.

[146] G. C. Kerner, *The Revolution in Ethical Theory* (Oxford, 1966),
pp. 148–49, 167.
[147] *Ibid.*, pp. 154, 158.
[148] *Ibid.*, p. 163.
[149] See above, p. 185.

To eliminate these differences, Hare in *The Language of Morals* suggests modifying and "enriching" the imperative mood in such a way that it is universalizable and can occur in any tense or person.[150] Analysis in terms of phrastics and neustics will, he thinks, effect this. The phrastic of an indicative sentence can be universal and in any tense or person; and it is possible to take the phrastic of any such indicative and make it into an imperative sentence simply by adding the imperative neustic. Thus, says Hare, we may take the indicative sentence "All mules are barren" and write it thus:

All mules being barren, yes.

The proper universal imperative sentence will then be written:

All mules being barren, please.

This differs in meaning from the imperative of ordinary language "Let all mules be barren" in that the latter can refer only to future mules, whereas the former is a fiat directed to all mules, past and present as well as future. Thus, if a mule in 23 B.C. produced offspring, this would not be a breach of the command "Let all mules be barren" said in 1970 A.D., but it would be a breach of a proper universal command uttered at any time.[151] In this enriched or modified imperative mood we can frame imperatives which are equivalent in meaning to ought judgments. "Instead, therefore, of the cumbrous terminology of phrastics and neustics, let us adopt the artificial word 'ought,'" says Hare. "This is to be defined as follows: if we take a proper universal indicative sentence 'All P's are Q' and split it into phrastic and neustic, 'All P's being Q, yes,' and then substitute for the indicative neustic an imperative one 'All P's being Q, please,' we may, instead of the latter sentence, write 'All P's *ought* to be Q.'"[152] The *"ought"* here is italicized and put in quotation marks to point the fact that Hare is not saying that this is how "ought" is used in ordinary language, but is simply seeing what modifications need to be made to imperatives before they can do the jobs ordinarily done by "ought."[153]

[150] *LM*, pp. 187–88.
[151] *LM*, pp. 189–90.
[152] *LM*, pp. 190–91.
[153] *LM*, p. 180.

Kerner's objection to all this is that whereas general ought judgments can be satisfactorily translated into Hare's modified and enriched imperative mood, *singular* ones cannot. The judgment (1) "One ought always to speak the truth" is equivalent to (2) "All things that are being said being true, please." But (1a) "You ought to tell him the truth" is not equivalent to (2a) "The thing you are about to tell him being true, please." According to Kerner, (2) is universalizable in the way that (1) is: both refer to all things that are being said. The singular (1a), being an ought judgment, is conceivably universalizable. But (2a), with which it is said to be equivalent, is in fact logically indistinguishable from a singular imperative "Tell him the truth." Therefore (2a) is not equivalent to (1a). Kerner says that, in order to make it equivalent, Hare had to rewrite it thus: (2b) "If you do not tell him the truth, you will be breaking the principle 'All things that are said being true, please' and I hereby subscribe to that principle."[154] He points out that (2b) is "not by any stretch of imagination an imperative of any kind or even like one, artificial or not." It is in the indicative mood. And so, he concludes, Hare's attempt to make out the logical similarity between ought judgments and imperatives, which is necessary if the former are to entail the latter, fails. The neustics of ought judgments, he maintains, must be quite different from those of imperatives. If this criticism can be sustained it appears to call in question Hare's basic belief that ought judgments are essentially prescriptive.

I do not feel convinced that it can be sustained. It strikes me as misconceived in at least two respects.

(i) If (2a) is no more than a singular imperative, then surely (2) is no more than a universal one, equivalent to "No lying." In that case the distinction which Kerner wishes to draw between (2) and (2a) in respect of universalizability does not hold. For universal imperatives are not universalizable any more than singular ones in the way that ought judgments are. The request for a U-type reason for them can be refused.

[154] Kerner, *op. cit.*, p. 164; cf. *LM*, p. 191. My numbering of the sentences here is different from Kerner's.

(ii) (2b) is Kerner's version of the following (2c) in Hare: "If you do not tell him the truth, you will be breaking a general '*ought*'-principle to which I hereby subscribe."[155] Kerner, it will be remembered, renders the general "ought" principle thus: "All things that are said being true, please," and no doubt he is entitled to do so in the light of Hare's remark that for "All P's being Q, please" we may write "All P's '*ought*' to be Q."[156] But has Kerner really taken Hare's point here? Was Hare substituting for (2a) something which was really not by any stretch of imagination an imperative as Kerner says? Hare goes on immediately after (2c) above to give a more formal version of his point. "More formally," he says, "we might write 'There is at least one value for P and one for Q such that (1) all P's *ought* to be Q and (2) your not telling him the truth would be (or was) a case of a P not being Q.' "[157] His intention seems to be to show that "You ought to tell him the truth" can be represented as the conclusion of a practical syllogism of which the major premise is "All that is said ought to be true," and the minor premise is "What you are telling him is something that is said." This analysis stands in contrast to that suggested by Kerner's contention that Hare had to substitute (2b) for (2a) above. If "You ought to tell him the truth" is analyzed in terms of (2c), i.e., of Hare's own analysis, then "You ought to tell him the truth" does not *state* that if you do not, you will be breaking a principle; nor does it *state* that the speaker subscribes to this principle. It invokes or applies a principle as the standard of judgment. In so far, then, as Kerner's criticism of Hare is to the effect that, in order to make (2a) equivalent in meaning to (1a), Hare had to rewrite (2a) as (2b), and (2b) is not, by any stretch of imagination, in the imperative mood, but is a straightforward indicative, that criticism fails. For it rests on a misinterpretation of Hare. Hare rewrites (2a) as (2c), *not* as (2b); and *furthermore* he gives a "more formal" rendering of (2c) which makes it quite clear that,

[155] *LM*, p. 191.
[156] Kerner, *op. cit.*, p. 164; *LM*, p. 191.
[157] *LM*, p. 191.

to his way of thinking, the latter is *not* simply a statement in the indicative mood.

I suspect that Hare would say that there is a more radical defect in Kerner's criticism. For Kerner takes it that, in modifying and "enriching" the imperative mood, Hare was attempting to show that ought judgments are equivalent in meaning to imperatives. But Hare has always insisted that they are *not* equivalent in meaning. His point has always been that ought judgments *entail* imperatives, *not* that they can be equated with them. I think he would say that his attempt to modify and enrich the imperative mood was intended simply to make it possible for entailments in any person or tense to be stated. So that, for instance, "He ought to have told the truth" can be said to entail a statable imperative in the third person singular and the past tense. However, it must be admitted that some of Hare's remarks in Chapter 12 of *The Language of Morals,* where he proposes this modified and enriched imperative mood, do read as if he is attempting to equate statements in that mood with ought judgments. For instance, in the first sentence of the chapter, he writes: ". . . let us imagine that our language does not contain any value-words; and let us then ask, to what extent a new artificial terminology, defined in terms of the imperative mood and of the ordinary logical words, could fill the gap which this would leave."[158] But, even if such remarks can be said to entitle Kerner to take Hare to be equating the meanings of ought judgments with imperatives, his criticisms of Hare are open to the objections which I have set out above.

(ii) Kerner's more radical criticism of Hare was that in conceiving of moral judgments as having two kinds of meaning, evaluative and descriptive, Hare misconceived both of these kinds of meaning. According to Kerner, Hare thought that, whereas the evaluative meaning of value words, like "good," is logically distinct from the appropriate criteria of application, the descriptive meaning of words like "red" is identical with their criteria of application. But Kerner argues in the first place that there is more to descriptive meaning

[158] *LM,* p. 180.

than sense and reference; descriptions, as such, have an illocutionary force which distinguishes them from other sorts
of speech-act. And, in the second place, there is more to
evaluative meaning than commendation (or whatever term
you choose to use for it). The commendation must be given
application; something specific must be commended, otherwise nothing is being said. In Hare's terms, as used by Kerner,
descriptions would be meaningless without their neustics; as
would evaluations without their phrastics.[159]

Kerner suggests that Hare confused two *levels* of meaning
(neustic and phrastic) with two *kinds* of meaning (evaluative
and descriptive) because he concentrated on single terms,
such as "good" or "ought," instead of full sentences. There
may be one-word sentences of course, but it is the sentence
which constitutes a unit of communication and "has meaning in the primary sense,"[160] the meaning of single words
being an abstraction from this. Some words or expressions
(e.g., "I promise," "I command," "Do," "I will"), considered
in isolation, have no criteria of application. But we do not
say that they lend a special kind of meaning to the discourse
or speech-acts in which they figure. We look on them as
being like Hare's neustics. Kerner thinks that moral terms,
like "good" and "ought," are very similar. They do not lend
moral judgments a separate kind of meaning, only a peculiar
illocutionary force. So, Kerner thinks, Hare's analysis of moral
judgments is unnecessarily complicated. Hare analyzed words
like "good" into two kinds of meaning; and meaningful
sentences into two elements, phrastics and neustics. He was
therefore operating with four factors, whereas, according to
Kerner, he could have got on very well with two: phrastics
(sense and reference) and neustics (illocutionary force). And
if he had restricted himself to these two, he would have
avoided the absurd position in which, says Kerner, he lands
himself, of maintaining that it is possible "to perform two
full speech-acts at once, to say two complete and separable
things in the same breath."[161] Kerner concedes that it would

---

[159] Kerner, *op. cit.*, pp. 150 ff.
[160] *Ibid.*, pp. 158–59.
[161] *Ibid.*, p. 147.

make sense to say that someone had described and persuaded
in the same breath, as the emotivists were wont to say. But
if one asks of a speech-act "Is this a description or a prescription?" "the proper answer seems never to be 'I am doing
both.'" Yet "in Hare's theory this would have to be the only
proper answer."[162]

Kerner notes that Hare regards the criteria of application
for words like "good" as identical with their descriptive meaning. This raises two questions: (a) what is the relation between the descriptive and evaluative meanings of these words?
and (b) what constitutes a reason for a value judgment?
Kerner thinks Hare's belief in two kinds of meaning: (a)
renders the former problem insoluble; and (b) necessarily
reduces reasons for evaluation to mere indications of contingent fact, namely of how the relevant evaluative terms are
used by individuals or communities.

In defense of Hare's position against these criticisms, I
think that at least three points can be made.

(i) It is no part of Hare's position that a *single* speech-act
may be both descriptive and evaluative (or prescriptive), at
least not in the way Kerner takes Hare to have thought that it
could. Hare seems to me to be clear that there are two quite
distinct things which you might be doing in saying "X is a
good person." You might be *describing* X: that is, informing
someone who knows what criteria of goodness you are invoking that X has certain qualities corresponding to these. In this
respect, you could, for example, intentionally inform the
members of a Conservative Association that X was not a thief
in saying that he was a good man, even though you yourself
did not consider respect for the institution of private property
a criterion of goodness. On the other hand, in saying that X
is a good man, you could be *evaluating* X; that is, grading him
by criteria to which you yourself do subscribe. In this respect,
in saying that X was good because honest, you would imply
your own approval of honesty. But these two sorts of remark
are not one speech-act. The circumstances and the intention of
the speaker determine, on any given occasion, *which* of them

[162] *Ibid.*, p. 148.

is taking place. Hare never said that they can both occur at once.

(ii) It is characteristic of value words like "good" that they can be used to revise their own criteria of application. Someone who hitherto has thought, for example, that a good man, as such, is one who never appropriates other people's property, may come to ask himself whether there may not be circumstances in which a good man, as such, might undertake what is called stealing. Now, could this logical characteristic of "good" and other value words be covered simply by saying that sentences containing such words have neustics of commendation? Surely, *within* the class of speech-acts with neustics of commendation there must be two subclasses: one in which value words are used in accordance with generally accepted criteria, and the other in which they are used to question these criteria. Hare's *way* of differentiating them, as having descriptive and evaluative meaning respectively, may of course be open to question; but that there is a difference which needs to be accounted for seems indisputable. It is not clear that Kerner recognizes the necessity for this difference or how he would account for it.

(iii) Kerner finds in Hare what he considers the absurd view that "we can give no reasons for our evaluations" and he thinks this due to Hare's mistaken theory about two kinds of meaning.[163] Whatever its source, Hare's view of evaluative reasoning does seem to resolve itself, in the last analysis, into consistency and nothing more. I form a value judgment. I can be asked a reason for it. Having given my reason, I am required, in order to qualify as a reasonable moralist, only to adhere to it consistently. Kerner, like others, finds this unsatisfactory because fanatics can be consistent. As I have already said,[164] it seems to me perfectly conceivable that there should be a form of discourse, quite properly called reasonable, in which being reasonable would amount to no more than being consistent. And it is conceivable that this is what moral discourse amounts to. As Hare has shown in his discussion of universalizability, if it is this and no more, many

[163] *Ibid.,* p. 159.
[164] Above, p. 208.

of the moves which we recognize as natural moves in moral argument are explained. However, the question can be asked: is there any logical limitation on what may be offered as a reason for a moral judgment? This is the question which, in one form or another, has cropped up repeatedly in our consideration of emotivism and prescriptivism. In the final section of the next chapter I will attempt to answer it.

CHAPTER 6. DESCRIPTIVISM

In this chapter I shall deal with some of the most recent developments in modern moral philosophy. In the first section, I shall set out some recent opinions on how a famous passage about the connection between "is" and "ought" in Hume's *Treatise* should be interpreted, and assess them. In the second section, the question will be asked: can moral ought judgments be grounded logically in what men want? The third section deals with an attempt to derive "ought" from "is" which has aroused much interest among modern moral philosophers. In the final section, I shall bring the story right up to date by outlining the debate currently in progress between prescriptivists, like Hare, and descriptivists, or neo-naturalists as they are sometimes called, such as G. J. Warnock and Mrs. Foot. Throughout this chapter my aim will be twofold: (i) to make it clear, within the terms of reference, precisely what contemporary philosophers are saying on the points at issue; and (ii) to form a critical judgment of their views.

I. THE INTERPRETATION OF HUME ON "IS" AND "OUGHT"

There is a famous passage in Hume's *Treatise* which in modern moral philosophy has frequently been interpreted as propounding the doctrine that "ought" cannot logically be derived from "is," that no value judgment follows from any statement of fact. Adherents of all the main types of ethical theory which have so far been considered in this book have been inclined to quote this passage in their own support. It runs as follows:

I cannot forbear adding to these reasonings an observation which may, perhaps, be found of some importance. In every system of morality, which I have hitherto met with, I have always remarked that the author proceeds for some time in the ordinary way of reasoning, and establishes the being of a God, or makes observations concerning human affairs; when of a sudden I am surprised to find that, instead of the usual copulations of propositions *is* and *is not*, I meet with no proposition that is not connected with an *ought*, or an *ought not*. This change is imperceptible; but is, however, of the last consequence. For as this *ought* or *ought not* expresses some new relation or affirmation, it is necessary that it should be observed and explained; and at the same time that a reason should be given for what seems altogether inconceivable, how this new relation can be a deduction from others, which are entirely different from it. But as authors do not commonly use this precaution I shall presume to recommend it to the readers; and am persuaded, that this small attention would subvert all the vulgar systems of morality, and let us see that the distinction of vice and virtue is not founded merely on the relations of objects, nor is perceived by reason.[1]

Though not referred to by either Moore or Ross, these words are quoted by their fellow intuitionist H. A. Prichard[2] in support of his thesis that ought questions are *sui generis*. The emotivist A. J. Ayer[3] claims, with this passage in mind, that his ethical theory rests upon a sound and respectable point of logic which had already been discovered by Hume, namely that "ought" does not follow from "is." Prescriptivism's leading protagonist, R. M. Hare, is most explicit of all in claiming Hume for a precursor and an ally. He refers to the logical impossibility of deriving "ought" from "is" as "Hume's law"[4] and declares himself to be its loyal adherent and stout defender.[5]

[1] *Treatise* III. i. 1, pp. 469–70. The page references to Hume's *Treatise* and *Enquiry* are to the Selby-Bigge editions. I have modernized the spelling and punctuation.
[2] *MO*, p. 89.
[3] Cf. above, p. 134.
[4] *FR*, p. 108.
[5] E.g., *FR*, pp. 108, 186.

The Accepted Interpretation

The interpretation of the famous passage is not in dispute among the representatives of these differing schools of modern ethical theory. Hume, in the above passage, says that in every system of morality which he has encountered a move is made from "is" to "ought." This move he speaks of as a "deduction": and he declares that it "seems altogether inconceivable" how it can be made. Intuitionists, emotivists, and prescriptivists who cite him have taken his word "deduction" to mean logical entailment and his phrase "seems altogether inconceivable" to be a typically ironical understatement for "*is* altogether inconceivable." They have taken his point to be that, from the premises (i) "ought" cannot be entailed by "is" and (ii) arguments are either deductive or defective, the conclusion follows that there is an impassable logical gulf between moral judgments and statements of natural, or supernatural, fact. This logical gulf, they say, is that to which Moore was referring when he spoke of the indefinability of "good," that which Stevenson had in mind when he differentiated beliefs from attitudes, and that which Hare claimed to be exposing when he contended that no description can be used to prescribe.

Such an interpretation of Hume's famous passage—for convenience we will call it "the accepted interpretation"—has recently come under attack. Some moral philosophers now reject it as completely misconceived. According to that accepted interpretation, Hume was arguing that there is *no* logical connection between "is" and "ought." Those who now reject it maintain the very opposite. Hume, they say, was arguing that there *is* a logical connection between "ought" and "is" and claiming that, whereas other moral philosophers had failed to explain it correctly, he was able to do so. For convenience, we will call this "a new interpretation" of Hume's famous passage. While there is agreement among those who offer a new interpretation that Hume believed himself able to resolve the is-ought problem, there is some divergence of opinion among them as to precisely *how* he thought himself able to do so.

In passing, the possibility should at least be recognized that the differences of opinion between exponents of the accepted interpretation and of a new interpretation respectively, and between those who offer one new interpretation and those who offer another, may be due to inconsistencies within Hume's moral philosophy itself. These conflicting interpretations may simply have fastened onto different elements in that philosophy which cannot in fact be reconciled. In support of this possibility, it could be said that anyone who, so to speak, reads Hume through modern analytical spectacles will detect seeming ambiguities in those passages which are usually referred to in an attempt to settle this controversy and to which we shall refer below. It can hardly be denied that a good deal has to be conceded, to the effect that we cannot expect in Hume the clear distinction between psychological and logical considerations which we should look for in a modern philosopher, if Hume is to be saved from all charge of ambiguity. However, when dealing with a philosopher of Hume's stature, there is always a presumption that we have failed to understand him rather than that he is confused. So, to begin with, we must assume that he had a self-consistent point to make about the connection between "is" and "ought" and ask whether the accepted interpretation or one of the new interpretations most faithfully represents this. We have seen what exponents of the accepted interpretation took his point to be. Now we turn to the question: how, according to his new interpreters, did Hume bridge the gap between "is" and "ought"?

New Interpretation No. 1

We will call the first new interpretation to which I shall refer, N.I. (1).[6] This does not reject the assumptions of the accepted interpretation that (i) Hume thought that "ought" (at least as used in those systems of morality which

[6] For this view cf. G. Hunter, "Hume on *Is* and *Ought*," *P* XXXVIII (1963), 150. Hunter acknowledges his debt to Professor G. Ryle. The papers referred to in this section by A. C. MacIntyre, R. F. Atkinson, G. Hunter, A. Flew, and myself are all contained in *The Is-Ought Question* (1969), edited by W. D. Hudson.

he was attacking) cannot be entailed by "is"; and (ii) he believed arguments to be either deductive or defective. Those supporting N.I. (1) simply claim that Hume eliminated the is-ought gap altogether by *identifying* ought propositions with certain is propositions. If this interpretation is correct, Hume's point was that it only "seems altogether inconceivable" how moral judgments can be deduced from statements of fact when you assume that such a move *needs* to be made. In fact it does *not*. For moral judgments *are* statements of fact. Such passages from Hume as the following are quoted in support of N.I. (1).

(i) From the paragraph immediately preceding the is-ought passage:
. . . when you pronounce any action or character to be vicious, *you mean nothing, but* that from the constitution of your nature you have a feeling or sentiment of blame from the contemplation of it (italics mine).[7]

(ii) From the section immediately following that which the is-ought passage concludes:
We *do not infer* a character to be virtuous, because it pleases: but in feeling that it pleases after such a particular manner, we in effect feel that it is virtuous (italics mine).[8]

Such passages have been taken to show that, in Hume's opinion, there is no need to account for an *inference* from "is" to "ought" because what ought propositions *mean* can be adequately *defined* in terms of "is."[9] Ought propositions simply state that certain objects cause the speaker, or the spectator, to have certain sorts of feelings. This interpretation makes Hume a subjectivist, i.e., one who takes moral judgments to *report* the occurrence of certain emotions.

Against it, some admirers of Hume claim that he was more of an emotivist than a subjectivist. They quite rightly set Hume's remarks in an eighteenth-century context. Hume, they say, was intent upon denying (i) the belief of the ra-

---

[7] *Treatise* III. i. 1, p. 469; cf. Hunter, *op. cit.*, p. 148.
[8] *Treatise* III. i. 2, p. 471; cf. Hunter, *op. cit.*, p. 149.
[9] Cf. also Hume, *An Enquiry Concerning the Principles of Morals*, Appendix I. i., p. 289; and Hunter, *op. cit.*, p. 149 n.

tional intuitionists that moral judgments such as "Promises ought to be kept" state necessary truths self-evident to all reasonable men; and (ii) the conviction of his religious contemporaries that to call anything wrong is to say that it is against God's will. In opposition to these systems of morality, they maintain, Hume was insisting that moral judgments are ultimately grounded in human sentiment. But of course the crucial question is: how so grounded? Professor A. G. N. Flew contends that we "get the emphasis wrong" if we think Hume's answer would have been that moral judgments *report* human sentiments. It is "so much better to say" that his "central insight" was that moral judgments *express* feelings of praise or blame.[10] Hume said, for instance, in an Appendix to his *Enquiry Concerning the Principles of Morals:* "And when we *express* that detestation against him [Nero] . . . it is not that we see any relations of which he was ignorant, but that, . . . we *feel* sentiments against which he was hardened. . . ."[11] The grounding in feeling lies in the fact that our judgment expresses our detestation. Flew does not pin his whole case to this one quotation, of course; nor does he claim for a moment that Hume was as clear and explicit in his emotivism as Stevenson or Ayer. He is fully alive to the point already made, that Hume did not differentiate psychological description from logical analysis in the way that a modern philosopher would. But Flew says in effect that just because of this, we ought not to take Hume too literally when he says that "X is vicious" means "I have a sentiment of blame from the contemplation of X," or that "virtuous" in "X is virtuous" is to be defined as "causes the speaker, or spectator, to have a feeling of approbation for X." All Flew claims is that Hume is closer to emotivism than to any other modern ethical theory. There seem to me to be better grounds for Flew's interpretation than for N.I. (1). If Hume thought that ought judgments are expressions of emotion (not statements to the effect that it has been experienced) then it

[10] A. G. N. Flew, "On the Interpretation of Hume," *P* XXXVIII (1963), 180; see note 6.
[11] Appendix I. ii., p. 291 (Flew's italics); cf. Flew, *op. cit.,* 182.

may well have seemed to him "inconceivable" how they should be deduced from statements of fact. The point of Flew's argument that Hume was an emotivist, not a subjectivist, is to defend the accepted interpretation.

New Interpretation No. 2

I turn now to a second new interpretation of the is-ought passage, which I shall speak of as N.I. (2).[12] We saw that N.I. (1) could allow the assumptions of the accepted interpretation that Hume (i) thought that "ought" (as used in the systems of morality to which he was referring) cannot be entailed by "is," and (ii) believed arguments to be deductive or defective. However, N.I. (2) rejects the second of these assumptions. On what grounds? We will begin with two exegetical points and then go on to wider considerations.

The accepted interpretation, it will be recalled, took Hume's word "deduction" in the is-ought passage to mean logical entailment, and his "seems altogether inconceivable" to be ironical. The second new interpretation challenges that exegesis on both counts. It takes Hume's "deduction" to mean simply inference. In the eighteenth century the word "deduction" appears to have been used of all discursive, as opposed to intuitive, reasoning.[13] In his other writings Hume himself sometimes speaks of what we call induction as deduction, referring to what we call deduction as "demonstrative argument." This is the ground on which N.I. (2) takes "deduction "to mean simply inference. But that interpretation does not go unchallenged. It is pointed out that Reid, Hume's contemporary, took the latter's "deduction" in the is-ought passage to mean entailment.[14] However, if there is any plausibility in N.I. (2)'s interpretation of "deduction," it means that one main support of the accepted interpretation is that much less secure. It may then be possible

[12] E.g., A. C. MacIntyre, "Hume on 'Is' and 'Ought,' " *PR* LXVIII (1959); see note 6.

[13] Cf. MacIntyre, *op. cit.*, pp. 460–61.

[14] Reid, *Essays on the Active Powers*, Chap. VII, referred to by R. F. Atkinson in "Hume on 'Is' and 'Ought': a Reply to A. C. MacIntyre," *PR* LXX (1961), 235.

that Hume was not discussing entailment, but some other way of passing from "is" to "ought."

Exponents of N.I. (2) also reject the accepted interpretation of Hume's "seems altogether inconceivable." Ironic this expression certainly is, if it means "is altogether inconceivable." But does it mean that? Because Hume is often ironic it does not follow that he is invariably so and that, whenever his words could be so taken, they must be. If there is, as we shall see that exponents of N.I. (2) believe, a possible non-ironic interpretation, we need not conclude that it is mistaken just because it is non-ironic.

Freed, then, from the necessity to read "deduction" as "entailment" and "seems inconceivable" as ironic, exponents of N.I. (2) have taken Hume to be saying in the is-ought passage that there is an explanation of the connection between "is" and "ought" which corrects the misconceptions of other moral philosophers on the point. So far from pronouncing the gap between "is" and "ought" to be unbridgeable, Hume was saying that it can be bridged. Put summarily, the way in which exponents of N.I. (2) think that Hume purported to bridge this gap is: by showing the reasonableness of inferring what ought to be done from a consideration of what is in the common interest. They draw a comparison between this move and induction. Their point is not, of course, that this inference is an instance of induction, but simply that it is like induction in a certain respect which I will now indicate. By induction we predict, for example, that the sun will rise tomorrow. But we cannot demonstrate that it will. All we have to go on is the fact that it has risen on every morrow within our experience, and it does not necessarily follow from this fact that it will do so again tomorrow. Therefore the principle of induction—that conformities within our past experience can, under certain conditions, provide a rational basis for predicting their repetition within future experience—admits of no logical demonstration. Is it therefore logically disreputable? Hume, it will be remembered, gave classic expression to the feeling that it is.[15] But such doubts about in-

---

[15] *Treatise* I. ii. 6; cf. MacIntyre, *op. cit.*, p. 454.

duction are derided by many modern philosophers. They are said to involve the confusion of supposing that the question "Is it reasonable to infer A from B?" must always in the last analysis mean "Does B entail A?"; or in other words that arguments are deductive or defective. In point of fact, however, deduction is one method of argument and induction is another. Each is appropriate to its own purpose and subject matter; deduction, to the demonstration of necessary conclusions; induction, to the prediction of contingent events.[16] According to exponents of N.I. (2), there is just the same sort of objection to regarding inferences from "is" to "ought" as either deductive or defective. Why should there not be a non-deductive method of argument, as appropriate for settling moral questions as induction is for settling questions about what the empirical facts are, or will be? Hume, we are told by exponents of N.I. (2), saw no reason against this. They take him to be saying in the is-ought passage that his moral philosophy indicates the appropriate non-deductive method of passing from "is" to "ought."

How precisely is he supposed to have conceived of that inference? Professor A. C. MacIntyre says that Hume believed that moral rules are justified if, and only if, they are in everyone's long-term interest. Against the possible objection that Hume made the transition from "Obedience to this rule would be to everyone's long-term interest" to the conclusion "We ought to obey this rule" by presupposing, as Hare for instance would, the major premise "We ought to do whatever is to everyone's long-term interest," MacIntyre argues thus:

"We ought to do what is to everyone's long-term interest" cannot function as such a premise for Hume since in his terms it could not be a moral principle at all, but at best a kind of compressed definition. That is, the notion of "ought" is for Hume only explicable in terms of the notion of a consensus of interest. To say that we ought to do something is to affirm that there is a commonly accepted rule;

[16] Cf. P. F. Strawson, *Introduction to Logical Theory* (1960), pp. 248–63.

and the existence of such a rule presupposes a consensus of opinion as to where our common interests lie. An obligation is constituted in part by such a consensus and the concept of "ought" is logically dependent on the concept of a common interest and can only be explained in terms of it. To say that we ought to do what is in the common interest would therefore be either to utter an aphoristic and misleading truism or else to use the term "ought" in a sense quite other than that understood by Hume. Thus the locution "We ought to do what is to everyone's long-term interest" could not lay down a moral principle which might figure as a major premise in the type of syllogism which Hare describes.[17]

How, then, does Hume make the transition made from "is in everyone's long-term interest" to "ought to be obeyed"? This is MacIntyre's answer:

> The transition from "is" to "ought" is made . . . by the notion of "wanting." . . . Aristotle's examples of practical syllogisms typically have a premise which includes some such terms as "suits" or "pleases." We could give a long list of the concepts which can form such bridge notions between "is" and "ought": wanting, needing, desiring, pleasure, happiness, health—and these are only a few. I think there is a strong case for saying that moral notions are unintelligible apart from concepts such as these. . . .
>
> The interpretation of the "is" and "ought" passage which I am offering can now be stated compendiously. Hume is not in this passage asserting the autonomy of morals—for he did not believe in it; and he is not making a point about entailment—for he does not mention it. He is asserting that the question of how the factual basis of morality is related to morality is a crucial logical issue, reflection on which will enable one to realise how there are ways in which this transition can be made and ways in which it cannot. One has to go beyond the passage itself to see what these are; but if one does so it is plain that we can connect the facts of the situation with what we ought to do only by means of one of those concepts which Hume treats under the head-

ing of the passions and which I have indicated by examples such as wanting, needing, and the like.[18]

In answering the question: do these remarks justify N.I. (2)? the following considerations seem to me to be apposite.

(i) First, a general comment. Hume had doubts about induction, as we have noted, which presupposed that arguments are either deductive or defective. Would it not, then, be rather surprising if he denied this disjunction when it came to arguments from "is" to "ought"? That is what MacIntyre takes him to be doing. Strange to say, MacIntyre expresses surprise that modern philosophers, while deploring Hume's doubts about induction, have been content with the accepted interpretation of the is-ought passage which assumes that arguments are either deductive or defective. He thinks that since modern philosophers reject that disjunction in the one case, they ought to have done so in the other. But this overlooks a difference between the two cases. Argument from past experience to predicted future experience is indisputably what we mean by "reasoning," when questions of empirical fact have to be settled in science or common sense;[19] but it is by no means so certain that the move from "is" to "ought" (whatever the "is" might be) is per se what we mean by "reasoning" in moral argument. So I do not think that it is inconsistent to say that induction is logically respectable, and yet to deny that the move from "is" to "ought" is. But however that may be, it would surely not be surprising, in the light of his doubts about induction, if Hume had the same sort of doubts about the move from "is" to "ought." This is what one might expect.

(ii) In the first of the above quotations, MacIntyre confidently affirms that "the notion of 'ought' is, for Hume, only explicable in terms of the notion of a consensus of interest." He supports this remark with three others which presumably purport to substantiate it by stating Hume's opinions.

---

[18] *Ibid.*, pp. 463–66.
[19] I leave aside here any consideration of the precise character of scientific thinking, e.g., whether or not it is hypothetico-deductive.

(a) "To say that we ought to do something is to affirm that there is a commonly acceped rule." Hume certainly did say things like the following:

> When therefore men have had experience enough to observe that, whatever may be the consequences of any single act of justice performed by a single person, yet the whole system of actions, concurred in by the whole society, is infinitely advantageous to the whole, and to every part; it is not long before justice and property take place.[20]

To say this is to say perhaps that *because* there are common interests there are rules of justice. But it is certainly not to say that the "ought" in these rules amounts to nothing more than a statement that the rules exist. (b) MacIntyre may be taking this point when he goes on to say: "The existence of such a rule *presupposes* a consensus of opinion as to where our common interests lie" (italics mine). But is even this interpretation of Hume's point, in a passage such as that just quoted, indisputable? When he there speaks of justice "taking place," does he mean that as a matter of *logical* fact its rules cannot *exist* unless it is observed that they will be in the common interest, or simply that as a matter of *psychological* fact they will not be *accepted* until that observation has been made? The answer may indeed be hard to determine but it does affect the sense in which the notion of a common interest *explains* the notion of "ought." (c) MacIntyre evidently takes Hume to be making the logical, rather than the psychological, point for he goes on: "An obligation is constituted in part by such a consensus and the concept of 'ought' is *logically dependent* on the concept of a common interest and can only be explained in terms of it" (italics mine). But this simply raises, and does not answer, the question: in what part? An exponent of the accepted interpretation would doubtless agree that, from the belief that X is in the common interest, it follows, according to Hume, that X ought to be done; but he would say that it only does so because the major premise, "Whatever is in the common interest ought to be done," is tacitly supplied by Hume. Hume's criticism of Wollaston has been taken to lend some support to this latter view. Wollaston believed that all immorality is, in the last analysis, lying—i.e., the denial of what is. For instance, that the wrongness of an ungrateful act to one's benefactor lies in the fact that such an act denies the truth that he is one's benefactor. On this, Hume trenchantly commented that, in Wollaston's "whimsical system," the immorality of denying what is the case is simply presupposed. In other words, you cannot get from "X is a lie" to "X is wrong" without the premise "All lies are wrong."

Does it follow then, as some have claimed against Mac-Intyre,[21] that according to Hume, similarly you cannot get from "X is in the common interest" to "X ought to be done" apart from the premise "Whatever is in the common interest ought to be done"? I think not. In the criticism of Wollaston, Hume's point was not simply that a major premise is presupposed, but that the question of its justification remains. He wrote: "I shall allow, if you please, that all immorality is derived from this supposed falsehood in action, provided you can give me any plausible reason why such a falsehood is immoral."[22] And if, as MacIntyre thinks, Hume would have said that this "reason why" will have to show that such falsehood is against the common interest, we cannot argue that because, in Hume's opinion, the move from "X is a lie" to "X is wrong" requires the premise "All lies are wrong," then the move from "All lies are against the common interest" to "All lies are wrong" must, in Hume's opinion, require the premise "Whatever is against the common interest is wrong." His opinion *could* have been that some such notion as that of "interest" effects the logical transition here from "is" to "ought." MacIntyre's main point, as we saw in the quotation on p. 258, is that Hume believed there to be a strong case for saying that moral notions are unintelligible apart from the concept of needing, or wanting, or some other such bridge notion. He takes Hume to have been sum-

[21] See R. F. Atkinson, *op. cit.*, 237–38; and my own article "Hume on *Is* and *Ought*," *PQ* 14 (1964), 250; see note 6.
[22] *Treatise* III. i. 1, p. 462 note.

ming up to this effect in the is-ought passage. Notice that *if* MacIntyre is right and *if* Hume was doing that, Hume's point was not (or not simply) that if we did not think that justice is in the common interest, we could not be psychologically induced to obey its rules. It was the logical point that, when an ought judgment has been delivered, the question "Why?" can be answered by an appeal to human interests, needs, or wants with a finality with which it can never be answered simply by an appeal to general moral principles.

Which Interpretation Is Correct?

Summing up so far, there seem to be three possibilities concerning the role which some such proposition as "We ought to do what is to everyone's long-term interest" plays in the moral philosophy of Hume. They are: (a) that it states a *general moral principle;* (b) that it states a *definition* of "ought"; (c) that it states a *rule of inference* by reference to which we can logically infer "ought" from "is." Exponents of the "accepted interpretation" come down in favor of the first of these. Advocates of N.I. (1) prefer the second. And protagonists of N.I. (2) are for the third possibility.

Two questions arise. They are: (i) which, if any, is the correct interpretation of Hume? and (ii) which view, if any, is correct, apart from the interpretation of Hume, as a solution of the is-ought problem? I shall conclude this section with some opinions about the first of these two questions. Then, in the next section, I shall turn to the second of them and consider, in particular, the views differentiated as (b) and (c) above—respectively, that "ought" may be defined in terms of interests or of "want," and that wanting constitutes a logical bridge notion between "ought" and "is."

What conclusion, then, must we come to about Hume's is-ought passage, in the light of these varying interpretations? I think the following:

(i) Hume seems to have affinities with both subjectivists and emotivists but cannot be said to belong unambiguously to either school. For reasons given above (p. 254), it is unsatisfactory to say that he simply regarded ought propositions as a special kind of is-propositions, but, equally clearly, he did not draw the sharp logical distinction between "is" and "ought" which a modern emotivist would draw.

(ii) Hume believed that it is the passions, not reason, which invariably move to action. Moral judgments, in so far as they are action-guiding, must be grounded in the passions. He wrote: "Upon the whole, it is impossible that the distinction betwixt moral good and evil can be made by reason; since that distinction has an influence upon our actions, of which reason alone is incapable."[23] He believed that moral judgments are in fact grounded in men's desire for that which is in their common interest. But it is very difficult to say what he took the nature of this grounding to be. Did he hold that it is only because they are in the common interest that the rules of justice, in fact, induce men to obey them, or that the fact that they are in the common interest logically constitutes the rules of justice? I can find no unequivocal answer to this.

(iii) Such understanding of Hume's is-ought passage as we can attain will be gained only by setting it firmly in its eighteenth-century context. The section of the *Treatise*, at the end of which it occurs, is entitled "Moral distinction not derived from reason" and that which immediately follows, "Moral distinctions derived from a moral sense." One thing seems certain. In the great eighteenth-century debate about the nature of conscience, Hume intended to refute the rational intuitionists and to side with the moral sense philosophers. But he seems also to have had a further intention: to refute those religious moralists, whichever side they were on, who wanted to ground morality in God's will. Hume rejected (he professes reluctantly) any such grounding. He wrote to Hutcheson in 1740: "I wish from my heart I could avoid concluding that since morality, according to your opinion as well as mine, is determined merely by sentiment, it regards only human nature and human life. This has often been urged against you, and the consequences are very momentous."[24] Some think that the derogatory reference in the

---

[23] *Treatise* III. i. 1, p. 462.
[24] *Letters* edited by J. Y. T. Greig, Vol. I, No. 16, p. 40, quoted by Flew, *op. cit.*, 180. On the debate between rational intuitionists and the "moral sense" school see my *Ethical Intuitionism* (1967).

is-ought passage to "vulgar systems of morality" which he is "subverting" is intended by Hume to apply only to religious moral codes.[25] But whether that is the case or not, it is certain that Hume believed morality to be grounded in human sentiments or interests and not in reason or the will of God.

(iv) I think we have to say, in the end, that Hume simply raised the question as to the *precise nature* of this grounding, but provided no clear answer to it. Morality, as such, he clearly took to have an intimate logical connection with human wants or needs. But was he saying merely that if we had no wants—if it made no difference to us what happened— then we should have no use for evaluative language, moral or otherwise? This is a view with which any emotivist or prescriptivist would agree. Is that what Hume was saying or more? And if more, what more? Was he saying that "ought" must be *defined* as "is wanted"; or that "ought" can be *inferred* from "is wanted"? Or what? The answer to these questions is not certain. We must conclude, I think, that to expect Hume to have come out clearly for one position or another is to treat him as though he were a philosopher of our own age and not of his own. I think that Hume did not take "We ought to do whatever is to everyone's long-term interest" as exclusively a moral principle, a definition, or a rule of inference, but as some amalgam of all three. Expositors, as we have seen, can find quotations which seem to support the view that Hume took it as each of them respectively; and I think there is no very clear preponderance in favor of one as against the others. That is why I say that, for us, Hume's famous is-ought passage, when set within the context of his moral philosophy as a whole, simply raises, but does not answer, the question of how wants or interests are related to obligations. To that difficult matter we must now turn.

II. OUGHTS AND WANTS

In the last section I referred to two possible opinions about the relationship between wanting and obligation. These were, to put them very succinctly: (i) that "ought" *means* "wants"

and (ii) that "wants" constitutes *a conclusive reason* for
"ought." We have considered the question: did Hume hold
either of these opinions? I now turn to the question: which, if
either, is correct?

Does "Ought" Mean "Wants"?

Is it true *by definition* of "ought" that we ought to do what,
in some sense or other, we want to do? The opinion has
recently been canvassed by some philosophers that we can
(logically) say in terms of "want" everything which, in the
normal course of events, we would ever wish to say in terms
of "ought."[26]

This opinion should, first of all, be quite clearly differentiated from others with which it seems easily to be confused.[27]
It is emphatically an opinion on a point of logic, not of
psychology. That is to say, it has nothing to do with whether
or not people will strive for X as strenuously if they think of
it only as what they want, as they would if they thought of it
as something which they ought to attain. Nor again, is it
relevant to ask whether or not talk in terms of "want" is less
or more effective in getting people to do what we wish them to
do than talk in terms of "ought." Perhaps it can be shown
that men fired by conscience are on the whole more successful
in attaining their ends than those inspired only by personal
ambitions; and, indisputably, it can be shown that the techniques used by advertisers and propagandists are more successful in persuading men that something or other is what
they want than the exhortations or admonitions of moralists.
But such considerations are nothing to the purpose. Our
concern is with the question: can we *say* in terms of "want"
everything which we now say in terms of "ought"?

The precise terms of "want" in question here may, of
course, be a matter open to much discussion. Someone who
believes in the universalizability of moral judgments, for instance, may wish to say that "I ought to do X" means, not

---

[26] E.g., M. Zimmerman, "The 'Is-Ought': an Unnecessary Dualism,"
M LXXI (1962); and D. H. Monro, *Empiricism and Ethics* (Cambridge, 1967). The papers by Zimmerman and Hanly, referred to in this
section, are contained in *The Is-Ought Question* (see note 6).

[27] See e.g., Zimmerman, *op. cit.*, pp. 56–59.

simply "I want to do X," but "I want to do X and I want others to do X"; and again, someone who thinks that the important feature of moral judgments is that they are over-riding may wish to say that "I ought to do X" means "X is what I most want to do." For the moment, however, I shall leave all such refinements aside and simply consider the question: are there any patent differences between the ordinary uses of the words "want" and "ought" respectively, which discredit the view that their meanings can be equated?

It has sometimes been held that the use of "ought" has to be supported by reasons, as that of "want" does not. Against this, it can be pointed out that, in many contexts, it is as natural to expect a reason for what is said to be wanted as for what it is said ought to be done. It is true that one feature which differ-entiates moral judgments from expressions of taste or descriptions of likes or dislikes is the fact that reasons are normally expected in the former case, as perhaps not in the latter. If I said "I ought to go on strike," and when asked "Why?" replied, "What do you mean 'Why?' I just ought," I should put my reputation as a reasonable man in jeopardy, as I should not if I said "I want to go on strike"—whether this was taken as an expression of, or a description of, my feelings—and when asked "Why?" replied that I just did. But such cases may not be indicative of any significant difference between "want" and "ought." For one thing, there are occa-sions on which it would be perfectly natural to turn aside the demand for a reason when one has used "ought." If I said, for example, "I ought to pay my debts" and, to the question "Why?" replied, "What do you mean 'Why?' I just ought," that would not be an unnatural thing to say. Moreover, not only are there some such occasions, but on all occasions when moral judgments have been voiced and a reason given, the latter seem to be constituted, in the last analysis, by an appeal to something which just is, or is said to be, the case. If, for example, having judged that capital punishment is wrong because it contributes nothing to the general happiness, I were asked, "But why does that make it wrong?" I would, if I were a utilitarian, have to reply "It just does." If there is a logical gap between "want" and "ought," then, whatever else may constitute it, it cannot be the fact that the justification of one, as against the other, rests upon that for which no further reason is, or can be, given. For, in the last analysis, they both do.

Another difference which has been thought to constitute a logical gap between "want" and "ought" is the putative fact that we can contradict each other in terms of "ought," but not of "want." Is there anything in this? If A said "You ought to do X" and B said "You ought not," it might be natural to say that they were contradicting one another. But, the argument goes, if "You ought" simply means "I want you to"; and "You ought not," "I do not want you to," A and B would not be contradicting one another. A's "I want you to" and B's "I don't want you to" could both be true. So, if "You ought" really does contradict "You ought not," it seems to follow that any definition of "ought" in terms of "want" must be misconceived. But does this follow? Let us consider for a moment why it seems so natural to say that A's "You ought" contradicts B's "You ought not." Undoubtedly, if a *single* speaker said "You ought and you ought not," this would be a contradiction. Anyone who took this to mean "I want and I don't want you to" would, moreover, agree that it is self-contradictory. But when we say that A's "You ought" is contradicted by B's "You ought not," are we simply assuming that what would be self-contradictory if one speaker said it must necessarily be a contradiction when its dicta are uttered by two different speakers? We certainly cannot say that *because* A's "You ought" and B's "You ought not" *do* contradict each other therefore they cannot mean respectively "I want you to" and "I don't want you to." This is begging the question. It is not logically necessary that they should be contradictory. If they did mean "I want you to" and "I don't want you to" respectively, they would not be contradictory. It has not been proved that they do not mean this.[28]

A further ground which has been offered for rejecting the definition of "ought" in terms of "want" is the fact that it

---

[28] A somewhat similar argument is used by Stevenson against Moore; see *The Philosophy of G. E. Moore* (Evanston, Ill., 1949), edited by L. A. Schilpp.

makes perfectly good sense to say that I doubt whether I ought to do what I want to do. This, we are told, cannot mean that I doubt whether I want to do what I want to do, because that does not make sense. But does it not? Would it, for example, necessarily be meaningless if I said to my wife, "I don't know whether I want to do what I want to do or what you want to do"? It might prove me an infuriatingly indecisive spouse, but it would not be gibberish.[29] "Want," of course, is being used in two different senses here. I am saying something like "I don't know whether I want (in the sense of 'most want' or 'want after reflection'—*sense 1*) to do what I want (in the sense of 'feel a strong desire at the moment'—*sense 2*) to do or what you want (in either of the two senses) to do." If "ought" were defined in terms of "want" (sense 1), then the statement "I doubt whether I ought to do what I want to do" could mean "I doubt whether I want (sense 1) to do what I want (sense 2) to do." It could, therefore, make sense to say that I doubt whether I want to do what I want to do, and so the simple contention that it could not, is not sufficient to dispose of the view that "ought" means "wants."

But can we simply say that "ought" means "wants" in either of the senses differentiated as 1 and 2? I do not think so. I think that there is a further distinction[30] which can, and must, be drawn, if there is to be any hope of equating the meanings of "ought" and "want." An illustration will help to make this distinction clear. Smith belongs to a religious sect which forbids its members to marry unbelievers, i.e., people who do not belong to the sect. Now consider this conversation:

> *Smith.* I do not want to marry Mary Jones.
> *Questioner.* Why?
> *Smith.* Because she is an unbeliever.

The questioner's "Why?" may be taken in two senses. He may be asking what *causes* Smith not to want to marry Mary

---

[29] Cf. Monro, *op. cit.*, pp. 208 ff.
[30] Cf. K. Hanly, "Zimmerman's Is-Is: Schizophrenic Monism," *M* LXXIII (1964); see note 26.

Jones. If that is the question, Smith's reply explains his not wanting to marry Mary Jones by bringing the latter occurrence under some such causal generalization as: whenever Smith finds that a girl is an unbeliever he loses all desire to marry her. But the questioner may be asking what *reason* Smith has for not wanting to marry Mary Jones. Then Smith's reply will explain his first remark by bringing it under some such general principle of selection, or classification, as "Never want to marry an unbeliever." Smith's "want" in "I don't want to marry Mary Jones" thus has two possible senses, corresponding to these possible interpretations of his questioner's "Why?" In one, "want" is used simply to describe Smith's psychological condition, a sense to which causal explanations are appropriate (call it the descriptive sense). In the other sense, Smith's "want" is being used to evaluate, or classify, Mary Jones; this is the sense to which principles of selection are appropriate (call it the classificatory sense).

If "ought" could be defined in terms of "want," it would have to be in terms of this latter (classificatory) sense, for "ought" is never used simply to describe a psychological condition, as "want" sometimes is. We noted above (p. 266) that it is as natural in many contexts to ask a reason for what is said to be wanted as for what it is said ought to be done. But we see now that these must all be contexts in which "want" is being used in what I have called its classificatory sense.

Remember that the whole point of the attempt to define "ought" in terms of "want" which we are considering in this section is to bridge, or rather eliminate, the logical gap between "is" and "ought." But if what I have been saying is correct, the only sense of "want" in which it might conceivably be used to define "ought" is one which leaves the gap as wide open as ever. Smith's move from the statement of fact "Mary Jones is an unbeliever" to the "classificatory" utterance "I do not want to marry her" is not a straightforward move from "is" to "want." "I do not want to marry her" is not a factual description of his psychological condition but, in some sense, an *evaluation* of Mary Jones. The logical gap between description and evaluation is still there, and can be bridged only by the principle of evaluation "Never want to marry an unbeliever." This principle, notice carefully, is necessarily synthetic. It could not be true by definition. If "not being wanted by Smith as a girl to marry" meant "being an unbeliever," then Smith's "I do not want to marry Mary Jones because she is an unbeliever" would not be, in any sense, an evaluation. It would simply mean "Mary Jones is an unbeliever because she is an unbeliever." And this same objection applies to any proposed descriptive definition of "not wanted by Smith as a girl to marry." All the logical objections to defining "ought" in terms of "is" apply to defining "want" (the evaluative, or classificatory, sense) in purely descriptive terms.

To summarize then: (i) "Want," if it is to define "ought," will have to be used in its evaluative, classificatory, or selective, sense—call it what you will—as distinct from its purely descriptive sense. That is to say, it will have to be used in the sense for which reasons, as distinct from causes, can be given. (ii) When it is so used, a principle of evaluation or selection is always logically necessary to bridge the gap between any statement of fact and any expression of wanting or not wanting. (iii) Such principles of selection are not analytic and so, however they bridge the gap, it is not by definition. Though I have attempted to defend it against some criticisms, I find myself unable, therefore, to accept this view that "ought" means "wants."

Does "Wants" Constitute a Conclusive Reason for "Ought"?

I turn then to the alternative view, that "wants" constitutes a conclusive reason for "ought." Wanting is said to be a bridge notion[31] by which we can (logically) pass from "is" to "ought." If I say that I ought to do X and am asked "Why?" so the argument goes, the reply "Because I want to do X" has a logical finality not shared by any other conceivable reply. If I gave any other reply, e.g., "Because doing X will be the keeping of a promise," etc., it would make perfectly good sense to ask "But why keep promises?", etc. However, it does not make sense to ask "Why ought I to do what I

[31] Cf. above, p. 258.

want to do?" If a man has a reason for doing anything, he has a reason for doing what he wants.

This line of argument is prima facie very attractive. What is the point of reasoning about action at all, if not to get what one wants? As Professor Kurt Baier remarks: "Our very purpose in 'playing the reasoning game' is to maximise satisfactions and minimise frustrations. Deliberately to frustrate ourselves and to minimise satisfaction would certainly be to go counter to the very purpose for which we deliberate and weigh the pros and cons. These criteria are, therefore, necessarily linked with the very purpose of the activity of reasoning. In so far as we enter on that 'game' at all, we are therefore bound to accept these criteria."[32] We can (logically) think of any such reason as "Because doing X will be the keeping of a promise" as a reason which I have *chosen* to adopt. We can think that I might *not* have done so. It is not taken for granted that I would be mad (insane), if I had not. But with "Because I want to . . ." the case is different. To quote Baier again: "There is a correct use of the word 'mad' and . . . people who prefer whatever they do not enjoy doing to whatever they do differ from normal people in just such fundamental and undesirable respects as would make the word 'mad' correctly applicable to them."[33]

What has wanting to do with being moral? I am going to draw a distinction which seems to me to be not unhelpful in this connection. It is between two questions, corresponding to two uses of the word "moral" (and its cognates). "Moral" may be used, so to speak, either to *evaluate* or to *allocate*. When, for instance, I say that a reason is a moral reason, I may be evaluating it as a morally good or right reason for doing something; just as, if I call a remark immoral, I may be taken to mean that it is wicked or vicious. On the other hand, when I say that a reason, or a remark, is moral, I may be allocating it as a move within the moral universe of discourse. "Nonmoral," or "amoral," is the customary opposite of "moral" in this sense. Corresponding to these two

senses of the word there are two questions which may be
asked: (i) Why do what is moral (in the former, or evaluative,
sense of "moral")? and (ii) Why be moral (in the latter, or
allocating, sense of "moral")? The former question looks for
a reason *within* the moral "language game"; the latter seeks
a reason *for getting into* that "game." I will take them in
turn.

It will be remembered that the question at the head of this
subsection is: does "wants" constitute a conclusive reason
for "ought"? This question could be approached in either
of two ways, corresponding respectively to the two senses of
"being moral" which I have just differentiated as the evaluating and the allocating. First I shall consider whether "wants"
constitutes a conclusive reason for "ought" in that it answers
conclusively the question: why be moral (in the evaluative
sense)? or: why be just? That will engage our attention in
the next subsection. In the next subsection but one, I will turn
to the question: why be moral (in the allocating sense)?
Why, that is, participate in the moral "language game" at all?
I will consider what wanting may have to do with that.

Why Be Just?

Mrs. P. Foot addresses herself to the question "Why do
what is moral (in an evaluative sense)?" in her paper, "Moral
Beliefs." She asks: why be just? And part of her answer runs
as follows:

> Is it true . . . to say that justice is not something a man
> needs in his dealings with his fellows, supposing only that
> he is strong? Those who think that he can get on perfectly
> well without being just should be asked to say exactly how
> such a man is supposed to live. We know that he is to prac-
> tise injustice whenever the unjust act would bring him ad-
> vantage; but what is he to say? Does he admit that he does
> not recognise the rights of other people, or does he pre-
> tend? In the first case even those who combine with him
> will know that on a change of fortune, or a shift of affec-
> tion, he may turn to plunder them, and he must be as wary
> of their treachery as they are of his. Presumably the happy

unjust man is supposed . . . to be a very cunning liar and actor, combining complete injustice with the appearance of justice. . . . Philosophers often speak as if a man could thus hide himself even from those around him, but the supposition is doubtful, and in any case the price in vigilance would be colossal. If he lets even a few people see his true attitude he must guard himself against them; if he lets no one into the secret he must always be careful in case the least spontaneity betray him. Such facts are important because the need a man has for justice in dealings with other men depends on the fact that they are men and not inanimate objects or animals. If a man only needed other men as he needs household objects, and if men could be manipulated like household objects, or beaten into a reliable submission like donkeys, the case would be different. As things are, the supposition that injustice is more profitable than justice is very dubious, although like cowardice and intemperance it might turn out incidentally to be profitable.[84]

Here, I think, Mrs. Foot gives at least two main reasons against any man opting out of being just, even if he is one of the strong. (i) If he is to do so successfully, he will have to deceive people into thinking that he is really a just man; it will be very hard to do this successfully all the time and he will suffer no small inconvenience in the attempt. (ii) Many of his relationships with other people will be depersonalized in the process; he will have to treat other people as things, not persons, and in so doing he will impoverish his own existence. Her conclusion is that being just satisfies wants which all men have or, in other words, that it pays to be good. This conclusion has been vigorously challenged by some other modern moral philosophers.[35] Their main objections to it are, I think, as follows.

(i) It seems to be contrary to fact. Whatever the "pay-off" is conceived to be—material gain, happy personal relationships, an easy conscience, etc.—the thought forces itself upon

[84] *PAS* LIX (1958–59), 103–4. Mrs. Foot's paper is contained in *The Is-Ought Question* (see note 6).
[35] E.g., D. Z. Phillips, "Does It Pay to Be Good?" *PAS* LXIV (1964–65).

us, after a moment's reflection, that perhaps it does not pay
to be just—or, at least, not always. The unjust, only too frequently, prosper, have a wide circle of friends, and sleep
untroubled by any qualms of conscience. Of course it may
be simply our shortsightedness which makes it appear to us
that unjust men are happy. In fact the unjust man may be
frustrating wants which all men have.

(ii) A more serious objection to the view that it pays to
be good is that we can (logically) never know that this is
the case until it is too late to offer it to any man as a reason
why he should do one thing rather than another. We cannot
(logically) know that it will have paid a man to do what is
just, rather than what is unjust—at any rate, in the long run—
until he is dead. Of course, if we hold the belief that there
is a life after death in which those who have lived unjustly
in this world will be punished in the next, then that puts the
argument on another ground altogether. But Mrs. Foot is not
putting it on that ground.

(iii) The gravest objection of all is that this whole notion,
that justice pays, misconceives the nature of morality. If there
were, to use a traditional word, a "heteronomous" pay-off to
justice, i.e., a pay-off in some nonmoral terms, then it would
follow that any man who has been just and has not enjoyed
this pay-off has suffered a disaster. That ("disaster") is the
very word which Mrs. Foot uses, in a paragraph immediately
following the one which I quoted, about a man who chooses
to die rather than be unjust. Surely this is a *reductio ad absurdum* of any view that the reason for being just is that it
pays "heteronomously." For even to die for justice is *not* a
disaster to the just man, as such. The only disaster he could
suffer, *qua just man,* would be for him to choose injustice in
order to avoid death.

So clear does it seem to some modern philosophers that
the view which we are considering is misconceived that they
reject even the idea that justice pays by being the means to
moral perfection. D. Z. Phillips approvingly quotes J. L. Stocks
to this effect. "Morality may call on a man at any moment
to surrender the most promising avenue to his own moral

perfection."[36] I find this point hard to take as it stands. It supposes that a man can attain moral perfection by doing something other than the right thing. But how? He might, of course, have to do something other than the conventionally right thing, or the thing which hitherto he has thought to be right. Again, he might be motivated in his pursuit of moral perfection by the thought of kudos which he will receive, or at least of which he will be worthy, when he is morally perfect, and then he is being just for the sake of some end to which justice is merely a means. It is, moreover, a homiletical commonplace that a man can be so careful of his virtue that he loses, or minimizes, it in the process. St. Cassian did not risk soiling his garments on his way to the divine presence by helping the wagoner stuck in the mud, but St. Nicholas did, and in consequence, when they reached that presence, St. Nicholas enjoyed a fuller measure of the divine favor than St. Cassian. But, of course, all this is not in dispute. If we leave it all aside, I cannot make sense of the idea that there could be any other "promising avenue" to moral perfection than doing what one ought. For what *is* moral perfection, if not doing what one ought?

This last contention, which I dispute, is not, however, essential to the main argument against the view that the reason for being just is that it pays "heteronomously." I find the rest of the argument very persuasive. It rests on a foundation which many moral philosophers, though diverse in other respects, have been at one in declaring firm. This foundation is the autonomy of morals. Kant said that the moral imperative is categorical, not hypothetical; Kierkegaard, that to will the good is to will one thing;[37] Moore, that "good" is indefinable; Hare, that evaluative discourse cannot be logically reduced to descriptive. All were saying, in effect, that the last appeal *within* moral discourse is to the justice of justice. The conclusive reason for being just is not that it pays or is what any man, or all men, want, but that it is being just.

The answer, then, to the first of the two questions which

---

[36] *Ibid.*, p. 59. Cf. P. Winch, *Moral Integrity* (Oxford, 1968), pp. 20–25.
[37] I owe this reference to Phillips, *op. cit.*, p. 52.

I differentiated above, namely the question: why do what is moral (in the evaluative sense of "moral")? or, in other words: why be just? is simply: because it *is* moral (in that evaluative sense of "moral"). The question: is it moral (or just) to do—ought one to do—what any man, or all men, want? is not self-answering. It might be self-answering, of course, if "want" were being used here in what I called above its "classificatory" sense. But that is not the sense in which those opinions I am here rejecting take the word. Taking the word "want" in their sense (i.e., the sense which I called the "descriptive" sense), we can say with assurance that "want" does not constitute a conclusive reason for "ought." *Within* the "moral language game," the mere fact that any man, or all men, want (in the "descriptive" sense) something does not constitute, in itself, a reason why anything ought, or ought not, to be done.

Why Be Moral?

I turn now to the other question which I am attempting to answer, namely, the question: why be moral (in what I called the "allocating" sense)? Notice that this question, unlike: why be moral (in the evaluative sense)? or: why be just? does not arise, so to speak, within, but *outside,* the moral universe of discourse. We saw that the answer to: why be just? cannot be: because it pays. But it does not follow, of course, that the answer to the present question cannot be that the reason for being moral is that it pays. Are there satisfactions which being moral maximizes, and frustrations which it minimizes, such that we can say that the reason for being moral (in the present sense) is grounded in what all men want?

Do all men want to be moral? The question is, of course, ambiguous. It may mean: if asked what they want, would they reply "To be (or to go on being) moral"; or, if we observed their other behavior, would it bear out that this is what they consciously desired to be? Alternatively: "Do all men want to be moral?" may mean: is it the case that only in being moral can they maximize certain satisfactions and minimize certain frustrations? They may, in this sense, want (or need) to be moral without realizing it. It is in this latter sense that I am taking the question.

In the former sense, the answer to it seems clearly to be that all men some of the time, and some men all of the time, do *not* want to be moral. I referred above to the anxieties which conscience breeds. We would all, I think, have some sympathy with the sentry in Masefield's *Good Friday* who remarks:

> I find sufficient trouble in what is
> Without my seeking what is right or wrong.

But the reply which he receives is:

> All have to seek her and the search is long.

Well, do they? And in what way "have to"? I shall consider very summarily three possible views as to why they "have to," held by those who think that they do.

(i) It has been argued that it is essential to a harmonious society that those within it should be moral. I am not sure whether Baier, in the following passage, is using "moral" in what I have called the allocating, or the evaluative, senses. But his words may be interpreted as using "moral" in the former sense; and so interpreted, they would represent the point of view to which I have just referred, viz., that it is essential to harmony within a society that its members engage in moral discourse or the moral "form of life." Baier writes: "The best possible life *for everyone* is possible only by everyone's following the rules of morality, that is, rules which quite frequently may require individuals to make genuine sacrifices." But he adds: "Outside society, people have no reason for following such rules, that is, for being moral."[38] He seems to be claiming here no more than that, *if* there is a society, then satisfactions will be maximized and frustrations minimized for all within it, if, and only if, each acts from reasons

[38] Baier, *op. cit.*, pp. 314–15.

which are moral. He is not, here at any rate, saying that morality is a necessary condition of society, but only of a harmonious society.

The *precise* point should be noted. Suppose some individual decides to opt out of his society. What reason can we give him for not doing so? Not, it would seem on Baier's view, the reason that if he refrains from opting out he will maximize satisfactions and minimize frustrations. All we can say to him is that, so long as he stays within society, the best life *for everyone* in it, *himself included,* is possible only if he acts from moral reasons. But why should he worry about "everyone"? Merely from the fact, if it is a fact, that certain wants (e.g., security of life) will be satisfied *for all* in his society only if each acts from moral reasons, it does not follow that these wants could not be satisfied for some individuals within society, of whom he may be one, who did not concern themselves at all with moral considerations. It seems impossible, on Baier's account of the matter, to give anyone a reason for not giving up morality within society. That is, if he is numbered among the strong, not the weak.

(ii) Perhaps in part to meet this sort of objection, some have argued that society itself is possible only if there is morality. Professor Peter Winch, in his paper "Nature and Convention," argues to this effect. Here again, I am not sure that Winch would accept my differentiation of the "allocating" and "evaluative" senses of "moral," or my interpretation of his points in terms of the former. However, I think that his words could be so interpreted. He says, "There could not be a human society which was not also, in some sense, a moral community."[39] If I understand him rightly, he goes on to argue that society is impossible without the sort of commitment, by its members to each other, which subsists only through the recognition of certain virtues *as such;* that is, without moral thinking. Communication in language, for example, is possible, not simply where there are rules for the use of words, but where those who communicate in general regard truthfulness as a virtue. If there were no recognition

[39] Peter Winch, "Nature and Convention," *PAS* LX (1959–60), 239.

of speaking the truth *as* something which ought to be done, then no communication would be possible. Looking wider, Winch says that "integrity . . . is to human institutions generally what truthfulness is to the institution of language. . . . To lack integrity is to act with the appearance of fulfilling a certain role but without the intention of shouldering the responsibilities to which that role commits one. If that, *per absurdum,* were to become the rule, the whole concept of a social role would thereby collapse."[40] And with it, of course, society.

It seems to me that a society without some commitment on the part of its members to each other is indeed inconceivable. But I am not convinced that the reasons which those within the society give to themselves, or each other, for this commitment must necessarily be *moral* ones. Winch recognizes that one might be led to Hobbesian conclusions about the agreement upon which society is (logically) based.[41] It could be a pact motivated purely by self-interest. For my own part, using the expression "want to be" now in the sense, "only so can they maximize satisfactions and minimize frustrations," I would say that men undoubtedly want to be *social.* But I do not feel sure, having regard only to the concept of society and what it logically implies, that, therefore, they necessarily want to be *moral.*

(iii) It does seem to me, however, that we can advance the sort of argument for being moral which Mrs. Foot advanced for being just. Her argument did not appear successful. But remember that we are now considering what constitutes, not a reason within, but a reason for getting into, or remaining within, the moral "language game" or "form of life." Even if it is correct to say that the only reason for being just is that it is being just, the reason for being moral, as I am now using the word "moral," could (logically) be that it pays, that only by being moral, by engaging in moral discourse, can men maximize certain satisfactions and minimize certain frustrations. "How is the unjust man supposed to live?"

[40] *Ibid.,* pp. 250–51.
[41] *Ibid.,* p. 240.

asked Mrs. Foot. She suggested: (i) that he will find it difficult, if not impossible, to do so; and (ii) that he will forfeit
much, if not all, of value in personal relationships in the
process. I ask, in my turn, how a man who opts out of being
moral (in the present—allocating—sense) is supposed to live. I
think the two points which Mrs. Foot mistakenly makes about
the unjust man may be made a fortiori about the amoral man.

(i) A man who decides to opt out of moral discourse will
find it difficult, if not impossible, to carry his decision into
complete effect. At so many points in human life moral issues
arise. Our man will have nothing to say on any questions
which arise in terms of fairness, obligation, justice, responsibility, and so on. Nor will he ever think to himself in these
terms. We assume that it will be easy enough for him not
to do so. But is this because we confuse what I called above
the allocating and evaluative senses of "moral"? The man
who gives up being moral in the latter sense is familiar
enough. He gets what we should call the wrong answers to
his moral questions; or, getting the right ones, he fails to put
them into action through perversity or weakness of the will.
But I am not speaking of the immoral man, but the amoral.
The latter opts out of morality in the sense that he ceases to
think or speak in moral terms. It is very hard indeed to be
such a man. I have had pupils, for example, who informed
me that they could find no use for moral discourse nowadays;
and then went straight on to tell me that I ought to opt out
of it too because it was harmful.

(ii) A second fact with which a man who gave up being
moral would have to cope is that many if not all personal relationships subsist, so to speak, in the moral universe of discourse. Their distinctive character cannot be described without
using some essentially moral terms, such as "trust," "loyalty,"
"obligation," "responsibility," etc. To say, for example, that
X is Y's father is to say more than that X contributed the male
element in the procreation of Y. If someone said to Y, "You
ought to look after X in his old age" and Y asked, "Why?"
the answer "He is your father" would be perfectly natural

and intelligible. It seems to be part of the meaning of "father," as we normally use the word, that anyone so described owes, and has owing to him, certain obligations. To the question why this is so we shall turn in the next section. Here all I wish to point out is that it is so. I am not, of course, saying that a man cannot have some sort of relationship with other people, even though he has ceased to conceive of his relationship with them at all in moral terms. Such a man can use other people for his own pleasure or profit. All I am saying is that he cannot experience any of those personal relationships which, if they are to be experienced at all, must be conceived of, to some extent, in terms of such notions as "trust," "responsibility," etc. It makes sense to say that, in opting out of such relationships, a man would be destroying himself. Whatever the defects of their philosophy as a whole, those existentialists who insist that the worst thing which can befall a man is that his personal relationships should be reduced from the level of I-Thou to that of I-It have a point. A man who treats other persons as things has, to that degree, ceased himself to be a man. To opt out of being moral is to opt out of being human.

I have gone beyond the question "Does 'wants' constitute a conclusive reason for 'ought'?" My answer to that was "No." "Ought," as here in question, is a word used within moral discourse and, as I have claimed, within such discourse, the last appeal can, always and only, be to the oughtness of "ought." But if it occurs to anyone to ask "Why use such discourse at all?" then my answer has been "Because of what all men want." And by speaking of what they want, I have not meant simply that which they would find it hard or impoverishing to be without, but that without which they could not be what we mean by being men—in other words, what they need. I shall return to the notion of a need below.[42] But first, I am going to say something in the next section about another way in which some modern philosophers have thought that the is-ought gap can be bridged or eliminated.

[42] Pp. 304–7.

III. INSTITUTIONAL FACT

Searle's Attempt to Derive "Ought" from "Is"

Professor J. R. Searle, in an article called "How to Derive 'Ought' from 'Is'" which was published in the *Philosophical Review*, 1964, and which has been the occasion of much discussion, says that the distinction between description and evaluation, fact and value, drawn by moral philosophers such as Moore, Stevenson, and Hare, is really a conflation of at least two distinctions: (i) that between different kinds of illocutionary force; and (ii) that between utterances which involve claims objectively decidable as true or false, on the one hand, and utterances which do not involve such claims because they are matters of decision or opinion, on the other. It has been assumed, he says, that the former distinction is a special case of the latter—that if something has the illocutionary force of an evaluation, it cannot be entailed by factual premises.[43] Searle sets himself to show that this assumption is false: that factual premises can entail evaluative conclusions. He does so by expanding an idea found in embryo in Miss Anscombe's writings, namely that of an "institutional fact."[44]

There are, Searle claims, different types of fact. Some facts presuppose institutions, others do not. They may be differentiated as "institutional" and "brute" facts respectively. Institutional facts are facts which exist only within our institutions; that is to say, within a system of constitutive rules. Constitutive (as distinct from simply regulative) rules create or define (and also regulate) new forms of behavior, as distinct from regulating antecedently existing forms of behavior. Eating is an antecedently existing form of behavior regulated by rules of politeness. Chess is a new form of behavior constituted by

---

[43] J. R. Searle, "How to Derive 'Ought' from 'Is,'" *PR* LXXIII (1964), 58. The articles by G. E. M. Anscombe ("Modern Moral Philosophy"), Searle, Flew, McClellan and Komisar, Hare, and myself, and the relevant passages in J. R. Searle, *Speech Acts,* are all contained in *The Is-Ought Question* (see note 6).

[44] Cf. "Modern Moral Philosophy" *P* XXXIII (1958), and "On Brute Facts," *A* 18 (1957–58); see note 43.

the rules of the game. Eating exists apart from etiquette; but checkmating does not exist apart from chess. "Brute" facts are, so to say, the factual raw materials out of which institutional facts are made. To each institutional fact certain other facts are "brute relative." The movement of certain pieces on a board is brute relative to checkmating; the utterance of "I promise" is brute relative to promising; and so on.

Searle contends that "many forms of obligations, commitments, rights, and responsibilities are similarly institutionalized."[45] He takes, for example, one such institutionalized form of obligation, namely promising. It is his intention to show that we can start with the "brute" fact that a man uttered certain words; then invoke the institution of promising in such a way as to generate institutional facts; then appeal to the constitutive rule of the institution; and so arrive at an evaluative conclusion. In this way, Searle purports to derive "ought" from "is." I will set out the stages of his putative derivation in greater detail.

(1) Jones uttered the words "I hereby promise to pay you, Smith, five dollars."
(2) Jones promised to pay Smith five dollars.
(3) Jones placed himself under (undertook) an obligation to pay Smith five dollars.
(4) Jones is under an obligation to pay Smith five dollars.
(5) Jones ought to pay Smith five dollars.

Searle says of this list, "The relation between any statement and its successor, while not in every case one of 'entailment,' is nonetheless not just a contingent relation; and the additional statements necessary to make the relationship one of entailment do not need to involve any evaluative statements, moral principles, or anything of the sort."[46]

What are the "additional statements" to which he here refers? Notice that Searle says that they consist of "empirical assumptions, tautologies, and descriptions of word usage"[47]

[45] Searle, *op. cit.*, 56.
[46] *Ibid.*, p. 44.
[47] *Ibid.*, p. 48.

and nothing more. The additional premises to which he refers
are as follows:

Between (1) and (2):
      (1a) Under certain conditions, C, anyone who utters
           the words (sentence) "I hereby promise to pay
           you, Smith, five dollars" promises to pay Smith
           five dollars.
      (1b) Conditions C obtain.
Between (2) and (3):
      (2a) the tautological premise: All promises are acts
           of placing oneself under (undertaking) an ob-
           ligation to do the thing promised.
Between (3) and (4):
      (3a) Other things are equal.
      (3b) the tautological premise: All those who place
           themselves under an obligation are, other things
           being equal, under an obligation.
Between (4) and (5):
      (4a) Other things are equal.
      (4b) the tautological premise: Other things being
           equal, one ought to do what one is under an
           obligation to do.

Some explanatory comments on these additional premises may
be useful.

Premise (1a) starts with "brute" fact and invokes the institution of promising to generate institutional fact. The brute
fact that someone utters the words "I promise," "in a proper
context," as Miss Anscombe would say,[48] "ordinarily
amounts to" the institutional fact that he promises. Premise
(1b) simply says that this is such a "proper" context. As
examples of the conditions fulfilled to make it proper Searle
offers: "that the speaker is in the presence of the hearer
Smith, they are both conscious, both speakers of English,
speaking seriously. The speaker knows what he is doing, is
not under the influence of drugs, not hypnotized or acting in
a play, not telling a joke or reporting an event, and so
forth."[49]

[48] Anscombe, "On Brute Facts," *op. cit.,* p. 71.
[49] Searle, *op. cit.,* p. 45.

Premise (2a) embodies the constitutive rule of the institution of promising, that to make a promise to to undertake an obligation. Just as, by undertaking to play chess or any other game, one commits oneself to the observation of certain constitutive rules, so, if one promises, one commits oneself thereby to certain obligations. *Within* the game of chess I cannot question or reject the rules; similarly, *within* the institution of promising, so to say, I cannot reject the obligation.

Premises (3b) and (4b) are simply tautologies, resting on ordinary usage of the words "obligation" and "ought."

The *ceteris paribus* clauses, premises (3a) and (4a), exclude the possibility that there is some reason for supposing that the obligation is void—step (4)—or that the agent ought not to keep the promise—step (5). What such reason could there be? Searle answers this question in a footnote.[50] The "other things being equal" between (3) and (4) excludes, for example, the promisee saying to the promiser, "I release you from your obligation," which would cancel the obligation. Between (4) and (5) "other things being equal" excludes the overriding of the present obligation by some other obligation, for example, by Jones's obligation not to pay Smith five dollars because his children will starve if he does.

Criticism of Searle

Searle's derivation of "ought" from "is" has been challenged in at least two ways. (i) It has been pointed out that there is a distinction between using the word "promise" as a detached reporter of verbal usage and as an engaged participant in the language of which it forms a part. If one changes from being a detached reporter to being an engaged participant, Professor A. Flew has maintained, this can only be by "commitment to the incapsulated values which alone warrants us to draw the normative conclusions"[51]—that is to say, by bridging the gap between "is" and "ought." Against this, I have elsewhere[52] raised the question: when one refuses to

[50] *Ibid.*, p. 47.
[51] Flew, "On Not Deriving 'Ought' from 'Is,'" *A* 25 (1965), 193; see note 43.
[52] W. D. Hudson, "The Is-Ought Controversy," *A* 25 (1965), 193.

use a word like "promise" as an engaged participant, what precisely is one doing? Surely, not just retaining a descriptive, or factual, element in the word's meaning, while rejecting an evaluative. One is rejecting a whole way of speaking; one is stopping using a word with all that word's implications. Flew seems to think that, by exposing the difference between a reporter of verbal usage and a participant in that usage, he is exposing the gap between "is" and "ought." But exposers of the naturalistic fallacy were not concerned to show what Flew has shown, viz., that where descriptions entail evaluations we can decide whether or not to use them as engaged participants. They were showing, or trying to show, that there is no description such that it validly entails an evaluation.

A possible refinement on the distinction with which I have just been working, between "a detached reporter of verbal usage" and "an engaged participant," is the distinction between: (a) someone who uses "promise" to mean simply uttering certain words (sense 1) and (b) someone who uses "promise" to mean undertaking an obligation (sense 2). It might then be said that, if Searle's premise (1a) above is really descriptive, all his move from his premises (1) to (2) proves is that Jones made a promise in sense 1. But in order to get from his (2) to (3), Searle has to prove that Jones made a promise in sense 2. In addition to (2a) above, therefore, he needs another extra premise between (2) and (3). And this has to be an *evaluative* premise. Searle himself takes account of this possible objection in his recently published book *Speech Acts* (Cambridge, 1969). He puts these words into the mouths of his critics against himself: "You prove that Jones made a promise in sense 1 and then assume that you have proved that he made a promise in sense 2 by assuming incorrectly that these two senses are the same. The difference between sense 2 and sense 1 is the difference between a committed participant and a neutral observer. It is both necessary and decisive to make this distinction between the committed participant and the neutral observer, for it is only the neutral observer who is making genuine factual or descriptive statements." Searle's reply to this is, I think, quite effective. He denies the charge of equivocating on senses 1 and 2 of "promise" by contending that sense 1 *does not exist.* As he says, "There is no literal meaning of 'promise' in which all it means is uttering certain words. . . . A sentence of the form 'X made a promise' is not lexically ambiguous as between 'X said some words' and 'X really promised.' 'Promise' is not thus homonymous."[53]

(ii) The other criticism of Searle to which I shall refer fastens on his *ceteris paribus* clauses, i.e., (3a) and (4a). As we saw, they are intended to secure that (to use Searle's own words[54]) "no reason to the contrary can in fact be given" why we should not move from (3) to (4) and from (4) to (5). We gave examples of what such reasons might be. That which is supposed to be excluded by these "other things being equal" clauses is the necessity for any *evaluation,* particularly between (4) and (5). Searle obviously has to exclude that necessity in order to carry through his attempt to get an "ought" in (5) from exclusively non-evaluative premises. He acknowledges, of course, that an evaluation may have to be made between (4) and (5) if there is a clash of obligations in any situation; but his point is that this does not need to be made in all cases and so it is possible to have counter-examples to the thesis that "ought" cannot be derived from "is." That is, if there is no obligation in conflict with that of promise-keeping in a given situation, we can move from (4) to (5) without an evaluation. Against Searle, the point is made[55] that his "no reason to the contrary can in fact be given" is either a statement of fact or a judgment. If it simply means that at this moment someone cannot, in fact, offer a reason why he does not have an obligation—perhaps because his mouth is stuffed with food—it is ridiculous to think that this makes an act obligatory which otherwise would not be. But, if we take the other alternative—that the quoted words are a judgment—is not that judgment necessarily evaluative? If it is, Searle has not got from (1) to (5) without an evaluative premise. Perhaps with this sort of objection in mind, Searle

[53] Searle, *op. cit.,* pp. 192–93; see note 43.

[54] *Ibid.,* p. 47.

[55] J. E. McClellan and B. P. Komisar, "On Deriving 'Ought' from 'Is,'" *A* 25 (1964), 32–36; see note 43.

says that he could, if need be, put the "other things being equal" into (5) which would then read: "Other things being equal, Jones ought to pay Smith five dollars." It would not then matter, from his point of view, if this *ceteris paribus* was evaluative. For he would have got from (1) to (5), i.e., to the evaluative conclusion, without any evaluative premises en route. However, (5) would not then be categorical, but hypothetical: *"If* other things are equal, then Jones ought to pay Smith five dollars." Searle cannot call the "ought" in (5) "categorical," as he does,[56] and include the *ceteris paribus* clause in (5).

While admitting the force of such criticisms, I have tried elsewhere[57] to defend Searle against them by arguing that his position can be held without any "other things being equal" clauses at all. "Other things being equal" between (3) and (4) purports to exclude possibilities such as that the promisee should release the promiser from his obligation. Why should not the exclusion of this possibility be included in the conditions C, referred to in Searle's premises (1a) and (1b)? Above I quoted a sample list of such conditions. There does not seem any reason why something like "the promisee has not released the promiser from the implications of what the latter has said" should not be included in them.

What of the *ceteris paribus* clause between (4) and (5)? This, we saw, is intended to exclude possibilities such as a conflict of obligations. But it is only necessary to exclude such possibilities, if their realization would inhibit the move from (4) to (5). Would it do so? Whatever difficulties there may be in deriving (5) from (4), the mere fact that Jones was involved in some other obligation besides that to pay Smith five dollars, does not seem to me to constitute such a difficulty. Suppose Jones has children who will starve if he pays Smith the five dollars. Why cannot we say that he ought to pay Smith and he ought to feed his children? True, "ought" implies "can." Jones can pay Smith. And he can feed his children. What he cannot do is both. But that is beside the pres-

[56] *Ibid.,* 48.
[57] Hudson, *op cit.,* 194-95.

ent point. How one ought to resolve the position when there are two things that one ought to do, not one, is a familiar problem in modern moral philosophy. It has exercised thinkers seemingly as different as W. D. Ross and J. P. Sartre; we saw, in previous chapters,[58] that the former talked about "weighing" prima facie obligations, and the latter urged his pupil simply to choose between them. But the fact that there is this problem does nothing to show that it is contrary to the ordinary uses of the words "obligation" and "ought" to say that if we are under an obligation to do X, then we ought to do X.

It is interesting to notice that, in *Speech Acts*, Searle restates his putative derivation of "ought" from "is" in substantially the same form as he gave it in the 1964 article, except that he dispenses now with the *ceteris paribus* clauses.[59] They were, he says, "a standing invitation to various kinds of irrelevant objections."

There was one such clause between (3) and (4) in the 1964 version. But Searle now says, "In order to get a straightforward entailment between 3 and 4 we need only construe 4 in such a way as to *exclude any time gap* between the point of the completion of the act in which the obligation is undertaken, 3, and the point at which it is claimed the agent is under an obligation, 4. So construed 3 entails 4 straight off" (italics mine).[60] And, in similar vein, "The essential point for the move from 3 to 4 is the tautology that when you place yourself under an obligation you are then and there under an obligation, even though you may be able to get out of it later, may have conflicting and overriding obligations at the same time, etc."[61] So, in his 1969 version, Searle rewrites the 1964 tautological premise, (3b) above, thus:

All those who place themselves under an obligation are (at the time when they so place themselves) under an obligation.[62]

[58] Cf. above, pp. 95 and 218.
[59] See Searle, *op. cit.*, pp. 177–82.
[60] *Ibid.*, p. 179.
[61] *Ibid.*, p. 180.
[62] *Ibid.*, p. 179.

This tautology, he now thinks, is enough to take us from (3) to (4).

There is another *ceteris paribus* clause between (4) and (5) in the 1964 version. But Searle says in his 1969 book, "Analogous to the tautology which explicates the relation between 3 and 4 there is here the tautology that if one is under an obligation to do something, then, *as regards that obligation,* one ought to do what one is under an obligation to do" (italics mine).[63] This is a revised version of the tautological premise (4b) above. Searle now sets out two possible senses in which (5) above—i.e., "Jones ought to pay Smith five dollars"—may be taken:

(5′) As regard his obligation to pay Smith five dollars, Jones ought to pay Smith five dollars.
(5″) All things considered, Jones ought to pay Smith five dollars.[64]

And he says, "Now clearly if we interpret 5 as 5″ we cannot derive it from 4 without additional premises. But equally clearly if we interpret it as equivalent to 5′, which is perhaps the more plausible interpretation given its occurrence in the discourse, we can derive it from 4. And regardless of whether we wish to interpret 5 as 5′, we can simply derive 5′ from 4, which is quite sufficient for our present purposes"[65]—i.e., to show that "ought" can be derived from "is." So, in his 1969 version, Searle rewrites the 1964 tautological premise, (4b) above, thus:

If one is under an obligation to do something, then as regards that obligation one ought to do what one is under an obligation to do.[66]

This tautology, he now thinks, is enough to take us from (4) to (5).

[63] *Ibid.,* p. 180.
[64] *Ibid.,* p. 181.
[65] *Ibid.*
[66] *Ibid.*

We noted above the criticism that Searle could not embody his 1964 *ceteris paribus* clause in (5), thereby getting—even though the *ceteris paribus* were necessarily evaluative—exclusively from is premises to an ought conclusion. For, it was pointed out, if the *ceteris paribus* is embodied in (5), then the "ought" in (5) becomes hypothetical—"If other things are equal, then Jones ought to pay Smith five dollars"; but Searle had already said in his 1964 article that the "ought" in (5) was categorical. With that criticism no doubt in mind, Searle now points out that: "even with 5 interpreted as 5′ the 'ought' is in Kant's sense a 'categorical' not a 'hypothetical' ought. 5′ does not say that Jones ought to pay up *if he wants such and such*. It says he ought, as regards his obligation, to pay up."[67]

And so Searle's conclusion is, I think, in line with what I have said concerning his *ceteris paribus* clauses above and elsewhere in my attempt to defend him against criticism which turned on these clauses. Searle draws his 1969 version of how to derive "ought" from "is" to an end with the words: "We rely on definitional connexions between 'promise,' 'obligate,' and 'ought,' and the only problems which arise are that obligations can be overridden or removed in a variety of ways and we need to take account of that fact. We solve our difficulty by specifying that the existence of the obligation is at the time of the undertaking of the obligation, and the 'ought' is relative to the existence of the obligation."[68]

Descriptivists and Prescriptivists

Does this kind of attempt to derive "ought" from "is" succeed? The nub of the problem is the question which is crucial between prescriptivists and some descriptivists. It is: can one logically separate, within the notion of promising, a factual, or descriptive, element from a normative, or evaluative, element? The prescriptivist would say that one can: the word "promise," as we ordinarily use it, incapsulates a general decision of moral principle, to the effect that promises ought

[67] *Ibid.*
[68] *Ibid.*, p. 182.

to be kept. Some descriptivists deny this. They ask the rhetorical question: when did I, when did anyone, *decide* that promises ought to be kept?

In support of the latter position, it could be pointed out that there does not seem to be any "engaged participant" use of the word "promise" where it is not taken for granted that an obligation is involved. However, the case is different with some other "institutionalised obligations." Consider this conversation:

A: You ought to help X.
B: Why?
A: He's your father and he's in need.
B: What has that to do with it?

This last sentence sounds bizarre. Surely we all know what that has to do with it. A ought to help X, if X is his father and is in need. Agreed. But, obligations to fathers are a matter about which there has been considerable development and change of opinion over the years. One might say, therefore, that these obligations *have* been decided upon, or discovered. It is not, therefore, unplausible to suggest, as a prescriptivist might, that the word "father": (a) describes certain facts, such as that X contributed the male element in the procreation of A; and (b) incapsulates a general moral principle to which we in our society have come to subscribe, namely that we ought to help the man who contributed the male element in our procreation, if he is in need.

However, those descriptivists who rest their case on institutionalized obligations will not have this. They insist that it manifestly will not do simply to hold that a statement of institutional fact "adds something non-factual" to the statement of the relevant "brute relative" facts.[69] Against this, the prescriptivist asseverates that what is added can *only* be nonfactual. Hare, for example, writes on Searle's derivation: "It may seem as if the 'brute fact' that a person has uttered a certain phonetic sequence entails the 'institutional fact' that he has promised, and that this in turn entails that he ought to

[69] Cf. Anscombe, "On Brute Facts," *op. cit.*, 70.

do a certain thing. But this conclusion can be drawn only by one who accepts, in addition, the non-tautologous principle that one ought to keep one's promises. For unless one accepts this principle, one is not a subscribing member of the institution which it constitutes, and therefore cannot be compelled logically to accept the institutional facts which it generates in such a sense that they entail the conclusion. . . ."[70]

There seems to be a difference of opinion here which it is impossible to resolve. Recall the conversation instanced a moment ago. Suppose B asks A what he means by saying that X is B's father, and A replies, "I mean he begat you," "I mean he brought you up," "I mean apart from him you wouldn't be here," etc. All these are the brute relative facts. But now suppose that B says, with reference to each, "But ought I to help the man who begat me (brought me up, without whom I wouldn't be here, etc.)?" These are open questions, all of which make quite good sense. Descriptivists would not deny it. But they would insist that "He is your father" is a statement of institutional fact and that "Ought I to help my faher?" is *not* an open question. There is more in the statement "He is your father" than in the sum total of the above statements of brute relative fact. What more? Quite simply, the more which renders "Ought I to help my father?" not an open question. The prescriptivists, for their part, would agree with that. They too would say that there is more in "He is your father" than in any of the other statements of fact and that it follows from this "more" that one ought to help one's father. But, while descriptivists insist upon calling this "more" an element of institutional fact, the prescriptivists insist upon calling it an incapsulated general moral principle.

Does it matter which we call it? It does not seem to me that either side, at the end *of this particular dispute,* has shown that their way of describing the "more" is the right one. Of course, if in the light of wider considerations there is on the whole a better case for prescriptivism than for descriptivism, or vice versa, then these wider considerations will

---

[70] R. M. Hare, "The Promising Game," *Revue Internationale de Philosophie* (1964), 126; see note 43.

weigh in favor of deciding here for one way of putting it rather than the other. All I am saying is that, in itself, the analysis of promising as an institutional fact does not appear to settle the matter. We must now go on to consider more widely the issues between the two schools of thought to which I have just referred.

IV. THE PROS AND CONS OF DESCRIPTIVISM

Moral philosophy is still very much alive. That makes it a rewarding subject to study. But it also means that any account of the latest developments in the subject must necessarily be inconclusive. Despite the advances of the last six decades, the question "What makes a judgment moral?" is far from settled. The center of interest at the moment is the debate which is in progress between the two schools of thought to which I was referring at the end of the last section and which are commonly known as prescriptivism and descriptivism respectively. Prescriptivism is a clearly defined point of view and the moral philosophy of its leading exponent, R. M. Hare, has already been examined in detail in this book. Some philosophers would perhaps take exception to my calling descriptivism a school of thought because this suggests that there is a clear-cut, positive set of opinions to which those called descriptivists subscribe. In fact, the latter, while at one in their rejection of prescriptivism, seem to be sometimes not very sure of, and certainly not completely united in, their positive opinions. So it is perhaps too early to speak of descriptivism as a school of thought. However, I shall not be deterred by that. The debate to which I shall refer in this section—whatever styles we give to those engaged in it—is undoubtedly going on and the outcome will be crucial so far as future developments in moral philosophy are concerned.

I shall take Mrs. Phillipa Foot and G. J. Warnock as leading representatives of what I have called descriptivism. Their attack upon Hare and the grounds from which it is launched will be outlined. Hare has defended himself against this attack and I will try to show how he does so. It will probably become evident early in the section that I consider

Hare to have had the better of the argument so far. But I will try to give as clear and fair a picture of the debate as I can.

For our purpose here, a descriptivist may be defined as someone who holds at least these two opinions: (i) that it is not always logically possible to separate the descriptive and the evaluative meanings of a moral judgment; and (ii) that the criteria applied in moral judgment are *not* in the last analysis merely a matter of free choice. I will deal with these opinions in turn.

Description and Evaluation

In order to consider the opinion that descriptive and evaluative meanings sometimes cannot be separated let us consider the remark "Smith is courageous." Hare writes of such a remark thus:

> There are certain ways of behaving, describable in perfectly neutral terms, which make us commend people as, for example, courageous. Citations for medals do not simply say that the recipient behaved courageously; they give descriptive details; and though these, for reasons of brevity, often themselves contain evaluative terms, this need not be the case, and in a good citation it is the neutral descriptions which impress. They impress us because we already have the standards of values according to which to do *that* sort of thing is to display outstanding merit.[71]

This comment assumes that a clear distinction can be drawn between: (a) the facts described by "Smith is courageous"; and (b) the speaker's commendation of Smith on account of these facts. Mrs. Foot sees no good reason to draw such a distinction. She says, with Hare in mind:

> What is this extra element which is supposed to be present or absent after the facts have been settled? It is not a

---

[71] Hare, "Descriptivism," *Proceedings of the British Academy* (1963), 121. The papers by G. E. M. Anscombe ("Modern Moral Philosophy"), P. Foot ("Moral Beliefs" and "Goodness and Choice"), and Phillips and Mounce, referred to in this section, as well as Hare's "Descriptivism," are all contained in *The Is-Ought Question* (see note 6).

matter of liking the man who has courage, or of thinking
him altogether good, but of "commending him for his courage." How are we supposed to do that? The answer that
will be given is that we only commend someone else in
speaking of him as courageous if we accept the imperative
"let me be courageous" for ourselves. But this is quite unnecessary. I can speak of someone else as having the virtue
of courage, and of course recognise it as a virtue in the
proper sense, while knowing that I am a complete coward,
and making no resolution to reform.[72]

Mrs. Foot's contention is evidently that she can *sincerely*
form the moral judgment that someone did well to be courageous, yet not assent to the entailed imperative "Let me be
courageous." But can she? Hare, it will be recalled,[73] built two
conditions into his contention that moral judgments entail
imperatives: (i) that the speaker will assent to the entailed
imperative *if,* and only if, he is sincere in his judgment; and
(ii) his assent to the imperative will be sincere *if,* and only
if, where he is physically and psychologically able to do so, he
acts accordingly. Hare recognized weakness of will as a
possible form of inability. Is Mrs. Foot simply saying, when
she speaks as she does at the end of the last quotation, that
she may suffer from such weakness of will and so not carry out
the imperative "Let me be courageous"? If so, there is nothing
at issue between her and Hare. Or is she saying that she can be
sincere in commending someone for the virtue of courage
and, though able to practice that virtue herself, not assent
to the entailed imperative "Let me be courageous"? If so,
then here again there may not be anything at issue between her
and Hare. For Hare[74] allows that I may say that another man
is a better man than I am in a certain respect, yet be under no
obligation to try to be more like him in that respect because
I am trying to be good in a different way from him. I suppose
an example might be a scholar who commends a business-
man's determination in getting things done without seeking to
emulate it because the life he leads calls for virtues of another

[72] Foot, "Moral Beliefs," *PAS* LIX (1958–59), 98; see note 71.
[73] Above, p. 169.
[74] *FR,* p. 155.

kind, such as perpetual self-criticism, which might well be inhibited by too much determination to get things done. However, in the case of courage, it is arguable that "all goes if courage goes" and so this is a virtue which good men of any kind need. I think Mrs. Foot is mistaken if she is forthrightly denying that when we commend someone for a virtue such as courage, we normally imply our assent to the imperative "Let me be courageous" (or whatever). If I commend Smith as courageous while I turn to run from a dangerous duty I invite the comment "How about you?" It would not be natural for me to answer with "What do you mean—how about me?" I know very well what they mean. If I am (a) sincere and (b) able, it is to be expected that, having commended Smith for being courageous, I shall be, or at least try to be, courageous myself. If I make no such effort, it will be assumed either that I cannot help being a coward or that I do not sincerely rate courage a virtue. *Ex hypothesi* the former alternative is excluded. We are left with the latter.

If descriptivists are mistaken about the logical relationship between descriptive and evaluative meanings in cases such as that which we have been considering, why are they mistaken? Why do they think that, when anyone calls a man courageous (or by any other such apparently descriptive-cum-evaluative expression, e.g., dangerous, cowardly, etc.), we cannot (logically) separate the descriptive element in what they say from the evaluative? Hare's account of why they are mistaken is along these lines.[75] There are two ways in which description may be logically connected to evaluation: (i) the evaluation may be supervenient upon the description; or (ii) the expressions used may be such that description and evaluation are in a certain way logically tied together within the description. If I say that anything is good, for example, I must have an answer to "What is good about it?"; that is the former kind of connection. On the other hand, if I say that a man has acted courageously, it will be odd[76] for me to add that he did not do the right thing. Such a remark need not be completely

---

[75] Cf. Hare, "Descriptivism," *op. cit.*, 125.
[76] Cf. P. H. Nowell-Smith, *Ethics*, pp. 84–87.

nonsensical. But it would mean that, from one point of view, what the man did was right in that it was courageous, but from another point of view it was wrong, e.g., because it was rash. The descriptive element in the word "courageous" is in that sense logically tied to the evaluative, or commendatory. Now, says Hare, the descriptivist lands himself in confusion because he commits two fallacies: (i) he equivocates on the two ways in which description is logically connected with evaluation (viz. supervenience and what I have called being logically tied), and (ii) he assumes that what is true of words must be equally true of things. That is to say, the descriptivist argues thus:

The evaluation, or commendation, of anything must be logically connected, in *either* of the two ways indicated (i.e., supervenience or being logically tied), with its description.

But: Some *words,* e.g., "courageous," are such that, in their case, the connection between description and evaluation is that which I have called being logically tied together.

Therefore: In the case of some *things* the connection between description and evaluation is that which I have called being logically tied together; e.g., we cannot describe what it is about a man which we are referring to when we say that he is courageous without at the same time evaluating, or commending, him.

This does not seem to me to be an unfair account of what Mrs. Foot is, in effect, saying and, of course, the argument is fallacious.

Criteria and Choice

Mrs. Foot, in her article "Goodness and Choice,"[77] claims that a connection with the speaker's choice is neither a sufficient nor a necessary condition for the use of terms such as "good." It would be a *sufficient* condition if all that were required to make my use of "good" in "a good X" appropriate were the fact that I am ready to choose the kind of X which

[77] *PAS* Supp. Vol. XXXV (1961); see note 71.

I have called good. It would be a *necessary* condition if, whenever I call an X a good X, one thing required to make my use of "good" appropriate were that I am ready to choose X's of the kind to which I refer. Mrs. Foot's contention is that in neither case is the if clause fulfilled. Is this contention correct? Consider these examples:

I. A: Smith is a good father.
   B: But he neglects his children.
   A: I know.
   B: Then why do you call him good?
   A: If I could choose, I would always choose for myself, or others, a father who neglects his children.
   B: Oh, I see.

Does B's last remark make sense? Does he "see"? Can A, that is to say, intelligibly call fathers good because they neglect their children, provided only that this is a reason which he chooses to have for doing so? He could, if the readiness of the speaker to choose in accordance with the criteria invoked were a sufficient condition for the use of "good."

II. A: Smith's son is a good lad.
   B: What do you mean?
   A. I mean that I would choose Smith's lad as a son any day.

Is that what A is saying? It is manifestly not all that he is saying, of course. But is it even *part* of what he is saying? It would be, if the speaker's readiness to choose in accordance with the criteria invoked were a necessary condition for the use of "good."

The answer to the questions which I pose after each of these conversations seems to be *no*. So, such examples as these appear to constitute *reductiones ad absurdum* of the views which Mrs. Foot is attacking. She attributes such views to Hare. In reply he contends that either: (i) Mrs. Foot is attributing to him views which he has never held, and there is really no difference of opinion between him and her; or (ii) she is maintaining a highly unplausible position.

To support this contention he calls attention to an ambiguity in the expression "conditions for the use of a word."[78] This latter expression, he says, may mean: (i) "conditions for a word being said to be used correctly to express what the speaker who calls a thing 'good' (for example) wishes to convey"; or (ii) "conditions for a thing's being said to be 'good.'" I take the relevance of this distinction to the point at issue to be, in Hare's intention, as follows:

The rules for the use of "good" are such that:

  (i) Suppose that a man said "X *is* good," we asked him "Why?" and he replied "I am ready to choose X (or things like X)." This reply (to use an expression of Mrs. Foot's) does not "legitimatize" his words. His being ready to choose X *is not* a sufficient, nor a necessary, condition of X's *being* good. He could be ready to choose X, and X not be good; X could be good, and he not be ready to choose it.
  (ii) Now suppose that a man says "I *think* X good," we ask him "Do you really?" and he replies "Yes. I am ready to choose X." This reply does "legitimatize" his words. His being ready to choose X *is* a sufficient, and a necessary, condition for saying that he thinks X good. If he is ready to choose it, we may safely say that he thinks it good; and if he thinks it good, we may safely say that he is ready to choose it.

If Mrs. Foot is simply saying that a speaker's being ready to choose X is neither a sufficient, nor a necessary, condition of X's being correctly said *to be* good, Hare has no quarrel with her. He claims that he has insisted upon this himself.[79] If, on the other hand, Mrs. Foot is saying that the speaker's being ready to choose X is not a sufficient, or a necessary, condition of his being correctly said to *think* X good, then Hare considers her contention "not very plausible."[80]

Hare's opponents, I think, would respond that all this is a missing of the point. Even if a distinction such as this can

[78] Hare, "Descriptivism," *op. cit.,* 127.
[79] *Ibid.,* 128; cf. *LM,* p. 107.
[80] Hare, *op. cit.,* 129.

be drawn between what is thought good and what is good, the question remains: is it open to anyone to choose what the criteria for determining goodness shall be? Whether the goodness in question is moral or not does not affect the point at issue. I have referred earlier in this book to Warnock's insistence, against what he takes to be Hare's position, that we must not confuse: (i) being free to decide for ourselves in moral questions *on the evidence;* and (ii) being free to decide *what evidence is.* He represents Hare's position thus: "I do not, it seems, decide that flogging is wrong because I *am* against cruelty; rather, I decide that flogging is wrong because I *decide to be* against cruelty. And what, if I did make that decision, would be my ground for making it? That I am opposed to the deliberate infliction of pain? No—rather that I *decide to be* opposed to it. And so on."[81] It seems to Warnock that if you allow this sort of thing—people making up, not only their own minds, but also their own evidence—all reasoning must necessarily be at an end. I argued above against Warnock's view that moral discourse is not essentially irrationalist if it amounts to no more than choosing reasons why things are good, etc., and being tested for consistency in one's choice. But I said that the question remained as to whether moral reasoning really does amount to no more than that. According to Mrs. Foot it amounts to more. One does not simply choose the criteria of goodness, moral or otherwise. Rather, in her words, "Criteria for the goodness of each and every kind of thing . . . are always determined, and not a matter for decision."[82] She admits what she calls "competition examples" as an exception; judges or examiners can, of course, decide quite arbitrarily what shall constitute criteria of goodness for the purpose of some competition.[83] But, these apart, is her thesis supportable? The kind of example with which she endeavors to substantiate it is "a good knife," "a good rider," "a good father," etc. A good knife, she thinks, is one which fulfills the purposes for which knives are normally used, i.e.,

[81] Warnock, *op. cit.*, p. 47; see above, p. 207.
[82] Foot, "Goodness and Choice," *op. cit.*, p. 47.
[83] *Ibid.*, p. 54.

cutting;[84] a good rider, one who achieves the characteristic
purposes of the rider, e.g., pleasure, exercise, locomotion.[85]
We cannot say that a good knife is one which rusts quickly
and justify this use of "good" simply by saying that that is
the sort of knife which we choose for our own use. Nor can we
say that a good rider is one who, like a clown in a circus,
rides in such a way as to make people laugh, and justify
this use of "good" simply by saying that that is what we
want riders to achieve by riding. Such is not, says Mrs. Foot,
"the language of mankind." Of fathers she writes: "Being
a good *father* must have something to do with bringing up
children, and more specifically caring for them. While opinions may differ as to what is best for children, and while more
or less of the children's care may be assigned to parents in
different communities, it is only within such limits that the
criteria of a good father will differ from place to place. If, in
a certain community, a man were said to be a good A in so
far as he offered his children up for sacrifice, 'A' could not
be translated by our word 'father.'"[86] In none of these cases,
according to Mrs. Foot, can a man simply choose what shall
constitute the criteria of goodness. Something is taken for
granted—the purposes to which things like knives are put, the
point of an activity like riding, the conduct we look for in
fathers. These impose a limit upon what the relevant criteria
of goodness can be. If a speaker did not adhere to these in
commending knives, riding, fathers—or whatever—we could
not understand him.

In reply to all this, Hare points out that when some things
are called good an explanation seems called for; but not
when some other things are called good.[87] To take the sort of
example around which this point in the discussion has re-
volved, suppose a man persistently clasps and unclasps his
hands as he sits idly in his chair and tell us that he thinks it a
duty to do so. We shall be puzzled. Why? Not, Hare would
say, because it is a "logical absurdity" for anyone to think

[84] *Ibid.*, p. 46.
[85] *Ibid.*, pp. 57–58.
[86] *Ibid.*, pp. 50–51.
[87] Hare, "Descriptivism," *op. cit.*, p. 129.

this; but because it is a "contingent improbability" that anyone should. Now suppose that someone explains that our handclasping man is a sculptor who fends off rheumatism by this exercise and does this so persistently because he thinks that he has a duty to finish certain works of art so that they will not be lost to posterity. We are puzzled no longer. There is nothing contingently improbable in a man thinking it his duty to bequeath as much pleasure to posterity as he can. But, apart from some such "background" explanation, it is odd for anyone to speak of clasping and unclasping his hands as a duty. But, Hare insists, odd, not because logically illegitimate, only because contingently improbable.

> The reason is that very few of us, if any, have the necessary "pro-attitude" to people who clasp and unclasp their hands; and the reason for this is that the pro-attitudes which we have do not just occur at random, but have explanations, albeit not (as the descriptivists whom I am discussing seem to think) explanations which logic alone could provide. . . . We do not have, most of us, any disposition to choose, or to choose to be, men who clasp and unclasp their hands. We do not, accordingly, think that men who do this are good.
> The explanation of our not thinking this is that such choices would hardly contribute to our survival, growth, procreation & c.; if there have been any races of men or animals who have made the clasping and unclasping of hands a prime object of their pro-attitudes, to the exclusion of other more survival-promoting activities, they have gone under in the struggle for existence. I am, I know, being rather crude; but in general, to cut the matter short, we have the pro-attitudes that we have, and therefore call the things good which we do call good, because of their relevance to certain ends which are sometimes called "fundamental human needs."[88]

Once we have called something a *"need,"* however, there *is* a logical connection between calling it that and saying that a good man, as such, must (logically) possess it. Hare does

[88] *Ibid.,* 131.

not, of course, deny this. He simply insists that the point to take is that this connection is between the *words* "need" and "good." He thinks that failure to take this point is the descriptivists' root error. They take truths about words for truths about things (cf. above, p. 298). From the fact that anything which is called a need must logically be called good, it does not follow that anything in particular must be called a need. One thing can (logically), just as much as another, be taken for a "fundamental human need"—to recall Hare's list above, nonsurvival, nongrowth, nonprocreation, just as much as their opposites.

Is There Anything Which Cannot Be Denied to Be Good?

If anything at all can significantly be said to be a need, then it follows that, equally significantly, anything at all can be denied to be a need. Hare implies that such is the case; that men can choose what they will take to be fundamental human needs; and that, however contingently improbable in the case of some things, it would not be absurd to deny that anything whatever was a fundamental human need. Is such really the case? Or are there some things which it would not make sense to say that a man did not need? The point to take is this. If, as Hare concedes, anything whatever which is called a need must (logically) also be called good; and if, as I am now suggesting might be the case, there are some things which it cannot be denied that men fundamentally need; then it follows that it cannot be denied that these latter things are good. The criteria for the application of "good," where human life and action are concerned, would thus not be entirely open to choice. If, for instance, it cannot be denied that survival is a need, then it cannot be denied that survival is good. And if it cannot be denied that survival is good, that gives the descriptivists their case.

Is there anything of which it would not make sense to say that men do not need it? Freedom from physical injury has been suggested as one such need.[89] It is said to be a want which all men have. For the moment, I am using the words

---

[89] See Foot, "Moral Beliefs," *op. cit.,* p. 95.

"need" and "want" interchangeably; later I shall consider briefly the difference between them. Do all men need, or want, freedom from physical injury? Mrs. Foot contends that they do. The proper use of one's limbs would seem prima facie to be something which all men want, if they can be said to want anything. Of course there are some apparent exceptions. People in lunatic asylums sometimes try to injure themselves quite pointlessly. Again, in special circumstances, people who are perfectly sane have wanted to injure themselves; when, for example, a "blighty wound" would take them out of the firing line. And it is just conceivable, as Mrs. Foot observes, that a man could have servants who did everything for him, so that he did not need his limbs in order to get anything which he wanted. But such cases are all beside the present point. We are speaking of the logical grounding of moral judgment and the lunatic by definition has no concern with that; again, injuries such as "blighty wounds" are the means to a greater freedom from physical injury, or the probability of it; and yet again, no one, however many servants he had, could know for certain that, to the end, he would not require his limbs to get anything which he might want. With these exceptions thus accounted for, will Mrs. Foot's contention stand? It has not gone unchallenged.[90] Those who oppose the view that there are some wants, or needs, which all men have, take at least two lines against it.

(i) They claim that as a matter of empirical fact there are no wants which all men have. Freedom from physical injury is certainly one of the strongest contenders for the title of such a want, but all men do not want it. There have been numerous examples in history of men who have *not* wanted, or needed, freedom from physical injury. Scholars, for example, have sometimes been grateful for disabilities such as deafness because these aided concentration; and saints have thanked God for their "thorns in the flesh." Of course it is one thing to be glad that you have a disability, once you have it, but another actively to seek it, when you do not. But I do not think that difference affects the argument. If some penitent but

[90] See D. Z. Phillips and H. O. Mounce, "On Morality's Having a Point," *P* XL (1965); see note 71.

incorrigible thief wanted, or felt the need, to cut off his hands
so that he would not be able to steal any more, should we have
to say, in the strictest sense, that his action lay beyond all
reason? We might not approve of it, but it would not be unintelligible. I do not think that Mrs. Foot really allows for such
exceptions, though she is careful to say that the desire for
freedom from physical injury does not necessarily provide
an "overriding" reason for action.[91]

(ii) The second argument against Mrs. Foot's contention is
that the whole attempt to discover wants, or needs, which
all men have, so that moral beliefs can be grounded in them,
is misconceived. The very reverse is the case. At least some
of men's wants are logically grounded in their moral beliefs
and not vice versa. Messrs. Phillips and Mounce offer an
example in support of this latter point.[92] A scientific rationalist is arguing with a Roman Catholic housewife about
contraceptives. He stresses the harm which having too many
children may do, the wants or needs which it may frustrate—
hazard to the mother's health, restriction on her career, poverty
in the family, the consequent limitation of the opportunities of
those who belong to the family, and so on. In reply the housewife stresses the honor which a mother has in bringing children into the world. The authors who use this example say:
"It seems more likely that the scientific rationalist was blind to
what the housewife meant by honor, than that she was blind
to what he meant by harm."[93] Are we to say that either of
them has wants, or needs, which he or she does not recognize?
Can either say to the other: "If only you had the experience
and the imagination to appreciate the evidence for the goodness of the view I am advocating, evidence, which, unfortu-
nately, is too complex for you to master, you would see that
what I want is good for you too, since really, all men want
it"?[94] The authors whom I am quoting think not. They do not
only say that the rationalist and the housewife have different
wants. They also claim that these two do not hold their re-

[91] Foot, "Moral Beliefs," *op. cit.*, 97.
[92] Phillips and Mounce, *op. cit.*, 317–19.
[93] *Ibid.*, 317.
[94] *Ibid.*, 318.

spective moral beliefs because they have different wants; but,
on the contrary, have different wants because they hold differing moral beliefs. They say of the housewife, for instance: "It
may be admitted that the majority of mothers nowadays want
to plan the birth of their children to fit in with the Budget if
possible, and regard the rearing of their children as a pause in
their careers. But this will not make the slightest difference to
the housewife of our . . . example. She believes that what the
majority wants is a sign of moral decadence, and wants
different things. But she does not believe because she wants;
she wants because she believes."[95] Notice that they do not
say that the rationalist and the housewife have simply *chosen*
to regard different things as needs and therefore as good.
Their claim is that these two speak out of different moral traditions. These authors are with Hare in holding that, in the last
analysis, the reason for a moral judgment cannot be the mere
fact that somebody wants something, but only that we ought
to do what we ought to do. But they are with Mrs. Foot in
rejecting the idea that men simply choose what shall be just or
unjust, good or evil; on the contrary, this is given in the moral
tradition within which they think or speak. The basic difference between the two people in their example is that the rationalist simply does not know what the mother means by
honor.

A Proposed Middle Way

The kind of view held by Phillips and Mounce has recently
been given an admirably clear statement by R. W. Beardsmore in his *Moral Reasoning* (London, 1969) with due
acknowledgment to his mentors. He claims to have steered
between Scylla and Charybdis, to have found in the views of
Phillips and Mounce a middle way between the mistakes of
Hare's prescriptivism and those of Mrs. Foot's type of descriptivism. He agrees with Mrs. Foot in thinking that Hare's
mistake is to regard form alone as constituting a moral
judgment. But he holds that Mrs. Foot is mistaken in at least
two ways about the content which constitutes moral judg-

[95] *Ibid.*

ment: (i) virtues such as justice should not be thought of as *means* to the realization of any end beyond themselves, such as what all men want, human flourishing, or whatever, as Mrs. Foot supposes; and (ii) there is not simply *one* ultimate descriptive meaning to moral judgments as she thinks, but there is a *range of concepts,* reference to any of which makes a judgment moral. The range of concepts just mentioned includes honesty, fidelity, truthfulness, justice, courage, etc., and their opposites, that is, anything which we would normally call a virtue or a vice. Beardsmore's main argument runs as follows: a judgment, purporting to be moral, which is not supported by a reason invoking some concept or concepts within this range would be *unintelligible.*

In assessing this argument I think that we must first of all recognize an ambiguity in the word "unintelligible." On the one hand, when we say that someone's opinion is unintelligible to us we may simply mean that we find it very odd. In this sense the beliefs of Jehovah's Witnesses or British Israelites are unintelligible to me, I cannot understand people who will not allow their children to receive vital blood transfusions and I think it arrant nonsense to say that the British are the chosen people. On the other hand, when we call a view unintelligible we may mean that the statement of it either is self-contradictory or employs some word or words in ways contrary to their normal use. The beliefs of Jehovah's Witnesses and British Israelites are not, or not all of them, unintelligible in this sense; I understand them even though I do not subscribe to them and they are not nonsensical in the way that self-contradictions are or statements which misuse words. Beardsmore is alive to this ambiguity in the word "unintelligible." I am not accusing him of being otherwise. But I do think that the existence of the ambiguity lends a plausibility to his argument for unwary readers which it would not otherwise possess.

Much is made in that argument of the fact that we learn to use moral language as we grow up in a community which has a specific moral code. I did not decide, for instance, to think that murder is wrong any more than I decided to speak the English language. I grew up doing both. It follows that, on first encounter at any rate, the view that murder is *not* wrong must have struck me as odd. In the former of the above two senses I must have found it unintelligible. And this is a logical "must." But, of course, in order to make out his case Beardsmore has to show that *some* such views as the view that murder is *not* wrong are unintelligible in the latter of the above two senses. He has to show that there is always some judgment, or judgments, of the same kind as "Murder is wrong" to which, in the last analysis, anyone making a *moral* judgment must (logically) subscribe.

A judgment like "Murder is *not* wrong" is certainly not self-contradictory. Though I did not grow up holding this view I may come to do so. Many people have held it, at least with reference to particular murders. However much we may disagree with them, we can make sense of what they thought. Beardsmore nowhere suggests that we cannot. So he is not saying that such judgments are unintelligible because self-contradictory.

He rests his case, as I understand him, on the ordinary meaning of the word "moral." If anyone delivers what purports to be a *moral* judgment, then it is in order to ask the reason for it. This reason, to be a *moral* reason, must (logically) invoke some concept or concepts from the range referred to above; it must invoke some recognized virtue or vice as such. Suppose somebody says, "Such and such a murder was not wrong" and we ask him why he thinks so. His reply may well be something like this: "Well, it was the only way of ridding the world of a man who was causing others great misery." Here beneficence is invoked. It is because we think the latter a virtue, Beardsmore believes, that the reason given makes sense to us and the judgment which it supports becomes intelligible as a *moral* judgment.

It should be noted that Beardsmore's view allows for rebellion, conversion, and development within morality. In a chapter called "The Rebel and Moral Traditions" he points out, for example, that Nietzsche's intention in attacking conventional morality may be interpreted in either of two ways: (i) as the rejection of a perverse morality in favor of a genuine—say of servility in favor of courage; or (ii) as the rejection of

one in favor of another from among possible genuine morali-
ties—say of the Christian ethic in favor of a Spartan ethic. But,
according to Beardsmore's view, Nietzsche's intention could
not intelligibly be interpreted as the rejection of the *whole
range* of concepts constituting morality, if Nietzsche is to be
regarded as in any sense a moralist. Intelligible moral judgments, Beardsmore holds, are always delivered *within* a
context, e.g., the context of Roman Catholic morality or the
ethic of scientific humanism. It does not make sense, he
contends, to think of a moral judgment being delivered outside
any such specific moral context. He has to recognize what is
patently true, that a man may change his context. A Roman
Catholic could (logically) ask himself "Is Roman Catholic
morality right?"; decide that it is not right; and give it up in
favor of the ethics of scientific humanism or something else.
But both these contexts, in so far as we can recognize them as
moral contexts, must, Beardsmore believes, be constituted
in the last analysis by some appeal to what we ordinarily
recognize as virtues or vices. What no one could (logically)
do is to make a *moral* judgment which rejected all these virtues
and vices as such.

Prescriptivists are committed to the opinion that the whole
content of morality could (logically) be rejected in a judgment
which it would be intelligible to call a *moral* one. We could
say, "It is not right to practice honesty, fidelity, etc., and refrain from practicing their opposites"—running through the
whole range of accepted virtues and vices. True, when someone asked a reason for this judgment it might be unlike any
reason which had ever before been given for a moral judgment so far as its content is concerned. But that would not
matter. The form of the judgment would be enough to make
it moral. Beardsmore is convinced that such a view is patently
false. He leans heavily upon a remark of Wittgenstein's in
Philosophical Investigations, p. 242: "If language is to be a
means of communication there must be agreement, not only
in definitions, but also (queer as this may sound) in judgments." Wittgenstein was not referring specifically to moral
language but Beardsmore takes this remark to mean, among
other things, that men could not make any sense of each

other's moral judgments unless there were some agreement among them not only as to form but as to content. I will not discuss whether or not this is a legitimate interpretation of Wittgenstein but simply take the point as it stands here. If all men evaluated things differently, would it follow that they could not understand each other's evaluations? Suppose that no two people in the world ever set the same price on anything. Would it follow that they could not know what pricing is or understand each other's prices? Surely not. They could still recognize the speech-act of pricing as logically distinct from any other speech-act. And they could still understand the man who said that the price of X was value 1, the man who said it was value $1 + 1$, the man who said it was $1 + 2$, right on to the man who said it was $1 + n$, whichever of these men they happened to be themselves. Theirs would certainly be a chaotic economy. If each insisted upon his own price there could (logically) be no commerce between them. But this would not be because they did not understand each other but because they refused to make any deals with each other. In much the same way men could not understand moral discourse unless they could recognize a moral speech-act as logically distinct from any other sort of speech-act. The form of the speech-act would have to be the same in all cases in order to make the speech-act a moral one. It would have to be moral evaluation (or pricing) which was going on. But would the content (the prices set) have to be the same? To say that, if not, there could be no moral agreement (dealing) is not to say that there could be no understanding of what was going on.

The question, then, to which Beardsmore's type of theory brings us back is: does the *form* of a moral judgment alone make it moral? That question will concern us for the remainder of this chapter.

Is Morality Logically Grounded in Human Needs?

In his *Contemporary Moral Philosophy* Warnock suggests[96] that there are at least these defining characteristics of moral-

---

[96] Warnock, *Contemporary Moral Philosophy* (London, 1967), pp. 52 ff.

ity: (i) a certain "psychological penumbra" of responsibility, guilt, remorse, etc., which surrounds moral judgment; (ii) certain principles of conduct which are (a) dominant or overriding in a man's life and (b) which he prescribes universally; (iii) a content or general topic, namely human *needs* or *wants*. What is the relationship of the last of these elements to the others? Is it true a priori that moral discourse has a certain logical form—prescriptivity and universalizability—while its particular content is a contingent matter? Or is a content of concern with human wants or needs a priori and the particular way in which we express this concern in moral discourse a contingent matter? Against Hare, Warnock inclines strongly to the latter view. The psychological penumbra, the overridingness, the universal prescriptivity, are, he thinks, characteristic of moral discourse *because* its content is concerned with human wants or needs. But why? Warnock says: "It would seem to me more natural to say that, for very many people, certain principles play a predominant role in their own conduct, and are applied universally in judgment of the conduct of others, because they are believed to be moral principles, rather than, in reverse as it were, that their being moral principles *consists in* their being treated as overriding and of general application."[97] And his reason for saying this seems to be that discourse *other* than moral may have the same psychological penumbra and the same features of overridingness and logical prescriptivity.[98] But, by the same token, may not discourse other than moral be concerned with human wants or needs—e.g., psychological, sociological, or historical discourse? May these not, that is, have the same *content* as moral discourse? You cannot, I think, claim to be talking about morality simply because you are talking about human wants or needs. It is a particular way of talking about them which makes your talk moral. The logical form of the discourse is certainly essential to its being moral, whether or not the content is also.

Warnock, however, goes on to make more telling points in

[97] *Ibid.*, p. 57.
[98] Cf. *ibid.*, p. 56.

support of his thesis that morality is logically grounded in human wants or needs. I will refer to two in particular, outlining them first and then offering some criticism. (i) He concedes that it is logically possible to deny that anything called a need, or want, is such; and, in so far as "need" or "want" is logically tied to "good," to deny that this thing, whatever it is, which we call a want or need, is good. Whether anything is good or not is, therefore, as Warnock puts it, a "matter of judgment." But, he says, "It is, I submit, quite clear that it is not always, not wholly or necessarily, a matter of *moral* judgment."[99] If a judgment is a *moral* judgment, that is to say, then "good" and other such evaluative terms used to express it will have a certain content in a concern with human wants or needs "simply because of what 'moral' means."[100] He urges us not to be bullied by prescriptivists out of the conviction, which we all have, that "it is a bad thing to be tortured or starved, humiliated or hurt. . . . That it is better for people to be loved and attended to rather than hated and neglected. . . ."[101] He thinks that it could be *demonstrated*, for example, that it would be morally wrong for him to induce heroin addiction in his children. He writes, "Anyone who . . . holds, while conceding the facts [*sc.* concerning the effect of heroin addiction], that . . . it would *not* be morally wrong for me to induce in my children addiction to heroin . . . shows either that he has not really followed the argument, or that he does not know what 'morally wrong' means."[102]

One implication of this argument, if it were valid, would be that what Hare called "fanaticism" is not a logically possible point of view *within* morality. Above we noted Hare's view that, in so far as a Nazi, for instance, was prepared to universalize his belief that Jews ought to be exterminated, that belief could properly be called a moral one. Warnock denies this. He explicitly restricts the appellation "moral ideal" in such a way as to exclude the ideals of the storm trooper. Such

[99] *Ibid.,* p. 61.
[100] *Ibid.,* p. 67.
[101] *Ibid.,* p. 60.
[102] *Ibid.,* p. 70.

ideals as are "openly destructive, or damaging, or pointless, or insane" cannot form part of any moral point of view.[103]

(ii) Conceding still that it is logically possible to deny that anything usually called a want, or need, is such, and so to deny that it is good, Warnock now argues that nevertheless such denials may not be *intelligible* to us. He asks, "There are, perhaps, no logical limits to what a person may be said to want; and doubtless there is nothing of which it can be said that necessarily everyone wants it; but are there not limits, nevertheless, to what a person may be said *understandably* to want?"[104] We have certain specific wants or needs as a matter of fact. Given the logical link between "need" and "good," it follows that goodness for us has a certain content. It is conceivable that it should have a different content for creatures with different wants or needs (e.g., Martians); and then we should simply not understand their use of "good."

These two points of Warnock's do not seem to me to be conclusive against the prescriptivism which he is attacking. I will comment on each in turn.

(i) Would it be unnatural to speak of the storm trooper's ideal as "moral"? There is no more moral term than "duty." During Hitler's war, it was not unknown for his troops to shoot hostages when a village had aided the Resistance. It would obviously be manifest nonsense to say things like "They shot them to entertain the other villagers." But would it be on the same level of nonsense to say, "In shooting those hostages, the troops did their duty"? Someone may object, "They did what they *thought* their duty." But it is at least arguably one's duty to do just that. Is it unintelligible thus to describe what they did as their "duty"? If, as I think, it is not, then one is not entitled to refuse to call their ideal a moral one, however much one may deplore it.

(ii) If we suppose that Martians would have different wants or needs from ours and so call different things good, is it true, as Warnock says, that we could not understand their "moral" talk? It is certainly true that we should not agree with it. But

[103] *Ibid.*, p. 59.
[104] *Ibid.*, p. 66.

we could recognize that they were commending things by their use of "good." And if to recall Warnock's list, the psychological penumbra, the overridingness, and the universal prescriptivity which characterize our moral discourse, characterized their discourse, then, despite the latter's very different content, should we not be able to recognize that they were doing the kind of thing which we call moral judgment, though with some fantastically different results? To understand another's discourse is to recognize the kind of speech-act which he is performing. To agree with him is to be prepared to perform a similar act with the same content. It seems to me that, whatever the content of a Martian's discourse, if he spoke of it as I speak, say, of the unnecessary infliction of pain, I should understand him, though I might well not agree with him.

Before concluding this subsection, I should like to call attention to what seems to be a possible point of rapprochement between prescriptivists, like Hare, and descriptivists, like Warnock or Mrs. Foot. The latter quite explicitly seek a logical grounding for morality in human wants, or more precisely in what all men want. Hare, I think, would wish to say that he does the same, in a sense. Notice two points: (i) It can plausibly be argued that there is some connection between wanting and assenting to an imperative. I think that Hare might say something like this: If you say that A wants to be (or to do) X, you properly express what you are saying that A *thinks*—supposing you need to express that—by saying "A assents to the imperative 'Let me be (or do) X.'" (ii) As we saw in the last chapter, according to Hare's universal prescriptivist utilitarianism, when we deliberate about whether or not X ought to be done, we are required to go the round of all the interested parties asking whether or not we would assent to the imperative "Let X be done," if we were in their shoes. On this requirement, recall Hare's own words, quoted above: we have to ask ourselves, "How much (as I imagine myself in the place of each man in turn) do I *want* to have this, or avoid that?" (italics mine).[105]

[105] P. 227.

Now, putting (i) and (ii) together, could it not be said that Hare grounds morality in what all men want? According to his view, as we saw in the last chapter, assenting sincerely to "X ought to be done" entails assent to "Let X be done." This means, in terms of (i) above, that wanting X to be done is a necessary condition of saying sincerely that X ought to be done. Again according to Hare, as we have already remarked, to judge whether or not X ought to be done is to consider whether one could assent to "Let X be done," if one were in the place of each interested party in turn. This means, in terms of (ii) above, that thinking X to be what all men concerned want is a necessary condition of saying sincerely that X ought to be done. As the debate between prescriptivists and descriptivists continues, it may well be that they will be able to resolve some of their apparent differences by considerations such as those to which I have just referred.

Nevertheless, while it may be said that both schools of thought ground morality in what all men want, I think there is a difference in the way that they do so which should certainly be noted and may turn out to be fundamentally divisive in the end. How does Hare do so? He thinks that we must take account of what all men want in order to be sure that we have calculated correctly what will maximize satisfaction. This was brought out in the subsection of the last chapter entitled "The Universalizability Thesis and Utilitarianism." If there I correctly interpreted Hare, it is logically possible, given his view, for the satisfaction of some fanatics in seeing all Jews exterminated to be greater than the satisfaction of all Jews in not being exterminated. There could be many who share this fanaticism and who would be satisfied by seeing all Jews exterminated. It *could* make sense to say that Jews ought to be exterminated because, when we have taken account of the wants of all concerned, the satisfaction of what these fanatics want would be the greatest satisfaction of wants which the case admits of. The point which I wish to make now may perhaps best be brought out by saying that, in Hare's case, "what all men want" means *any* wants which men may have. Whatever wants there are in a given situation must be taken into account in calculating what will effect the greatest satisfaction of wants.

How do Warnock and Mrs. Foot interpret "what all men want"? What would they say of a want such as that of the fanatics to whom we have just been referring? We have seen, in this subsection, that Warnock holds that anything as "destructive, or damaging, or pointless, or insane" as what such a fanatic would want cannot form part of any moral point of view. In grounding morality in "what all men want," Warnock and Mrs. Foot appear to be doing something different from Hare. In their case "what all men want" does not mean any wants which men may have, but *certain specific wants which all men, as such, do have*. They are saying, in effect, that there *are* such wants, e.g., for freedom from physical injury, and that, unless a judgment is directed to the satisfaction of these wants, it cannot (logically) be a *moral* judgment. It is one thing to say with Hare that a judgment is moral only if it takes into account the relevant wants of all those concerned; but another thing to say with Warnock and Mrs. Foot that a judgment is moral, only if it is directed to the satisfaction of certain wants which all men have and which determine what is, and what is not, relevant.

Flourishing

Considerable use has been made in this chapter of the notion of a need, and in particular, of a fundamental human need. I think the time has come to look at this notion a little more closely. The following points seem to me to be important.

(i) There is a difference between wants and needs. Hitherto, I have used these words as virtually identical in meaning. I do not think that that invalidates anything which I have said, but we must now note that they do not, strictly speaking, mean the same thing. The difference beween them can, perhaps, best be put like this. Anything can (logically) be wanted for its own sake; but nothing can (logically) be needed for its own sake. To the question "What do you want that *for?*" it is possible to reply "I don't want it for anything. I just want it."

But to the question "What do you need that for?" it would never make sense to reply "I don't need it for anything. I just need it."

(ii) There are (at least) two senses of "need." They are: (a) Men may need something in the sense that they cannot, empirically or logically, exist as men without it. In this sense, it has been said, for example, that it is empirically and logically impossible for a man not to be moral (in what I called the "allocating" sense of "moral").[106] (b) Men may need something in the sense that, while they can exist without it, their existence cannot be a *good* existence without it. In this sense, it might be said that growth in body and mind, companionship, having children, etc., are fundamental human needs.

(iii) What, in the light of the distinction between these two senses of "need," is the connection between "need" and "good"? (a) If we are using "need" in the sense defined under ii.a., then "need" *is not* logically tied to "good." If it is simply the case that men could (empirically or logically) not exist without X, the question is nevertheless open as to whether or not X is good. We cannot take it for granted that because something is necessary to man's existence, it is therefore good. (b) If, on the other hand, we are using "need" in the sense defined under ii.b., then "need" *is* logically tied to "good." If it is the case that men could not have a *good* existence without X then it cannot be denied that X is good (in that sense).

(iv) A view has become fashionable recently which grounds moral reasoning in the notion of human flourishing. "Flourishing" is sometimes defined as the fulfillment of certain needs.[107] It will be remembered that I said above[108] that the answer to the question "Why be just (or 'moral' in what I called the evaluative sense)?" is, in the last analysis, "Because it is being just (or 'moral' in the said sense)." But those who hold the view to which I am now referring consider this to be a mistake. They say that the answer to "Why be just (or in the

[106] See above, pp. 276–81.
[107] Anscombe, "Modern Moral Philosophy," *op. cit.*, p. 7; see note 71.
[108] P. 275.

said sense 'moral')?" is, in the last analysis, "Because in so doing you will flourish." If I have understood them correctly, those descriptivists who take this line would say two things at least with regard to such flourishing. They would say: (a) that the statement "Flourishing is good" is true, but not simply true by definition of the *word* "flourishing"; and (b) that it nevertheless would not make sense to say "Flourishing is not good." That is, they would say: (a) that it is not the case that, in calling anything "flourishing," we are begging the question as to whether or not it is good; yet (b) it is the case that "Is flourishing good?" is not an open question. If this view is correct, then, to put the point another way, we can derive an evaluation from a description, an "ought" from an "is." From "Act, or state of affairs, X will constitute human flourishing," we can deduce "X ought to be done (or brought into being)."

This view, that moral reasoning is logically grounded in the notion of human flourishing, seems to have been gaining in popularity among moral philosophers over the last decade. But it is open to objection. If we are speaking of "flourishing" as definable in some such way as "the fulfillment of a need (or needs)," I think we can see why the view referred to has seemed so plausible to many; but also why it does not hold good. The word "need," as we noted, is ambiguous. Now, it seems plausible to hold to iv.a. above—i.e., to the opinion that the statement "Flourishing is good" is not true simply by definition of the word "flourishing"—*because* "need" can be taken in sense ii.a. above—i.e., the sense in which (as we noted under iii.a.) the word "need" *is not* logically tied to the word "good." But then again, it seems plausible to hold to iv.b. above—i.e., that it makes no sense to say "Flourishing is not good"—*because* "need" can be taken in sense ii.b.—i.e., the sense in which (as we noted under iii.b.) the word "need" *is* logically tied to the word "good." It is this ambiguity in the word "need," given that flourishing is defined in terms of need, which lends credibility to the opinion that, from the factual statement "X is flourishing," we can logically deduce the value judgment "X is good."

But it is a specious credibility. We cannot make this deduction. If, on the one hand, we stick to "need" in sense ii.a., it is *not* an open question whether there is anything to which the word "need" applies, since obviously some things are empirically, and logically, necessary to the existence of man; but it *is* an open question whether any such need is good. We cannot just assume that because something is necessary to human existence, it is good. Circumstances could be conceived in which it would make sense to say that whatever is necessary to man's existence is bad. If, on the other hand, we stick to "need" in sense ii.b. it is *not* an open question whether what is needed is good, since by definition it must be so; but it *is* an open question whether there is anything to which the word "need" applies. We cannot just assume that growth of body or mind, for instance, are needs in this sense ii.b. It would not be self-contradictory to say that a man needs to be stunted or stupid; though of course it would be self-contradictory to say this and then to deny that being stunted or stupid is good.

The argument for grounding morality in the notion of "flourishing" then proceeds thus. There are some things which constitute human flourishing, are there not? (This means: are there not some things which are needs *in sense ii.a.*—things, that is, which, given a certain definition of "man," man cannot empirically or logically do without?) Undoubtedly there are, whatever definition is given to "man." Again, is it not good to flourish? (This means: is not anything which is a need *in sense ii.b.* also good?) One cannot without self-contradiction deny that it is. It seems to follow that the things which constitute human flourishing cannot be denied to be good. And so, the argument goes, once we have established what these things which constitute flourishing are, we can demonstrate that anything either is, or is not, good, simply by asking whether it is one of them, or the means to one of them. But, of course, this whole argument only works because of the ambiguity in "need."

Ethics and Anthropology

Must we, then, dismiss the view that moral thinking is logically grounded in the notion of human flourishing, as altogether misconceived? I think that perhaps there is more to be said and offer the following considerations in support of that opinion.

(i) There does seem to be some connection between anthropology and ethics, that is, between what it is believed that man *is* and what it is believed that he ought to do. I think this is true in the case of at least some types of ethical theory. Utilitarians believe, with Bentham, that nature has placed man under the governance of two sovereign masters, pleasure and pain, and, with Mill, in the social feelings of mankind; and when it comes to what man ought to do, they say that he ought to seek the greatest happiness of the greatest number. Evolutionists believe that man is a product of evolution; and that he ought to do what will be conducive to evolution. Marxists think that human nature takes the shape which it does under the pressure of economic forces; and that what is right is what furthers the aims of the workers in the class war. Existentialists believe that in man, existence precedes essence; and that the worst thing a man can do is to live as some kind of slave when he could live as a free being. Religious moralists think that man is God's creature; and that God's will is what man ought to do. Surely there is *some* connection between the "is" and the "ought" in some, if not all, these cases.

(ii) However this connection is to be explained—and I readily concede that its explanation may not be as simple a matter as I shall make it appear—there is one thing which it would plainly be untrue to say about it, and two things which would be, to say the least, unplausible. (a) It is manifestly not true that proponents of the differing ethical theories to which I have referred all agree as to what the facts concerning human nature and existence are, and differ *only* in which of these they select for approval or disapproval. There is, admittedly, some possibility of overlap in what they take man to be; utilitarians and religious moralists, for example, could agree about what man is. But there is clearly some divergence; for instance, existentialists certainly do not hold the same anthropological beliefs as Marxists. The differences which I have in mind here may, of course, be metaphysical. Nothing depends, for my argument's fate, on whether they are meta-physical or empirical. The only relevant point is that they are matters of putative *fact*. They are beliefs to the effect that something *is* the case concerning man. (b) It would be un-plausible to say that the anthropological beliefs of those who subscribe to each type of theory are logically grounded in their respective moral beliefs. Someone who wished to take that line might, for instance, argue that the point which I am making amounts to no more than that "ought" implies "can": that it makes no sense to say that men ought, for example, to live as free beings unless they can. But my point amounts to more than that. Surely it would be putting the cart before the horse to say, for instance, that religious moralists believe that man ought to obey God's will, and, since man could not do that unless he were a being who lived under God's govern-ance, the religious moralist *therefore* believes that that is what man is. (c) Even less plausible would be the opinion that it just happens to be the case that, in each type of ethical the-ory, the respective anthropology and ethic subsist together. This would supply no explanation of the indisputable fact that the anthropology is frequently invoked in order to make the ethic intelligible.

(iii) The question then becomes: just how is it invoked? In reply, I will first hark back to the disagreement between the rationalist and the Roman Catholic mother.[109] It was said that they had different wants because different beliefs. But these different beliefs, it should be noted, were not, or not simply, moral beliefs as to what is good or what ought to be done. The rationalist and the mother disagreed as to what the *facts* are, where human existence is concerned. The mother believed that she and her children were immortal souls, living under the governance of a God, who forbids the use of con-traceptives and upon whose approval our ultimate destiny de-pends. The rationalist believed that he and his fellow men were simply creatures of space and time, living under no God, and free to do whatever they chose. Now let us suppose that

[109] Above, pp. 306–7.

someone is puzzled by the mother's moral beliefs and someone else tries to dispel his puzzlement. Imagine this conversation:

A: She thinks that using contraceptives is wrong.
B: Really! How odd.
A: It's not odd. She believes in God and thinks that he forbids their use.
B: Oh, I see.

Why does A's second remark dispel B's puzzlement? Are we to say that what B "sees" is that the mother's position concerning contraceptives resolves itself into this "practical syllogism":

Major premise: Whatever God forbids ought not to be done.
Minor premise: God forbids the use of contraceptives.
Conclusion: Therefore contraceptives ought not to be used.

In such a case, when told the mother's factual belief (the minor premise), B supplies a general moral principle (the major premise) and "sees" that the mother's moral judgment (the conclusion) follows for anyone who accepts these premises, as he takes the mother to do. This seems to me a possible way of explaining how, in such an instance, a factual belief about human nature or existence can make a moral judgment intelligible to us.

(iv) But now consider another similar imaginary conversation:

A: He thinks that men ought never to take their opinions about what to do ready-made from others.
B: Never?
A: Never.
B: That's odd.
A: It's not odd. He believes that in man existence precedes essence.
B: Oh. I see.

If we try to explain how the factual belief makes the moral judgment intelligible by invoking, in this case as in the last, some major premise, then the question arises as to what that major premise could be. Here, B has a minor premise to work with, viz. "In man existence precedes essence"; and a conclusion, viz.: "Men ought never to take their opinions about what to do ready-made from other people." What major premise does he need to supply so that the former renders the latter intelligible?

Very tentatively, I suggest that it is some such major premise as this: "Whatever will give rise to the flourishing of man, as what he is taken to be, ought to be done." What B "sees" will then be the following explanation of the existentialist's position:

(1) Whatever will give rise to the flourishing of man, as what he is taken to be, ought to be done.

(2) Man is taken to be a being in whom existence precedes essence.

(3) Therefore whatever will give rise to the flourishing of man as a being in whom existence precedes essence ought to be done.

(4) Never taking one's opinions about what to do ready-made from other people gives rise *ceteris paribus* to the flourishing of man as a being in whom existence precedes essence.

(5) Therefore never taking one's opinions about what to do ready-made from other people is what one ought to do.

If there is anything in this—i.e., in my suggestion that B would need to supply the major premise which I have supposed in order to "see" that A's "He believes that in man existence precedes essence" explains the existentialist's moral judgment— then the following comments are, I think, apposite.

(a) Notice that this major premise recognizes a limit on what, for any given moralist, may count as "flourishing." I am well aware that "flourishing" is itself an evaluative word; and that, within any school of thought, such as existentialism, opinions may differ as to what constitutes it. But not limitlessly. What, for instance, could we make of an existentialist who said, "Men flourish by taking their opinions about what to do ready-made from others"? He would be contradicting himself, not because, as an existentialist, he subscribes to the moral principle that men ought not to take their opinions about what to do ready-made from others, but because, as one, he believes that man is a being in whom existence precedes essence and, when asked, "What is it to be such a being?" one of the things which he says in reply is that it is to be someone who *does not* take his opinions about what to do ready-made from others. Any being who did take his opinions about what to do from others would, in the existentialist's eyes, *cease* to be a man. It follows that, on the existentialist's lips, "Men flourish by taking their opinions about what to do ready-made from others" is self-contradictory. So far from flourishing, as *men* they would cease to be men in his eyes.

I realize that there are at least two objections which may be raised to the claim which I am making here. (1) It may be said: "Men, in the generally accepted definition of that word, can, and frequently do, take their opinions about what to do ready-made from others. So the existentialist's definition of "man" is stipulative. And, when one tries to make sense of it, it is clearly persuasive. It is the existentialist's way of saying that he thinks men ought not to take their opinions about what to do ready-made from others." I am strongly tempted to accept this objection and say no more. But I cannot quite bring myself to believe that it is damning. When the existentialist states his anthropology, surely he is saying, however unclearly, that he believes man to have certain characteristics or potentialities which other beings lack. In particular, man has a kind of freedom which enables him to form his own opinions about what to do. Men may not exercise this freedom and those who have it may come to have it no longer, as the existentialist recognizes. But his definition refers to something which (however mistakenly, if he is mistaken) the existentialist believes that man *is,* not that he ought to be. Given that you say, as the existentialist does, that this is what man *is,* you cannot (logically) go on to say that he flourishes by not being this. (2) The second objection which may be raised to what I am here claiming is as follows: "By your

talk of 'flourishing,' in effect, you are denying that it ever
makes sense to say that a man ought to destroy himself.
But what about self-sacrifice? With perfectly good sense, many
teachers have said that this is what men ought to practice
even to the extent of laying down their lives." This objection
is, I think, beside the point which I am making. The latter
turns on the existentialist's definition of "man." Given that
definition, I am simply pointing out, there is something which
it would be self-contradictory to say. Nevertheless, the present
objection is interesting if we take up the reference to self-
sacrifice. Is it not significant that those who advocate self-
sacrifice usually present it as a path to self-realization? "He
who loseth his life shall find it." However difficult it may be
to make sense of this, and I do not personally find it difficult,
the fact remains that to those who advocate it, and to those
who heed them, self-sacrifice appears to be a duty *because* it
is the way to some kind of self-realization. A moralist who
advocated self-destruction *simpliciter*, who said "Men ought
to destroy themselves" and left it at that, would surely be
saying something which, we should find, though not self-
contradictory, certainly irrational and unintelligible. We
should say that he was mad. This brings me to the next main
point which I want to make.

(b) The major premise "Whatever will give rise to the
flourishing of man, as what he is taken to be, ought to be
done," is not just one general moral principle among others.
I venture to suggest that subscription to it might be called
a test of rationality. If a man used moral language to commend *not* doing whatever would give rise to the flourishing
of man as what he took man to be, then we should consider
him irrational. Anyone who subscribed to existentialist anthropology, for instance, and at the same time said, "You ought
to take your opinions about what to do ready-made from
other people," would not be considered simply to hold an
unusual ethical opinion. He would be thought mad, or, at best,
hopelessly muddleheaded. Why? It may be argued that, since
"flourishing" is an evaluative word, the major premise in
question reduces, in the last analysis, to "Whatever ought to be
done ought to be done." And to deny this would of course be

irrational because self-contradictory. But that does not dispose of my point. I am saying that, even if "human flourishing" simply means "what ought to be done," there is nevertheless a limitation on what may be intelligibly said to constitute such flourishing, which is imposed by what man has been said to be—assuming of course that he has been said to be something. Having said that man is such-and-such we cannot go on to say that he ought to do just anything whatever, without any possible risk to our reputation for rationality. I have illustrated my point—that there are some things such that, if we said that man ought to do them, given our anthropology, we would be thought irrational—from the case of existentialism. I am not sure that it can be illustrated as effectively in the case of every ethical theory. But even if the connection between ethics and anthropology holds in only some cases, it needs explaining.

It might help to make the sort of explanation which I am proposing clear, if I digress for a moment and recall what some philosophers of history[110] have said about historical explanation. Suppose a historian is asked why Cromwell had King Charles executed. He tells the story in such a way that it becomes clear that Cromwell had to take this step in order to protect his insecure authority against the challenge of a man who could invoke all the mystique of kingship in his support. The historian and those who accept his explanation obviously subscribe to the principle that it is "the thing to do" for men like Cromwell to take such action against men like Charles. I do not mean the moral thing to do, of course. I mean simply that, in so far as we consider it reasonable to take the kind of action which Cromwell took, we understand his action when it is pointed out that it was that kind of action. This sort of explanation, in terms of generally accepted views about "the thing to do," stands in sharp contrast to any explanation of an event which shows it to be the kind of thing which generally happens. The Cromwells of this world do *not* always take such action to protect themselves against the Charleses. We are not being told that they

[110] See e.g., W. H. Dray, *Laws and Explanation in History* (1957).

do. The explanation appeals, not to our beliefs about what always happens, but to our views about "the thing to do." The point of this digression into the philosophy of history is to bring out what I mean by saying that subscription to the above major premise—"Whatever will give rise to the flourishing of man, as what he is taken to be, ought to be done"— is a test of rationality. Using *moral* terms like "good" and "ought" in order to commend the flourishing of man *as what we take him to be,* is "the thing to do" with such language. If anyone is not doing this, then what he is doing does not make sense to us.

The practical significance of what I have been saying, if it is correct, is at least twofold: (1) It gives us a weapon against opponents. When we are arguing with someone about a moral issue, we are entitled to ask him how he would answer the question "What is man?" Then, if he replies to this inquiry, we are entitled to raise the further question as to whether or not his anthropology is logically compatible with his ethic. He cannot simply brush the question aside by appealing to the is-ought dichotomy. Can he, as a reasonable man, subscribe to both his anthropology and his ethic? It makes sense to ask. It is possible that he cannot. Whatever a man says in terms of "is" may not be formally contradicted by whatever he says in terms of "ought"; but, even so, we could conceivably convict a man of using moral language in a way which goes against "the thing to do" with it, if he couples some moral judgments with some is-beliefs. And should he reply, "Well, that's the thing that *I* do with it," we are entitled to point out that the mad and the muddleheaded can always make that reply. (2) What I have said above has the further practical consequence that it makes some foundation in fact for moral judgment at least conceivable. We *may* eventually settle the question "What is man?" By "settle" I mean "secure general agreement about." Highly improbable it may be, but not inconceivable. If we ever got—and in so far as, within limited groups, we do get—such agreement, we could—and we can—show that, given the relevant anthropology, there is a limit upon what may be said in terms of "ought." A limit, that is, on what may be taken to constitute the flourishing of man, as what he is taken to be, and so upon the moral judgments which may be intelligibly or reasonably expressed. This being so, disciplines which inquire into the nature of man could shed some light upon ethics. I have in mind the human sciences (such as physiology, psychology, sociology) and also religion. I merely point this out. It is beyond the scope of this book to pursue the relevance of science or religion to morality any further.

CHAPTER 7. ACTION AND RESPONSIBILITY

Moral judgments presuppose action. They do so in the sense that they are delivered upon, and intended to guide, actions. Unless action is possible, moral judgments lose their point. If we cannot make sense of the concept of action neither will the concept of moral judgment be intelligible to us. It is true that states of affairs, as well as actions, are the subject matter of moral judgments. But these states of affairs are always such as can be created, preserved, destroyed, or changed by human actions of one kind or another.

Other sorts of speech-act, besides moral judgments, are action-directing. The action presupposed, however, is not always necessarily the same. We begin to see the nature of the action presupposed by moral discourse when we ask ourselves what *other*, or what *more*, such action necessarily is than the action presupposed by other forms of action-directing discourse. For example, the "hidden persuaders" of the advertising world direct action; but this is action in a minimal sense, if indeed it can be called action at all. Subliminal advertising is designed to create an influence, to cause consumers to buy certain goods. In the chapter on emotivism, we saw that moral judgments cannot be so conceived. It follows that the action which they presuppose is something other, or something more, than the action which subliminal advertising presupposes. The difference between this sort of action-directing discourse and moral judgment is a big one. In other instances, the difference is not so great. When, for instance, we were discussing prescriptivism, we encountered the view that moral judgments have logical affinities with imperatives and decisions. A man delivering a moral judgment is certainly more

like a sergeant uttering a command, or an umpire ordering
a man out of the game, than he is like a "hidden persuader."
But there are still important differences, as prescriptivists have
fully recognized. Sergeants and umpires direct action, but the
action here presupposed is not altogether the same as that
presupposed by a moral judgment. A sergeant sends his men
marching around the barrack square, but if he is so incompe-
tent that, in the end, he has them marching off the square
and over the vegetable garden, it is not their fault. An umpire
gives batsmen out and sends them marching back to the pavilion, but if he wrongly gives some batsman out and, in consequence, the latter's team loses, it is not the batsman who is
to blame. Compare such cases with that of a man upon whose
actions or affairs another man passes a moral judgment. In
delivering the moral judgment, the other man entails an imperative—"That is wrong" *ceteris paribus* entails "Don't do
that." Again, in delivering the judgment, the other man implies a decision of principle—"That is wrong because you
gave your word not to do it" implies "Whatever is the breaking of a promise is wrong." Even so, the man upon whom
the judgment is passed cannot absolve himself from responsibility for the consequences of obeying the imperative, or accepting the decision of principle, as the soldiers in the vegetable garden, or the batsman on his way back to the pavilion, can. The action presupposed by moral judgment is the
man's *own* action in some sense, or to some degree, that the
actions of the soldiers or the batsman are not their own.

    In some instances, the difference between moral judgment
and other forms of action-guiding discourse appears to be
quite small. Descriptivists, as we saw, think that morality has
a certain content. If that is so, then presumably people can
be taught that such-and-such actions are right or wrong, or
how to behave in such-and-such situations, as they can be
taught any other body of knowledge. This suggests an analogy
between moral judgment and tutorial advice or instruction.
Is the action presupposed in each case the same? A tutor's
words are action-directing and presuppose that the pupil concerned can get certain books, read them, embody what he
learns in essays, take advice about how to produce an essay,

etc. If, however, the tutor is stupid or uninformed, a pupil can hardly plead this as an excuse for failing his examinations, as the soldiers in the vegetable garden, or the batsman on his way back to the pavilion, can plead that what they were doing is the fault of the stupid sergeant or the careless umpire. True, it is not altogether absurd to blame failure in an examination on bad tutoring. And, I suppose, one could say that it is not altogether absurd to excuse someone's immoral conduct by pointing out that he has been misguided by those who delivered moral judgments to him. Nevertheless, this latter move is intelligible only in unusual circumstances: say, where the person thought to have been misguided is very young, or of subnormal intelligence, or in some other such way exceptionally placed. Moral judgments guide actions. And the actions which they guide are normally taken to be, in an unqualified sense, the actions of the person being guided. That moral judgments have been addressed to him never absolves an agent from responsibility for what he does, as he may be absolved from that responsibility by the fact that "hidden persuaders," army sergeants, cricket umpires, or even university tutors have been at work on him. The action which moral judgment presupposes is, in the fullest possible sense, an agent's *own* action. The question which will concern us in this chapter is: how precisely are we to conceive of the kind of action which moral discourse presupposes? That is one of the questions which have engaged the attention of philosophers throughout the entire history of their discipline. In the first section of this chapter, I shall have something to say about how one of the greatest of classical philosophers, Aristotle, answered it. But, in the main, I shall be discussing the way in which contemporary philosophers have dealt with it. A book on modern moral philosophy would be incomplete without some consideration of their treatment of the concept of responsible action.

I. NEGATIVE CONDITIONS OF RESPONSIBLE ACTION

The action which moral discourse presupposes is, in a word, voluntary action. Aristotle gave it as the essential characteristic

of voluntary action that it has its origination within the agent.[1]
If we accept this definition, then the action which moral discourse presupposes is in some sense *free* and in some sense
determined. It is *free,* on the one hand, in the sense that the
agent can originate it and also can "not-originate" it. There
would be no point in telling an agent that he ought to do what,
as a matter of empirical fact, he could not do; just as it
would be nonsensical to enjoin him to do, or blame him for
not doing, what is logically impossible. "Ought to do" clearly
implies "can do," where the "can" is both logical and empirical. But, equally clearly, it implies "can not-do" in the sense
"can refrain from doing." We should neither commend nor
censure an agent if he could not have refrained from doing
what he did under any conditions whatever, e.g., even if he
had chosen to do so.

These, then, are the senses in which the action, presupposed by morality, is free. It is *determined* in the sense that
it is always conceived as proceeding from an agent. Action
is always *done;* it never merely occurs. That is to say, there
is always assumed to be an agent, or agents, to whom the
origination of the action can be attributed. We shall have to
consider more carefully below what this relationship is between an action and its agent and how it differs, if at all, from
that between an event and its cause; but at the moment I
simply wish to affirm that a voluntary action is always conceived in some way to originate in the choice, intention, will,
or whatever, of an agent, or agents, and is, to that extent
and in that respect, determined to be what it is. The point is
important because some moral philosophers in their anxiety
to defend the freedom of the will have contended that voluntary acts are entirely *un*determined.[2] The mistake here will
be seen if we ask how in fact we differentiate, say, the voluntary activity of striking someone from the mere movement
of an arm in the throes of a disease such as *locomotor ataxia.*

---

[1] *Nichomachean Ethics* III.
[2] E.g., C. A. Campbell, "Is 'Free Will' a Pseudo-Problem?" *M* LX
(1951), and *On Selfhood and Godhood* (1957), Lecture IX and Appendix B; E. F. Carritt, *The Theory of Morals* (1928), Chap. XV, and
Ethical and Political Thinking (Oxford, 1947), Chap. XII.

We do not do so by conceiving of the former as undetermined and the latter as determined. There is determination in both cases; the difference lies in where we locate it. In the former case we locate it *within* the agent, i.e., we think of him as striking his victim from choice, intentionally, voluntarily; in the latter case we locate the determination *outside* the agent, i.e., we think of the movements of his arm as events causally connected with other events, namely his illness and its effects, the latter being conceived not as anything which he has done but as misfortunes which have befallen him.

Our original question: how is the action, which moral discourse presupposes, to be conceived? has thus become: what conditions, negative and positive, must be fulfilled if the action, which moral discourse presupposes, is to be free and determined in the required senses? Aristotle gave two of these negative conditions in the discussion of voluntary action to which reference has already been made. First and most obviously, action will be voluntary if and only if it is not due to external compulsion. Suppose that, while driving my car, I were pushed in the back by one of my passengers and consequently swerved into and injured a pedestrian on the pavement. Such an accident would be spoken of normally as something which had happened to me as well as to my victim. Secondly, according to Aristotle, action is voluntary in the required sense if and only if it is not due to the agent's ignorance. If I had run that pedestrian down because, unknown to me, my brakes were faulty and, when applied, made my car swerve into him, the accident would not have been considered my doing. Of course, in the case of both these negative conditions, viz., not due to external compulsion, and not due to ignorance, numerous qualifications need to be added, as Aristotle himself noted. What precisely constitutes external compulsion? If someone who is holding a gun to my head orders me to do something, I have a choice between obeying him or disobeying, between doing what he says or getting myself shot. Would doing what I am told to do in such circumstances be considered a voluntary action or not? All kinds of circumstances will have to be taken into account—

e.g., how I got into that situation in the first place, what effects would follow upon my choice one way or the other, etc.—before one could say whether this was a case to which moral judgment was appropriate or not. Similarly, in the case of ignorance, we cannot say that a man is neither free nor responsible simply because he is unaware of what he is doing. To quote Aristotle's example, a drunken man may be unaware of what he is doing, but "he might have helped getting drunk, and this is the cause of his ignorance."[3] Allowing for all such qualifications, then, we may say for a beginning that in order to be free and determined in the required senses an action must not have been done under external compulsion or from ignorance. It must, to use Aristotle's terminology, be "that whose origination is in the agent, he being aware of the particular details in which the action consists."[4]

So far so good. But we must look much more carefully at the distinction between what an agent would be said to have done and what he would not, between what we should say originated within him and what without. If I ran a pedestrian down because I had a sudden heart failure or a blackout, provided I had not had any previous grounds for expecting these misfortunes to befall me, this would be considered a clear case of origination outside the agent. But suppose I run someone down because I suffer from a form of megalomania and this makes me drive crazily fast under certain circumstances. Suppose again that while I am driving a hazard presents itself and, losing my nerve, I swerve wildly and run someone down. Is the origination in such cases within or without the agent? It certainly may be within at one remove, so to speak: had I known about my megalomania or my nervousness and what a menace they might make me, I could, and indeed should, have refused to take a car out. But are the conditions which we describe as megalomania or nervousness themselves external or internal to the agent? I think that most people today would say that psychological mechanisms such as megalomania are certainly a form of illness

[3] *Nichomachean Ethics*, 1113b.
[4] *Ibid.*, 1111a.

comparable to heart failure or a blackout. An agent could not normally control his megalomania, any more than he could control heart failure, by an effort of will. Conditions such as that which I called nervousness (cf. cowardice, anger, etc.) are more difficult. A man who told us that he swerved into a pedestrian simply because he felt nervous might be telling us no more than that he swerved into that pedestrian. But then, he might be telling us more. Evidence of the agent's nervousness, which goes beyond any particular action, might exist: he might always have perspired, grown wild-eyed, trembled, acted without thinking, etc., when certain traffic conditions obtained around him. His doing so on the present occasion could therefore have been predicted. In such case, nervousness explains his conduct in the same way as *mutatis mutandis* megalomania would. The important question, as I have already suggested, where such explanations are offered is: to what extent is the agent's conduct under his own control? One way of discovering that is to see whether moral praise and blame can, as a matter of empirical fact, influence his behavior. In conditions such as megalomania, it seems clear that they cannot; but in conditions such as nervousness sometimes at least they appear to do so. Here we find moral discourse not simply presupposing voluntary action but helping to define it.

It is important to notice that opinion changes concerning what has, and what has not, its origination within the agent. Our great-grandparents would probably have felt little sympathy for the view that a man who behaved recklessly to the danger of other people was suffering from a form of illness. They would have said that he was simply a wicked or irresponsible man. Today, however, there are those who would consider even nervousness, such as that of the motorist in our example, to be external to the agent. And it is certainly within the bounds of possibility that, as the psychological study of character traits develops, conduct due to a nervous disposition will come to be thought no more a man's own fault than that due to compulsive psychological mechanisms such as megalomania. The line dividing what is within from what is without the agent is, from time to time, redrawn and there is no reason to suppose that it will remain forever where it is now generally considered to run.

II. POSITIVE CONDITIONS OF RESPONSIBLE ACTION

So far we have considered only *negative* conditions of voluntary action: it must not be due to external compulsion, ignorance, compulsive psychological mechanisms, such as megalomania or kleptomania, nor, maybe, to dispositions such as nervousness, cowardice, etc. Now we must turn to a *positive* condition. Action is voluntary, if and only if it is done of the agent's own choice. But what is meant by "of the agent's own choice" and, in particular, how is his choosing to do X related to his doing X? There has been much discussion of this question in recent philosophy. G. E. Moore raised it in his *Ethics* and what he had to say about it there will be our point of departure. J. L. Austin took up the discussion and, characteristically, called attention to complexities and subtleties in our talk of voluntary action, which other philosophers had tended to overlook. Austin's treatment of the question has been, and still is being, analyzed and criticized by philosophers. We shall consider what he and some of his critics have said. I must warn the reader that the discussion, at this point, will become somewhat involved. But I will try to keep the issues clear. Some philosophers recently have given a good deal of thought to how our talk about actions is logically related to our talk of bodily movement. We shall conclude our discussion with some consideration of that question. In the remaining sections of this chapter, therefore, I shall discuss three lines of thought. These may be summarized as follows: (i) The view that action is voluntary when a certain causal condition, namely the agent's choosing to do the action, is fulfilled, and so belief in free will is quite compatible with belief in determinism. (ii) The view that "can" is a categorical, independent verb which does not require an if clause to complete its sense. (iii) The view that there is a logical or conceptual gap between the language of intentional action and that of causally connected events, so that anything said in either of these cannot without loss or change of meaning be expressed in terms of the other.

Is Free Will Compatible with Determinism?

G. E. Moore put forward the first of the above views in the well-known discussion of free will in his book *Ethics*. He suggested that "I can do X" should be analyzed "I can do X, if I choose"; or, as he remarked, to avoid "a possible complication" perhaps it would be better to say "I shall do X, if I choose."[5] What precisely he had in mind here by "a possible complication" is not quite clear. J. L. Austin seems to have thought that what Moore had in mind—perhaps subconsciously—was a possible confusion of (a) the opinion that the verb "can" always requires an if clause in the sentence to complete its sense (which is suggested by "I can, if I choose") with (b) the opinion that the meaning of "can" may be reproduced by some other verb with an if clause appended to it (which is suggested by "I shall, if I choose").[6] At the time, Austin was arguing the case for the view to which we shall refer below, namely that "can" is a categorically independent verb which does not require an if clause to complete its sense, and he took Moore's substitution of "I shall, if . . ." for "I can, if . . ." to be tacit recognition of the correctness of the view. But it seems to me much more likely that what Moore really had in mind, when he spoke of "a possible complication," was the inevitability of an infinite regress, if "I can" is analyzed "I can, if I choose." The "can" in this latter sentence would, in its turn, have to be rendered "can, if I choose" and so *ad infinitum*.

But let us turn from such inconclusive matters to questions which we can answer with more confidence. What sort of "if" did Moore intend the "if" in "I can, if I choose" or "I shall, if I choose" to be? That he intended it to be an "if" of causal condition is clear because his whole object was to arrive at an interpretation of voluntary action which would be compatible with the belief that everything has a cause.[7] If we allow then that we are dealing with a causal condition, shall we take the if clause to state a *sufficient* or a *necessary* condition? Shall we say that an act is voluntary only when, if the agent chooses to do it, he can, or will, do it (sufficient condition); or simply that it is voluntary only when, if the agent does not choose to do it, he cannot, or will not, do it (necessary condition)? It is again not clear which view Moore himself took. He wrote, "Many of our actions are under the control of our wills, in the sense that *if*, just before we began to do them, we had chosen not to do them, we *should* not have done them, and I propose to call all actions of this kind *voluntary actions*."[8] At first sight this may suggest a necessary condition: if we had not chosen to do them, we should not have done them. But Moore did not say "if we had not chosen to do them" but "if we had chosen not to do them" and so his words are open to the interpretation that they state a sufficient condition: if we had chosen not-to-do them, we should have not-done them.[9] The really important question, however, is not the purely exegetical one as to what Moore took the if clause to state, but what it should, as a matter of logical fact, be taken to state. Does the if clause, in fact, state a condition and if so, a sufficient or a necessary one?

Let us first consider the view that the if clause in "I can do X, if I choose" states a *sufficient condition*. The obvious and immediate objection to this is that my choice, or decision, to do an action is never in itself sufficient to cause the action. Other conditions constituting my ability and opportunity to do the action must necessarily be fulfilled. This is recognized by those who take the view which we are now considering. Professor K. Baier, for example, claims that when we add ". . . if I choose" to "I can do X," we imply that all necessary conditions constituting my *possession* of the ability and opportunity to do X are satisfied, and simply state the suffi-

---

[7] Moore, *op. cit.*, pp. 131–32.
[8] *Ibid.*, pp. 10–11.
[9] Cf. K. Baier, " 'Could' and 'Would,' " *A* Supp. Vol. 23 (1963).

cient condition of my *exercise* of the power to do X.[10] There are, however, two difficulties at least in Baier's position. (i) His declared aim, it should be noted, is to uphold Moore's attempt (see above) to reconcile free will and determinism. It is, however, logically impossible for Baier's way of interpreting the if clause, as stating a sufficient condition, to be correct and determinism to be true. This can be shown as follows. If my doing X, were I to do it, would be a voluntary action, then, were I *not* to do X, it would nevertheless be true that I could have done it, if I had chosen. If Baier is correct, ". . . if I had chosen" here states a sufficient condition. But if determinism is true, for any act X which is *not* done, there will be a sufficient condition of its not being done. Now, according to Baier's way of interpreting it, "if I had chosen," when taken to state a sufficient condition, as we saw, implies that all the necessary conditions of my being able to do X are fulfilled. One of these must obviously be that the sufficient condition of X's *not* being done is *un*fulfilled. But, if determinism is correct, then, as long as X is not done, the nonfulfillment of this sufficient condition is impossible. So Baier's way of interpreting the if clause is not compatible with determinism.[11]

(ii) A further difficulty arises when we consider what may or may not be inferred intelligibly from "I could have done X, which I did not do, if I had chosen." Notice first that, in the case of "If p then q" where the "if" is of sufficient condition, the contrapositive "If not q then not p" can be inferred; but we cannot draw from "If p then q" either of the inferences, "If p or not p then q" or "q" *simpliciter*. Compare this with the case under discussion. The contrapositive of "I could have done X, which I did not do, if I had chosen," supposing this to state a sufficient condition, would be "If I could not have done X, which I did not do, then I had not chosen." Austin seemed to think that this makes no sense, but I cannot see why, on the face of it, it should not be taken as a statement of sufficient condition. However, we *should* nor-

[10] *Ibid.*, p. 24.
[11] K. Lehrer, " 'Could' and Determinism," *A* 24 (1963–64).

mally draw from "I could have done X, which I did not do, if I had chosen" inferences which, as pointed out a moment ago, do *not* follow from a statement of sufficient condition; namely, (A) "I could have done X, which I did not do, whether I had chosen or not." (If p or not p then q) and also (B) "I could have done X, which I did not do" (q *simpliciter*). This fact counts strongly against the view that we are dealing here with the "if" of sufficient condition.[12]

We turn then to the view that the if clause in "I could have done X which I did not do, if I had chosen" states a *necessary* condition. This view has been developed by Professor D. J. O'Connor.[13] Let us consider what may or may not intelligibly be inferred when it is so regarded. The usual form of a statement of necessary condition is "If not p then not q," which yields the contrapositive "If q then p." Statements of the form "If p then q" may sometimes state a necessary condition. For instance, it is not odd to say, "If we take the nine fifty-five, we shall be in London by one o'clock," where taking the nine fifty-five is not the sufficient condition, but only one of the necessary conditions, of our reaching London by one o'clock. We can, then, if we are so minded, take "I could have done X, which I did not do, if I had chosen" as a statement of necessary condition equivalent in meaning to "I could not have done X, which I did not do, if I had not chosen" (If not p then not q). Its contrapositive will be "If I could have done X, which I did not do, then I had chosen" (If q then p). This is intelligible. It tells us that one of the necessary conditions of my doing X is my choosing to do it. What of the two inferences (A) "I could have done X, which I did not do, whether I had chosen or not" (If p or not p then q) and (B) "I could have done X, which I did not do" (q *simpliciter*)? These, as noted above, are inferences which we should normally draw from "I could have done X, which I did not do, if I had chosen"—call this (C). Clearly, they do *not* follow from (C), understood to state a necessary con-

[12] Cf. Austin, *op. cit.*, pp. 157–58.
[13] D. J. O'Connor, "Possibility and Choice," *PAS* Supp. Vol. XXXIV (1960).

dition, if "could" in (C) means the same as "could" in (A)
and (B). Advocates of the view that the if clause in (C) states
a necessary condition save the situation by interpreting the
"could" differently in (A), (B), and (C) respectively. Its
function in each case, they would say, is "to warn the hearer
that the operation of the verb it modifies is subject to certain
conditions but without specifying their number or their nature."[14] If we call this number N in the case of (B) "I could
have done X, which I did not do," it becomes N — 1 in the
case of (C) "I could have done X, which I did not do, if I had
chosen" and N — 2 in the case of (A) "I could have done X,
which I did not do, whether I had chosen or not." "Could"
does not mean the same in each case; but the total number
of necessary conditions is the same in all three cases and so
the inferences are valid. When the main clause ("I could have
done X, which I did not do . . .") is subject to only one
necessary condition (". . . if I had chosen") then (C) is
equivalent in meaning to "I *would* have done X, which I did
not do, if I had chosen." Taken as a statement of necessary
condition ("If p then q": equivalent, see above, to "If not p
then not q"), this yields the contrapositive "If I would have
done X, which I did not do, then I would have chosen" ("If
q then p"). The latter is an intelligible statement of necessary
condition. And no questions arise concerning the inferences
"I would have done X, which I did not do, whether I had
chosen or not" (If p or not p then q) or "I would have done
X, which I did not do" (q) because we do *not* normally draw
such inferences from "I would have done X, which I did not
do, if I had chosen."

This view, that the if clause in "I could have done X, which
I did not do, if I had chosen" states a necessary condition
seems more plausible than the view that it states a sufficient
one. However, it is not free from difficulties. "I could have
done X, which I did not do, if I had chosen," as equivalent to
"I could *not* have done X, which I did not do, if I had *not*
chosen" (necessary condition), means that my ability to do it
was conditional upon my choosing to do it. Had I not chosen

[14] *Ibid.*, 9.

to do it, I should not have been able to do it. But the whole point of "I could have done X, which I did not do, if I had chosen" is to claim that I had the ability to do it, even though I did not choose to exercise that ability.[15]

There is a formidable difficulty which applies equally to the views that the if clause states a sufficient condition and that it states a necessary one. Both views imply that in the case of a voluntary action, X, we are talking about two distinct occurrences, viz. my choosing to do X and my doing X. There are at least two objections to accepting this. (i) We do not always have adequate empirical grounds for affirming that there are these two occurrences when an agent does something which he can do. Sometimes agents are not aware of having first chosen to do an act and then having done it; and there may be nothing evident in their behavior to support the contention that two such occurrences have taken place. Sometimes, of course, we can differentiate the choice or decision to act from the action itself. I may, for instance, decide which film to see and then some hours later go to see it. Such choices have been called "prospective" to distinguish them from cases of "immanent" choice where we cannot identify any occurrence, distinct from the agent's starting to do the action, as his choosing to do it.[16] (ii) The view that when I do what I can do this is not one occurrence but two —an act and the act of choosing to do it which is its precondition—leads to an infinite regress. The act of choosing is itself doing something which the agent can do. So it must also be not one occurrence but two: choosing to choose to do and choosing to do, and so on. The only way of avoiding this infinite regress is to say that choosing to do X, unlike doing X, is something which an agent does unconditionally. But what valid grounds could there be for saying this? Why should there be two occurrences if I choose to do what I can do but not if I choose to choose to do what I can choose to do?

To the former objection it might be replied that it amounts

---

[15] Cf. Lehrer, "Could and Determinism," *op. cit.*, 27.
[16] O'Connor, *op. cit.*, 13–14.

to no more than saying that the choice, which is a precondition of voluntary action, is frequently obscure. We must improve our techniques of observation, it might be said, so that we can identify what causes agents in varying situations to start to do what they start to do. We shall thus be able to give some content to the notion of choice as a precondition of action.[17] But whatever content we gave to it, we should still be left with the latter of the two above objections. As long as we interpret the condition that action is voluntary, if and only if it is done of the agent's own choice, in such a way that there is an if clause of causal condition (". . . if I choose") in the analysis of "I can do X," we have on our hands the problem of how to avoid an infinite regress. This raises doubts about the whole interpretation of ". . . if I choose" here as a statement of causal condition. What if it does not state a causal condition at all?

Does "Can" Require an If Clause to Complete Its Sense?

J. L. Austin contended that some, at least, of "the things we ordinarily say about what we can do or could have done"[18] show that the "if" in "I can if I choose" is not, or not always, the "if" of condition, but rather the "if" of doubt or hesitation. He said that we can on different occasions and in different contexts give many different interpretations to "I can, if I choose" and suggested the following among others:

"I can, but do I choose to?"
"I can, but perhaps I don't choose to."
"I can, but then I should have to choose to and what about that?"
"I can, I have only to choose to."
"I can whether I choose to or not."

and so on. What is common to them all, said Austin, is "that the *assertion*, positive and complete, that 'I can' is linked to the *raising of the question* whether I choose to, which may

[17] Cf. *ibid.*, 14.
[18] Austin, *op. cit.*, p. 179.

be relevant in a variety of ways."[19] "I can whether I choose to or not," for instance, does not mean "I can on condition that I choose and likewise on condition and I don't." It means "I can, but whether I choose to or not is an open question."[20]

But now let us consider "I could have done X, which I did not do, if I had chosen." "I can, if I choose" implies that the choice *has not* taken place; so there is room for doubt or hesitation. But "I could have done X, which I did not do, if I had chosen" implies that the agent *has* already chosen and acted, so the possibility which existed before he did X, of his choosing or not choosing to do it, exists no longer. What happens then to Austin's suggested rephrasings, if adopted *mutatis mutandis* in the case of "I could have done X, which I did not do, if I had chosen"? We certainly cannot say "I could have done X, which I did not do, but did I choose to?" nor "I could have done X, which I did not do, but perhaps I didn't choose to," and possibly others of Austin's suggested rephrasings would be equally unacceptable. However, what would be wrong with "I could have done X, which I did not do, I had only to choose to"? This rephrasing makes sense. But it has been urged against Austin that it does so only if interpreted as a statement to the effect that my choosing to do X would have been a sufficient condition of my doing it; and, since a choice has in fact occurred, namely my choice not to do X, "I had only to choose to" cannot express either doubt or hesitation.[21] But against this in turn, surely it is the case that, at the time to which we would be referring, the time at which I could have done X, if I had chosen, there may have been doubt or hesitation. I do not see any compelling reason why "I had only to choose to" should not be interpreted as indicating that there was such doubt or hesitation.

Austin recognized that "could" and "could have" are frequently used in forming subjunctives and in such case they require a conditional if clause, or its equivalent, to complete

---

[19] *Ibid.*, p. 160.
[20] *Ibid.*, p. 160 note.
[21] Lehrer, "Could and Determinism," *op. cit.*, 22.

their sense. But he affirmed that "can," "could," and even "could have" frequently function as indicatives of the independent verb "can." He wrote:

> It is quite true that "could have" *may* be, and very often is, a past conditional: but it is *also* true that "could have" may be and often is the *past (definite) indicative* of the verb *can*. Sometimes "I could have" is equivalent to the Latin "Potui" and means "I *was* in a position to": sometimes it is equivalent to the Latin "Potuissem" and means "I *should have been* in a position to." Exactly similar is the double role of "could," which is sometimes a conditional meaning "should be able to," but also sometimes a past indicative (indefinite) meaning "was able to": no one can doubt this if he considers such contrasted examples as "I could do it 20 years ago" and "I could do it if I had thingummy." It is not so much that "could" or "could have" is ambiguous, as rather that two parts of the verb *can* take the same shape. Once it is realised that "could have" can be a past indicative, the general temptation to supply if-clauses with it vanishes: at least there is no more temptation to supply them with "could have" than with "can." If we ask how a Roman would have said "I could have ruined you this morning (although I didn't)," it is clear that he would have used "potui," and that his sentence is complete without any conditional clause. But more than this, if he had wished to add "if I had chosen," and however he had expressed that in Latin, he would still not have changed his "potui" to "potuissem"; but this is precisely what he *would* have done if he had been tacking on some other, more "normal" kind of if-clause, such as "if I had had one more vote."[22]

While agreeing with Austin that "could" and "could have" may function as forms of the independent verb *can* and so not require a conditional if clause to complete their sense, M. R. Ayers thinks Austin was mistaken in concluding that they are therefore not subjunctives.[23] Austin evidently thought that an if clause, explicit or implicit, is a necessary condition of the

[22] Austin, *op. cit.*, pp. 163–64.
[23] M. R. Ayers, "Austin on 'could' and 'could have,'" *PQ* 16 (1966).

subjunctive mood; he takes it that no conditional if clause means no subjunctive. But there are two objections at least to Austin's view that "could" and "could have," without an *if* of condition, are indicatives.[24] (i) If "could" and "could have" are forms of the present and past indicatives respectively of *can*, then they must serve as alternatives to the more normal forms, namely "can" (present indicative) and "could" (past indicative). But they do not. "I could (present) run one hundred yards in ten seconds" does not mean the same as "I can run one hundred yards in ten seconds"; nor does "I could have run one hundred yards in ten seconds" mean the same as "I could (past) run one hundred yards in ten seconds." (ii) Austin refers to "could have" (normally past subjunctive) as sometimes the past *definite* indicative and to "could" as the past *indefinite* indicative. (We may assume that he would similarly have called "could" [normally present subjunctive] sometimes the present *definite* indicative and "can" the present *indefinite* indicative.) The difference, drawn by grammarians, between a definite and an indefinite tense is that the former refers to one definite occasion while the latter does not (e.g., *definite* present and past indicatives: "I am writing," "I was writing"; *indefinite* present and past indicatives: "I write," "I wrote"). Presumably this was the ground on which Austin intended to differentiate "could have" (past definite indicative) from "could" (past indefinite indicative). (And similarly, though he does not deal explicitly with the present tense, "could" [present definite indicative] from "can" [present indefinite indicative].) But if so, he is clearly in error. We can see from the following examples that the difference between "can" and "could" (present tense) and between "could" and "could have" (past tense) is not that, in each case, the former (can, could) does not refer to a definite occasion, while the latter (could, could have) does. "I could (present) get it at any time" makes good sense, as does "I can get it only at the right time"; and "I could (past) not get it even at the right time" makes good sense, as does "I could not have got it at

[24] Cf. Ayers, *op. cit.*

any time." These objections cast considerable doubt on Austin's treatment of "could" and "could have" as indicatives.

Ayers, who offers them, contends however that the subjunctives "could" and "could have" may be used, not to make conditional statements, but simply to indicate the speaker's belief that "the power, ability, possibility, capacity or potentiality in question is not, or was not, or will not be, exercised or actualised."[25] His supporting examples are: "I could be at home now," "This car here could do 100 m.p.h.," "John could have won." It does not follow, of course, that if the relevant power, etc., has been exercised or actualized, the subjunctive ascription of power, etc., is false. Rather would this confirm that ascription. It is true that John could have won if, unknown to the speaker, he has won. But again it does *not* follow that the subjunctive ascription can be verified *only* if there is evidence that the power, etc., has been exercised or actualized. It may well be true that John could have won even if he has not. Ayers insists that the subjunctive "John could have won" is not a form of, but is equivalent in meaning to, the indicative "John had the power to win"; and that neither is equivalent to "John has won," "John is winning," or "John will win." Evidence which would verify the claim that John has the power to win (indicative) would also verify "John could have won" (subjunctive), but this goes no way toward showing that the latter is not a real subjunctive.

The point at issue in all this, it will be remembered, was whether or not *can* is an independent verb, not a mere auxiliary which requires another verb to complete its sense. A consideration, which suggests that it is, is as follows.[26] Compare (A) "I may do X" and (B) "I may not do X," where "may" expresses possibility, not permission, with (C) "I can do X" and (D) "I cannot do X." While (A) and (B) can both be true in the sense that it is possible at a given time that I will do X and possible also that I will not, (C) and (D) cannot both be true, for "I cannot" contradicts "I can" as "I may not" does not contradict "I may." One way of accounting for this latter

[25] Ayers, *op. cit.*, 119.
[26] See O'Connor, *op. cit.*, 19–20.

350 Modern Moral Philosophy

fact is to say that "not" in (B) attaches to the main verb: "I may not-do X"; whereas in (D) the "not" attaches to "can": "I can-not do X." If this explanation is acceptable, then it counts in favor of the view that forms of the verb "can" have an unconditional sense. For it would seem that, whereas auxiliaries like "may" merely affect the tense, mood, etc., of their main verbs and so can hardly be negated, a verb which may be negated, as "can" may, must have some core of meaning of its own. But this is not conclusive. "Can" could conceivably be more than a modal auxiliary like "may," without having an *unconditional sense* of its own independent of any other verb. O'Connor points this out, in rejecting the view that "can" is an independent verb and defending his own view that, in the analysis of "I can" as "I can, if I choose," the if clause states a necessary condition. He argues from the fact that it is more natural to use "can" than "may" in a sentence such as "He can pass the exam if he works hard," and more natural to use "may" than "can" in a sentence such as "He may pass the exam if he is lucky," to the conclusion that "can" is more appropriate than "may" where the conditions to be fulfilled are internal to the agent (work) rather than external (luck). On this view the verb "can" in its various forms would have a twofold sense: "first the general vague concept of *possibility* (shared with "may") and then the notion that the realisation of the possibility is, so to speak, internal to the subject of the verb."[27] But against this there is still the objection, which we have already noted, that such a view takes action of one's own choice to be invariably not one occurrence but two.[28] We have seen something of the difficulties in that view. We must turn now to an account of voluntary action which seeks to avoid them.

The Language of Action and the Language of Event

It is held by many contemporary philosophers that when we say X was done of an agent's own choice, we set X within a

[27] *Ibid.*, p. 19.
[28] Above, p. 344.

logically distinctive conceptual scheme.[29] We are not saying
that two causally connected *events*—choosing to do X and doing X—have occurred; we are saying that X is an *action,* something done by an agent. That there is this logical distinction
between conceiving of X as an event, or series of events, and
conceiving of it as an action has been argued from the following considerations among others.

Suppose, to take up again an illustration already used,
that my car mounts the pavement and injures a pedestrian.
If we say that this was not of my own choice, we are saying, in
effect, that it was an *event,* something which happened. "Why
did it happen?" will then be the appropriate question if we are
seeking an explanation of this event. Any appropriate answer
will connect it causally with another event, or other events,
under some covering law or laws. The explanation may be very
complicated, but it will be entirely in terms of generalizations
to the effect that whenever an event of one kind occurs an
event of another occurs as its consequent. We understand what
happened when we know the causal law, or laws, under which
it falls. If, however, we say that I drove my car on the pavement and injured a pedestrian of my own choice, we are
saying, in effect, that this is an *action,* something which was
done. "Why did you do it?" or "Why did he do it?" will now
be the appropriate questions, if an explanation is sought, and
any appropriate answer will be in terms of agency, e.g., "I
(He) did it to avoid a head-on crash," "I (He) did it because
I (he) hated that pedestrian and intended to run him down."
To understand such an explanation is not to know that a
certain kind of thing always happens, given certain precondi-
tions, and that this is a case in point. Drivers do *not* always,
under any statable conditions, mount pavements in order to
avoid head-on crashes, nor, fortunately, do they always try to
run down people whom they hate. To understand the above
explanations of my action is to see that what was done was in
accordance with some principle, or principles, of action ("Al-

[29] See e.g., S. Hampshire, *Thought and Action* (1959) and *Freedom
and the Individual* (1965); A. I. Melden, *Free Action* (1961); D. F.
Pears and others, *Freedom and the Will* (1963); G. E. M. Anscombe,
Intention (Oxford, 1963); etc.

ways swerve to avoid head-on crashes," or "Always injure those whom you hate, if you get the chance") to which the person who gives, and the person who accepts, the explanation subscribe.[30] By "subscribe" here I do not mean "approve of" nor "conform to." I mean rather "recognize as a thing *to do* in the given circumstances." I may subscribe in this sense to "Always swerve to avoid head-on crashes" as a principle of action and yet not, in practice, conform my own actions to it. And again I may disapprove strongly of people who injure those whom they hate and yet see some point in doing so. An action is explained when the person who offers the explanation and the one who accepts it hold in common certain norms of behavior and where the action has been shown to be a case in point. One must add that in any community there are certain generally accepted norms of behavior, which constitute in that community what "rational conduct" means. Explanations of action which hope to win general assent must appeal to these. There are conceivable answers to the question "Why did you (he) mount the pavement and injure that pedestrian?" which would be utterly unintelligible to most people: e.g., "Because the pavement was six inches high," "Because that pedestrian had red hair," etc. They are unintelligible in the sense that in our community they would not be considered, except by those who were thereby shown to be irrational, the thing to do in the given circumstances.

We may note in passing that some philosophers have equated voluntary action with rational action, i.e., to quote one of them, action which "can be influenced or inhibited by the adducing of some logically relevant consideration."[31] They reject the view for which, as we saw, Moore put up a case: that free will and determinism can be reconciled. Action is free when it is directed, as sometimes it is to all appearance, solely by reasons; and reasons are logically quite distinct from causes of any kind. Some determinists have replied that they would not for a moment deny that deliberation, i.e., reasoning about what to do, can influence or inhibit action. Nor, again, would

---

[30] See above, p. 327.
[31] A. C. MacIntyre, "Determinism," *M* LXVI (1957), 34.

they deny that it serves as a criterion of whether behavior is voluntary or not to discover whether or not the adducing of logically relevant considerations can influence or inhibit it. All they insist upon is, to quote, "that these [deliberations] are in their turn determined."[32] Does this mean that it is not the reasonableness, as such, of an argument for action, A, which determines what an agent does, but something "within" the agent which, when he is confronted by A, as one argument among others for the same course of action or alternative ones, predetermines his acceptance of A? If it does, there are some fairly obvious grounds for treating such a view with, to say the least, caution. We are familiar with cases where an argument for a course of action is accepted by an agent because he is predetermined to accept that argument and no other: we say that these are cases of rationalization to differentiate them from cases of genuine reasoning about action. The determinists referred to say, in effect, that this distinction between rationalization and genuine reasoning must be replaced by one between rationalizations which most people engage in and those which are peculiar to off-beat individuals here and there. Is this theory plausible? Its proponents do not allow that it is empirically falsifiable: wherever there is a reason for action it *must* have a determinant "within" the agent who accepts it, and if we cannot discover this at once, we must press on with our psychological investigations until we do. It would inspire more confidence in the determinists' guiding-principle if they could show that, in reasoning at large about action, certain types of argument invariably appeal to certain types of agent. But this they have not shown. In so far as they have shown anything of the kind, they have certainly not shown that *all* reasoning about action is rationalization. Take this example. If it could be shown to a middle-aged don that, in virtue of his long-standing habits of thought and action, he is predisposed to regard all arguments for increasing "productivity" in universities, as based on a category-mistake, how would he react? He would, if he were a reason-

---

[32] A. Flew, "Determinism and Rational Behaviour" *M* LXVIII (1959), 378.

able man, have been put on his guard and, in consequence, he would examine more carefully his reasons for thinking that the said arguments are based on a category-mistake, in order to ensure that they were well-grounded. The important point to take here is that it is logically possible for a man to react in this way to *any* such deterministic account of his reasoning processes; and as long as that is logically possible, it seems to be logically impossible, in principle, for the determinist to carry his explanatory program through to completion. It always makes sense, that is, to treat it as incomplete. To this point we shall return below.[83]

Wittgenstein wrote of the two conceptual schemes, that of action and that of event, in the following way:

Examine these two language games:
(a) Someone gives someone else the order to make particular movements with his arm, or to assume particular bodily positions (gymnastics instructor and pupil). And here is a variation of this language-game: the pupil gives himself orders and then carries them out.
(b) Someone observes certain regular processes—for example, the reactions of different metals to acids—and thereupon makes predictions about the reactions that will occur in certain particular cases.
There is an evident kinship between these two language-games, and also a fundamental difference. In both one might call the spoken words "predictions." But compare the training which leads to the first technique with the training for the second one.[84]

It is odd to speak of orders as predictions but let us leave that. The point is that training is required in order to play a language game and that this training differs in the case of these two games. Part of the training will necessarily be in what Wittgenstein elsewhere called the "tacit presuppositions"[85] of a language game. We should not give planets, stones, or trees orders because it is not a presupposition on

[83] See below, pp. 358–60.
[84] *PI*, 630.
[85] *PI*, p. 179e.

which we deal with such phenomena that they are sources of action and so can obey orders; but we deal with men on this presupposition. Similarly, it would be meaningless to "explain" an event such as the rising of the sun by saying that it had chosen to rise; but it is not meaningless to explain an occurrence such as that of my mounting the pavement in order to avoid a crash, or to injure a pedestrian, as done of my own choice. Another way of saying that an act was done of the agent's own choice is to say that it was intentional. Wittgenstein spoke of the intention as "lying in" the action.[36] He said, "Why do I want to tell him about an intention too, as well as telling him what I did?—Not because the intention was also something which was going on at that time. But because I want to tell him something about *myself*, which goes beyond what happened at that time."[37]

Precisely how far and in what respects the intention takes us "beyond what happened at that time" is a complicated matter. It has been suggested that it does so in two ways: (i) "it provides us with a better understanding of the action itself by placing it within its appropriate context" and (ii) "it reveals something about the agent himself."[38] What, for example, is my intention in raising my arm? It may be to raise my arm and nothing more. But it may be to greet a friend, to hail a taxi, to signal that I am about to turn right, etc. In each of these latter cases when you know my intention, you know more about the *context* of my raising my arm (that it occurs when I am vis-à-vis a friend, etc.), and that is why you understand more fully what I am doing. You also understand *me* more fully. It tells you that I am, to some degree, a careful driver when you know that I gave a hand signal; that I am, to some degree, adequately financed when you know that I hailed a taxi; and, to some degree, a sociable chap when you know that I raised my hand in greeting a friend. For our present purpose I think the important point to grasp is that knowing the intention takes us, in the above ways, "beyond what hap-

[36] *PI*, 644.
[37] *PI*, 659.
[38] Melden, *op. cit.*, p. 102.

pened at that time" because of what an intention is. It is *not*
a cause. It *is* the description of an action which its agent would
accept, provided only that he was not out to deceive himself
or anyone else and understood the meaning of the words being used.

It seems to follow from all this that an agent is in a privileged position to know what he is doing of his own choice.
What others know of the context of his action and of him
may enable them to surmise with varying degrees of accuracy
what he is doing. For instance, if people see me mount the
pavement when another car is heading toward mine, they will
most likely say, "He was avoiding a head-on crash." But they
could be wrong. I, on the other hand, know what my intention
was. I cannot be mistaken about what description of the action
I would accept, as others may be. Professor S. Hampshire
makes this point thus: "It seems to be characteristic of an
intentional action that a man who accuses the agent of answering the question 'What are you doing' wrongly, accuses
him either of deliberately lying, or of misdescribing his own
activity in some more or less trivial way. It seems that he can
never accuse him of simply not knowing what he is doing, of
sheer ignorance in this respect, without implying that his action is not intentional."[39] The agent is in no such privileged
position when what has happened (an event), not what he
has done (an action), is under discussion. If, because I am
pushed in the back or my brakes fail, my car mounts the
pavement and runs down a pedestrian, knowledge of these
causally connected events is open to everyone who looks into
what has happened and I am no more likely to be right about
that than anyone else.

That there is a logical or conceptual gulf between the language of action and that of event becomes clearer still when
we recognize that what is said in the one language cannot be
translated into terms of the other without loss or change of
meaning. Some behaviorist psychologists have attempted to
describe and explain human actions as complex patterns of
physical movement; but it has been pointed out that, though

---

[39] Hampshire, *Thought and Action*, pp. 94–95.

some bodily movements are necessary conditions of any action, it has yet to be shown that any *particular* movements are either necessary or sufficient conditions of any action.[40] The same bodily movements may be used in performing quite different actions and the same action can be performed by means of quite different bodily movements. For instance,[41] the bodily movements employed in writing one's name may be used in the following actions and others: signing a check, giving an autograph, or authorizing a representative. Equally, the same act of paying a debt may be performed by the bodily movements involved in signing a check, or in handing over coins, etc. "In other words, the criteria which we imply in judging that two bodily movements are the same or different are quite other than the criteria which we use in judging that two actions are the same or different."[42]

Given that this is so, however, the question arises: does what is said in one of these languages impose any limitation on what may be said, in the same connection, in the other? The answer seems to be that it does and the following illustration has been offered by G. J. Warnock in support of this answer. Suppose a physical determinist were to describe a certain process of matter in motion and show that, given the antecedent physical setup, these movements could have been predicted; and suppose that these movements are those involved in Smith's kicking Jones on the shin. The deterministic account of these movements does not entail any specific description of *what Smith did;* he might have been kicking Jones, but then again he might have been beginning a dance in which his foot accidentally collided with Jones's shin, or carelessly showing Jones his new shoelaces, etc. The deterministic description, however, is not compatible with *any* account *whatever* of what Smith did; it could not be true, for instance, that what he did was to keep both feet on the ground. What

---

[40] Cf. R. S. Peters and H. Tajfel, "Hobbes and Hull—Metaphysicians of Behaviour," *British Journal for the Philosophy of Science* (1957–58), p. 36, referred to by A. C. MacIntyre, "The Antecedents of Action," in *British Analytical Philosophy* (1966), edited by B. Williams and A. Montefiore.

[41] I borrow these illustrations from MacIntyre, *op. cit.*

[42] MacIntyre, *op. cit.*, p. 212.

it comes to, then, is this according to Warnock: "Given the physical set-up, nothing could have occurred except what did occur; that is, matter could have moved *only* as in fact it did move. Now what the man in question *did* is certainly not thus determined, but the question left open here is surely only this: what, given that matter so moved, *might the person have been doing?* Certainly there will be a variety of possible answers to this question. But it seems clear that the range of possibilities will not be *the same* as that which we should normally consider as possible answers to the question *what he could have done.*"[43]

However, *before* Smith acted, were the only possibilities open to him those compatible with our determinist's predictions concerning certain physical movements? Could Smith not have kept both feet on the ground if he had chosen to do so? It is certainly true that, when an action *has been done*, the description in terms of bodily movement of what has occurred will only be compatible with *some* descriptions of action. The same bodily movement description, for instance, would fit Smith's beginning a dance as well as Smith's kicking Jones, but it would not fit Smith's keeping both feet on the ground. To say this, however, is to say nothing about what Smith could have done before he acted. Suppose a determinist has predicted that, the physical setup being what it is, certain physical events will occur, namely those involved in Smith's kicking Jones. This prediction can only be fulfilled if a certain sequence of events takes place. If Smith hears of the prediction, can he not interfere with this sequence and so falsify the prediction? It only makes sense to say that he cannot (logically)⁔ if in this account of this sequence the determinist has included an account of how Smith will behave when he hears about it; only so far, that is, as the sequence includes the decisions which Smith will take when he gains the inductive knowledge on which predictions of his actions are based. But this lands us in an infinite regress. Smith gains such-and-such inductive knowledge of his situation—that the physical setup is so-and-so and if there is no interference

⁴³ G. J. Warnock, "Actions and Events," in Pears, *op. cit.*, p. 78.

with it, it will result in such-and-such action on his part—and then asks himself, "What shall I do, this being the case?" Suppose his knowledge increases and he learns what his answer to this will be. This has only increased his knowledge of the situation in which he may act. Once again he can (logically) raise the question, "What shall I do, this being the case?" And so *ad infinitum*. His decision is systematically elusive to the determinist's account of his situation: he can "step back" from inductive knowledge of the situation even where this includes predictions as to what his own decisions will be. As Hampshire puts it: "In deciding upon action, there is an unavoidable stepping back process, which entails that any inductive knowledge of what we will, or would, do, or decide to do, in the natural course of things is knowledge of the situation that confronts us: and in respect of this situation, once recognised, it must be true (logically must) either that we intend to alter it in some way, or that we intend to leave it as it is and allow events to take their natural course. That is, it must be true that we have some secondary intention. And, if we do not take this secondary intention into account, we cannot know what we will do."[44] This, it has been felt by some, is "straining thought and language";[45] and indeed it is, if we take it to mean that there is an unobserved psychological occurrence in such cases, namely the decision to let things ride. But this is not the claim which is being made. It is conceivable that an agent should answer questions about his future action solely with predictions and not at all in terms of decision. It is instructive to compare this with the somewhat similar case of a man who answers questions about his duty by estimating the pleasurable or painful consequences of alternative courses of action and not at all in terms of obligations. In the latter case, it would make sense to say that the agent had formed an implicit moral judgment (that one ought always to seek pleasure and avoid pain) even if he is unaware of it, and this, not in the sense that he had gone through the unobserved psychological step of deciding to be an ethical

[44] In Pears, *op. cit.*, pp. 89–90.
[45] P. L. Gardiner in Pears, *op. cit.*, p. 92.

hedonist, but in the sense that assent to some moral judgment is a logical implication of the fact that what he says is said in answer to a question about duty. In the same way, the argument could go, it is a logical implication of the fact that what an agent says is said in answer to a question about his own action that, in saying it, he has formed a secondary intention. Even, that is to say, if his answer is in terms of predictions, not decisions, it is an answer to "What shall I do?" and, as such, expresses an intention. It may be claimed that the study of human behavior will eventually reach a stage of development—or, at least, that there is no evident reason why it should not—at which a psychologist will be able to predict with certainty how any given agent will answer the question "What shall I do, this being so?" in any given situation. But this claim overlooks the infinite regress to which attention has already been called. Suppose it is predicted (P1) accurately that A will do such and such an action. Now suppose that A comes to know of this prediction and the evidence on which it is based. What decision or secondary intention will he form? Suppose this too can be predicted (P2). But suppose he learns also of P2. What secondary intention will he form about his situation now? This calls for another prediction (P3). But suppose he learns of P3. This calls for P4. And so on *ad infinitum*. To say the least, it seems from this that no psychologist could (logically) complete a deterministic account of human behavior.

There are some considerations, however, which make one dubious about the hard and fast distinction between the language of action and that of event, which has been drawn above. I will briefly refer to, and comment on, one or two of these in conclusion.

(i) In support of the point that what is said in the language of action cannot be translated without change or loss of meaning into the language of event, and vice versa, it was pointed out that the same bodily movements may be used in performing quite different actions and the same action can be performed by quite different bodily movements. Some doubt suggests itself as to whether this is necessarily so. Let

us take the above examples: the same bodily movements involved in writing one's name may be used in signing a check,
giving an autograph, or authorizing a representative; and the
act of paying a debt may be performed by the bodily movements of signing a check, handing over coins, etc. Is it perhaps
arguable that, if we were told *more of the story* this would
not be so in either case? The bodily movements involved in
writing one's name on a piece of paper are the same in all
three of the above actions; but in each case there is more to
the bodily movement story than that. Different bodily movements, additional to signing one's name, are involved in each
case: for examples, opening one's checkbook, finding a blank
page in an autograph album, reading the text of an authorization respectively. It would be bizarre if, having signed a check,
one handed over one's checkbook to the person for whom it
was made out just as it would if, having signed an autograph
album, one tore out the page and handed that over; and it
would be bizarre if one carefully read all the printed matter
in one's checkbook or in an autograph album before signing,
as one would be well advised to read the whole text of an authorization before putting one's name to it. All I am saying
is that if the bodily movement story were more *fully* told in each
case, the possibility of confusing one activity with either of
the other two might disappear. In a similar way, it would
seem, if the story of the intention, which, as we saw, fills out
the context of the action, were more fully told in the case of
paying a debt, there would no longer be any doubt about
whether this was by check or coin of the realm. It may well
be, of course, that in each case, i.e., the bodily movement story
and the story of the intention, when enough has been told to
avoid the possibility of *certain given* alternative descriptions
in the other language fitting the case, *some other* conceivable
alternative descriptions in the other language would do so.
For instance, when we have filled out the bodily movement
story in a given case so that it is quite clearly a case of signing
a check and not an autograph album, we may need to tell
more of that story to indicate whether this is a case of signing
the check fraudulently or honestly. And similarly when we
have filled out the story of the intention so that a given case

of paying a debt is quite clearly a case of paying by coin and not by check, we may have to tell more of the story to make it clear whether this was a case of paying a debt or trying to make a good impression. Allowing for all such qualifications, is it conceivable that a point can always be reached where the bodily movement story is so complete that it will fit only one action, or the intention story so complete that it will fit only one set of bodily movements? If this is conceivable, the particular ground, which we are here considering for the point that what is said in the language of action cannot be translated without loss or change of meaning into the language of event, and vice versa, will collapse.

(ii) However, it may still be claimed that, although when we tell the whole story only one account of bodily movement fits any given action and vice versa, the two descriptions of what is going on are logically quite distinct. If this claim is made, the question remains as to what the ground for it might be. Some philosophers seem to take it for granted that events cause events and cannot (logically) cause actions and that this is a ground for the above claim. But is this ground firm? Suppose that every time something goes wrong with my car, I lose my temper and kick it. This would be stupid conduct, of course, but it might well occur. There is no doubt that in such a case I would perform an action, viz., kicking my car. It would make perfectly good sense to say that the breakdown of my car had *caused* my action. Now, someone might remonstrate with me for such ridiculous conduct and say, "You are at the mercy of your car. That's silly. What are we going to do about it?" My reply might be, "You're right. I shall control myself. Next time it goes wrong, I will simply send for the garageman." In so saying, I have, true enough, "stepped back" from my situation. But the fact that I can do so does not alter the fact that until I was remonstrated with, a Humean causal generalization "Whenever his car goes wrong, he kicks it" could be formulated and was indeed true. Actions, it would appear, *may be caused* by events.[46] It seems that we must look for the ground of the difference between action

[46] Cf. MacIntyre, *op. cit.*, p. 222.

and bodily movement elsewhere than in the contention that it makes no sense to speak of actions being caused.

(iii) Neither of the two foregoing considerations, (i) and (ii), of course, shows conclusively that acts are logically reducible to bodily movements or vice versa. It is perfectly conceivable that (a) only one account of bodily movement would fit any given action or vice versa, and again that (b) events may cause actions or vice versa, *even though* actions belong to one conceptual scheme and events or bodily movements to another. But so long as we take it that there is a logical gulf between actions and events, it seems to me that we have on our hands a problem to be solved and a possibility to be reckoned with. I will say a word about each in conclusion.

The problem is how to resolve the Cartesian dualism of a view which sees certain occurrences always in two distinct lights: as sequences of bodily movements and as intentional actions. Does my intentionally turning on to the pavement just happen to occur at the same point in time and space as the physical movement of my arm which brings down the steering wheel? We are left with an order in which things *are caused* and another in which things *are done*. But the question is: what is the relationship between them? It does not seem to be an altogether comfortable solution to say simply that they are two different ways of looking at some common object.[47] Is their relationship then an ineluctable mystery? If light is to be shed upon it, this can only be when some kind of logical connection between action and event has been made out. Many philosophers feel that they cannot be expected to rest content until it has.[48]

The possibility to be reckoned with is that the language of action will drop out of use. As an agent's behavior is causally connected ever more closely with events or conditions in his body or psyche, the room left for any practical use of the language of action could conceivably diminish. It may be true

[47] As e.g., by F. Waismann, "Language Strata," in *Logic and Language,* 2nd ser. (Oxford, 1955), edited by A. Flew, pp. 30–31, referred to by MacIntyre, *op. cit.,* pp. 217–18.

[48] For a recent discussion of attempts to resolve the dualism see G. N. A. Vesey, "Agent and Spectator," in *The Human Agent,* Royal Institute of Philosophy Lectures, Vol. 1 (1968).

that the agent could *logically* still "step back" from his body, his brain structure, or his compulsive psychological mechanisms and ask, "What shall I do, this being so?" And no doubt, at the least, he would have to form a "secondary intention" whenever he was confronted by the inductive knowledge on the basis of which his conduct was predicted. But there could conceivably come a time when there was no *practical* point in doing so. As Wittgenstein remarked, language games may become obsolete and get forgotten.[49] Consider an example. The language of animism is logically irreducible to that of natural science, but this is not regarded by most modern men to be a reason for affirming that there are two orders, that of spirits and that of things. The language which presupposes spirits inside stones, trees, and other phenomena serves no useful purpose in our dealings with nature and therefore we have dropped it. Could it be that, in a similar way, the language which presupposes action and agency will come to serve no useful purpose in our dealings with human beings? This seems at least conceivable. The language of action would then be obsolete in the way that the language of animism is. What would go with it? If the language of action went, moral language for one thing, would presumably go with it. We might still conceive of moral discourse as a kind of propaganda and regard "moral" expressions as useful in certain contexts: e.g., if "You ought not," as a matter of experience, stopped people from doing what we do not wish them to do more effectively than "Don't." But this would not be moral language as we know it. The assumption that the point of such discourse is to furnish free agents with reasons for action is essential to moral discourse as we know it. I am not, for one moment, saying that I think that the language of action *will* become obsolete. I am merely saying that, logically and empirically, it could. I invite the reader to ponder the extent to which any such development would change the character of human life. As I see it, the changes would be radical. And one of the most radical of all would be that moral discourse as we know it, and the forms of life which it constitutes,

[49] *PI,* 23.

would become, at best, fading memories. I go so far as to say that their demise would make whatever came afterward not recognizable as what we mean by human life. The end of morality would be the end of man. In which thought, perhaps, there is a moral. But it is no part of the purpose of this book to draw it.

INDEX